# Generations of the Holocaust

# GENERATIONS

# OF THE

# HOLOCAUST

EDITED BY

## *Martin S. Bergmann*

AND

## *Milton E. Jucovy*

*Basic Books, Inc., Publishers*     *New York*

The editors gratefully acknowledge permission to use the following poems: The epigraph on page v is a passage from "Esthétique du Mal" by Wallace Stevens, from *The Collected Poems of Wallace Stevens*, copyright © 1954 by Wallace Stevens and reprinted by permission of the publishers, Alfred A. Knopf, Inc. The final epigraph, "Everyone Has a Name," by Zelda, an Israeli poet, was translated from the Hebrew and is copyright by Marcia Falk and appears in *The Burning Bush: Poems from Modern Israel*, published by W. H. Allen of London in 1977.

Library of Congress Cataloging in Publication Data

Main entry under title:
Generations of the Holocaust.

Bibliography: p. 317
Includes index.
1. Holocaust, Jewish (1939–1945)—Psychological
aspects—Addresses, essays, lectures. 2. Children of
Holocaust survivors—Psychology—Addresses, essays,
lectures. 3. Holocaust survivors—Psychology—
Addresses, essays, lectures. 4. Children—Germany—
Psychology—Addresses, essays, lectures. 5. Psychology,
Pathological—Addresses, essays, lectures. I. Bergmann,
Martin S., 1915–      . II. Jucovy, Milton E.
D810.J4G46      940.53′15′03924      81–68405
ISBN 0–465–02666–4      AACR2

It may be that one life is a punishment
For another, as the son's life for the father's.
But that concerns the secondary characters.
It is a fragmentary tragedy
Within the universal whole. The son
And the father alike and equally are spent,
Each one, by the necessity of being
Himself, the unalterable necessity
Of being this unalterable animal.
This force of nature in action is the major
Tragedy.

WALLACE STEVENS

# *Contents*

# Contents

# Contents

## PART IV

### Theoretical and Clinical Aspects

# Acknowledgments

THE WORK of the Group for the Psychoanalytic Study of the Effect of the Holocaust on the Second Generation, from which the major portion of this book has been distilled, could not have begun without the vision, inspiration, and dedication of Dr. Judith Kestenberg. She provided the inspiration for an ongoing, in-depth investigation of how the trauma inflicted upon victims of the Holocaust could be transmitted from one generation to the next, and also edited part III. Jane Isay, co-publisher of Basic Books, prompted the organization of the collected material into a cohesive and unified work. We are grateful for her encouragement and confidence. The grant awarded by the Psychoanalytic Research Fund of the American Psychoanalytic Association facilitated work on many aspects of the study.

We wish to thank the members of the study group, and also the many colleagues who presented their own case material to the group and whose cooperation and generosity helped crystallize our insights and conclusions. Several others played signal roles in the completion of the final manuscripts. Deborah Buhler aided in transcribing great masses of material from the taped discussions made in the course of the investigation. Dr. Linda Zierler Jucovy assisted in the preliminary organization and refinement of the manuscript, and Jon R. Jucovy translated chapter 8, "The Return of the Persecutor," from the German and re-edited it. The skillful and meticulous copy editing of Phoebe Hoss of Basic Books is greatly appreciated.

We are deeply indebted to Dr. George E. Gross, director of the Treatment Center of the New York Psychoanalytic Institute; to Mrs. Beryl Oppenheimer, director of Social Service, and Mrs. Helen Riethof, administrative secretary, at the institute's Treatment Center; and to Katherine Wolpe, Ruth Reynolds, and Jeannette Taylor for help with the bibliography. We are also grateful for the contributions of members of the Israel Psychoanalytic Society and for the collaboration of the Frankfurt Holocaust Study Group.

# Acknowledgments

Parts of chapters 4 and 7, "Survivor-Parents and Their Children" and "A Metapsychological Assessment Based on an Analysis of a Survivor's Child," have been published in the *Journal of the American Psychoanalytic Association* 28, 1980, pp. 775–804. Chapter 8, "The Return of the Persecutor," was read at the meeting of the German-speaking Psychoanalytic Societies in Bamberg on 30 March 1980, and has been published in the *Jahrbuch der Psychoanalyse* 12, 1981, and in *Beitraege zur Theorie und Praxis* (ed. W. Loch and F. W. Eichoff [Bern-Stuttgart-Vienna: Hans Huber]). It appears here, with permission from Hans Huber. Chapter 13, "Recurrent Problems in the Treatment of Survivors and Their Children," was presented in an abbreviated version at a meeting of the American Psychoanalytic Association, held in New York in December 1979, as part of a panel on Research in Progress.

# List of Contributors

MARIA V. BERGMANN, Ph.D., a member of the Group for the Psychoanalytic Study of the Effect of the Holocaust on the Second Generation, has served on the faculty of the New York Freudian Society since 1961. She is the author of psychoanalytic publications on promiscuity, acting out, problems of narcissism, and female sexuality.

MARTIN S. BERGMANN, co-chairman of the Group for the Psychoanalytic Study of the Effect of the Holocaust on the Second Generation, serves on the faculty of the New York Freudian Society. He is a member of the board of the Psychoanalytic Research and Development Fund, and associate editor of *Imago*. He is co-editor of *The Evolution of Psychoanalytic Technique* (Basic Books, 1976).

M. DONALD COLEMAN, M.D., is a psychoanalyst in Westchester, New York, and assistant clinical professor of psychiatry at Albert Einstein School of Medicine.

ANITA ECKSTAEDT received her medical degree in 1962. She undertook her psychoanalytic training at the German Psychoanalytic Association and became a member in 1974. She has worked as a neurologist at the Sigmund Freud Institute in Frankfurt am Main and, since 1974, has been a training analyst with a private practice in that city.

YOLANDA GAMPEL, Ph.D., is a clinical lecturer in the psychology department at the Tel Aviv University in Israel, as well as a senior lecturer and clinical supervisor in the School of Psychotherapy, a graduate division of the Medical School of Tel Aviv University. She is also a full member of the International Psychoanalytic Association.

GERTRUD HARDTMANN, M.D., has been a psychiatrist specializing in child psychiatry and forensic psychiatry. Beginning in 1977, she was professor for Social Educational Theory at the Technical University in Berlin for three years. She currently practices psychoanalysis.

JAMES HERZOG, M.D., assistant professor of psychiatry at Harvard Medical School and staff psychiatrist at the Children's Hospital Medical Center, runs

# List of Contributors

the latter's Clinic for the Development of Young Children and Parents and is director of training in clinical psychiatry. He practices psychoanalysis and teaches at the Boston Psychoanalytic Institute.

MILTON E. JUCOVY, M.D., is a training and supervising analyst at the New York Psychoanalytic Institute and the President of the New York Psychoanalytic Society. He is a supervising psychiatrist at Long Island Jewish-Hillside Medical Center. He is the author of psychoanalytic publications on transvestitism and the co-editor of *Style, Character and Language*, the collected papers of Victor H. Rosen.

JUDITH S. KESTENBERG, M.D., is a founding member and secretary of the Group for the Psychoanalytic Study of the Effect of the Holocaust on the Second Generation. She is a psychoanalyst; clinical professor of psychiatry, Division of Psychoanalytic Education, New York University; professional lecturer, Down State University, New York; co-director of the Center for Parents and Children, sponsored by Child Development Research; and the author of *Children and Parents* (Aronson, 1975).

MILTON KESTENBERG, an attorney in private practice in New York City, has been handling restitution cases for survivors in cooperation with German lawyers and has appealed on behalf of his clients in restitution offices and higher courts. He is a founding member of the Group for the Psychoanalytic Study of the Effect of the Holocaust on the Second Generation.

MARION M. OLINER, Ph.D., has a private practice in psychoanalysis and psychotherapy. She is a faculty member of the training institutes of the New York Freudian Society and the Institute for Psychoanalytic Training and Research.

LUTZ ROSENKÖTTER, M.D., is a member of the German and the International Psychoanalytical associations. He is a training and supervising psychoanalyst at the Sigmund Freud Institute in Frankfurt and a practicing psychoanalyst. His writings reflect his interest in the impact of current history on psychoanalytic treatment.

ERICH SIMENAUER, M.D., is a member of the International Psychoanalytical Association, an honorary guest of the British Psychoanalytical Society, and a member of the Berlin Psychoanalytic Institute. He is the author of numerous papers on the theory and practice of psychoanalysis and on literature, art, and ethnology. His books include *Rainer Maria Rilke, Legend and Myth* (1953), *Der Traum bei Rilke* (1976 and 1980), and *Felix Mayer, Schopferische Sprache und Rhythums* (editor, 1959).

# Generations of the Holocaust

# *Prelude*

THUS FAR, attempts of historians, creative artists, and scientists to comprehend fully the dark forces unleashed during the Holocaust have met with limited success. Many survivors have warned us that we can never fully understand their experiences. Elie Wiesel has asked, "How do you tell children, big and small, that society could lose its mind and start murdering its own soul? How do you unveil horrors without offering at the same time some measure of hope?" (1977, p. 6). Undertaking even an approximate scientific study of this period of infamy, and of the legacy of evil which followed it, poses an almost insuperable challenge. One may feel it presumptuous to attempt—rationally, soberly, and objectively—to describe the indescribable and to speak of the unspeakable. Yet our hope is to achieve understanding out of living memory as seen through a prism of psychoanalytic discipline that has already illuminated much of what shapes and determines human behavior.

The very term *Holocaust* has been criticized. Some critics claim that it has a euphemistic ring and covers the general concept of genocide, thus diminishing the Jews as victims of Nazi tyranny. Lucy S. Dawidowicz (1976) has affirmed, however, that it is precisely the term the Jewish people themselves have chosen in the English language (*Shoah* in Hebrew) to describe their fate of persecution and death. She points out that, on a superficial level, the word denotes great destruction and devastation, but that its etymological roots suggest a more specific Jewish interpretation. It derives from the Greek word *holokauston*, a translation in the Septuagint for the Hebrew word *olah*, which means "what is brought up." Translated into English, *olah* can mean "an offering made by fire unto the Lord" or a burnt offering. The implication is that once more the Jewish people are sacrificial victims, and that the Holocaust is another link in the chain of suffering and martyrdom. We are also reminded that the chronicles and liturgical poetry of the period of the First Crusade (1095–99) evoke the image of the *Akedah*, the binding for the sacrifice of Isaac, as the antecedent of later Jewish ordeals, and hence as a rationalization for them. One important difference must be underscored: however the story is interpreted, the life of Isaac was spared, human sacrifice was abjured, and animal sacrifice substituted. While the recurrent pattern of persecution that has been the Jewish historical experience claimed many lives and caused untold suffering, the catastrophe of the Holocaust, involving the death of six million and the agony of many others, transcends all previous ordeals. One half of world Jewry living in Eastern Europe was consumed, and an entire civilization destroyed.

The concept adopted by the Nazis in devising the Final Solution was the fulfillment of an ideology of hate—an apocalyptic end in itself. Sophisticated technology was applied to the organized and relentless slaughter of a people—a slaughter on a scale surpassing any anti-Semitic crimes of the past. In *Why War?* (1932, pp. 214–15) Freud, who was hardly an optimist in the last decade of his life, expressed the hope, in his answer to a question of Einstein's,* that the process of civilization and the evolution of culture might enable the human race to govern instinctual life and help to internalize aggressive impulses. Freud was writing in a period of apparent enlightenment and emancipation—a period that ended in ashes and skeletons, and the disappearance of the rich and lively culture of European Jewry.

## Aftermath of the Holocaust

The war in Europe was over in 1945; the concentration and death camps were liberated by the advancing Allied forces, and the long night gave way to dawn. The scattered survivors tried to find a place among the living once again. Some attempted to take up life again in the countries and towns from which they had been deported, only to find desolation and, in many places, a reception that was inhospitable, even hostile. Large numbers of the impoverished and stateless were cared for temporarily in displaced persons camps, waiting for visas to emigrate to more congenial places abroad. Many survivors who tried to find their way to Palestine before 1948, when the State of Israel was established, were intercepted and turned back to internment camps in Cyprus. Those who succeeded in reaching the shores of the "Promised Land" were only a short time away from the ordeals of the War of Independence and the onslaught of the Arab armies following the evacuation of British mandate forces after the United Nations vote to create a Jewish state. A fairly

* In a letter to Freud of 30 July 1932 (Freud 1932, Vol. 22, p. 201).

# Prelude

sizable number of survivors were able to make contact with family members in the United States and other countries in North and South America.

During these first years after the war, the energies of the survivors were absorbed in finding their way back to some semblance of conventional life. Most had to learn a new language, search for other occupations, and meet some of the challenges of a society in a foreign land. Many families clung together in their new neighborhoods, creating new ghettos, hoping to re-create their original communities, surrounded by an alien culture, which, though not usually physically threatening, nevertheless regarded them at best with an ambivalent mixture of awe and mistrust, the very embodiment of a past the survivors wanted to forget. It was rare for an entire family to have survived intact. New partners, more often than not fellow survivors, had to be found, and new families started. While life was safer and certainly more bearable, adaptation was by no means easy.

The shock and the drama of liberation, and the need to deal with the plight of the victims of Nazi persecution, helped mobilize action and kept survivors visible in the eyes and conscience of the world for a short time. Then, for at least two powerful reasons, a curtain of silence descended. First, for close to a decade, intense individual and collective defense mechanisms functioned to ward off preoccupation with, and memories of, traumatic experiences. From the psychoanalytic point of view, the Jewish people can be seen not only as a socioreligious group, but also as a group united by common trauma. Jews are admonished to remember their history: "If I forget thee O Jerusalem, let my right arm wither, let my tongue cleave to my mouth if I do not remember thee." A Jew must remember the destruction of the Temple and the scattering to the Diaspora, the Exodus from Egypt at every Passover, the threats of the Amalekite enemy, and the genocidal plots of Haman at the time of Purim. The list is long indeed.

Despite a long history of pogroms and exiles, persecutions and suffering, there was nothing in it to prepare the Jewish community for Hitler's Final Solution. Occurring frequently in archival documents about the Holocaust are such statements as: "Nobody told us; we couldn't imagine or believe what we saw." During this period of latency—the decade after 1945—the compelling need of the survivors was to deny and repress their experiences. The Hebrew writer Aharon Appelfeld, who arrived in Israel after liberation from a concentration camp at the age of twelve, gave the following retrospective account:

After liberation the one desire was to sleep, to forget and to be reborn. At first there was a wish to talk incessantly about one's experiences; this gave way to silence, but

5

learning to be silent was not easy. When the past was no longer talked about, it became unreal, a figment of one's imagination. The new Israeli identity, sun-burned, practical, and strong, was grafted upon the old identity of the helpless victim. Only in nightmares was the past alive, but then even dreaming ceased.

What appeared to be a moderately healthy and adaptive way of dealing with the Holocaust could be achieved only with massive denial and repression of the traumatic period. It is not surprising that, eventually, the intolerable memories of the past returned to haunt the survivor.

At times the defenses were so massive as to survive extensive analytic work. A woman who was in two analyses had been removed from the Warsaw ghetto and raised secretly by a Catholic family. Both her parents had been killed and she was later reclaimed by an aunt. She said:

> For years I claimed in a big way that I did not suffer from the war, that I was a privileged child in the ghetto (which is true, privileged to have survived, if this is a privilege). I was lucky to have been much loved by my mother and aunt who raised me and still another aunt. Then this whole defensive edifice gave way little by little. The much-loved child really suffered a succession of abandonments. My aunt saved me by taking me out of the ghetto and then when I was ten she abandoned me by leaving for Israel. It was just revenge, for I had survived her daughter and her sister. The privilege is a heavy burden to bear. . . . Life seems very hard to me and I live it from day to day without projects, as if I could only hold my head above water, and incapable of doing the least bit for others.

Ernst Kris (1956) has shown how tenacious an autobiographical myth can be. For this patient, the conviction of being "lucky" survived the first analysis and crumbled only after the death of her aunt. Still, the second analysis did not quite overcome the depressive core that was hidden behind the conviction of being fortunate.

The second reason for silence, apart from the need of the survivors to forget, had to do with the world's need to forget. E. Rappaport, a psychoanalyst and survivor of Buchenwald, reported:

> I survived a concentration camp but I regularly made the observation that people did not really want me to talk about my experiences, and whenever I started they invariably showed their resistance by interrupting me, by asking me to tell them how I got out. (1968, p. 720)

And Wiesel wrote:

> Had we started to speak, we would have found it impossible to stop. Having shed one tear, we would have drowned the human heart. So invincible in the face of death and the enemy, we now felt helpless. . . . We were mad with disbelief. People refused

6

to listen, to understand, to share. There was a division between us and them, between those who endured and those who read about it, or would refuse to read about it. . . . We thought people would remember our experiences, our testimony, and manage to suppress their violent impulses to kill or to hate. (1977, p. 5)

Psychiatrists and psychoanalysts also neglected to confront the psychological problems of survivors. When plans for rehabilitation of the traumatized population were first formulated, material assistance was emphasized, and psychiatric issues were ignored. One notable exception to this extraordinary oversight was Paul Friedman (1948, 1949) who, in surveying mental health among Jewish displaced persons in Europe, had paid special attention to the problems of children under the auspices of the American Joint Distribution Committee. He had also helped to establish a program of mental hygiene for Palestine. Friedman's work thus was one of the earliest efforts to focus attention on the vast psychic trauma which would later be exhaustively investigated and described in detail.

Perhaps temporal and emotional distance were necessary before the survivors were able to remember and before mental health professionals were themselves ready to deal with the problem. In the early 1950s, the German Federal Republic undertook to provide restitution to the victims of the Nazi regime. Apart from material assistance to be provided to the State of Israel, the German government agreed by law to indemnify individual victims for damage to their health as well as for other hardships. The legislation, called *Wiedergutmachung* (literally, "making good again"), was complicated and created what could be considered almost a new legal specialty among attorneys who represented their victimized clients in pressing claims (see chapter 3). Because medical and psychiatric examinations were necessary to prove a link between the previous persecution and the current symptoms and maladaptation, a large number of psychiatrists were able to collect a volume of case histories through interviews with those survivors who sought indemnification. It must be emphasized that discrepancies and distortions were bound to occur when interviews for reparations were involved, compared with situations where individuals were seeking treatment. An interviewing psychiatrist, no matter how empathic and gentle, might project an image of authority to a survivor who would naturally have powerful reasons for mistrust and suspicion of any doctor chosen to evaluate the mental status of himself and his family. Data collected from treatment sessions rather than from interviews were meager at that time, as there was again a natural reluctance for survivors to seek treatment for psychological impairment—a reluctance based in large part on their need for denial, repression, and isolation of traumatic memories and on their consciousness that no one, not even a survivor-therapist, could readily understand and empathize.

## Psychoanalytic Investigations

The theoretical position of psychoanalysts, many of whom were classically Freudian in orientation, particularly in respect to trauma, did not appear sufficient to conceptualize and explain the bewildering array of symptoms presented by the survivors who were examined. Freud, in *Beyond The Pleasure Principle* (1920), defined as traumatic any experience that succeeds in breaking the so-called stimulus barrier. He spoke of an excitation from outside that is powerful enough to break through the protective shield. This is actually a metapsychological assumption and not, strictly speaking, a clinical observation. It rests on a series of assumptions that, in turn, are also based on abstract and unverifiable laws: for example, that the human organism is equipped with an apparatus to protect the individual from overstimulation. A further such law is that this hypothetical apparatus can function only within a certain range of stimuli: if it is subjected to a massive dose of stimuli, the barrier will break down, and a state of shock and disorganization will ensue. A few years earlier, in the *Introductory Lectures* (1916c), Freud had already stressed that the term *traumatic*—as applied to an experience that presents the psychic apparatus with stimulus too powerful to be dealt with in the normal way, within a short space of time—has no other meaning than an economic one. The definition assumes that trauma is temporary—that, having suffered it for a brief period, one returns to a relatively innocuous and nonthreatening state. The definition could not encompass a situation where for months and years one daily confronted death and degradation, and where existed a new reality totally at variance with the framework of social and moral reality that one had once taken for granted.

In accordance with this classical psychoanalytic view of trauma, psychoanalytic theory has operated with three models for the understanding of psychopathology: the model of trauma, which emphasizes the undermining of psychic functioning from without; the model of development arrest, manifesting itself in fixation points of the libido, or in the failure of certain ego functions to develop; and, finally, the model of intrapsychic conflict, where one is unable to resolve conflicts between psychic structures. While these three models

# Prelude

operate at times in isolation, they can also be combined and interweave. A trauma can thus cause developmental arrest as well as intrapsychic conflict.

When the traumatic neuroses were first observed in the First World War, they were cited, by psychiatrists who disagreed with Freud, as proof that danger to self-preservation can be a cause of neurosis, and as indicating that he was mistaken in insisting on the sexual etiology of neurosis. In response, Freud stated: "It would seem highly improbable that a neurosis could come into being because of objective presence of danger, without any participation of the deeper levels of the mental apparatus" (1926, p. 129). This belief was, in turn, based on another—namely, that there is nothing in the unconscious that corresponds to the annihilation of life. He continued: "I am therefore inclined to adhere to the view that the fear of death should be regarded as analogous to the fear of castration . . . one of being abandoned by the superego powers of destiny, so that there are no longer any safeguards against danger" (p. 130). Phyllis Greenacre defined traumatic conditions as "any conditions which seem definitely unfavorable, noxious, or drastically injurious to the development of the young individual" (1971, p. 277). This formulation seems to omit the possibility of trauma having a psychologically deleterious effect on the adult. In a similar vein, Anna Freud wrote: "External traumas are turned into internal ones if they touch on, coincide with, or symbolize the fulfillment of either deep-seated anxieties or wish fantasies" (1967, p. 241). These views were difficult to reconcile with the observations of those who were grappling to understand, within a framework of psychoanalytic theory, the symptoms of survivors of the Holocaust.

Gradually reports dealing with survivors' psychological problems, many of which arose only years after liberation as late effects of persecution, began to appear in the psychiatric journals during the early and middle 1960s. The data were collected largely from surveys in the United States and abroad, and from personal interviews; some were obtained from survivor patients treated in psychotherapy. Several of these pioneer efforts should be mentioned, but they cannot all be noted in this preliminary survey. William G. Niederland was one of the earliest to study defenses employed against the stresses of life in concentration camps (1961) and to describe the psychiatric disorders that appeared both early and late (1964). Paul Chodoff, too, described some of the late effects of the concentration camp syndrome (1963); as did L. Eitinger, in Norway, who drew a harrowing picture of the prisoners' terror and helplessness and of the physical cruelty, including starvation and beatings, to which they were subjected (1961). In Israel, H. Zvi Winnik, who had chaired a symposium sponsored by the Israel Psychoanalytic Society in 1966, reported on the psychopathology and treatment of the victims of the Nazi persecution (1967a).

The problems of the survivor came to international attention in a psychoanalytic setting at the 1967 congress of the International Psycho-Analytical Association held in Copenhagen, the proceedings of which were published in 1968. A symposium took place entitled "Psychic Traumatization through Social Catastrophe," with participants from several countries, including Erich Simenauer, H. Zvi Winnik, William Niederland, Emmanuel De Wind, Martin Wangh, and Klaus D. Hoppe. The general tone of the discussion seemed to suggest that the traditional way in which psychoanalysts had regarded the effects of trauma lacked certain important elements that might help one to understand and treat victims who had emerged from the Holocaust with significant psychological impairment. In this symposium the participants stressed the permanent injury to the ego as expressed in alteration of personal identity, psychosislike clinical pictures, and other major sequelae that seemed to substantiate the view that previous personality might play a less than major role in the symptoms of the survivor. When it comes to the discussion of problems of technique, analysts differ as to the relative significance they assign to the roles of abreaction, insight, efforts at reconstruction, the recovery of childhood memories, and the analysis of the transference. In the treatment of survivors, these varying emphases were particularly sharp: there was no general consensus about which category or modality of technique might prove most helpful. De Wind (1968), for example, stressed trying to help the survivor to deal with aggression. He believed that warded-off aggression was behind both the prevalence of chronic depression as well as the frequent somatic illnesses among survivors. He also felt that if other channels were blocked, the survivor often directed aggression toward offspring, thus perpetuating the original traumatic impact of the Holocaust. Wangh (1968) believed that the main work to be done with survivors was to help them to mourn. Because of the extreme circumstances of the Holocaust—particularly for those in concentration camps, where behavior had meaning only for survival, and the difference between life and death was arbitrary and unpredictable—memories often usurped fantasies in the survivors' mental life. Some psychoanalysts felt that it might be therapeutic to attempt to reactivate fantasy life.

SURVIVOR SYNDROME

However one chooses to assess the evidence, and whether one agrees with the assertion that previous personality plays but a minor role in the symptoms

# Prelude

seen among survivors, or remains a proponent of the traditional psychoanalytic theory of the pathogenicity of trauma, the group of symptoms described by Niederland (1968) as the "survivor syndrome" was one landmark in the psychoanalytic study of Holocaust victims. Before sketching this syndrome, an important qualification must be noted: we have no intention of suggesting here that the appearance of this syndrome was universal, or that its symptoms were totally unique and exclusive. Although we have historical evidence of other tragedies involving genocide, we do not have comparable psychoanalytic data for any master plan for the deliberate extinction of a group of people who were regarded as unfit to inhabit the earth with other mortals. While some psychiatrists have claimed that, as a result of their ordeals, survivors of other and more recent man-made and natural disasters may show similar symptoms, this opinion has been regarded by others as trivializing of the Holocaust. We firmly adhere to the opinion that those survivors who present symptoms reveal a conglomerate complex of psychopathological consequences that is palpable and recognizable. It must, however, be emphasized that, in recovery, many survivors have shown an unusual degree of psychic strength and resilience and have adapted to the renewal of their lives with great vitality. (It is likely that people who survived had great psychic strength to begin with.) Many have achieved remarkable success and, perhaps because of their need for continuity and compensatory life-affirming attitudes, have inspired their children to be energetic and dedicated to responsibility and service.

The symptoms of the survivor syndrome, as described by Niederland, are multiple and varied; but his study and observation of nearly one thousand victims indicated consistently recurring manifestations: anxiety, chronic depressive states, some disturbances of cognition and memory, a tendency to isolation and withdrawal, many psychosomatic complaints, and, in some extreme cases, an appearance that suggested to him a similarity to the "musulman" or "living corpse" stage of concentration camp prisoners who had regressed to such apathy and hopelessness that death was imminent. The most prominent complaint cited was anxiety, which was associated with the fear of renewed persecution. Applicants for reparations interviewed by Niederland presented themselves as huddled and silent figures. They suffered from numerous physical symptoms mainly connected with the gastrointestinal tract and the musculoskeletal system. Depressive equivalents appeared as feelings of fatigue, a sense of heaviness, and emptiness. Disorders of sleep were common and included the fear of falling asleep as well as early morning awakening. Patients dreaded their nightmares, which evoked the terrifying experiences of the past. Social withdrawal and seclusiveness were seen in many cases, and a sizable number showed a striking inability to verbalize the traumatic events they had suffered. Under the circumstances of having to report such experiences to an examiner who might have been seen as the representative of authority and thus viewed with suspicion, it would probably be extremely difficult to assess the often puzzling selective silences.

Two books—*Massive Psychic Trauma* (1968), edited by Henry Krystal, and *Psychic Traumatization: After Effects in Individuals and Communities* (1971), edited by Krystal and Niederland—have consolidated the early psychoanalytic studies of the Holocaust.

One haunting aspect of the depression seen in survivor families was an inability to mourn appropriately for dead relatives—a mourning that would have allowed for gradual decathexis of the lost object and subsequent internalization. The lack of opportunity for the dubious luxury of adequate mourning was an unbearable deprivation and led to later problems. Some survivors clung to a belief that family members or dead children might magically reappear. Others, who became the parents of children born after liberation, saw the children in their new families as revenants and frequently named them for children in their first families who had been killed during the Holocaust. These children were often passionately protected; and, when they became ill or were even mildly injured, the response of the parent was often more intense than in an average family or even in one where a child had died from illness or accident.

THE ROLE OF PRE-HOLOCAUST PATHOLOGY

Some examples might highlight the question of what constitutes a trauma: whether neuroses of the pre-Holocaust period had any effect on the survivor syndrome; and whether the clinical picture can be clearly related to childhood events. Paul R., who suffered from intense anxieties and obsessional thoughts about contracting an illness, notably cancer, seemed nevertheless healthier than most of the survivors' cases presented at the international symposium on trauma in 1968. An analysis of several years' duration was conducted without parameters. His Holocaust experiences were not ignored, but the bulk of the analytic work dealt with the patient's relationship to his father and, to a lesser extent, with his mother. It differed from an ordinary analysis in that its main task was to help Mr. R. to mourn important losses of family members in the Holocaust. The patient's attitudes toward his own children were similar to those of parents who are distant from their children, but did not seem to incorporate significantly the events of the Holocaust. His children had been named for the dead parents of his father; but the names were modified to sound less Jewish, as a precaution against potential anti-Semitism in the country to which he had emigrated. The transference of Mr. R. was characterized by a remarkable lack of interest in his analyst, and by the unshakable belief that the latter was Gentile (actually the analyst was himself a survivor) and knew nothing about Judaism or the Holocaust. A challenging problem of technique emerged from a study of Mr. R.: should the traditional anonymity of the analyst be maintained in the classical manner to the very end of the treatment, or should it be breached in an effort to mobilize further and perhaps crucial material?

A fascinating case was recently reported by A. Freedman (1978), with published discussions by H. P. Blum (1978) and H. Roiphe (1978). The patient was a survivor of the Warsaw ghetto and had developed an unusual perversion after the war. Analysis was conducted with hardly a reference to his experiences in the ghetto, even excluding his participation in the heroic and doomed uprising there. All the ingredients of the perversion were accounted for and explained in the analytic work by the life history of the patient and by the intrapsychic conflicts he had developed before the Holocaust. Although the patient lost his family in Europe, helping the man to mourn seemed to have played no significant role in the treatment, which apparently came to a satisfactory conclusion with relief of the presenting symptoms and resolution of major conflicts.

Such apparently polarized differences in the data pose formidable questions for psychoanalytic theory and technique. As we scan reports of analyzed patients who were involved in the Holocaust, the conduct of the analyses appears to reflect three major patterns: the Holocaust may be taken into account in a clear and definite way as a particularly powerful factor in the patient's psychopathology; it may be largely ignored in the analytic work; or there may be an intertwining of pre-Holocaust private pathogenic elements with the trauma suffered during the Holocaust.

Our clinical experience substantiates convincingly many of the findings gathered through interviews, other large-scale surveys, and psychotherapy conducted by the early pioneers in Holocaust research. Two clinical vignettes may further serve to underscore the problems we face in differentiating private pathology from that induced by the Holocaust. Another reason for presenting these vignettes derives from the fact that both patients were in their early adolescence when they were apprehended by the Nazis and taken to a concentration camp. Mary-Anne S., an intelligent and acutely perceptive woman of nearly fifty, came to treatment because of almost constant guilt feelings, of anxiety that fluctuated in intensity but was rarely absent, of excessively low self-esteem, and of various somatic complaints. She was a frequent visitor to hospital emergency rooms because of symptoms referable to her gastrointestinal and cardiovascular systems. Although she had a prolapsed aortic valve, her cardiac complaints seemed psychically overdetermined. Cautioned by her physicians to give up smoking, she nevertheless continued to smoke at least one pack of cigarettes a day. Born in Europe, she was married to a native American who had some creative talent but worked at a technical job that he despised. His uneven temperament and disappointment in his career contributed to marital discord. The couple had two grown children: an older daughter, who was a high achiever in her beginning professional career, but showed signs of a larval anorexia and of potential problems in her relationships with men; and a younger son, who seemed healthy and well adjusted and was showing promise of becoming successful in business management and administration.

Mrs. S. was born to an affluent middle-class Jewish family in a Western European country that was invaded by the Nazis early in the Second World War. When she was ten, the family—consisting of her parents, her brother, and herself—were captured by the Nazis and sent to a concentration camp, where they spent nearly five years before they were liberated. All survived except her father, who contracted dysentery weeks before the Allied armies arrived.

She rarely spoke to anyone about her experiences, but she readily did in treatment. She recalled the horror of their lives in the camp, where one lost any sense of wanting to live until the next day. She recalled little actual fear or anxiety and no memories of intense hatred for the guards. She was able to see her family, and one thing that sustained her was the thought that, if the situation became totally unbearable, then at least she could look forward to death. She recalled two incidents with great intensity and clarity. One day she was out in the yard marching with her group, when she caught a glimpse of beets piled in a heap. Barely twelve at the time and desperately hungry, she impulsively broke formation and ran to grab a beet. A guard saw her, drew his pistol, and shot at her—and missed. The other recollection involved a formerly very attractive and elegant older woman prisoner who had befriended the girl soon after her arrival at the camp, and whom she saw, after a considerable lapse of time, looking like an apparition and barely alive.

All through the imprisonment, Mary-Anne S.'s close relationship with her father, who was cheerful and optimistic and predicted the end of the persecutions, was a sustaining factor. She recalled with sadness his last days: exhausted by dysentery and pneumonia, he died in her arms, but she knows she has not been able to mourn him adequately. Even now she cannot go to memorial services during the High Holy Days because she cannot pray with people who have lost less than she feels she did. After liberation she returned to her native city, where her mother was soon remarried to a man whom the patient resented and disliked. When he died, they emigrated to the United States, where her brother became successful and affluent. She remains constantly guilty, worries about her mother, children, and husband, cannot leave home for a vacation trip because she will not leave her dog with a stranger, and is continually afraid her mother will reproach her for some fancied neglect. Her only gratification is her work, which she performs skillfully and conscientiously.

At first timid and cautious in treatment, she has shown increasing trust but continues to employ a cynical and "flip" manner to ward off strong affects. She castigates herself and frequently makes her own interpretations, because accepting something from the therapist would place her in his debt and put her at a disadvantage. She keeps track of the time and calls a halt to her sessions. She consistently pays her bill at the end of the month before she receives it. It makes her uncomfortable to allow herself to be in anyone's debt. As far as could be determined, Mrs. S.'s early development does not suggest a potential for the sustained and chronic disability shown in her adult life. In many ways the guilt, self-deprecation, tendency to somatization, withdrawal from most contacts, and moderate to severe xenophobia, all conform to the complex of symptoms seen as late sequelae of Holocaust trauma. The relatively good adaptation made by her mother and brother makes her difficulties stand out in even bolder relief. It would not be rash to speculate that the age at which she suffered the trauma made her particularly vulnerable, that her Holocaust experience was a strong organizing factor in the development of severe symptomatology.

For comparison and contrast, we can consider the clinical picture presented by Jacob C., who was imprisoned in a concentration camp also as a young adolescent. In this case, problems of specificity are more complex and difficult to identify, and thus indicate some of the methodological problems faced in a research project of this nature. Mr. C.'s major reason for seeking treatment was an inordinate and consuming jealousy involving his wife and a man she had known some years before her marriage. He was constantly preoccupied by thoughts about their relationship and had florid fantasies about the sexual relationship they might have had.

A trim, intense, and good-looking man in his mid-forties, he described his suffering and his background in a thoughtful manner. He was born in an

Eastern European *shtetl*, most of whose members were ultra-orthodox, and their fealty was to a particularly rigid and authoritarian rabbi. Mr. C. was vituperative about what he saw as their fanaticism, narrow-mindedness and hypocrisy. His father had been ill with tuberculosis for a number of years and finally died when Jacob was twelve. For months afterward, Jacob was troubled by dreams and fantasies about the Angel of Death. The family was bitterly impoverished after the father's death, and the son was sent, according to custom, to the homes of various neighbors for meals. He described bitterly how he was treated as a beggar and given dregs to eat. Shortly after the father's death, his younger sister took ill and died of some infectious disease.

By this time the Nazis had overrun the area where he lived; and when he was thirteen, he and his mother were herded into a boxcar and sent to Auschwitz. They were separated at the entrance to the camp, and he never saw his mother again. For at least three days afterward he cried incessantly. He tended in his descriptions to gloss over the apathetic, brutalizing, and dehumanized life in the camp, but said that he grew to dislike many of his fellow prisoners and felt mistrustful of them because they seemed to be concerned only for themselves. He admired and respected prisoners who had some leftist political discipline. He was later sent to a labor camp in Germany. After liberation, he joined a left-wing Zionist group and made his way to Israel, where he worked on a kibbutz for several years before emigrating to the United States in his early twenties. He studied, entered a business, married a young American woman, and embarked on his new life with energy and enthusiasm. However, he had always a lingering bitterness about the past, sometimes directed more fiercely against his life in the *shtetl* than at that under the Nazis. His generalized wariness erupted acutely when he discovered in his home a book that had been inscribed to his wife by her former man friend.

In treatment it did not take long for his mistrust to crystallize in a formidable and unyielding resistance. He had some knowledge of psychoanalytic procedure, but he expressed grave doubts about using the couch. He had seen several consultants before coming to his present analyst, and expressed strong reservations about each one. He also verbalized sharply polarized feelings about his analyst. On the one hand, he felt him to be reasonably intelligent, caring, and humane, but also wondered if the analyst's skills and intellect were sufficient to deal with his problems. Mr. C.'s objections then focused on feeling that the analyst was perhaps too Jewish. He observed that, in the waiting room and office, there were many books and pictures that dealt with Jewish themes, though in reality he was exaggerating. He reflected that the books and pictures might remind him of his childhood community which had treated with contempt the poor little orphan he had been. He also wondered if psychological treatment was really what he needed, and asked for more time to make up his mind. At one point he developed severe coryzal symptoms* which he attributed to allergies; he claimed it was uncomfortable to use the couch under these physical conditions. When he was asked if the outpouring of fluid from his nose and teary eyes could be connected with his crying when he was separated from his mother in the camp, he accused his therapist of jumping to premature conclusions. On the other hand, he said that the analyst listened too much and did not offer him enough interpretations. On the following day he appeared with dry mucous membranes, smiled, and said that the pollen count must have dropped precipitately. Now able to use the couch, he told of a recent dream in which he is standing on a rock in a barren place. The landscape about him is bleak and forbidding; off to one side he notices buildings that look like a concentration camp. He knows somehow that there are Nazis nearby who are rounding up Jews, and that he has to escape. However, the landscape is so threatening that he feels it is almost better to allow himself to be taken. He was perplexed by the dream and not able to associate to it productively. The analyst commented that Mr. C.'s difficulty in committing himself to the analysis might be reminiscent of his feelings of impasse during the time of the Holocaust. Mr. C. said that this sounded like an interesting point. At the next hour he said that this was not a recent dream but actually one he had told some time before to the psychiatrist who had been seeing the family because he and his wife were having some problems with their children. Mr. C. felt that he had been given a more sensible interpretation at that time. When he was asked what he thought about his need to test and trap his analyst by rearranging the truth in this way, he became intensely angry, reproached the analyst for accusing him of lying, and said that he was terminating treatment.

The foundering of the therapeutic process might have been predictable at the outset. Mr. C.'s symptoms, the outlines of his character structure, and his pattern of "shopping" for a therapist, suggested serious character pathology and paranoid qualities. On the basis of the rather brief experience, it would be difficult, at best, to determine how much of Mr. C.'s mistrust was related to earlier pre-Holocaust conflicts, and how much to his incarceration and separation from his mother during early adolescence. Later discussion will consider some of these theoretical and technical problems encountered in the treatment of children of survivors, including the influence of certain countertransference attitudes that can contribute to, and escalate, difficulties.

* Acute inflammation of the membranes of the nose. (Ed.)

For a number of years, further studies and emendations focusing on the psychological problems of survivors used the concept of the survivor syndrome as a base and a common denominator. The label stuck and became offensive, as Helen Epstein (1979) pointed out. In her words, it implied "an insidious disease contracted by every Jew who had survived the Holocaust" (p. 176), and ignored complexities and variegated patterns of life in survivor families, and also comparisons with other groups who had suffered during the reign of the Nazis. Aside from the fact that this point carried to extremes could trivialize the fate of the Jewish people in the Holocaust, Epstein's argument is intrinsically sound:

> The term "Survival Syndrome" did not address itself to . . . beneficent changes in personality. It seemed to imply that a defective human mutant had been created, intrinsically different from you and me. Novels and films had elaborated on this characterization, portraying survivors either as saints and martyrs, people who had survived the worst and could do no wrong; or alternatively, as little more than shells of their former selves, near-criminals, who had stooped to inhuman measures in order to prolong their lives. (P. 177)

The polarization—frequently encountered in psychoanalytic work—between the wish to be "special" and an "exception" and the abhorrence for labels and stigmatization is a human quality, and it is difficult to strike an acceptable balance.

## The Second Generation

As time passed, and the Holocaust became distant history for all but a few individuals and families, a new generation of children born to survivor families was growing up. Yet little or nothing appeared in psychiatric or psychoanalytic literature about the effects of the Holocaust on the second generation, although doubtless many of the children were sophisticated and well educated and had access to sources of treatment. Perhaps, like their parents, they were wary of psychological treatment; or when they did engage in it, the Holocaust was not recognized, by either patient or therapist, as a problem to be solved.

Some of the first reports about the second generation came from Canada. V. Rakoff (1966, 1969) described his experiences in treating adolescent children from survivor families. He noted disproportionate numbers and some severe symptomatology among such patients, but qualified his opinion by pointing out that not all survivor families had psychologically conflicted children who required treatment. He described three cases in some detail, noting that two of his patients had made suicidal gestures before the age of twenty. At first glance they might have resembled patients selected at random from an average sample of the clinic population, but they showed certain common features that had to be given special and serious consideration. They had an excessive need to curb the normal aggression and rebellion common in adolescence, and seemed to be struggling with conflicts arising out of a need to fulfill expectations their parents had for them. These missions for redemption, they anticipated, would magically undo, or at least partially compensate for, the unendurable losses of the parents' generation. Many of these children became obedient achievers, but many broke under the strain. It may be claimed that this pattern of children living out parental hopes and ambitions is not an unknown phenomenon; it was common among immigrant populations and seen in Jewish families who emigrated from Eastern Europe during the early part of this century. However, in survivor-families, the expectations and the need for children to make up for parental trauma are greater than in other generations.

With J. Sigal (1971, 1973) and the additional work of B. Trossman (1968) in Montreal and Krystal (1968, 1971) in Detroit, further data and clinical material began to accumulate. (We have already emphasized that a mental health professional can draw conclusions only from data collected from patients who seek help, and cannot report findings from a population that has not sought professional aid.) A survey conducted by interview techniques or questionnaires has certain limitations imposed by the methodology and can erroneously indicate an absence of pathology. However, Sigal and Rakoff (1971) compared adolescent children of survivor-families with a control group of teen-agers and found more evidence of disturbance and impaired adaptive behavior in the survivor-group, as well as greater feelings of alienation and greater evidence of dependence on parents. Differences in the two groups were explained as a result of the preoccupation of survivor-parents with the losses they had incurred, which presumably made them more sensitive to their children's normal activity and sometimes aggressive behavior than average parents would be.

Trossman's work (1968) with children of survivors at a student mental health clinic elicited a number of common features. He found overprotective parents who seemed to encourage phobic responses in children. He also described instances where a child was exposed to continued verbal assaults in being used as an audience for parents' accounts of their harrowing experiences. Such assaults, he felt, were likely to contribute to guilt and depression in a child. There is, in this connection, the difficulty of determining which has a more salutary effect and which a more traumatic one: the endless account of tribulations or the silence practiced by many survivor-parents in their well-intentioned wish to spare their children stories about the traumatic past. The "pact of silence" may frequently encourage a child to elaborate fantasies that are even more frightening and pathogenic. It appears that the recounting of parental experiences depends more on how they are told and in what spirit, on whether the information is used to inform and educate or is employed as a threat. Other common features found by Trossman include the transmission to offspring of a suspicious attitude to an external world perceived as hostile and the almost impossible expectations from children to provide meaning to the empty lives of parents.

Krystal has emphasized that survivor parents might, without conscious intention, encourage in their children aggressive behavior that they could not permit themselves to express to their own martyred families. Conversely, as we have said, clinical observations have indicated that survivor parents frequently have less than an average degree of tolerance for aggression on the part of their children, even when it is age appropriate and well within the range of expectable active behavior. It is also possible that identification with a brutally aggressive oppressor may have served as an important unconscious mechanism to master the helplessness experienced by survivors during their captivity. Projection onto one's children of such aggressive fantasies may later serve an ongoing defensive purpose.

In Volume II of *The Child in His Family: The Impact of Disease and Death*, edited by E. J. Anthony and C. Koupernik (1973), an entire section is devoted to a symposium on children of the Holocaust. Opening with some editorial comments by Anthony (p. 355) and introductory remarks by Judith S. Kestenberg (pp. 359–61), additional contributions are included by authors from the United States, Canada, and Israel. Anthony begins eloquently by referring with compassion and sensitivity to some of the paradoxical attitudes stimulated by survivorship, and then turns almost immediately to a discussion of the impact of Hiroshima, which had been studied by Robert J. Lifton (1967) and the landslide at Aberfan, Wales, which killed 114 children. One can only hazard a guess about the curious emphasis in this editorial comment: it is as if the Holocaust is so overwhelming emotionally that an immediate comparison to other catastrophic events is necessary to reduce it to an acceptable scale. Kestenberg, in her introductory remarks, comments on her own experience in the treatment of a young adolescent whose recovery was facilitated when the impact of the Holocaust on his parents was brought into the treatment. She suggests a number of questions for the symposium to consider: among them are the readiness of the analyst to face such disturbing problems, and the problem of whether psychoanalytic work can uncover any-thing unique in the dynamics operating in children of Holocaust survivors. She further brings to our attention the scanty literature based on psychoana-lytic work with children of survivors, and also cautions us to acknowledge the strengths as well as the weaknesses and vulnerabilities we may encounter as we increase our clinical experience with patients whose families have been victims of the Holocaust.

A large section of the symposium was devoted to presentations based on those that had been given at the Congress of Child Psychiatry held in Jerusa-lem in 1970. These included studies conducted in Israel on survivor-families by means of interviews, psychological tests, and, in some instances, psycho-therapy. D. R. Aleksandrowicz (1973) investigated the potential effects of Nazi persecution, posing the question whether psychic scars carried by people who survived their ordeals affect the mental health of their children. He asked whether the children show any typical or specific symptoms related to traumas suffered by their parents. Families with grossly disturbed parents were excluded from the study, and the methodology did not include any sta-tistical analysis. The conclusions drawn were therefore purely impressionistic. The thirty-four families studied were described as falling into two main groups. The first showed families with "parental disequilibrium," where the survivor parent seemed strong, capable, and intelligent and had married a spouse beneath his or her level, socially and intellectually. Parental authority in these cases was out of balance, with one parent respected and the other despised. The other group comprised families where the survivor-parent suf-fered from "affective deficiency" which had been attributed by other re-searchers to the need for massive repression of traumatic memories. The pic-ture of cultural conflict in children of survivors described by observers in other countries was not obvious in Israel, where acculturation in a Jewish state seemed sharply to reduce a sense of alienation. The author concluded that emotional scars left by concentration camp experiences may result in problems in the second generation but are only one factor in a complex of pathogenic influences. Where problems were found, they did seem to be re-lated to the emotional scars of the survivor parent. The author recommended that further comparative studies with other parent groups might throw addi-tional light on the question of the transmission of trauma incurred during the Holocaust.

H. Klein, in the same section, reported on a systematic study conducted in Israel between 1967 and 1969 on twenty-five survivor families living on kib-butzim. Three survivors received psychotherapy; the data were otherwise gathered from interviews and testing. The group was fairly homogeneous: the families came from a lower middle class Polish background, and most were adolescents during the war and affiliated with Zionist youth organizations. An important finding in this group, many of whom had fought with partisan units, was the seeming absence of individual and family psychopathology during early developmental phases. They had come to the experiences of the Holocaust after growing up in a warm and supportive atmosphere, perhaps a determinant of their survival.

The destruction of their familiar world disrupted feelings of security and self-representation, and these survivors could not experience and work through ritualized grief and mourning for the loss of loved ones. There ensued considerable denial and a form of magical thinking about resurrection of lost families which the survivors could only gradually abandon. Only after they had done so could libidinal energies be employed toward developing new love relationships and rebuilding a community. An important characteristic of this group, which may have accelerated acculturation, was that their individual and collective rebirth coincided with the re-establishment of a Jewish state. Klein's poignant vignettes illustrate the vulnerabilities and adaptive mechanisms seen in these families. One man who had spent five years in a ghetto and a concentration camp, encountered a German kibbutz volunteer in the fields: rage welled up in him, but he mastered it and presented the grapes he had cultivated, saying, "Your father gave my father Cyclon B. I am giving you the fruit of the land of Israel." They both cried and were then able to relate to each other as individuals rather than as stereotypes.

Klein feels that a profusion of fantasy life serves as a coping mechanism for both generations, frees ego restrictions, and aids neutralization of aggressive energy. Children's fantasies can provide a sense of security and cathartic relief from anxiety; and those that involve themes of danger, death, and salvation can have a favorable effect on the resolution of the Oedipus complex in sons. Internalization of the father image as a victim of aggression and as a hero can diminish castration fears and encourage identification with a benign father image. In adolescence, revival of oedipal conflicts can bring to the surface an identification with father as hero along with a reduction of fear and anxiety about the self—a phenomenon noted during military service. Such an outcome might serve an adaptive function in a besieged country like Israel, but would do so at the expense of intensifying projection and mobilizing aggression against the external world. However, Klein and other researchers have observed that survivors and their children have a profound fear of being sadists or aggressors. Realization of their successful defense of Israel made survivors uneasy, unaccustomed as they were to being victors rather than vanquished; and they had a great need to justify any aggression as temporary and purely defensive.

Parent-child relationships in survivor-families were found to be characterized by a pattern derived from the primary motif of restoration of the lost family and undoing of destruction. Beginning during pregnancy, a number of women expressed fears of being changed from good mothers to witches who might give birth to monsters—an internalization of their persecutors' attitudes toward them. In some cases obsessive fears were based on real experiences when younger siblings or offspring were killed. Feelings of self-degradation derived from the Holocaust were expressed in the view of oneself as a prostitute or a hungry animal and created anxieties about one's potential for adequate mothering. These anxieties occasionally resulted in miscarriage, amenorrhea, or periods of sterility. Klein distinguishes between the obsessive fears of survivor-mothers and fantasies of neurotic mothers. Real experiences are the basis for fears in the former group; while, in the later, preoccupations and obsessions about the unborn child are rooted in pre-oedipal or oedipal conflicts. Some mothers felt that their emotional and physical responses to a first-born child was not adequate during its first months of life. They were overprotective and had a need to provide food. Repetitive persecutory dreams of being trapped with their children in a concentration camp confirm the interpretation that parental fears represented an expectation of a return of persecution. Children shared parents' fearful attitudes, and they all had difficulty separating from each other—a problem that was accentuated at times of illness and during war.

Survivor-parents spend more time at home with their children than do other kibbutz families. There is a great display of affection, overprotectiveness, and openness, understood by psychiatrists as a re-emergence of feeling suppressed during the Holocaust and as a recathexis of restored love objects, combined with defensive attitudes against anxiety about new losses. Expressions of closeness are even more evident when the parents relate their past and when real danger is confronted. The very concept of "family" is highly charged for survivors, and there is more discussion about relatives than in other kibbutz families, where children do not sustain parents' memories as intensely. Survivor-parents see their children as sources of security and gratification and maintain high expectations for them, with a special emphasis on intellectual achievement. Some difficult periods for mother-child relationships occur during the anal period, when the child experiments with autonomy and separation, and during adolescence, which frequently corresponds to the period of the parents' traumatization in the Holocaust.

Along with other researchers, Klein emphasizes that the experience and expression of mourning is central in the life of survivors. He underlines how the kibbutz provides an environment where unresolved mourning can be worked through. On Israel's annual day of commemoration, the community mourns together. This affirmation of the meaning of the past is perceived by both Klein and the survivors as a positive force for the future, linked to the rebirth of the Jewish people in the state of Israel. The children participate in the mourning ritual and replace for their parents the generation that perished. These observations led Klein and his colleagues to suggest that collective rituals undertaken at various levels can allow families and individuals to work through feelings of shame, anger, and fear and to release emotional energy that might otherwise be misdirected. The value of these studies indicates the great importance of making comparative studies of the dynamics of survivor-families in several societies, so that the varied responses to trauma, both pathological and adaptive, can be further illuminated.

Three contributions in the symposium addressed themselves to psychoanalytic work with children of survivors and are notable because of the relative dearth of such reports in psychoanalytic literature. M. Laufer (1973) presented the analysis of Stanford H., an adolescent boy who had been born after his father died in a concentration camp. The mother remarried when the child was just over the age of four, and died during his adolescence—a set of special circumstances that made it difficult to isolate problems uniquely connected with the boy's being the child of a survivor. Despite high intelligence, the boy did not do well at school, a blow to his mother who expected him to become an intellectual as his father had been. When the mother became seriously ill, he was not prepared for her death by either his stepfather or his grandmother. His mother died when the boy was fifteen, eight months after he had begun analysis. Feeling unable to cry, he was shocked and full of guilt because he could not show any overt grief. He would not change his clothes, refused to see people, but assumed responsibility for shopping and cooking in the home. An early concern of the analyst was about Stanford's potential for suicide, because of remarks the boy had made indicating a wish for death. A less ominous view was to regard them as expressing both an identification with his dead father and aggression toward him as—in the boy's view—a passive victim of the Nazis. Analysis of his inability to touch his penis following his mother's death led to the uncovering of incestuous fantasies and of some earlier ideas that his mother might have been a prostitute and that he was illegitimate.

Analytic work helped Stanford with his mourning and with plans for the future. He entered a technical career instead of trying to become an intellectual; his choice was understood to be connected with fantasies that his father had died of starvation, and gave him the adaptive opportunity to play a nurturing role. Stanford continued to do well; and when he expressed a desire to leave analysis after four years, the analyst agreed. His progress has been followed to his present age of twenty-five, and Stanford has functioned adequately.

Laufer (1973) saw pathology as overdetermined by four major themes or areas of conflict: damage to normal infantile omnipotence because of the father's inability to survive; a feminine identification with the victim; the inhibition of aggressivity that tied him to his mother and made his adolescent sexuality feel dangerous; and the disturbed relationship to his own body observed in his attitude to death, seen as a fantasy of reunion with the dead father and mother. Despite overdetermined special aspects of the patient's developmental history, Laufer felt it was possible to recognize areas of vulnerability which seemed characteristic of children of survivors.

In the published discussion, M. Williams (1973) questioned the detrimental impact on Stanford's development from hearing stories of the dead father and being rescued by the mother. The author saw preservation of omnipotence which led the boy to feel special and may have served a later adaptive purpose. She questioned the intensity of the identification with the victim, emphasized the vitality and enterprise of the mother, and called attention to her insistence that her son undertake treatment, a rather uncommon experience in general and even less common in survivor-families. The suicidal potential was not regarded as seriously by Williams as by the analyst. She felt it was difficult to make a definitive evaluation of the effects of the trauma, and stressed the importance of assessing each patient as an individual. Solnit's discussion (Laufer 1973, pp. 371–72) focused on the role of fantasy in the formation of identifications and pointed out how such fantasy is often discouraged in orphaned children. The ability of a mother to encourage fantasy may help to explain the variety of personality and character types seen in children of survivors.

L. Rosenberger (1973) maintained firmly that children of survivors show no distinctive pathology, and that any differences seen derive from the particular handling by parents as a reflection of their own personalities. She distinguishes two types of survivor parents: those who disregard the child's emotional needs and are obsessed with providing food and material things to prevent the hunger and deprivation they experienced; and those who identify with the growing child, using him or her for the gratification of their own narcissistic needs. Rosenberger presented a rather schematic analysis of a late adolescent with school problems and depression. Despite initially dismissing the Holocaust as a crucial experience, Rosenberger cited several examples contrary to that opinion, and concluded that only after assimilating his father's concentration camp experiences did it become possible for Stanford to report dreams and associate freely.

E. Furman's contribution (1973) to the symposium was organized around the presentation of the analytic work done with a three-and-a-half-year-old boy, Franz M. She cautioned, as have others, that any clinical picture one sees as a psychoanalyst is based on a combination of influences derived from individual personality development, upon which is superimposed the traumatic experience. Franz seemed utterly lacking in basic mastery: speech, independent eating, and self-differentiation. He feared being overwhelmed from within and without—a fear that he warded off by trying to control people and objects. When this failed, he had severe anxiety and tantrums. There was an intense primitive relationship between mother and son. She was tyrannical and controlling in some areas and treated him as a narcissistic extension of herself in others. The father was a remote student who expected his son to behave like a much older child. Both parents had come from Eastern Europe: the mother from an orthodox community, and the father from an assimilated one. When the Nazis came, the mother was forced to betray her aunt and uncle in an effort to save her parents. The mother and her parents survived a concentration camp, while the rest of the family were killed. The father, who had also survived a camp, met his wife after the war and emigrated to the United States after their marriage. A detail worthy of emphasis is that Franz was the survivor of twins, the other of whom had died soon after birth. An important complication of Franz's development was the intermittent and fluctuating care of him by the mother and the maternal grandmother. The child was forced to accommodate to two polarized worlds: he was urged to become an "American" boy, while remaining in the parochial world of his grandparents. The description of the treatment is as much a testimony to the helpful education provided by the therapist to the mother, as it is an explanation of the analytic work that facilitated Franz's development. In concluding, Furman indicated the importance of providing the boy with appropriate information about the Holocaust and also stressed the need to study individual cases intensively and to avoid tempting generalizations.

A report that should be included in a review of the scanty literature dealing with classical analyses of individuals who have been influenced by the events of the Holocaust, is that by S. Brody (1973) about Günter S., the son of a refugee—a report that is intended to show connections between a specific historical event, a father's flight from Nazi persecution, and an aspect of the son's neurotic conflicts during adolescence. Brody concluded by offering a hypothesis that when a father has been sought by police and regarded as a criminal, that very external reality can have profound effects, regardless of actual guilt. In this case, it appeared sufficient to facilitate Günter's projection of his oedipal wishes onto the father, and thus to lead him to perceive the father as the oedipal criminal. Brody emphasized the interplay between the inevitable instinctual forces and the actual historical event that can shape defenses and the ultimate character formation of a patient.

Another recent paper, which is not based on psychoanalytic material but is noteworthy for touching on diagnostic issues that seem particularly relevant to children of survivors, is the report by S. Axelrod, O. L. Schnipper, and J. H. Rau (1980) on hospitalized children of survivor-families. The clinical data presented by the authors raise some important and seminal questions about the nature of the regressions and the ego functions one may see in some young people who might be regarded as showing schizophrenic symptoms, but who may have to be regarded in another light when more closely scrutinized.

A trend that has recently developed among many members of the second generation should not go unmentioned. Some of these young people who were frequently interested in one or another of the helping professions, began to band together in groups to discuss some of their common concerns and problems. Among the mental health professionals who were active in forming these groups and acting as leaders and facilitators were Y. Danieli (1980) and E. Fogelman and B. Savran (1979, 1980).

Judith S. Kestenberg had for a number of years been interested in examining the effects of the Holocaust on the second generation. Her ideas had been sharply crystallized by analytic work done with a young patient (1972) who had behaved in a bizarre way and treated the analyst as a hostile persecutor. She then devised and sent several hundred questionnaires to colleagues in several countries, inquiring if they had analyzed any children of survivor families and whether the analyses indicated any special features. The questionnaire was used to prepare the programs for a congress on child psychiatry in Israel in 1970; it was also used for a colloquium sponsored by the American Psychoanalytic Association in 1971 (reported by S. M. Sonnenberg [1974]). Kestenberg learned from her inquiries that only a few of such children had been analyzed, and—as Epstein (1979) has aptly pointed out—was able to draw more certain conclusions about the analysts than about the patients. She found that many analysts showed an amazing indifference to the problems, and that many were startled because it had never occurred to them to link their patients' dynamics to the history of their parents' persecutions. It was largely because of Kestenberg's initiative and inspiration that a study group was organized to investigate the effects of the Holocaust on the second generation, through psychoanalytically derived material, in a systematic and large-scale way.

The study group has been meeting regularly since 1974, once a month whenever possible. Each meeting is devoted to the detailed study of a patient who is being treated, or has been treated, by one of the psychoanalysts in the group or by an invited guest. The discussion centers first on the general problems presented by the case, and on diagnosis, phenomenology, dynamic and genetic questions, and problems of technique. Then the focus usually shifts to the relevance of the Holocaust for a better understanding of the general functioning and psychopathology encountered in the patient. The particular interest of the group is whether survivor-parents can transmit to, and influence conflict and psychopathology in, their offspring as a result of trauma incurred during the Holocaust; and if they can, what form this transmission may take. Grappling with the problem of specificity has been difficult. Investigation is constantly faced with the complex, interwoven strands of what may be called the "private pathology" of the patient and of what may be exquisitely related to the Holocaust—a paradigm of the attribution of pathogenesis common to all psychoanalytic research methodology. Most of the clinical pictures encountered showed a wide variation and conflicts and symptoms that would be difficult to differentiate from those found in children of other traumatized groups or even from a population that is considered average in our own culture. The child of a Holocaust survivor is exposed to the Holocaust as filtered through the experiences of the parents. The Holocaust thus becomes but one aspect, and a significant one, of the relationship of the parents and the family to the child.

Over the course of six years, thirty-four cases have been studied in depth. Thirty of these patients were either adult survivors (one was persecuted as a child), refugees or children of refugees, or children whose parents survived the Holocaust in concentration camps or as partisans or ghetto fighters. Twelve children of survivors were patients who were in psychoanalysis and nine had been seen in psychoanalytic psychotherapy. One psychotherapy case was an adult survivor whose child was in the group of survivors' children seen in psychoanalysis. The remaining eight cases fit into a miscellaneous group who had encountered the Holocaust either in adulthood or childhood in varying circumstances ranging from dislocation as a refugee to a concentration camp victim. These eight patients were all in psychoanalysis. The remaining four patients, all in psychoanalysis, are the children of Nazis.

# Prelude

The opportunity to investigate case material in detail was afforded the study group by the cooperation with German colleagues who shared their experiences with us at conferences and discussion groups.

## Children of Nazis

Part III deals with problems encountered in psychoanalytic work with children of Nazis. No social experience known is comparable to surviving a concentration camp, but the destructive effect of Nazi ideology on German children was nevertheless profound. Children of Nazis are also victims. Comparing the two groups leads to a deeper understanding of the interaction between ego and superego pathology.

A number of German colleagues who have shared their experience in analyzing children of Nazi parents have contributed to this volume and enriched our knowledge. They, too, have had to grapple with problems of specificity in conceptualizing their methodology, and to deal with the question whether the preoccupation of their patients with the Nazi era is a defense to ward off earlier pathogenic influences or vice versa. No matter how the issues are viewed, those of the young generation in Germany, as Kestenberg pointed out (1977), still need to come to grips with their consciences, not just with their victims.

The studies included in this volume are still in progress. Nearly every case report that has been scrutinized and discussed illuminates an aspect of the problem which has been in shadow before. Yet one is reminded of Freud's words: "When you think of me, think of Rembrandt. A little light and a great deal of darkness."* The editors and contributors hope that this book will shed further light to help children of survivors within the framework of psychoanalysis and that it will demonstrate that psychoanalysis can make a valid contribution to trauma stemming from the interaction of individual pathology and social catastrophe.

---

* This quotation of Freud's was reported to Martin Bergmann over a quarter of a century ago by Paul Federn, a member of Freud's earliest circle.

# PART I

# The Background

# 1

# *The Background of the Study*

PEOPLE WHO ESCAPED from Nazi persecution before and during the Second World War, and those who were liberated by Allied troops and came out from hiding after the war, attempted to forge a new existence in countries other than their own. But when they approached people who did not share their fate, they were faced with a mixture of disbelief and pity and frequently with a wall of silence (Porter 1978; Danieli 1980). Before and during the war, refugee agencies assisted the displaced persons. At the end of the war, the help offered the victims was insufficient; and the horror of their experiences, discovered by the liberators and described in diaries of victims, was overshadowed by the general trend to restore the shattered image of Germany and to forget the Holocaust. The world wanted to forget the unbelievable; perhaps believing might have interfered with the extension of help to the defeated who were to be rehabilitated, denazified, and indemnified for what the Allied armies had inflicted upon them. Psychiatrists and other mental health professionals, among them victims themselves, were not immune to the mass denial that prevailed during and after the Holocaust. (For exceptions, such as Friedman 1948 and 1949, see our Prelude to this volume.)

Internists and psychiatrists played a role as consultants to government and private agencies helping survivors, but the latter's plight did not begin to receive the legal and medical attention it deserved until West Germany passed its restitution law in 1953. Many victims of persecution felt that money would not restore their losses, and they refused the monetary amends of West Germany. Other victims felt that restitution was owed to them and had to be accepted because it constituted an admission of guilt on the part of Germans. Many victims were so debilitated and impoverished that they needed the money awarded to them and could not afford to refuse it, even if this meant that they had to submit to traumatizing and humiliating interrogations (see chapter 3). The official admission of guilt on the part of the one-time persecutors also served to diminish the collective guilt of the bystanders who had allowed Hitler to dispossess, torture, and kill millions of people but had not attempted to rescue and provide refuge for them.

The tortuous legal process of the restitution practices delayed payments to sick victims; and not until many years later was there any acknowledgment of damage to the victims' mental health. Required to submit reports about the health of survivors, many psychiatrists and psychoanalysts began the investigation of what was later called the "survivor syndrome" by Niederland (1961). (For the early and later literature about survivors' mental health, see Grubrich-Simitis 1979 and the Prelude to this volume.) There ensued a discussion of whether survivors could or should be treated with psychoanalysis (Symposium 1967); and only a handful of analytic procedures were undertaken (Winnik 1967a and b, 1968). Attention was paid rather early to child-survivors, some of whom were analyzed in London (A. Freud and Dann 1951; Gyomroi 1963; Wolfheim 1966). Many more analyses were completed of refugees from the persecution than of survivors of concentration camps. There was a reluctance to analyze patients whose terrible past could be re-lived in analyses. One gains the impression that the analysts themselves could not yet listen at a time when they themselves were participating in the mass denial of the extent of the trauma. It was easier to deal with the less excessive traumatization of the survivor dubbed "refugee," who was "only" threatened with genocide and robbed of his or her identity. In 1968, H. Winnik presented excerpts from two psychoanalyses: one of a survivor who was a child during Nazi persecution and was hidden by a Christian family; and another of a patient, born to survivor-parents after the war. These two cases,

"marginal" from the point of persecution, exhibited typical symptoms of the "survivor syndrome" without having actually been internees of concentration camps. These cases prove how far-reaching the sequelae of such persecution can be and that they may appear even in the second generation, the children of the persecutees. (P. 301)

In discussing their own reluctance to face the facts of the Holocaust, Williams and Kestenberg (1974) began to speak of a latency period that had to be traversed before one could give up the denial and repression of the unspeakable terror (see also Sonnenberg 1974). The period of long latency served as a distancing maneuver from the trauma that could not be averted. Analyzing a survivor before a successful working through of denial, and ignoring the patient's past, led to countertransference problems, which interfered with analyses of survivors and their children. Moses (1978) spoke of having been with others "a partner to the denial of the impact" not only of the Holocaust but also of several wars that threatened the state of Israel. During the 1973 war, the vulnerable Israeli defenders, many of them survivors or their children, were helped by a support system of psychological first-aid stations. Israeli psychiatrists rose to the occasion; their readiness paralleled the awakening of psychiatric attention to the Holocaust when there was an immediate and practical need to write reports for survivors to ensure restitution payments. When reality demanded that psychoanalysts step in actively to remedy rather than endure long periods of helpless listening, feelings of guilt were reduced, defenses decreased, and research could begin.* However, most of the research was based on interviews and psychotherapy rather than on psychoanalyses. To the degree that restitution laws were looked upon as amends and enabled the previously passive onlookers to mobilize themselves, they were a welcome sign and psychologically helpful. However the nature of these laws, and the sometimes insidious way in which they continued the persecution of victims, impeded the progress made by the survivors and their advocates (see chapter 3). Moneys were obtained for the treatment of survivors; but little attention was paid to their children, who were reared by traumatized parents, frequently retraumatized by the restitution-centered investigation of their past (Krystal 1968; Wangh 1968, 1969; Kestenberg 1972, 1974).

## *Analyses of Children of Survivors*

Children of survivors had been seen in consultations, treated with psychotherapy or psychoanalysis for some time; but until the late 1960s there was no acknowledgment of a possible connection between their problems and the traumatization of their parents (Winnik 1967, 1968; Krystal 1968; Wangh 1969). By then, Germany had spent more money on restitution than planned, and German attitudes were hardened with the ignorance and increased denial of a new generation that did not learn about the Holocaust in school (Kestenberg 1977, 1981). The laws did not provide for the undoing of the genocide or for the rehabilitation of Jewish generations, but were concerned with hard economic facts. A man or woman whose capacity to earn money was impaired because of persecution was entitled to restitution. A sojourn in a concentration camp of over a year was automatically presumed to be a cause of "damage." Otherwise proof of damage had to be given that, owing to being Jewish, one had been thrown out of one's house, one's place of business had been shattered, one's job given to a Nazi, one's money and valuables confiscated, one's life threatened, and one's children expelled from

---

* Danieli (1981) examined systematically the countertransference in the psychotherapy of Holocaust survivors and their children. She came to a conclusion, that the obstacle psychotherapists encounter in the treatment of these patients is part of a general reaction to the Holocaust, shared by the general population.

school: none of these abuses warranted the assumption that one had suffered impaired capacity to earn money and damage to health. Even less credibility was attached to the need to treat failures in parenting which would lead to no obvious loss of income. No connection was seen between the attempts to depreciate and annihilate the Jewish seed and the Jewish survivors' capacity to propagate and parent children of average expectable emotional health.

Many survivors rehabilitated themselves and raised children who made an excellent adjustment. Some survivors, however, began to seek help and bring their children to the attention of psychiatrists. When in 1969–70 a questionnaire was sent to child analysts in the United States and abroad asking whether they had treated children of survivors, the answers showed that "20 children of survivors, who themselves were not subject to persecution, have been analyzed" (Kestenberg 1972, p. 3) or were being analyzed at that time. There was considerable difficulty in collecting data from reliable sources; and in some cases it became evident that the analysts did not connect the parental Holocaust experiences with the children's material in analysis. This type of isolation would become institutionalized by highly trained researchers. An example is the ample material in the Hampstead Clinic in London where many survivors and many survivors' children had been analyzed; but their records cannot be found, because their highly specialized index did not include the item "survivor."* In the accounts of a few cases analyzed in the Hampstead Clinic in London which were made available by the analysts themselves, no reference was ever made to the parents' experiences in the Holocaust; but in one instance there was discussion of these experiences with the survivor-parent. Another typical example is that of a child analyst who was apprised, in the first analytic session, of the child's ideas about the parents' Holocaust experiences; the analysis continued and was terminated without any reference to this material. The analyst acted like the silent survivor parent who does not want to talk about the Holocaust. Many years later when the interest in survivors' children became universal, the analyst remembered the case and instituted a follow-up.

By the time the Group for the Psychoanalytic Study of the Effect of the Holocaust on the Second Generation was formed in 1974†, the majority of analyzed patients were adult children of survivors. No case of child analysis

* Joseph Sandler, personal communication.
† The members of the Group for the Psychoanalytic Study of the Effect of the Holocaust on the Second Generation included: Karolina Bein, Maria V. Bergmann, Martin Bergmann, Ari Falick, Elizabeth Gero-Heymann, Milton E. Jucovy, Shirley Jucovy, Milton Kapit, Hannah Kapit, Judith Kestenberg, Milton Kestenberg, Muriel Laskin, Ruth Lax, Yehuda Nir, Marion Oliner, Oscar Sachs, Martin Silverman, Jack Terry, Muriel Winestine, Liselotte Weyl, and Simon Weyl.

was presented during the deliberations of the group, despite the fact that there are now young children of survivors who had been victimized early in life.

The interest in children of survivors was revived when many of them reached adulthood and themselves became members of the helping professions. Groups were formed in which adult children of survivors could unload their feelings and discover that they have much in common. In Israel, the International Congress on the Psychological Adjustment in Time of War and Peace originated the Holocaust Study Group. Shamai Davidson (1972) now heads the Institute for Holocaust Studies in Tel Aviv. Groups were formed in the United States as well, and the teaching of Holocaust history followed in the footsteps of the introduction into colleges of courses on African History. The survivor-author Elie Wiesel took a pioneering role in this type of youth education. In the United States, a Holocaust Study Group was founded by psychologist L. Podietz. Helen Epstein's article in the *New York Times* (1977) and her book *Children of the Holocaust* (1979) indicated the interest that the children of the Holocaust survivors themselves were taking. Eva Fogelman and Bella Savran (1979, 1980) began to conduct short-term awareness groups for survivors' children, from which the creative, multidisciplinary group the Second Generation arose in Boston. Yael Danieli (1981; Hays and Danieli, 1976) founded the Group Project for Holocaust Survivors and Their Children. There are many more projects that cannot be listed here.

Despite the growth of interest in survivors' children, psychoanalytic data were scarce and difficult to find. Gradually, as the children of survivors themselves began to focus on their common heritage, they took the initiative to seek psychoanalytic treatment, and many more analysts began to pay attention to a subject that was no longer tabooed by society at large. This new attitude, however, did not become universal and did not pertain to child analysts. We can only speculate that the widespread avoidance of material from analyses of children is at least partially caused by Western culture's attitude toward children. Because of the relative weakness of their egos, we are more protective of them and hope that their young lives can be spared facing the Holocaust horrors. We hesitate to reveal to them that adults cannot always protect them; more than that, we hate to diminish their trust in the adult world by conceding that Nazi adults victimized their parents and did not shun the killing of children. Most of us would rather not talk to children about murder, and we tend to present death to them as a natural occurrence in old age (E. Furman 1974). Child analysts are not immune to the universal idea that children are better off denying and repressing rather than facing fears of a reality that transcends childhood fantasies. The conspiracy of silence may well be shared by the survivor-parents and the psychoanalysts themselves. Parents do not wish to acknowledge that their experiences have affected their cherished babies. Most parents tolerate it better when their children begin to focus on their Holocaust experiences in adolescence, the time when all young people scrutinize their parents with a critical eye while struggling to obtain independence from them. When adolescent offspring of survivors act out or become confused, their behavior forces parents to seek help (Sigal 1973). When the separation from parents is not completed in adolescence, young adults seek analyses for a variety of reasons; until recently, they rarely asked for treatment of symptoms and attitudes related to their parents' Holocaust experiences.

By the time the Group for the Psychoanalytic Study of the Effect of the Holocaust on the Second Generation was formed, there was already considerable controversy regarding the question whether there was indeed an effect of the Holocaust on the second generation. Whether parents' reactions to their past traumatization could exert a specific influence upon their children, was an open question. Although the period of "latency" was over, it was still noticeable that psychoanalysts, analytic candidates, and their supervisors were paying scant attention to the fact that an offspring of survivors was being treated. It was assumed that analyses would yield more data than psychotherapies regarding the transmission of parental traumatization to a child. It was expected that if a specific "survivor's-child syndrome" could be detected, analysis would reveal it with greater precision than would other forms of treatment or interviews. How accounts of analyses, conducted without reference to the Holocaust, could be of use in this investigation, was another important question to be considered. There was a disagreement among members of the group about who should be considered a survivor's child. Should only those who had been in concentration camps, in ghettos, or in hiding be considered survivors, or should we include in our study those who had escaped torture and those who escaped the Holocaust in the early days of the Third Reich? Since each survivor may have reacted differently to traumatization, we had to consider his or her pretrauma personality and family background as well as the time and conditions of persecution. Finally, we had to consider the influence of the new country in which the survivor had settled and the reciprocal influence between children and parents. Could we separate the individual development and individual psychopathology of our patients from traits and symptoms that were connected to the parents' Holocaust experience? Could we find a common link among children of survivors as specific as the common bond among obsessive patients? It was clear that a multifaceted task faced investigators of this complex problem:

# The Background of the Study

1. To locate psychoanalytic accounts of children of survivors and to have analytic colleagues come to our meetings to discuss their cases with us.

2. To confront the presenter of the case with questions that would help him to remember what he might have ignored or repressed during treatment, and to reconstruct the influence of parents on the child's personality—a task difficult to accomplish from analyses of adults.

3. To define who was considered a survivor and who was a child of a survivor; to re-examine the popular belief that those parents who had been most severely traumatized produced children with survivor's-child syndromes, while so-called refugees did not (Winnik 1968, p. 3).

4. To look for, in each case, the features that linked the patients' development to the Holocaust which their parents had endured.

5. To compare the findings in different cases and pinpoint the degree to which the main features of all cases had a common matrix rooted in the experiences of one or both parents.

## Finding Cases

Faced with the formidable task of finding suitable case material, the group was helped considerably by the discovery of accounts of analyses conducted in the treatment centers of psychoanalytic institutes; many of these accounts alluded to the parents' experience during the Holocaust only on the face sheet of a patient's application. Since 1974, psychoanalytic case histories have emerged from various cities in the United States, from Israel, and from Germany. As the investigative work of the group became better known, colleagues have come forward and volunteered to present material. Greater interest in this topic was followed by invitations to group members to give lectures on the subject (Jucovy 1978; Kestenberg 1977, 1978). Not infrequently, we were told by analysts that, upon listening to us, they realized that the analysis had not progressed because they had not paid attention to a patient's disguised allusions to the Holocaust. We had such reports from survivors' children as well. In one such instance, the patient was secretive and was acting out hiding in response to his father's pretending to be Christian to avoid persecution.

## Eliciting Latent or Forgotten Material

As case histories were scrutinized and discussed with analysts who were treating children of survivors currently or had done so in the past, it seemed at first impossible to find out anything about the experience of those patients' parents in the Second World War. Gradually techniques of inquiry were developed that helped the analyst to recall material that had not been included in the patients' protocol transcript but that emerged in follow-up interviews or continued analysis. One such aid was the question, "After whom was the patient named?"—posed with the idea that a child named after a grandparent or a sibling killed by the Nazis would indeed feel it a burden to have a name that reverberated with doom (Blos 1968). Scrutiny of the manifest content of dreams for images of the Holocaust—such as fires, escapes, shooting, uniforms, or boots—helped us to investigate the overdetermination in dreams, whereby repressed wishes were condensed with representations of Nazi persecution.

Eventually it was recognized that the parenting wishes and the parenting attitudes of the analysands must be examined in detail, with special attention to conflicts derived from the German genocide threat. Because each case was different, and each analyst as well, one had to take into consideration the patient's preoccupation with problems objectively unrelated to the Holocaust, the analyst's selection of what is to be analyzed and when and how, as well as the supervisors' directions to the students—directions that, in some cases, constituted admonitions not to be interested in the Holocaust. The parameter used by child analysts to inform young patients of their parents' past, or to instruct the parents to do so (Kestenberg 1972; Furman 1973; Rosenberger 1973), was not applicable to the adult patient; but the questions arose whether the parent was unable to tell the child about his or her past, or whether the child was reluctant to ask. What were the patient's feelings about such questions? At what point of the analysis did he or she feel free enough to ask a parent? What stood in the way of the analyst who could not ask a patient about a parent's past? Some analysts were stunned to discover that they had ignored or forgotten pertinent material related to the Holocaust.

An important finding that evolved from this "detective work" was the refinement of critical evaluations of certain data about parents in the light of history (Podietz 1975). Knowledge of what had occurred, when and in what place, helped to clarify some distortions or omissions that could be used by parents, patients, or therapists to circumvent or ignore the effect of the Holocaust on the children of victims. In one instance, a patient who had all along

# The Background of the Study

questioned her mother's account of the latter's experience in Poland, could confront her with appropriate questions only when she, the patient, discovered through reading history, that what she had been told was historically inaccurate. An analyst who did not know the historical data himself, could not help a patient to understand or to organize his question. Sometimes analysts thought that a patient's parent had been in Auschwitz, but did not realize that Auschwitz inmates were all tattooed with a number and thus that such a thought could be verified. Patients obtained information not only from direct disclosures from parents but also from parents' remarks addressed to each other or to friends. Reading and attending study groups was a source of information frequently shunned by patients. We learned that a claim that there was no connection between the parents' Holocaust life and the patient's life, or that an account—in the professional literature—in which such a connection was not acknowledged, would have to stand the test of further inquiry before we could accept it.*

As we have pointed out before, we had to take into account the various personalities of the parents as well as the children's constitutional endowment and the traumata they themselves had experienced in childhood. Pre-Holocaust and post-Holocaust cultural differences had to play an important role in the development of the patients. We might have expected to see an essential difference in the psychoanalytic accounts of different cases and from different countries. It came as a surprise that the manner in which Holocaust material was presented openly or in disguise in the analyses of children of survivors was essentially the same in the United States, in Israel, and in Germany, despite the fact that each case preserved his or her own individuality on the basis of parental and individual experiences and cultural influences in the land of the parents' origin and in the land where they brought up their children.

---

* A case in point is Heinz Kohut's (1971 and 1977) account of Mr. A.: "Two events which affected the family fortunes decisively when the patient [Mr. A.] was six and eight years old respectively." The threat of the German armies overrunning the country interrupted the son's close relationship with his father. When the patient was six, the family had to flee when the Germans invaded the country. In consequence of the German invasion of the country to which they fled, once more everything was lost when the patient was eight years old. Kohut acknowledged (1971, p. 60) that the "father's extreme, sudden and unpredictable mood swings during the oedipal and preoedipal period" were at least in part responsible for the patient's structural defect. However, when Kohut was asked to provide the material that would allow us to search for a connection of the pathology with Holocaust experiences, he felt certain that such a connection did not exist (personal communication). He had discovered that the "hub of the patient's psychological defect . . . related to the traumatic disappointment in the idealized father image in early latency" (p. 61). However, it did not seem likely that the father's degradation by the German invaders, and his failure to stand up to them and maintain his business, was a crucial issue in the child's loss of faith in him.

## Definitions as Limitations and Refinement

The majority of the cases studied involved children of survivors who were born after the Second World War had ended in Europe. Only a few patients had been subjected to unusual hardship themselves in camps, in hiding, through expulsion from school and hurried escape. This latter group were considered survivors themselves. An example was a child who at the age of two had escaped from Europe with his parents. In his adulthood, he dreamed about traveling on water, on the basis not only of his parents' experiences but also of his own. It remains an issue of further study to explicate how such dream images might differ from the emotional impact of experiences in which a patient did not personally participate. An investigation of such cases will have to await the accumulation of further evidence.

The category of survivor's child was reserved for those who were born after parental liberation and were not themselves subject to persecution. It was much more difficult to define who is a survivor-parent. As might be expected, there has been some controversy about this issue. No doubt, threats, dispossession, and exile are not as far-reaching and massive a trauma as torture, starvation, illness, prolonged confinement, forced labor, and the daily escape from extermination. However, because our investigative interest focused primarily on one aspect of a survivor's functioning—namely, one's ability to parent and one's need to transmit traumatic experiences to one's offspring, the following characterization of parent-survivors has been proposed as the most useful for this study:

a survivor is one who as a result of Nazi persecution suffered the loss of love as a member of a social group, had to mourn the loss of self and objects as well as institutions, and has been bombarded by sado-masochistic events—not fantasies—which threaten to disrupt his psychic organization. His task is to rebuild it, and he can do so as he creates a new generation, free of survivor-guilt.

(Kestenberg 1972, p. 11)

Many researchers and students of the problems of the "Second Generation" take it for granted that only survivors of massive trauma are to be included in their investigations. In some instances, Holocaust survivors are included under the heading of all survivors from manmade disasters (Sigal 1978; Lifton 1967 and 1969). In the Group for the Psychoanalytic Study of the Effect of the Holocaust on the Second Generation, there were presented a number of cases whose parents had not been in camps or ghettos but had managed to escape the clutches of the Nazi tide before 1938–39. A detailed review of the differences in sequelae depending on the nature of the parental experience is still incomplete; but this author and others have called attention to the fact that much of the data collected and sometimes characterized as specifically influenced by parental persecution inflicted by Nazis, were derived from cases that should technically be called children of refugees (Brody 1973; Winnik 1968). There does indeed seem to be a greater kinship between problems of Holocaust survivors and refugees than between Holocaust survivors and survivors of natural or other manmade disasters, such as floods, earthquakes, war, and slavery. There seems to be little doubt on the part of those who hold this view that a parent who has lived under threats, and has suffered from daily torture, physical deprivation, and starvation, is likely to have a different influence on children from that of a parent who has lost only a position in society or material possessions. Yet there is a common link among these parents that warrants further attention.

## Parents' Holocaust Experiences and
## Patients' Emotional Development

### LINKING FEATURES

As the investigations proceeded, the dynamics of each case was studied with special reference to the issue of parents' survival—whether through liberation or escape. Stimulated by the rigorous thinking of several investigators in the group who watched over scientific methodology and compared findings with cases unrelated to the Holocaust,* it became clearer that it was unwise to anticipate an *absolute* specificity linking a parent's Holocaust experience with a child's traits that were unique and exclusive and could not be found in others who were not children of Holocaust survivors. This problem has been discussed in relation to many other questions arising in the course of scientific psychoanalytic investigations; one prominent example arose out of attempts to link obsessive traits to strict toilet training in childhood. The latter does not always result in an obsessive-compulsive personality, and it is certainly not true that all obsessives had a strict toilet training. Yet evidence of some linkage is clinically verifiable and justified. As the process of distinguishing between individual characteristics and those that could be derived from the Holocaust developed, it became necessary to explore as well whether

---

* Outstanding among them were Muriel Winestine and Jack Terry.

the findings depended on the usual linkage between parental behavior and a child's development (Sigal 1978). Gradually it appeared that there was something distinctly different between the need of a survivor's child to live in a parent's Holocaust past and the usual and expected identifications that all people have with their parents (chapter 5).

## THE COMMON MATRIX

Although there is general agreement that a definitive survivor's-child syndrome has not emerged (chapter 7), there does seem to be a similarity both in content and in metapsychological features. For example, the question of how a parent survived—whether he or she was guilty, base, betrayer, or hero—becomes a central theme in the analysis of survivors' children. Another central theme is the preoccupation with specific experiences of the parents, such as starvation, details of persecution, and loss of family members. It is almost universal for a child of a survivor family to grapple with the conflict of whether one should dwell on the Holocaust or whether to forget it. These themes are not necessarily conscious in patients, and many layers are present that require patient analysis and working through. A person with an eating problem may go through life suffering from a conflict in the oral phase without connecting the problem with the fact that, to the parents, food was a means of survival in a far more literal sense than to an average overanxious parent (Rosenberger 1973). The theme of survival may not appear in an analysis but, instead, may color every experience, as if it were always of immediate concern. It can thus affect the quality of the drives, the ego, and the superego and, in doing so, is an extremely important aspect of a survivor's child's profile. Both the content of survivors' children's fantasies and the structure of their psyche may be part of a normal survivor's-child complex (see chapter 7).

The question regarding the manner in which parents may transmit their experiences to their children is certainly a complex one. Childhood experiences influence parenting patterns, and survivors' parenting functions are obviously conflict-laden in many instances. They may transmit to their children the message that they, the children, must justify their existence by becoming a living monument to the triumph over the Nazis' nearly successful annihilation of the Jewish people (Kestenberg 1972). The issue becomes even more complicated when survivor parents had been persecuted during their own childhood or adolescence. In these instances, repetition of the trauma in relation to the children may be bound by two factors: identification with the parents' own parents, who "abandoned" them, and identification with the persecutors, who became authorities in lieu of the degraded and killed parents.

44

# The Background of the Study

It is also important to inquire how far a survivor-parent has succeeded in the process of rehabilitation, so that an appraisal can be made of how much self-esteem the child can gain by identification with that parent. The total background of the survivor-parent is therefore contingent not only on pre-Holocaust and Holocaust experiences but also on post-Nazi sources of persecution and discrimination (see chapter 3). Before considering clinical examples that lead to a metapsychological assessment of survivors' children, one must keep in mind that not only the past, but also the present, problems of survivors play a role in the manner in which they feel and act as parents of the second generation. In studying their background, we must be aware not only of the various problems besetting survivor-parents, but also of how they organize these problems in the wake of their Holocaust experiences.

**2**

# The Experience of
# Survivor-Parents

AN UNDERSTANDING of the special problems faced by children of survivors requires an examination of the unusual and anomalous position in which survivor-parents find themselves. One must consider especially the impact of the Nazi Holocaust on parental self-esteem and trust in parenthood, and the nature of post-Holocaust extension of persecution which undermines children's trust in their survivor-parents and tries the coping mechanisms of children of survivors (chapters 3 and 4).

## The Nature of the Trauma

Every natural and man-made disaster threatens the survival of a group of people and renders its victims powerless. Krystal (1978) defined adult trauma as "surrender to inevitable danger" (p. 113). Freud's concept of the traumatic neuroses was predicated on cases of "shell shock" during the First World War.* The situation of helplessness and the inability to protect oneself seemed to require a reliving and a mastery of the traumatic event in the dreams of those affected by traumatic neuroses. To the degree that Nazis assaulted their victims and rendered them helpless, survivors also suffer from recurring dreams of persecution. Their children sometimes share their dreams even though they were not overwhelmed by sudden shocks in their own experience (Winnik 1968). These shared nightmares can become an integral aspect of the parent-child relationship. They can be curative in nature and thus precious, to be retained at all costs until the trauma is sufficiently attenuated to fade as a shocking memory.

* For the controversial aspect of Freud's trauma theory, see the Prelude to this volume.

# The Experience of Survivor-Parents

The following example may indicate the intuitive awareness of a need to preserve such shared dreams in the service of mastery of such trauma. A mother and daughter both suffered from Holocaust dreams and were referred to a dream laboratory where a medication was offered to curtail and suppress the dreams. On the day of the appointment, mother and daughter departed for an unexpected vacation. It seems likely that, through these dreams, mother and child are united in a special way, linking survivors of the Holocaust and their children. The child behaves as if he or she had been present during the parent's specific traumatic experience which is experienced by both in repetitive dreams. Many of these dreams do not refer to a one-time traumatic event like "shell shock" but are condensations of many traumatizations in which one type of persecution becomes the organizer of the others— for instance, dreams of shooting, explosions, or pursuit by attackers. These are also representations of infantile interpretations of reality and as such can be related to pre-genital and genital infantile impulses.

Some authors refer to "strain trauma," as opposed to "shock trauma"; the former makes the individual more vulnerable to the latter (Solnit and Kris 1967). References are also made to the summation of partial traumata which must be distinguished from the concept of "cumulative trauma," developed by M. M. R. Khan (1963). Every painful event is experienced as a loss and as a punishment (Krystal 1978)—especially by children. H. Krystal distinguishes between the infantile form of trauma, which is an unbearable state of distress, and the adult form of trauma, in which the individual surrenders to inevitable danger and progresses from anxiety to abnormal states, ending perhaps in "psychogenic death." Ilse Grubrich-Simitis (1979) postulates that the traumatization of the second generation is due to Khan's cumulative trauma caused by the mother's chronic insensitivity to her infant. Grubrich-Simitis cites various factors affecting the survivor-mother, such as her regression and the blunting of her perceptions that contributes to her becoming the source of her children's traumatization. This view contrasts with that of authors (Krystal 1968; Danieli 1980, 1981) who observe survivors' children's symbiotic attachments to their families from whom the children are unable to separate. Insensitive mothers have difficulty developing a mutuality, characteristic of the normal symbiosis between mother and child (Erikson 1959; Benedek 1949; Mahler et al. 1975). J. Sigal (1973) assumes, with the concurrence of Anna Freud, that survivor-mothers belong to the group of "preoccupied" parents, comprising also alcoholics and depressed individuals. H. Klein, who studied survivor families in a kibbutz (1973), described how, despite their fears and their ambivalence toward their offspring, survivor-parents see them as sources of security and gratification. Frequently preoccupation with children's safety is based on the parents' fear of the return of the persecution. Dov Aleksandrowicz (1973), who studied lower middle class survivor-families in Israel, hypothesized that there were several survivor-family constellations. He focused especially on families with a parental disequilibrium, where the survivor-parent married someone below his or her status and looked down at the spouse, and on those with an affective deficiency syndrome. The latter was also noted by Sigal and Grubrich-Simitis. L. Rosenberger (1973) divided the parents she had seen in a clinic in Tel Aviv into those who disregard their children's emotional needs, and are obsessed instead with the need to provide food for them, and those who identify almost totally with the growing children, reliving their childhood through them or identifying with their own deceased parents. Recently Y. Danieli (1980), in her studies of survivor families in New York, categorized them as victims or fighters—as numb families or those "who made it." She pointed out that different demands were made on children in each different family atmosphere, but also cautioned that the distinctions should not be rigid because the traits she described overlapped in many families.

Regardless of the different attitudes in individual survivor families, the child born after Hitler's defeat represented a victory over the persecutor and yet created guilt about the many who had died, especially in the survivors' close families who could only symbolically be revived in the child, born in liberty. Whatever the nature of the trauma or of chronic traumatic conditions, the theme of being abandoned and abandoning prevailed. Whether through shared dreams, shared fantasies, or intricate reciprocal acting out, an illusion was created that parents and their post-persecution children had been together before the latter's birth (Klein 1973). Perhaps an important aspect of this illusory togetherness is a reassurance to the parent that he or she had never been abandoned and alone and had never forsaken his or her own family members. For the child, it can create an understanding of the parent, and an admission to the magic circle of those who have survived a nightmarish reality and are tied together by a special bond of common fate and common guilt (Epstein 1979). Perhaps through this bond the child can replace a mother, a sibling, or a close friend who perished and left the victimized parent to his or her misery, survival, and guilt. The child thus is a source of reassurance and confirmation of denial while, at the same time, bearing the traces of unmourned loss. In some cases, the child becomes the monument of mourning (Kestenberg 1972; Grubrich-Simitis 1979) and thus part of a mourning ritual of which the Nazi victim was deprived.

Accounts of survivors reveal that meeting a relative or a person from one's home town in a camp had a reassuring quality (Bornstein 1967). Belonging and not being alone restored, to some degree, the loss of infantile trust. It seemed that even dying together, rather than alone, was more tolerable, as it created the illusion of going to sleep under the watchful eye of the mother. By separating parents from children, husbands from wives, and siblings from each other, the Nazis systematically re-created conditions comparable to those of an infant abandoned by his mother. Krystal's (1968) distinction between infantile and adult trauma blurs when we take into account the regression evoked by the separation from loved ones and by the reduction of adults to physically dependent creatures forced to give up their adult status and assign it to the persecutor. A similar regression-inducing technique that made the persecuted dependent on their persecutors, was to degrade parents in front of their children and thus destroy the images of protecting and loving caretakers. Where family members of two generations were allowed to stay together, the physical and mental deterioration of a parent before the child's eyes would make the father or mother dependent on the child, and the child's survival was frequently linked to his or her ability to abandon the parent (see the moving account of Elie Wiesel 1972a). Children in latency or adolescence became old before their time; many of them literally became breadwinners through smuggling (Eisner 1980).

Adults who came from loving families could regress to the point where they retrospectively lost faith in their parents. Some veered between idealization of the lost family and a bitter accusation of not being protected. In many instances—perhaps in all—the extended "holding environment" (Winnicott 1965)—creating faith in the government, in one's teachers, in one's culture, or in God—collapsed, contributing to the helplessness and regression of those individuals who did not have support from their fellow inmates (Kogon 1950). Nazi tactics, featuring deception and lies, permeated and poisoned the atmosphere; and the German people, many of whom were friends of individual Jews, learned not to protest Jewish persecution (Simenauer 1978). An example is the lie about deporting Jews to labor camps where they would receive humane treatment. People who were anti-Semitic from the start—as were many Poles—were indoctrinated against Jews by such songs as "Hitler's wonderful, Hitler's grand, He put the Jews to work" (Donat 1978, p. 13). The lie contained therein is that Jews do not work but enslave others to work for them—a notion that Hitler reversed.

A. Donat (1978) also described the unreality of an experience when he was arbitrarily and unjustly attacked as "Jew liar" by a storm trooper who came to plunder his food supplies. By deceiving, indoctrinating, yet intimidating the non-Jewish population and bribing their followers with material goods and elevation in status, the Nazis gave the Germans, including their children, a feeling of power and prestige and a superior sense of belonging. The values of all but a small minority of the non-Jewish population seemed to change, as their superegos and ego ideals became invaded and corrupted by the Nazi doctrine. In their own ranks, the Nazis reversed the status of children versus adults, by encouraging children to report their parents' unfaithfulness to Hitler, the supreme leader who took the place of the father. Some of the older generation succeeded in saving their children's integrity, and a few were able to help victims of the propaganda. Children of the persecuted lost faith in their parents who had been forsaken by their community. A parent did not need to be tortured in a ghetto or a concentration camp to lose authority and his or her image as protector and nurturer. For a parent to be degraded, called names, and assaulted was a trauma no child could cope with.

In a sensitively written book for young people, Doris Orgel (1978) described the experiences of Inge, a twelve-year-old girl, with the "Devil in Vienna." Carrying nothing but their toothbrushes, her father and grandfather were taken away by the SS; and when they returned at night, they were dirty and disheveled after having been forced to clean the streets of the city, egged on by jeering Viennese crowds. Through her enduring friendship with the daughter of an SS man, Inge found ways of evading the Nazis and helping the family escape the country. Her ability to accomplish this was an integral part of her growing up. Her friend and the friend's mother were loyal, Christian, and helpful. They disagreed with the greedy, inhuman SS father. Remaining unspoken was Inge's reproach to her parents who did not protect the family, particularly to her father who mistrusted her loyal friend. However—despite his inability to stand up to the Nazis and preserve their home, Inge's school, their friends, and, indeed, all of their life in Vienna—in comparison with the coarse, sadistic Nazi father, Inge's father gained in stature.

Even when there was more threat than actual trauma, the Nazi assault on normal trust in parents had the effect of trauma. Even in the remote possibility that none of their kin and friends were killed, family members felt the loss of their selves and their impotence in face of a mass attack on their values. The loss of one's background and of one's feeling of group belonging, and the forced disruption of a familiar way of life, compounded the undermining of identity by the massive assault on one's heredity. Departing from Vienna, Inge left not only comfort, status, and material wealth but also her home and school, the familiar streets, and the expectation of fairness and justice in the world. One compensation was her father's assurance that his love for Inge made it worth struggling rather than giving up in suicide as a childless friend of his had done. Yet, even in the face of his enduring love, the entire family's past lost its continuity with the present and the future, and they were cast adrift, friendless, homeless, and rootless (see H. Strauss 1957 on *Entwurze-lungsneurose* ["uprooting neurosis"], and Sterba's 1968 report on uprooted adolescents).

Against the background of degradation of the Jewish community, there was the exaltation and adulation of the Germanic race, pure-bred and perfect (Podietz 1975). Orgel describes how Inge discovered with shame her envy of the singing and marching groups, from which she was excluded because of her Jewishness.* When in school Jewish children had to move to the last row to yield the front desks to Aryans; only the fact that Inge's best friend had preserved her former values and moved to join the "exiled" Jewish children, allowed Inge to preserve the cohesiveness of her ego at a time when a new identity was being built by a mirroring friend. Because she eventually succeeded in convincing her father of the fidelity of her Gentile friend, the entire family regained trust in one another and in the possibility that decency could emanate from the external world. However, it remained to be seen how the family's strength and value systems would be tested in other lands. As the Nazis expanded their conquests, Inge's family had to flee from two other countries before they could reach the United States of America.

By rendering their victims helpless, robbing them of their defenses, and reducing them to infantlike creatures whose relationship has been endangered and whose anaclitic needs have been intensified because of physical deprivation, the Nazis insinuated their psychotic values into the minds not only of their adherents but also of their victims (Kestenberg 1977, 1981a). Even in the relatively short time in which Inge's family experienced their degradation and exclusions, the Nazis succeeded in undermining their values and their self-esteem. The most important aspect of this fictional account of the Viennese-Jewish exposure to Nazi sadistic grandiosity is the depiction of the rescue of Inge's self-image by being able to rely on a friend, a non-Jew who was antipathetic to Nazi ideology. Not every Jew was that fortunate. Many were betrayed by former friends and some Jews betrayed each other. It has been suggested that the Nazis' need to degrade Jews was a projection of feelings of despair of the many Germans who had lost their fathers or become disillusioned with them (Mitscherlich 1979; Simenauer 1978). The more the Nazis shattered the image of a Jewish progenitor, devoted to his children, the

---

* A similar experience was recounted by a creative German analyst whose father had forbidden her to join the Hitler Youth. As a result, she had to remain at home when all the other children in her class could go on outings where they had a lot of fun. The pressure on German children whose parents tried to save them from Nazi values, was tremendous; and not all could resist it (see introduction to part III).

easier it was for the Germans to worship Hitler, whose image rose from the ashes of the exalted German and the annihilated Jewish father, who stood for their devalued paternal image.

Regardless of his experiences during the Holocaust, the survivor-parent is charged with the restoration of parenthood, in both the physical and the psychological senses. The more prolonged and the more extreme the persecution, the more intensified was his regression to a sado-masochistic relationship. The ultimate surrender to the Nazis implied the surrender—through death, castration, or starvation—of one's ability to propagate. The ultimate victory of the survivor was to undo the trauma inflicted where the Jews were traditionally most vulnerable. Their seed was being destroyed, and their parenthood was in question. The degree of sado-masochism that was generated was influenced by the intensity and duration of actual torture and deprivation. The degree of helplessness depended on the degree to which the ego was shattered and the superego altered. One or another of the changes in the psyche was more pronounced, but the essential assault on the superego and the ego ideal was never lacking. To the degree that parenting is affected by superego demands and by aspirations of the ego ideal, survivor-parents had a special task before them—a task perhaps unparalleled in the history of mankind.

## Comparison with Other Traumata

Certain types of trauma like floods, earthquakes, or assaults by enemy bombing have the effect of sudden peril to life comparable with First World War shell shock. The subsequent deprivation and helplessness as well as the uprooting from homes compounds the assault on the ego. However, none of this assault is based on total abandonment and attempted genocide. Traumatic acts of nature evoke organized attempts to help people survive and to avert long-term deprivations for survivors. There is time and provision for mourning for those who have perished, and there is less degradation of values or shifting of guilt upon the affected. Hiroshima victims (Lifton 1967)—disfigured and threatened with loss of fertility as well as with various physical illnesses and late sequelae to the bombing—as traumatized as they were, were not subject to a continuous, systematic, and organized assault as a people nor were they singled out as a group that is less human and not worth living.

The Nazi bombing of England and the American bombing of Dresden cost many lives and left many people homeless. Loss of liberty in concentration camps has been compared to trauma experienced by prisoners of war who were mistreated and exposed to various brainwashing techniques. Yet there was an escape for these prisoners—an escape that might frequently have involved accusations of treason, but that still could elevate the prisoner from utter despair and hopelessness to a measure of activity and a relative sense of restored well-being. In none of the foregoing traumata was there the threat of the destruction of one's seed and the branding of the seed as vile and defective. In Nazi Germany a Jew who changed religion and ostensibly accepted the values of the Aryans, was condemned with other Jews, despite the efforts of the Church to claim him or her as its own. The converted Jew's seed was still tainted, and his or her children could not be redeemed. If the tenet of one's own "evil" was accepted, there was no atonement or conversion possible.

A comparison that is perhaps closer to the experience of the Jewish people during the Holocaust is the degradation of the black slave population kidnaped from Africa, shackled and starved in the galleys of ships carrying them to a land of bondage. One of the most dreaded fates they could suffer was the separation of families, wives from husbands and parents from children, when they were sold to new owners by cruel and heartless masters. Yet there was no threat of genocide, and capable work could please the slave holder. The production of children was encouraged to enrich the master. Although a slave was considered to be property and less than human, he or she was still valuable; a Jew who worked was starved and treated as totally worthless. There were slave holders who were more humane than others. In the new land—and more particularly in the domain of a benign master—one could have some sense of self and place and could look for protection to one's owner and, once converted, to a new God who promised ultimate redemption. By contrast, the Jewish slave under the Nazis had nothing to look forward to. One could no longer trust one's neighbors, and the circumstances of life were unpredictable. Trust had become an undesirable commodity, and survival often became associated with utter dehumanization. The feeling of being left all alone, perhaps even by God, was degrading enough; but one of the most poignant indignities that one might endure was the feeling of guilt for surviving, perhaps at the expense of others—a psychological position that interfered cruelly with the completion of mourning for dead relatives and friends.

In any discussion of man-made traumata, special consideration must be given to the Turkish slaughter of the Armenian people, an example of genocide upon which Hitler modeled his plans to kill Poles. He must have surmised that the Allies would not readily come to the rescue of Jews or Poles, and said before he began his campaign of extermination:

Our strength is in our quickness and our brutality. . . . I have given the order, and will have everyone shot who mutters one word of criticism. . . . Thus for the time being I have sent to the east only my Death's Head units, with the order to kill without pity or mercy all men, women and children of the Polish race or language. Who still talks nowadays of the extermination of the Armenians?*

(However, according to Nazi doctrine, only the Polish intelligentsia, who threatened to resist enslavement by a "superior race," were to be exterminated; the rest of the Poles were to become slaves and for that reason were not allowed to get an education over and above the first few grades. Jews were expelled from schools altogether, and theirs was the "final solution"—genocide. Some Polish children were selected for Germanization and sent to the Reich for special training. Thus, the Poles could survive either as slaves or as new Aryans [Pilichowski 1980]).

During the First World War, Armenians had been expropriated, sent on death marches, starved, and killed.† Some historians claim that only one-half million Armenians survived out of a total of two million in Turkey. The unprecedented scale of atrocities and killings occurred when Turkey was an ally of Germany. Individual German clergymen entreated their government to intervene on behalf of the Armenians, but to no avail. It became evident that the government of Kaiser Wilhelm II did not wish to "interfere" in the internal affairs of its ally. The suspicion remains that by accusing the Armenians of siding with the Russians against the Turks, Germany had instigated the Turks to commit these atrocities—a tactic that would ensure Turkey's loyalty to the German cause.

One must pause to ask the inevitable question: was there, indeed, no difference between the genocide of the Armenians at the hands of the Turks and that of the Jews perpetrated by the Germans? This question is extremely difficult to answer, and there may even be doubts about the need to ask it. In raising it, one must keep in mind a certain paradoxical element. It would appear that aggression and overt cruelty were more common in the ways of the Turkish nation and the Middle East in general at that point in history, while Germany was considered to be the most enlightened and civilized nation in

* Speech at Obersalzburg, 22 August 1939.

† The following sources have been relied upon in discussing the history of the Armenian genocide: El-Ghusein 1975, Gebarski 1963, Tashjian 1965, and Toynbee 1975. Indebtedness is expressed by the authors and editors to Dr. H. Martin Deranian of Worcester, Massachusetts, for his cooperation in supplying this bibliography. For a biography of an Armenian survivor, see Kherdian 1979.

Europe. However, Germany's encouragement of the Armenian massacre may provide some clues to its perpetration of the sadistic atrocities of the Nazi era. There were parallels between the Turkish Armenians and the European Jews. Both were considered to be industrious and wealthy; both maintained high allegience to their families. Envy of Armenians, Greeks, and Jews in Turkey paralleled the envy of Jews in Europe who were reputed to control the sources of wealth and to exploit non-Jewish nationals. The incentive for the general population to support its government's punitive actions was the same in both Turkey and Germany. Enriching oneself through expropriation and plunder at the expense of Armenian merchants in Turkey and of Jewish merchants in Germany was justified because both ethnic groups were branded enemies of the nation. Jews were held responsible for the loss of the First World War in Germany. Armenians were continually accused of plotting with Russia. Both ethnic groups had shown allegiance to their countries and had fought valiantly in the service of their respective governments. At first, the Germans spared their Jewish war veterans; but soon these, too, were imprisoned and disenfranchised, as had been the Armenians who had won battles for Turkey. The Armenian massacre has been referred to as genocide, but there are some decided differences between the atrocities committed against the Armenians, and the Nazi "final solution" which involved the total annihilation of Jews. Many Armenian girls were rescued and given out to harems. Children were converted to Islam and kept in orphanages. This alternative was not possible for Jews under Hitler. One was a Jew no matter what religion one had adopted. While the similarities were great, the total mercilessness toward Jews, especially for Jewish children, makes the Nazi Holocaust unique in the history of the world.

All comparisons of tragedies are invidious, and this brief comparison with other traumata does not do justice to the ordeals of traumatized people. There is no doubt that all traumatic events have a similar effect on the victimized population; yet each situation is different. The point made here is relevant to the topic of the background of parents who are survivors of the Holocaust. What they have in common is the threat to their continuity as a people and the degradation of their seed as not worthy of propagation. According to the Nazi laws, God's chosen people who were to be multiplied like the sands on the shore, were abandoned and destined to become but ashes, used to fertilize the conquerors' lands.

## Liberation

After liberation, many survivors were near collapse. As soon as they were even partially recovered, they instituted a search for their families; when reunion was not possible, many remarried and formed new families. They sought to undo the threat of genocide and turned from passivity to sometimes frantic activity. They looked to their children for the restoration of their good name. Less well known were the vigorous and intense attempts of refugee parents, who had escaped before ghettos and camps could swallow them, to undo their losses and their degradation by bearing children who would prove the worth of the Jewish seed.

When the psychic structure of an individual is in a state of disequilibrium, as happens under conditions of assault on one's ego and superego, one becomes regressively dependent on external sources of support in the reformation and reintegration of structure. Refugees who escaped from Europe before the height of the Holocaust looked to their host countries for such aids. However, many countries would not admit refugees and they had to travel from one place to another in repeated attempts to escape the persecutors. Owing to the reluctance of strangers and the refusal of relatives in the countries of immigration to provide succor, the refugees were isolated in new ghettos and quarters where they huddled together and shared their memories about the past. Many lost their loved ones, family and friends.

Survivors who were liberated from concentration camps often faced the fact that, for many of their comrades, liberation had come too late. Many died after liberation of illnesses contracted in the camps and of the irreversible debilitating effects of starvation. Some of those who survived required hospitalization before they could be totally freed. Where nurses and physicians acted in a humane way, the healing environment constituted a first step in the regaining of trust in the outside world. However, the German hospitals where many survivors were cared for, were manned by German nurses and doctors, who could be easily identified with Nazis. In many displaced persons camps, survivors behaved as if they were still in concentration camps; indeed, children of survivors later dreamed of authorities of displaced persons camps as dressed in Nazi uniforms. Even where there was good will and a desire to help, the benevolent workers in agencies were unprepared to be the objects of the hate and suspicion survivors had felt for their Nazi guards—a displacement of feelings analogous to transference. Acting out in the displaced persons camps led to delinquencies that perpetuated the Nazi myth of Jewish moral inferiority. While many adults were placed in displaced persons

# The Experience of Survivor-Parents

camps before they were able to reach their final destination, many children were placed in foster homes, distribution centers, and orphanages. Some children found refuge with non-Jewish families in Sweden and France, and still others were smuggled into Palestine to become part of the "Youth Aliya," a system of rehabilitation whereby many children were placed in kibbutzim. Some children who had been hidden in convents during the Second World War, had been converted to Christianity and turned against their Jewish parents who claimed them (Donat 1978). After liberation, the emerging, and even swelling, sequelae of survivors' problems, the illnesses, the turmoil, and the disruption of families constituted a disaster of such magnitude that the Allied occupying forces and their relief agencies were not prepared to cope with it. In many instances, liberation came as a shock because it provided a freedom for which the survivor was not prepared.

For many years to come, perhaps forever, survivors suffered from decreased resistance to illness, from sequelae of mistreatment and starvation, and from mental anguish (Pilichowski 1980). In trying to get to a land where they could experience safety, the survivors were driven by an active goal: they were seeking a promised land, a delivery from slavery, and a reacceptance by their God as chosen people. The disappointment was inevitable, especially since, in the minds of survivors, harsh external reality in new countries could easily become confused with the psychotic reality of nazism. Adaptation was a difficult task for which aid was needed; but the real cure was a self-cure, and its goals were high:

1. Regaining all that was lost in a new territory, with new people.
2. Undoing the threat of annihilation and genocide.
3. Restoring one's self-esteem through reinstitution of a pre-Holocaust superego that would be mirrored by the esteem of the community and perpetuated in one's children.
4. Circumventing the mourning process by the fantasy of reincarnation of the dead in one's children. This also served to maintain the illusion that one had not been left alone.
5. Trying to undo the passage of time during which the Holocaust took place (Schieffer 1978) by starting time anew in the company of children and thus creating continuity between the pre-Holocaust life, the present, and the future.

To accomplish all this and more, the survivors' foremost priority was to be good parents to their children. No matter how parents tried to accomplish this goal, many expected near perfection from their children. The return of the idealization of parents required the idealization of children who reincarnated them. By being naughty or otherwise deficient, children committed a crime and cast doubt on the validity of Jewish worth and the Jewish right to procreation. Rebuilding one's life, finding a new occupation, and providing a good milieu for one's children were allied restitutive measures of which some of the sickest survivors were capable. Under even the best external conditions, however, they were burdened by the continual fear that a holocaust would recur as their nightmares did. They were plagued by questions of what was safest for the children: living in a Jewish or a Gentile neighborhood; becoming famous and well known or hidden in a crowd; talking about one's cruel fate or burying the past in silence; seeking revenge or forgiving; creating many children to defy genocide or having none as a precaution against further child killings; for one's children to be good and self-sacrificing or bad and powerful like the Nazis who survived. Many survivors had "an insatiable and precocious thrust to conceive and bring new life into the world" (Schieffer 1978, p. 84); yet such frantic pursuit of new life would frequently be fraught with anxiety and repudiation of life. In the face of this burdensome inner reality, a benign external reality was needed to uphold and confirm sublime goals and to allay anxiety and guilt in regard to the return of the Holocaust. Perhaps with such a reality, peaceful living could have been attained, the dead could have been mourned, and premature turning to children might have been avoided.

## *The Post-Nazi Era and the German Indemnification Law*

Interspersed throughout the chaotic situation after liberation were islands of peace where good will prevailed and Jews and Christians desired to rehabilitate victims, find their lost families, and steer them toward the establishment of a new existence. Many survivors returned to their home towns where they hoped to find relatives and old possessions. Finding one's loved ones was a rarity, and recouping possessions was not easy. People who now occupied Jews' former apartments were hostile to the returnees. The old places where people had lived did not look the same. It was better to return to Germany to DP camps and to hope for resettlement. However, countries that had refused to rescue Jews from Hitler's atrocities, were not eager to receive the wretched people who had survived the ordeal. For instance, rules and regulations prohibited American consuls from issuing visas; and Great Britain interned those who tried to get to the Holy Land without permission, and granted few permissions.

Once resettled, the survivors had to contend with learning a new language and understanding new customs. In the United States and in other countries as well, the local population was wary of refugees who might take their jobs away. People were wary of survivors. Some people thought that there must have been a secret reason why these people had been persecuted. An ingrained sense of justice made it difficult to believe that human beings could institute sadistic attacks on other human beings without some kind of justification. Terror was evoked by the stories of survivors, and the prevailing feeling was that they should forget the unspeakable past and learn to look toward the future. Like the refugees before them, survivors learned to be silent and to avoid evoking anxiety and guilt in others in order to be accepted by them into a foreign humane society. Survivors knew they could talk freely when they socialized with each other (Epstein 1979); yet they still felt that they had to be cautious in a world that did not want to hear what they had to say. The new environment did not successfully counteract the survivors' uncanny foreboding that they were not wanted anywhere and that the Holocaust would recur.

The wish to be reunited with what had been lost, people and possessions, was intense. Obviously the losses could not be recouped, and disappointment was inevitable. Many refugees and concentration camp victims looked upon the lack of restitution as a new assault upon their integrity. In this atmosphere, children began to grow: even though they were burdened by the demands made on them to rehabilitate their parents, they also drew strength from their efforts to rebuild the images of their parents and of themselves. However, this process was greatly impeded by current events that reinforced distrust in authorities.

The law and procedures adopted by West Germany in the 1950s, when its government took over the indemnification of victims of persecution that had begun under the Allied occupation, proved a mixed blessing. Many of the survivors were too ill to work consistently; many could not find work in their previous occupations. Needy and ill survivors looked forward to the pensions and/or lump sums from Germany that would enable them to support their families and pay their medical expenses. Others, who were not financially dependent on indemnification, derived a great deal of comfort from the fact that the injustice done to them was being acknowledged.*

Opinions were divided whether one should accept so-called blood money from the Germans. Some survivors thought that money could not make up for the degradation; others felt that one must give the Germans the opportunity to redeem themselves. Still others looked upon the restitution as something due to them—never enough, but better than nothing.

---

* The inequities of this law and of its practices are described in some detail in chapter 3.

# THE BACKGROUND

Under conditions in which the survivors needed to prove their damages and justify their claims, the past was revived. Enforced remembering brought on a distinct feeling of renewed persecution, renewed interrogation, disbelief, and degradation. In many instances, children had to accompany their parents to help them present their cases. Children witnessed the questioning of a parent's veracity and became aware of his or her anxiety and fear of self-contradiction. Some parents did not discuss the German indemnification with their children and many were ashamed to admit that they accepted money from "Nazis." Children began to wonder whether their parents' claims were legitimate. They sometimes suspected that there was something wrong with what their parents called their "pension." In one such case, the son revealed in analysis that despite his mother's secrecy he always knew when the monthly check arrived. The German consulate was on the letterhead, but his mother would open the letter furtively. When he had an opportunity, the son held the letter up to light and saw there was a check in it. The son wondered why his mother never talked about the German restitution, and he had the feeling that she was paid by the Germans to keep quiet.

A greatly disturbed survivor had allowed her father to handle her claim not only when she was a child, but also when she grew up and was a parent herself. Disassociating herself from her claim, she had denied that she had been harmed by her persecution in her early childhood. During her analysis she recognized that her anxiety and depression were an aftermath of persecution, and she applied for payments for her treatment. She was able to tell the German doctor who interviewed her how badly she felt and how panic and depression interfered with her functioning as wife and mother and in her work. The doctor pointed out to her that she had a husband, children, and a profession, and that she should be happy with these achievements. The patient was stunned. Her newly acquired ability to admit to the Germans that they had made her sick, was put into question again. She began to doubt her analyst's opinion that she needed to come five times a week in order to feel better. Perhaps the German doctor was right that she should be happy with what she had and disregard her anxiety and depression. She thought that the compensation she received earlier was fraudulently obtained by her father.

A survivor's son asked his mother to give him the accumulated restitution money. He felt that he had been wronged by her and that he was the true victim of the Nazi persecution: by mistreating her, the aggressors had made her too ill to care for him properly; thus, the money was due to him.

## *Conclusion*

The task of survivors' children who are becoming adults is to understand their parents' past experiences without degrading or idealizing them. In one sense, this task is not different from that of any other young person growing into adulthood. Yet, it *is* different in that it concerns a reality that defies trust in human nature and creates obstacles to the young person's need to understand history as a basis for the present and the future. The already disturbed trust in humanity is further jeopardized by current events that may be experienced as a renewal of persecution, and by the actual continuation of persecution manifested in the flare-ups of anti-Jewish feelings and anti-Jewish terrorism, and in discriminatory procedures that protect ex-Nazis.

# 3

# Discriminatory Aspects of the German Indemnification Policy: A Continuation of Persecution

AT THE END of the Second World War, the people of Germany were embittered and tired. They felt abused by the indiscriminate bombing of their cities, especially Dresden. They felt abused by the Russian occupants who subjected them to famine, rape, expropriation, and humiliation. They were in no frame of mind to think about the victims of nazism.

Many Germans denied knowledge of the crimes committed. They had subscribed to the idea of German superiority, they had been aware of discrimination against a whole people, but they did not know about the extermination camps, such as Auschwitz or Treblinka. Yet there were many Germans who disapproved and felt responsible. Some realized, belatedly, that they had seen, they had known, but they had done nothing to combat the atrocities. Among these Germans was the Reverend Johannes Schlingenseider, who wrote:

God knows it, we thought only of the church instead of resisting Hitler with the same strength the thousand times greater injustice spread in the world. In our city of Barmen, right before its gates, was the concentration camp Kamna. We saw all the atrocities that took place there. Therefore, we had to know what happened in Dachau, Oranienberg, Flossenberg, Theresienstadt and all the other places of horror. . . . We cannot excuse ourselves that we did not know about all of it. . . . Why did we not make the smallest effort to stop the mass transport of Jews? (1977)

When Germany introduced the indemnification program to compensate the Nazi victims, the good intentions of its originators were from the beginning marred by inconsistencies and pitfalls which eventually led to a continuation of the persecution via "legal" channels.

## The Indemnification Law

Almost immediately after the Second World War, upon the discovery of the atrocities committed by the Nazis and the plight of survivors who were emaciated and near death, the three Western allies—Britain, France, and the United States—promulgated laws and regulations, in their respective occupation zones, that were designed to restore to their prewar state the health and the economic conditions of the victims of persecution. These laws were administered by officials of the occupation forces in each zone, and judges were designated to resolve conflicts and interpret the law in their respective occupation zones. The extensive aid given to Germany pursuant to the Marshall Plan and the withdrawal of the occupation forces from West Germany were coupled with a pledge by Germany to continue the restitution program without narrowing the scope of commitment to the survivors.

From 1949 until 1953, the individual states in West Germany issued their own regulations based on those published by the occupying forces. When the Federal Republic was formed, these various laws were adopted in a uniform law of September 1953 which supplemented the restitution laws of the states and contained a clause that promised a "not less advantageous basis for compensation as those presently prevailing laws in the states of the American occupation zone." The Paris Memorandum of 23 October 1954 affirmed: "Persons who were persecuted because of their nationality with contempt of human rights shall receive appropriate compensation for permanent damage to their body."

As there was no precedent in history for a codified indemnification law, the German legislators had a difficult task. Credit is due to Chancellor Konrad Adenauer, who courageously worked for the enactment of the law.

The Federal Indemnification Law of 1953 (*Bundesentschädigungsgesetz*, or BEG) and its amendments have a broad scope of provisions to indemnify victims of Nazi persecution for material and health damages. In addition, West Germany entered into treaties with individual countries for lump sum compensation and these countries awarded war damages to their own nationals.

This discussion of the BEG limits itself to the so-called health claims that affected the lives of the indigent, needy survivors whose permanent injuries and personal tragedies did not allow them to work to their full capacity.

The indemnification program as a whole has affected the lives of a whole generation of survivors and also their children, regardless of whether they received compensation, whether their claims were rejected by the West German authorities or whether they had refused to accept badly needed money out of moral principles.

The health provisions allowed for the payment of a pension to a claimant whose working capacity was permanently impaired, and whose impairment was related to the persecution. The pension was paid retroactively to 1958—when the claim was filed—and was coupled with a reimbursement for medical expenses. The claims had to be filed by 1958 but certain corrective amendments (mostly decisions of the *Bundesgerichtshof* [the supreme court of the German Federal Republic]) extended the time for filing with reference to the group of claims affected by each amendment. Many of these claims are still pending in administrative agencies and courts in West Germany. (The only claims that can be asserted as of this writing relate to individuals who left Russia after 1965. These claims should have been filed by 31 December 1981, but this deadline may be extended.) At all times the granting of an award depended on a truthful report of the persecution to which the claimant was subjected and by a correct statement of facts related to the claim (represented in paragraph 7 of the law).

To file a health claim a survivor had to complete the necessary forms and furnish affidavits of witnesses and medical certificates regarding his health. These papers were submitted to the German Indemnification Authority (hereafter referred to as authority). The authority requested supplementary information and evidence, compared it with records available in West Germany—a procedure taking many years—and referred the claimant to a physician, appointed and sworn in by the German consulate. This physician, referred to as *Vertrauensarzt* ("confidential physician"), had to be licensed in the country in which he practiced. However, since he had to give his reports in German he was usually German-born. The *Vertrauensarzt* furnished the authority with his medical findings. He had to decide the degree of the claimant's disability. No award was made if he adjudged the claimant to be less than 25 percent disabled.

# Discriminatory Aspects of the German Indemnification Policy

Disability means an impairment of the earning capacity of the individual as a result of damage to health, due to Nazi persecution. The pension is affected by the degree of disability. The minimum compensable disability is 25 percent. If the damage is less than 25 percent, the German authority takes the position that the impairment is not sufficient to warrant any compensation.

If the decision of the *Vertrauensarzt* was negative, that is—under 25 percent—the claimant could request a re-examination, especially since the physician could be influenced by a clash with the claimant. Each negative decision was subject to a request for a review by the authority which, however, did not reverse the opinion of the *Vertrauensarzt* but sometimes ordered a re-examination of the claimant. However, a favorable opinion of the *Vertrauensarzt* could be challenged by the authority. Appeals could be made to courts, and courts would also order re-examinations of claimants. The procedures were lengthy. A *Vertrauensarzt* not only was held in some way responsible for a re-examination but also had to produce an explanation for any discrepancies in various letters, forms, and completed questionnaires.

From the above description, it is clear that abuses were possible. As time progressed, abuses became more frequent and new regulations were invoked to delay and refuse claims.

## Shortcomings of the Indemnification Law

The BEG contains a preamble that provides that the laws shall be applied "in the spirit of warmhearted and generous indemnification for the injustice committed taking into consideration the whole range of possibilities provided by the law." However, the restitution process fell short of its ideals. Indeed, a claimant most often felt terribly wronged. One expected *Wiedergutmachung* ("reparation") and instead was degraded and humiliated not only in one's own eyes but, dismayingly, also in the eyes of one's children.

The second generation may find it hard to comprehend why a country like the Germany of today, which espouses high moral principles, persecuted their parents, placed them in concentration camps, and now adjudges them to be liars and cheats—without any guilt on their parents' part. As such doubts are created, those of the second generation have asked themselves how their parents survived while the rest of their families perished, and six million innocent people were murdered. Did their parents sell out to the Nazis? They have witnessed many years of struggle for restitution, with old wounds being reopened and all the dehumanization and suffering being relived. The indemnification proceedings are extended indefinitely so that before they are concluded, a claimant may die and the claim then lapse. But when a claimant dies, the child may still question his or her parent's veracity, because there was no verdict or because the rejection of the claim seems to indict the parent as a liar. When one claimant was told by his caseworker that his claim was denied because he had "cheated" the authorities by making an inaccurate statement, he tore his shirt and screamed, "Kill me, I cannot face my family."

The granting of a decision was always contingent on an applicant's truthfulness in supplying the data regarding his or her persecution. Any error is equally damaging. If one gives the authorities a wrong age, one forever forfeits one's claim. In a sense, one is adjudged unworthy of receiving indemnification because one is a liar and a cheat who, under false pretenses, is trying to extort money from Germany. One is enjoined to record each item of one's past and then produce an affidavit from witnesses testifying that they had been with the claimant in, for example, Auschwitz or Belsen-Bergen. When the Red Cross furnished Germany with the Arolsen records of victims in camps, the authorities discovered certain inaccuracies. They discontinued the payments already awarded to the affidavit givers, and refused the claims of the applicants. It did not matter that one had indeed been in a concentration camp; what counted was that one made an inaccurate statement and was to be punished for it. Thus, the degraded Jew who was to receive an official acknowledgment of the wrong done to him or her was instead indicted and pressed into a position of having deserved the persecution and thus of not needing to be remunerated for the ill health that resulted from it.

The decisions relating to false statements are issued as a result of the unusual paragraph 7 of the Indemnification Law. This paragraph is so broad that it covers not only willful acts but also wrong statements caused by negligence, even in cases where in actual fact the claimant is entitled to restitution.

While it is a general principle of law that a false claim must be denied, the false statement must be relevant, meaning that if the truth were revealed, the claim would be denied. However, the official commentary on the German Indemnification laws goes counter to this principle. Under paragraph 7, compensation can be refused for "inaccurate statements which were made merely for simplification in the presentation of evidence" (*Aktenzeicheu* "Docket number" EU163/54 Munich). In addition, claims are dismissed for the use of "improper means," which applies "even to those misstatements which could not affect the desired indemnification." The applicant for restitution does not have to know that his or her statements had been objectively inaccurate (BSH RZ 57, 120;61,380).

Inaccuracies are frequently caused by the fact that documents have to be submitted in German, a language in which the majority of claimants are not well versed. Most of them speak Yiddish and Polish and have difficulty communicating with the lawyers processing the claims. But paragraph 7 served as an excuse for denying awards. And, as time passed, the interpretation of this paragraph became increasingly broader. While in the 1950s inaccurate statements attributable to a claimant's poor mental health were excused, they later became sufficient to warrant a rejection of the claim.

In a recent decision, a claim was denied because a witness made a statement that he had seen the claimant in 1943, while in reality he had seen him in 1942: in 1943, the witness was in the concentration camp Mauthausen and could not have seen the claimant or anybody else in hiding. Obviously this was an insignificant error; but the restitution authority wrote:

The authority is in all cases [acting] in the interest of determining the truth, relying on paragraph 7, B.E.G. Besides, the claimant has made other contradictory statements in this case. The claimant received an award for treatment for his nervous ailment. This award is not cancelled.

What the "other contradictory statements" were was not disclosed.


## Prejudicial Interpretations of the Law and Discriminatory Practices

### THE ROLE OF PSYCHIATRISTS

At first only physical injuries were considered for indemnification; and only since 1965 were psychiatric conditions recognized as caused by the persecution. However, according to old psychiatric theories adhered to in Germany as far back as the 1920s, any traumatic experience, no matter how severe, could have only a temporary effect on the individual. All permanent disorders were considered genetic and thus unrelated to persecution. In this view, manic depressive illness and psychosis such as schizophrenia are hereditary; they are rarely caused by outside damage.

An influential psychiatrist whose writings prompted the German court to move away from this view and to rule in favor of restitution for psychiatric disorders of survivors was K. P. Kisker. In his book on the psychiatric evaluation of victims of Nazi persecution (1961), he conceded that the emotional damage caused by persecution can be so severe that it can result in psychosis. He described the case of a five-year-old Hungarian youngster who, in the period of deportation of Jews from Hungary in 1944, was, together with his parents and siblings, subjected to mass shooting. He lay for days among the corpses until, half-starved, he was rescued by local people who hid him until liberation. After the war the boy, who was then six or seven years old, was so disturbed that he hid between tables and benches because he was afraid of all adults. He was taken to an orphanage and kept there until as an adolescent he went to Israel. There he was continuously afraid of imaginary agents and had to be permanently hospitalized with the diagnosis of "schizophrenic persecution complex." Kisker used this example to explain that, in his opinion, schizophrenia cannot be created by persecution but that a traumatic experience may be the determining factor in eliciting the psychotic outbreak. The patient was declared disabled and awarded a pension.

However, this case was an exception. In addition, as time progressed, the German psychiatrists and even Kisker himself tried to label every psychosis as schizophrenia and every schizophrenia as genetically determined and therefore not *verfolgungsbedingt* ("caused by persecution"). In a discussion with American psychiatrists, Ulrich Venzlaff, a professor at the University of Göttingen, pointed out that "only in schizophrenia which existed before the persecution, or in cases of clear-cut constitutionally conditioned problems, can we rule out the influence of persecution as a contributory cause" (1968, p. 110). A few years later, recognition of persecution as a probable cause of psychiatric illness had become practically nonexistent.

Psychiatrists in the United States (especially Niederland 1964; K. Eissler 1960; Wangh 1971; Schur, personal communication) had pressed for a change in the interpretation of the law, so that the survivors could receive funds for psychiatric treatment. But when in 1965 courts ruled favorably, other matters came up which led to injustices due to a perversion of the meaning of the law as a result of psychiatric opinions.

Professor Venzlaff (Herberg 1971, p. 107) reported the following case. A young German half-Jew served in the German army and fought in France, Belgium, and Russia. Upon the discovery that he was half Jewish he was expelled from the army and sent to Auschwitz. It was bad luck for the indemnification authority that the journal of the armed forces contained an entry that the "half-Jew" was totally healthy when discharged from the service. The *Vertrauensarzt* diagnosed a severe permanent psychic damage, coupled with burns, fractured bones, and other ills. Seven years after he had filed the claim, the claimant wrote a letter to the authority, complaining that the restoration of pension to a former Nazi takes less time and is subject to fewer demands of

# Discriminatory Aspects of the German Indemnification Policy

evidence than his own claim. In response, the authority wrote the *Vertrauensarzt*, indicating that the claimant was a psychopath, as shown in his letter. Since a psychopatic condition is considered to be genetic, a reevaluation of the case was ordered.

Problems resulted from the consistent view of German psychiatrists that one who as a child spent the first two or three years of life in a concentration camp or in hiding, will not remember the details of that suffering and cannot be permanently damaged. No modern psychiatric research supports this view. Wangh (1971) described a very ill young woman who spent two years of her infancy in Theresienstadt. He quotes a German professor's statement that "damages in the neurological field are not probable. A permanent damage after the persecution is not supported by other findings. We know of Anna Freud's Theresienstadt children who were separated from their parents that their disturbances disappeared after a given time" (p. 270). In rebuttal Wangh quoted Anna Freud's discussion (1960) with John Bowlby on this subject: "These children who had undergone repeated traumatic separation from birth or infancy onward . . . from preadolescence onward displayed almost without exception withdrawn, depressive, self-accusatory or hostile mood swings." In a personal communication to Wangh, Anna Freud wrote that it never crossed her mind that anyone could doubt the harm created by such adverse circumstances (see also chapter 2). These findings were confirmed by Keilson's (1979) longitudinal study of Dutch children who had been hidden during the Nazi regime or deported to concentration camps. He discovered that not only the first traumatization (that is, the separation from the parents) was decisive for further development, but also later sequences of traumatizations such as changes of hiding places for fear of discovery by the Germans.

First-hand experiences with clients were even more convincing than the reading of psychiatrists' reports. A young, attractive woman, Sarah D., suffered from learning disabilities, fear of public transportation, stranger phobia, and depression. She had made three attempts at suicide by taking poison, jumping from a second-story window, and slashing her wrists. She knows that she was born in a concentration camp, that her father died there, and that her mother saved her. However, her claim for restitution was rejected on the ground that there could be no causal relationship between her early childhood experience and her present condition. When she had her claim re-examined by a sympathetic *Vertrauensarzt*, the doctor said: "If I find her disabled and entitled to a pension, I shall be reversed in Germany. She married two years ago and is a good housewife. I will suggest a lump sum settlement for her disability. This will be sustained" (personal communication, 1970).

Moshe L. was seven years old when his mother was killed after his father had been taken away to a labor camp. He was sent with his twin brother to a camp where, in his presence, his twin was slaughtered. However, his application for a pension was rejected. The *Vertrauensarzt* considered it a classical case where a severe traumatic childhood experience does not have to leave a scar on the individual.

Moshe L. had graduated from a rabbinical school in a displaced persons camp. He was employed as a shipping clerk in a small company, was married, and had two children. His case was referred by the Jewish Nazi Victims Organization.

Mr. L. came to the attorney's office with his wife, who was also a survivor. During the entire discussion he did not utter one word; his wife said that this was his usual way of behaving. She explained that a co-worker picked him up for work and, once there, directed him to his work. Moshe L. then performed his work like an automaton. In the evening the same co-worker brought him home. Moshe L. did not talk to his family. He stared at the ceiling and then retired to the bedroom. At night he screamed because of terrible nightmares. After particularly severe nightmares he usually stayed home from work. In his presence, his wife announced that she was waiting for him to get a pension so that she could divorce him. She felt that she could not take it any longer, and that she had children by him only because he raped her.

The general secretary of the Jewish Nazi Victims Organization secured a statement from the rabbinical school Moshe L. had attended to the effect that the children in the displaced persons camp had been too disturbed to attend a regular school, so the teacher would read a phrase and the class repeated it. After two years of attendance, a certificate was granted to everyone. Moshe L. had clung to a particular teacher but spoke to no one else. He had never played with other children. Because of this additional document, the decision regarding Moshe L.'s pension was finally reversed. Yet most of the information had been available to the original *Vertrauensarzt*, who had disregarded it as irrelevant.

## Further Persecutory Practices

While psychiatrists and authorities were originally friendly and attempted to help the survivors, the situation gradually deteriorated. As Germany realized that increasingly more claims were being made, and that a great deal of

# Discriminatory Aspects of the German Indemnification Policy

money had to be expended, authorities began to change regulations and change the way they applied them, and to make individual dispositions that were discriminatory within the context of their own restitution law. While in the beginning it was not much of an issue, increasingly attempts were made to find discrepancies that were irrelevant to a claim, such as a place of birth or age. People who were already receiving pensions for health reasons were reexamined. An alleged difference between American and German psychiatry was emphasized, and the opinion of the *Vertrauensarzt* fell in line with the policies of the authorities. He could find that, while a patient was disabled, the disability caused by persecution was only 24 percent and thus the claimant was not entitled to any compensation at all. Protests filed against such findings and requests for reexamination by another doctor were consistently refused.

The requirement of a 25 percent disability to obtain indemnification excluded those who, despite severe emotional illness, were able to earn enough or even more than enough money to support their families. Their right to pursue happiness was abrogated. Earning a good salary was the sole issue at stake.

DELAYED DAMAGES

To obtain payment for treatment and for a pension commensurate with the loss of earning ability, the survivor was forced to procure statements from physicians describing the damage and proving that he or she had been treated since liberation. Only *Brückensymptome* ("bridge symptoms") were recognized as valid; they had to be present at the time of liberation and treated at that time and since. So-called *Spätschäden* ("delayed damages") were not recognized, at least not at first.

Proof was very difficult to obtain especially as regards mental illness. After liberation, attention was paid primarily to the physical illness of the disease-ridden and starved survivors and hardly any notes were made about the emotional state of the patients. In an article on psychoanalytic technique (1960) Kurt Eissler described the case of a shoemaker who spent several years in a concentration camp. His father and two children were murdered along with his two sisters and their children. He was starved, beaten over the head until he became unconscious, and attacked by dogs. He lived in constant fear of murder by torture. Compensation was paid to him for loss of freedom in the camp and approximately four hundred dollars additionally for his physical exhaustion, but no pension for disability was awarded. German authorities found that the claimant has been treated in a displaced persons camp shortly after the war for an ear infection. In the record was the remark: "thirty-six-year-old man, nourishment and strength good except for severe damage to teeth; no findings of illness of inner organs." This finding sufficed for the rejection of his claim to a pension.

Many physicians who had treated survivors were deceased and their records were not available. Some physicians were hostile because patients had left them to seek help elsewhere, and refused to submit their records to the attorneys. Some doctors consistently refused to release their original records and only produced transcripts or at best photostats which, however, were not acceptable to the authorities. All but the original records were rejected and doctors' certificates were characterized as *Gefälligkeitzeugnisse* ("certificates of accommodation") of no probative value. Statements under oath were not accepted, as if physicians and even pharmacists were part of a conspiracy to defraud Germany. All this was applied indiscriminately even in cases where the *Vertrauensarzt* confirmed that the mental illness was related to persecution. Many survivors fell ill later in life, but their symptoms were clearly triggered by events that reminded them of their past under the Nazis.

Anna L. was a superintendent's wife. She worked hard and never went to doctors because she did not believe they could help. About twenty-five years after her liberation from Auschwitz, the couple were told by the owner of the building that they must vacate the apartment because a new superintendent had been hired. Anna "recognized" the woman landlord as the Nazi guard who had whipped her when she collapsed during forced labor. She had to be hospitalized for a long time, but her claim for a pension was refused. Fortunately, the courts gave credence to hospital records that were dated just after her liberation and reversed the decision of the authority.

Leo F., who had escaped from the cattle train that was taking him to Auschwitz, lived in an inconspicuous manner until in 1959 he received a routine telephone call from the Internal Revenue Service to arrange the inspection of his books. He fell into a panic: the Gestapo was coming to get him again. He was convinced that the IRS agent would come in a Gestapo uniform. Leo F.'s nephew, a physician, tried conventional medication but to no avail. Mr. F. had to be taken to the hospital where he was given shock treatment. He complained that his hospital bed was full of ants that were crawling all over his body as they had done in the small camp he was interned in before being sent to Auschwitz. While still suffering from these delusions, he died. Mr. F. never filed a claim for fear of coming in contact with German authorities. Had he filed a claim, however, it would have been rejected, since he had not consulted a physician other than his nephew since the end of the war.

# Discriminatory Aspects of the German Indemnification Policy

In the 1970s, the rules related to *Spätschäden* ("delayed damages") were liberalized by a decision of the supreme court, but only to the extent that the causal relationship between illness and persecution was presumed (accepted without proof) in those survivors who had been concentration camp inmates for over a year. Some concentration camps, however, were looked upon by the German authorities as less terrible than others, and confinement in them for one year was credited only with two or three months' hardship.

In 1969 a conference was arranged to study the medical and legal aspects of severe *Spätschäden*. Physicians and jurists from many countries attended. When the head of the authority was invited to participate, he replied that since by then 95 percent of all claims had been completed the conference served no current purpose. This statement was grossly untrue (Nes-Ziegler 1971, p. 10).

De Wind, a Dutch psychoanalyst and a survivor himself, has done an extensive study of mental sequelae of persecution (1949). In the 1969 conference he attributed the negative attitude of German evaluators of survivors' claims to the horror they felt when going through files in order to understand the full extent of the damages. It is his opinion that only very few people in Germany are willing to undertake such an ordeal (1971, p. 332).

## THE CONSULTING PHYSICIAN

In the 1960s a new institution, one not provided for in the Indemnification Law, began to take over. This was the *Beratender Arzt* (consulting physician), who did not see the claimant but only read the report of the *Vertrauensarzt* and could overrule his opinion. Behind this procedure lay the contention that medical science is not universal: there is an American medical science and a German one. In cases where a claimant was examined by a doctor who practiced in the United States, the *Beratender Arzt* evaluated the record and scrutinized the report of the doctor for fear that he had been contaminated by American psychiatry. An example where the *Beratender Arzt* did not see the claimant will throw light on the difficulty in evaluating a claimant's condition based on the record alone.

A recent claimant whose application was rejected by the opinion of the *Beratender Arzt* offered to go to Germany at the expense of a relative to be examined in person by the specialist who had rejected her claim. The offer was accepted. After personally examining her, the *Beratender Arzt* reversed himself and affirmed the favorable decision of the American physician. The restitution authorities then referred the file to another physician, in Germany, who, on the basis of information in the file and without seeing the claimant, recommended rejection of the claim. The authorities concurred.

73

Some attorneys processing claims believe that the *Beratender Arzt* have become gradually more hostile to the claimants, and point particularly to the young German psychiatrists who are exposed to literature denying the Holocaust or who feel that they are protecting the generation of their parents who are being accused of committing the most hideous crimes in history. But economics also plays a crucial role. One German psychiatrist reported that his chief in the hospital admonished him to protect the *Fiscus* (Treasury) and reminded him that he was an employee of the state.

### FAILURE TO COOPERATE

Another prejudicial practice, one not provided for in the Indemnification Law, was the rejection of a claim due to the alleged failure of the claimant to cooperate with the authorities (*Mangels Mitwirkung*). In a typical case, the victim filed the claim on time and in full compliance of the law. For months he heard nothing, and then a letter arrived from the authorities requesting additional data and supplementary documentation, all of which had to be supplied by a deadline. If the claimant was ill—perhaps as a result of the persecution—or if he or she had moved or the attorney delayed contacting the claimant at the new address, the deadline could not be met and the case was rejected. Had a claimant been late in filing the original application, he or she could have made a so-called "late" filing, but failure to respond to a letter on time, regardless of cause, resulted in rejection. Such rejection was clearly arbitrary and designed to cut down on awards.

Dora M. was two years old when she was shipped with her family to the Lemberg ghetto, where she almost died of starvation. She was smuggled to peasants' homes and later hidden in a hole in the ground. At other times, she hid in a chicken house or remained "like a piece of wood" under a bed in constant fear of discovery. Her mother was caught and killed when she was trying to visit her daughter. Her brother was killed by being thrown out of a window. Her claim was rejected primarily because her father, ill himself, had failed to fill out a questionnaire that came to him by mail. The attorney mistakenly concluded that the case was withdrawn. Upon coming of age, Dora tried to reopen her case, but her claim was rejected several times until at last, after several years, the court ruled in her favor because she was a child and should have been protected as a ward of the court.

In other cases, the very illness that resulted from the persecution may make it impossible for a claimant to respond on time. The degradation and the fears of its repetition that make it impossible for the victim to cooperate promptly with any authority or even with her or his attorney, prevent the awarding of money that could be used to treat this condition.

## DELAYING TACTICS

If a claim is not brought to a successful conclusion before the victim's death, his or her case is closed. As of this writing, according to information given by attorneys, 50 percent of claims have been denied, 15 percent are still pending in courts, and only 35 percent have been resolved in favor of the claimants—all of this after the humiliation to which they have been inevitably subjected.

Each state in the German Federal Republic maintains its own indemnification office and some are known for favoring refusals or delays in granting awards. The slowest processing takes place in Hessen and Rheinland-Pfalz. When a file is referred to the *Beratender Arzt* he holds it for six to seven months. If he requires an expert opinion, this part of the proceedings extends over ten months, and that does not complete the case. The authority may require clarification from the *Vertrauensarzt* and refer the case to another physician, the *Oberbegutachter* (higher evaluator) for a new examination. Should there be a discrepancy between these examiners, the matter is referred back to the *Beratender Arzt*. This again brings the file into a dormant stage for six to eight months. In addition, every few years the authority orders a reevaluation of the earnings of the claimant. Lastly, cases are appealed in courts. In the supreme court a case takes eight years for determination. As a result of complex proceedings and court litigations, cases are still pending on claims filed over twenty years ago.

In a discussion at the April 1979 meeting of the Swiss Psychoanalytic Society in Zürich, Peter Riebesser, a German psychiatrist, stated:

I come from Germany where I am employed in a psychiatric clinic. There, I made half a dozen evaluations for indemnification as a child psychiatrist. These are cases which have been processed for an average of fifteen years, and our evaluation was the tenth one. The people were interrogated for the tenth time. It is obvious that some inconsistencies were stated or screen memories brought forward. That is obvious. Then, some court psychiatrist discovered an inconsistency and said that untrustworthiness had been proven. This is a continuation of the persecution.

To me, it was very depressing and evil when the now thirty-five to forty-year-old claimant had to travel to Germany for the second, third, or fourth time to convey once more his or her life story to a German psychiatrist (these claimants came from adjoining countries such as Belgium). I was furnished with sixteen-page minutes and had to ask questions about miniscule items to eliminate pseudo-inconsistencies.

These were bad situations and I can understand that some claimants refused to come to Germany. Pursuant to indemnification rules, someone who was born in and spent two years in a concentration camp, but does not remember his suffering, or one born in 1946 to persecuted parents, is not recognized as damaged by persecution. And I, a second generation of the German persecutors, had to evaluate my contemporaries who had been persecuted by my forebears.

The protracted processing of claims constitutes not only a great hardship to the survivors, but also a substantial burden on the administrative and judicial agencies of West Germany. The cost of processing the claims is staggering while the harassment of claimants creates ill will all over the world. The magnitude of the abuse by the German authorities becomes evident when we compare their indemnification law and practices with those of other countries. For instance, in Norway restitution is given to victims imprisoned or otherwise mistreated during the war, either for racial or political reasons. The Norwegian statute of 1946, as amended in 1968, provides that the authority has the burden of proof as regards an applicant's claim that he was ill due to persecution. His statements are taken as true unless the authorities can prove otherwise. The procedure was simplified to provide for speedy and liberal processing of claims, with the pension awarded ranging from three to four thousand dollars a year. In Holland, the government funded the Jewish Committee to assist victims of Nazi persecution in the collection of evidence. After the evidence was obtained the committee would request that the government pay all medical expenses as well as pension to the disabled individual and this request would be granted.

## An Attempt to Improve Proceedings

In sporadic appearances in Germany in 1977 and in the Congress on Child Analysis and Social Work at the University of Kassel (1979) this author advocated that the entire indemnification program would be best served if a procedure similar to that adopted in Holland were to be instituted.

Recently, such a practice has been adopted in a new German law. Unfortunately it concerns only two types of inequity and remedies them in a rather modest way: by considering applications of victims who (1) for compelling reasons were not able to file their claims on time; and who (2) left the Iron Curtain countries after 1965. Before this law was passed, victims who had to remain behind the Iron Curtain until 1965 were not entitled to compensation and thus were punished for the fact that Russia and its satellites refused them permission to emigrate.

According to the new West German law, a special fund has been set aside to be processed by the Conference of Jewish Material Claims against Germany to the limit of 400,000,000 deutsche marks. The Claims Conference has offices in New York, Tel Aviv, and Frankfurt. The New York office is headed by a well-known Jewish leader, Saul Kagan, whose presence assures humane treatment for the claimants. Unfortunately the allotment of funds is limited to a total of 5000 deutsche marks (equivalent to $2,500) per person, and no provision is made for medical expenses. The inequities persist as far as the extent of the indemnification is concerned. One who has been a victim of persecution, robbed of his belongings, of his social status and his identity and severely damaged in body and soul some forty years ago, must now prove economic hardship before he or she can obtain as a maximum the inadequate sum of $2,500. If one is 80 percent disabled, one can, upon reaching the age of sixty-two (for women) and sixty-five (for men), receive this sum without having to prove a causal connection between one's persecution and present disability. If one cannot prove an 80 percent disability, one can receive a smaller sum for loss of freedom in a concentration camp or for punitive arrest.

Sonia L. was in Kiev in September 1941 when her husband, her six-year-old child, and her parents were murdered by the Nazis in her presence. Her three-month-old baby died in her arms and she herself was shot in the shoulder but managed to escape. She remained in a hiding place until liberation in 1944. All her belongings had been confiscated by the Germans. Because she arrived in the United States after 1965, no provision is made for a pension or for medical expenses for this ill and indigent person. All she is entitled to is a lump sum not exceeding $2,500.

## Conclusion

Chancellor Adenauer and those who coauthored the BEG did not intend only to carry out Germany's commitment to the Allies. The codifiers were trying to express their total condemnation of nazism and a desire to make up for the atrocities committed against victims who had been persecuted in the lands occupied by the Nazis.

Adenauer intended to rehabilitate Germany in the eyes of the civilized world as well as in the eyes of the young generation in Germany. By being truthful about the infamous past, he sought to revive the culture for which Germany had been admired for two centuries. When West Germany entered into the Luxembourg agreement with Israel (1952) to cover the major cost of absorbing refugees from Nazi persecution into Israel, and the Arab League threatened a boycott, Adenauer reaffirmed that the Federal Republic would "stick to its word."

Yet, despite his best intentions, Adenauer and his associates did not exclude such inequities as the infamous paragraph 7 from the Indemnification Law. Could it be that the legislators projected onto the survivors the legislator's guilt about the deception perpetrated by the Nazis upon their Jewish victims?

To induce them to willingly go to destruction, the Nazis lied to Jews about their destination when they sent them to labor and extermination camps. The Nazis pretended to give the Jews autonomy by instituting *Judenräte* (Jewish Councils) which, in reality, had to recruit Jews destined for deportation and murder. The Great Lie that is still to be seen at the gates of Auschwitz—*Arbeit macht frei* ("Work liberates")—and of Dachau—*Freiheit Für Fleiss und Tugend* ("Freedom for industry and virtue")—introduced the deportees into slavery, starvation, illness, and death. By a terrible irony, the Jews, whom the Germans traditionally characterized as cheats, were easily deceived because of the Germans' tradition for veracity. The German legislators, still imbued with both stereotypes, were unable to confront themselves with the lies of those who were both Nazis and Germans and instead acted as though Germans still had to protect themselves against Jewish deception.

While in the early years of claim processing minor misstatements were not held against claimants, and paragraph 7 was only infrequently invoked, the need to prove the claimant's lack of veracity and to institute penalties for lying increased gradually as Germany felt drained by expenditures and the younger generation did not want to take responsibility for Nazi crimes. Alexander and Margaret Mitscherlich (1970) believed that the inequities of law and procedure were caused not by economic problems but rather by the fact that the younger generation had become imbued with their parents' defenses against the past and were eager to escape the shadow of horrible events that could not be undone.

In 1978, responding to the data presented here and to Mitscherlich's opinion on the subject, Gertrud Hardtmann thus characterized her own feelings, which represent those of many enlightened Germans whose parents opposed Hitler:

# Discriminatory Aspects of the German Indemnification Policy

We are dealing only with the survivors and have to be thankful for each single person who survived the persecution. We have burdened ourselves with enough guilt and each survivor relieves us. At least, we can make good partially to the survivor for what we have done. For the generation of children and people born after the war, this may not be clear, since undoubtedly it is the guilt of the fathers for which they are liable in a political and moral sense.

In my opinion the simple proof that a man was exposed to discrimination, persecution and pain in body and soul should be sufficient for a minimum award. It may be possible that we lack sufficient means to satisfy the claims of the survivors. Then we must state so openly. It would be unfair to burden the claimant with this by simply denying his claim.*

We must not forget that despite the flaws in the Indemnification Law and the inequities of its practice, many people have been helped by it to live in more secure economic conditions. Over and beyond economics, Germany's acknowledgment of guilt and of its desire to atone was psychologically significant. There is hope that Germany will overcome its Nazi past by examining more closely the effect of Nazi ideology upon their second generation who constitute the bulk of present-day German officials, physicians, legislators, and judges.

* Personal communication.

# PART II

# The Survivors'
# Children

# 4

# Survivor-Parents and
# Their Children

## Introduction

ALTHOUGH the severity of the trauma and the time of its occurrence have a direct bearing on the quality of a survivor's parenting, and although each survivor has a different background and one's "social syndrome" (Porter 1978) varies from one place of refuge to another, the children of survivors face a unique psychological task whether they are in America, Canada, Europe, or Israel. Many features are common to most, if not to all, cases of survivors' children that we studied. However, what emerged from the years of group discussions is a conviction that it would not be accurate to subsume their common problems under the heading of "survivor's child syndrome," comparable with that described by Niederland (1961) for survivors (see the Prelude). Some of us felt that we might be dealing with a complex or a constellation of features, which differed in quantity and import from patient to patient. To call it a "syndrome" rather than a "complex" would imply a pathology that is not always in evidence. Many of the features do not contribute to the formation of pathology, and some are expressions of strength. In addition, we must keep in mind that opinions expressed here—based as they are predominantly on material from analyses—should not, without further study, be extended to include survivors' offspring who did not seek analysis.

In the following accounts of cases, the central concern is with parents and children whose relationship has been molded by the overpowering threat to the survival of a whole people. Under the shadow of genocide, everyone was faced with the question, Shall we survive in our children and children's children and thus give an unequivocal answer to the attempt to extinguish us? To achieve this goal, survivors had to repeat, rework, and transform the trauma of the past into a new way of life. On the road toward this goal, they encountered obstacles. The cases illustrate some of the ways survivor-parents involved their children in the Holocaust.

Throughout, one should keep two ideas in focus: the connection between the parents' Holocaust experiences and the material presented by the patients; and the manner in which the survivor-parents' open or hidden messages were transformed and expressed in the themes their children selected.

## Ways of Children's Involvement in Their Parents' Holocaust Past

Parents habitually pass on to their children what their own parents have done to them. Children also become subject to the influence of their parents' acting out of infantile traumatic experiences. The same is true for the family life of survivor-parents; yet there is something different about their interest in and demands on their children. This difference can be seen in a wide range of survivor-parents: those who endured the Holocaust as children, adolescents, or adults; those who hid during the war; those who were fugitives on the run, refugees escaping to the hardships of Russia or to the wealth of the United States; those who starved; and those who slaved in labor camps, in ghettos, or concentration camps.*

### PARENTS WHO WERE CHILDREN DURING THE HOLOCAUST

Children who survived without parents felt the loss of protection very keenly. Those who survived as a group in Theresienstadt (A. Freud and Dann 1951) exhibited special features of precocity and self-reliance as well as attachment to the group rather than to an adult. The taming of their drives did not proceed in a normal way. Although they shared with each other and cared for all group members, their aggressiveness, their fears, and their need-oriented behavior interfered with the development of the ego and of the precursors of the superego. It was difficult for such children to find their place in a new society, and this difficulty was compounded in adolescence when their

* It must be stressed that neither the small sample presented here nor the total case load of the Group for the Psychoanalytic Study of the Effect of the Holocaust on the Second Generation is large enough to cover all aspects of the problems faced by survivors which were transmitted to their children.

84

great need to be loved and their deprivation were coupled with a very low self-esteem (Gyomroi 1963).

N. Wolffheim (1966) reported about children who were admitted to a camp in Windermere, England, before they could be placed elsewhere. Even after they left Windermere, they were plagued by memories of their trauma. Death meant to them that a person was killed. Some told of witnessing their mothers' murder. At the same time they did not want to think about their past. The analysis of a child from Theresienstadt who arrived in Windermere at the age of four and a half, revealed his preoccupation with sadistic fantasies that were concocted from memories and accounts of soldiers and dealt with shooting, the killing of his mother, and other atrocities. A child of seven and a half reported about her first impressions of Camp Windermere. She had thought it was a prison where all people cried and wept because others wanted to kill them. She explained that she came from Germany where people were imprisoned and murdered, and that she did not know that things were different in England. Adolescent children frequently chose careers that were linked to survival in camps. Many of them wanted to be undertakers or cooks. The latter was also the career choice of M. Laufer's (1973) patient, a child of a survivor-mother whose father had died in a concentration camp.

Both Anna Freud and Wolffheim were confident that these young children would overcome their traumata without a great deal of damage. This early impression was not born out by facts (Wangh 1971). A recent survey by Shalom Robinson (1979) in an Israeli mental hospital revealed that the psychic damage to children traumatized during the Holocaust was most severe in those who were persecuted before the age of three. Fewer than half of the controls who had survived the Holocaust in Russia, were diagnosed as psychotic; but the damage was less pronounced, and fewer had persecutory ideas, than those who survived in camps and ghettos and in hiding. In agreement with H. Wijsenbeek (1977), Robinson found that the sequelae of traumata in concentration camp victims were not "much different from those found in the group that survived through hiding" (1979, p. 212).

Young children who survived with one or both parents or with siblings, displayed an intense attachment to their families, but respected children more than adults. Younger siblings looked up to their older siblings as heroes, and the older children felt responsible for the younger (Wolffheim 1966). That type of relationship would continue after liberation and would cast a shadow on post-Holocaust development. As these young victims grew up, they repeated with their children not only what their parents and siblings had done to them, but also emulated the treatment they had received at the hands of the cruel, hostile persecutor whose image merged both with the punishing and the protective parent.

### PREOCCUPATION WITH DEATH

In his infancy in Slovakia, Harry R. was repeatedly entrusted to Gentile families who were supposed to hide him on the former estate of his grandfather. His mother was taken by the Nazis, but his father and older brother found Harry and remained with him in a labor camp until liberation when Harry was six years old.

Analyzed in his adulthood, Harry R. presented a picture of a driven man who made frequent demands on his father and his older brother. When he was alone, he was anxious; when he was cared for, he was demanding. He seemed to look upon the concentration camp as a steady, protective environment, primarily because, while there, neither his father nor his brother ever left him. He did not look upon the Nazis as his persecutors and was sure that all adversity that befell him was due to his father's cruelty. In this brief report only the effect of these attitudes on his parenting modes will be examined.

Having attained some success in a profession, Harry married and produced three children, one after the other. He complained about them incessantly, yelled at them, and singled out one or another of the children for severe physical punishments. At first, he did not realize that he was emulating his father who, he thought, had "persecuted" him in this manner throughout the better part of his childhood. Yet, he felt that he was better than his father because he cared for his children and was tender and loving toward the family. Analysis revealed that a mixture of cruelty and affection was the trait of his inconsistent father, who had remained close to him and his brother throughout both his early ghetto and his camp experiences. After liberation, the separation from his father, who went off to work, and from his brother, who attended school, became unbearable to six-year-old Harry, who came home much earlier than either of his protectors. In their absence he felt threatened with annihilation. The fear of being alone and uncared for remained with him and interfered with his functioning as an adult. He transmitted this fear to his children as he continually berated his wife in front of them, pointing out that she did not take good care of them and let them run around in rags, hungry and unsupervised. At the same time he incessantly complained about his father and brother, behaving as if together they were a pre-oedipal mother. When he was a child he had idealized them, and separation from them brought on a disillusionment that made him feel more dead than alive. In transference he veered between idealizing and depreciating the analyst. In states of idealization, he was an understanding father who talked to his children as the analyst spoke to him. In times of depreciation, he attacked the children ferociously and hated himself for it. Throughout, his highest ideal was to be a good provider and an exemplary father to his children. They could support his endeavor with an excellent performance or throw him into depths of despair with a bad mark in school. Yet, they understood that his tempers were not necessarily related to the misdeeds for which they had been assaulted.

The most important theme in Harry R.'s life as a father was his preoccupation with survival and killing. Yet he repressed the events of his pre-latency life that caused him to be tempted to "kill" his children and rescue them from failure. Separation and neglect were conceived as death, and a child's failure to conform threatened the survival of the whole family. Repression was not as profound in the fathers presented in the next section, who suffered persecution during latency; but separation and abandonment were predominant themes in all.

HIDING DURING LATENCY YEARS

Interviewed by researchers who conducted a father study, Joseph S. reported that he was four when he and his family escaped from Germany, and eight when he had to leave his new home and hide in various farmhouses and orphanages until the Nazis left the country he lived in after the family's escape. His father survived because the nature of his work had kept him away from their Hamburg home.

As an adult, Mr. S. worked day and night even though his occupation did not call for it. He never felt appreciated by his wife and children but took interest in the children and their progress. He yelled and fought with his eight-year-old daughter, Rena, chasing her until she ran away and hid from him. He took special interest in his younger child, John, who had difficulty in toilet training. The problem came to a peak when John was four years old, the age at which Joseph had had to leave his childhood home. It was John who, through his revelations, led the researchers into discoveries of his father's past, while Rena supported her father's denial of its traumatic events.

In a joint interview with John and his father, the latter was faced with John's bus phobia and asked directly whether he, Mr. S., had ever been taken to a hiding place in a bus. He denied it immediately, while John looked at him as if he knew better. Then Mr. S. became pensive and remembered a bus trip to a farm where he found refuge.

Mr. S. was very anxious about John's wetting the bed at night. He took him to the toilet himself, but could not always remember to do so. After an initial denial, he recalled that he had wet himself in a hiding place, and his father was asked to remove him. It was noteworthy that four-year-old John was chosen to re-enact his father's experience of incontinence at the age of eight or nine. There is great likelihood that Joseph, at the age of four, had reacted with incontinence to the traumatic events of his leaving Germany. The episode at the age of eight seems to have been a regression to a previous traumatic departure from home.

John not only helped his father to work through crucial traumatic events of the latter's Holocaust childhood; in his fantasies, he also rescued those his father had lost. John revealed to the interviewer that he looked upon his feces as re-creations of his dead grandparents, on the paternal and the maternal side. It was interesting to note that both parents reinforced John's fantasies. His non-survivor mother had not been able to complete the mourning for her own parents and she too remembered wetting accidents in her childhood. This case illustrates the intricacies of joint parenting, where a survivor is joined by his spouse in getting a child to relive the parent's past in an old, yet a new way and to act out the rescue of losses sustained by both parents. The next case, explored even more cursorily, allows only a bird's-eye view of a survivor father's effect on his family.

Karl F. spent several years of his latency working on farms, hiding from the Nazis. Separated from his parents, in constant fear of being captured and killed, he had to move on several times to seek new places of hiding. Interviewed in his adulthood in the context of a father study, he spoke of his desire to go on vacation. He persuaded his wife to leave their young children at home and go off with him on trips to Europe, especially to the land of his persecution in childhood. When he was home, his mind was elsewhere. He was with the children and yet absent.

His wife, herself not a survivor, seemed in collusion with her husband to re-enact his Holocaust separation experiences. However, what stood out most was not easy to connect with the hardships of physical and mental absenteeism that both parents inflicted upon their children. Mr. F.'s eyes habitually darted to and fro as if he were constantly on the lookout for danger, and this attitude was mirrored by the demeanor of his twelve-year-old son. Mr. F.'s peculiar haunted look was implanted in his younger son's face by the age of five months and settled there during a premature rapprochement crisis at fourteen months.

Mr. F. practiced the role of an absent father in identification with the father of his childhood who could not protect him. His absence, real or acted out, also seemed to be the result of his identification with the absent persecutor who did not see him and thus could not kill him. At the same time, he was repeating his childhood need to move on to new places, by getting away from his children and leaving them in a state of watchful alertness, lest some unknown evil would befall them.

## TRANSMISSION OF FEAR

At the age of twelve, Mirelle G. was referred for analysis because of her asocial attitude and her peculiar behavior. A thin, pinched-looking girl, Mirelle was mute except for occasional brief sentences. From time to time she produced a thin-lipped smile, but most of the time she looked away, surveying the interviewer surreptitiously. Most of the information that follows was obtained from Mirelle's parents. Although both parents, as schoolchildren, had to escape from Rumania to Russia, the focus here is primarily on the role Mirelle's father, Mr. G., played in the life of Mirelle and her nine-year-old brother. In the family constellation, Mr. G. acted as the aggressor toward, and Mrs. G. as the defender of, the children. Herself subservient to her husband, she cast him in the role of the relentless persecutor, while she accused herself of inexperience as a young mother.

Mirelle's father presented a picture of his own childhood deprivation and of his resourcefulness. He explained that soon after the family had arrived in Russia, his father was taken into the Russian army while he, Mr. G., was separated from his siblings and placed in an orphanage. In order not to starve, he scavenged and stole food in company with other boys from the orphanage. The family returned to Rumania after the war, but as soon as he, Mr. G., grew up, he got married and immigrated to Belgium where he fathered two children, Mirelle and her brother. Later Mr. G. moved to the United States in order to improve his finances further. Trying to build up his diamond business, he worked very long hours and insisted that the mother help him in his office.

Mirelle was lonely for Belgium and did not know the language and customs of the new country. To make friends she began to associate with delinquent children. She was preoccupied with getting food and acquiring objects. Lonely, frightened, and anxious to get help, she would go on a long bus trip to reach her analyst. Upon her arrival there, she would not talk except to explain how dangerous the journey had been and how no one would meet her when she arrived home. Her house, she felt, was not a home, and she had no real friends.

Each morning, her father admonished her younger brother to behave better, to wash his hands, or to sit straight. As a result, the little boy could not eat, and Mirelle herself felt that she must cook for herself to survive. Mirelle's father did not speak to the children except to chastise them. Both parents seemed to connect Mirelle's journey to the analyst with the father's trips to Russia and back to Rumania. They were anxious, worrying what would befall Mirelle during the bus ride, yet they would not take time off to drive her.

Mirelle's autistic and delinquent features were reminiscent of those exhibited by children of survivors who were diagnosed as psychotic. Afraid to speak to people, distrustful of her parents, she could not communicate. She seemed to live in a past with which she was not herself familiar; and one gained the impression that a multiple reality, that of her parents' past and of her own past in Belgium, interfered with her understanding of her present reality in the United States.

Both parents repeated their pasts in various ways, with abandonment, desertion, and hunger as important themes, as were dangerous journeys, delinquencies, and problems with new languages. Moreover, Mirelle's father continually sought an outlet for his identification with an aggressor. He looked down on his degraded father and tried to blame him for his misfortunes. He deserted Mirelle in identification with this deserting father. Mr. G. looked upon the child as an aggressor while at the same time attacking her. Only when the father understood how much Mirelle longed to be spoken to did he start to feel closer to the girl. When he began to speak to Mirelle, and the latter was able to respond, father and daughter met halfway on a common ground. It seemed to both of them that society at large or people in general were against them, and that there was danger on streets and buses. Mirelle's father did not form an image of the persecutors from whom he had to run, and neither did Mirelle. Appeasing people whom they mistrusted and getting things from them was an indiscriminate method of protection. Moving on, looking for a place of refuge representing parental protection, was a necessity for both parents and the child.

All these fathers most ardently wished to provide security for their children. Most of them continued to live in fear of abandonment to an unknown, unseen aggressor, and conveyed this fear to their children and to their wives. Unable to form a clear image of the object of their fears, unable to look to their parents for the assurance of survival, they developed a generalized suspiciousness of the society in which they lived. Perhaps children who have seen the Nazi persecutors with greater clarity could transfer their fears onto certain people rather than disperse those fears, mistrusting and fearing all. Harry R., who had spent his early years in a work camp, had visions of bombs falling and of shots fired at children, but he repressed the image of specific Nazi guards and expected cruelty from his father instead.

# Survivor-Parents and Their Children

For adolescents, the problem of identity and the quest to give up the parents loom supreme. Degradation and annihilation of the parent by outsiders facilitates the identification with the aggressor. The normal adolescent regression can combine with the repression during persecution to obscure their respective influences and to hinder the process of adolescent reorganization of ego and superego.

ACTING-OUT BEHAVIOR

Gretchen B. was sixteen and a half when she was referred for analysis by a refugee organization. Her mother had been sick for five years with cancer and finally died when Gretchen was ten or eleven years old. In the last year of her mother's life, Nazis began to boycott and loot Jewish businesses. Storm troopers invaded Gretchen's father's place of business and took his money at gunpoint. A short time after, they forced themselves into Gretchen's home and threatened or injured the father. Unable to support himself, the father managed to send his three older children out of the country; but he had to place Gretchen and an older sister in an orphanage, where they remained for four years. He committed suicide shortly before his younger children were rescued and brought to the United States to live with relatives. When Gretchen reached the age of sixteen and a half, the aunt with whom she lived complained that she quarreled, provoked, lied, and stole and alternated this behavior with fearful withdrawal. Placed elsewhere, Gretchen ran away, threatened suicide, blamed herself, and was ashamed. Feeling unwanted, she would fall ill with nausea, stomach trouble, and headaches, which she associated with her mother's cancer.

Gretchen began her analysis with complaints and provocations. She demanded that the analyst call her relatives to get things from them. She skipped appointments, came an hour too early or an hour too late. She invaded the waiting room and rattled the blinds, and she barged in the office, rummaging through books and throwing things. At one point in the treatment, she hit the analyst. She behaved like a hostile intruder, and her facial expression exuded maliciousness. The analysis of her provocative behavior took the treatment into her early years of training, her early misbehavior (which she thought had caused her mother's sickness), her resentment of her mother when she fell ill, her envy of her siblings, and the feeling of being abandoned and discriminated against in Germany and currently. Between bouts of somatic complaints and attacks against the analyst, Gretchen would confess how much she missed her mother and father. She revealed that she knew her father would "die" because on his last visit to the orphanage he had brought all the jewelry that was left. Her own suicide threats were based on her identification with him. At one time she had a fantasy that the sky opened and her parents came down. She frequently abandoned the analyst but would return to try again, especially when her interest began to shift to boy friends, whom she sought out in lieu of her older brothers who lived far away. The analysis of her rejection-provoking behavior when she craved love enabled her, at the age of nineteen, to form a relationship with a young German refugee who proposed marriage. He promised to be her mother, father, brother, and analyst and demanded that she stop treatment. No doubt, his rescue fantasy fulfilled his own survivor needs.

Gretchen seemed to live fairly happily with her husband and her children until seven years later when she developed an acute psychotic episode. It was occasioned by the "loss" of her brother-in-law, who decided to get married. Gretchen construed this as an abandonment which she connected with the loss of her mother and her brothers. She seemed oblivious to the fact that she was a wife and a mother; she was headed toward the "snake pit," and identified with the heroine in the 1949 film of that name. Repeated hospitalizations followed, and shock treatment was initiated. Gretchen's husband reacted to her illness by his own "breakdown" which necessitated the placement of the children in the country. When he recovered, he was prompted by his family to abandon Gretchen and remove the children from her influence. Thus, at the end, Gretchen had to be taken away and disappear from her children's life as her mother and father had disappeared.

The case was out of the analyst's hands, but had the analyst known that psychosislike episodes, simulating schizophrenia, are not unusual in survivors (and their children), she might have intervened and gotten the patient back into analysis.* Still in a period of denial of the effect of the Holocaust, the analyst had failed to interpret the patient's transparent identification with the Nazi storm troopers (who were just then being tried for their "psy-

* Marion Oliner has expressed the view that many of these pseudoschizophrenic episodes, in which the fate of persecution was repeated in a psychosis, were hysterical in nature and should be treated accordingly. In fact, a consulting psychiatrist had this diagnosis under consideration in Gretchen B.'s case. Two cases of survivors' childrens' psychoses were presented to the group, and their treatment bore out Oliner's view (see chapter 14). However, the interference of parents who had a stake in keeping a child in a psychotic reality, comparable to their past Nazi reality, interfered in the treatment of one of these cases (see also Axelrod et al. 1980, Kestenberg 1972, Lipkowitz 1973, and Rakoff et al. 1966). (See also chapter 10.)

chotic" crimes). Not until asked to give a report in connection with Gretchen's pending appeal for restitution did the analyst begin to understand the patient's retrospective equation of guilt about her mother's illness and death with the guilt of the Nazis who caused her father's downfall. Not until the analyst began to explore the dynamics of survivors' children did he suspect that the outbreak of Gretchen's psychosis may have been an anniversary reaction. One of Gretchen's children then was the same age as she, Gretchen, had been when her mother took sick. A follow-up interview revealed that Gretchen felt as abandoned by her children as she had felt abandoned by her parents and her siblings. Although bitter about it, she seemed to accept it in a fatalistic way.

THREE GENERATIONS OF HOLOCAUST SURVIVORS

When Lucienne P.'s mother came out of a concentration camp at seventeen, she weighed fifty pounds, had had her hair shaven, and was amenorrheic. The husband she later acquired had also spent his adolescence working and starving in a Nazi concentration camp. After liberation they were taken to France and were given shelter by Christians. The girl, Lucienne, born of this marriage, quickly picked up her parents' troubled demeanor. They had little appreciation of the fact that she was a child, and demanded adult performance from her. She was left alone a great deal when her parents worked. When she was disobedient, she was told by her father that she should have choked when she was born. Throughout her childhood and early adolescence, she was beaten and degraded by both parents, but more so by the father. She found solace in the house of a Christian friend; and when she grew up, she converted, abandoned her family, married a Christian, and had a child. Lucienne P. vowed to take much better care of her little boy than her parents had of her as a child. Yet she could not maintain a loving attitude; the boy seemed ungrateful to her in the way she had appeared ungrateful to her parents. Feeling abandoned, working like a slave, unloved, rejected by Jews and Gentiles, she was part of an actuality that seemed to her to have no reference to her past and certainly none to her parents' past. Despairing, getting into depths of depression, and surviving was the central theme of her life. Each spring when there came the anniversary of the liberation from concentration camps, she was especially vulnerable without knowing why. She seemed fixated in an adolescent stance, as if she was forever reliving a series of degradations that were followed by a liberation. These sequences were based not merely on her identification with her parents' past but also on actual recollections of her parents' behavior toward her. When, through psychotherapy, she was able to appraise her parents more realistically, she reported how they alternated between persecuting her and expressing their love for her. It became apparent that both her parents looked upon her as their persecutor, and that she continued their parental attitude in relation to her own child.

In Gretchen B.'s case we have a first-hand account of a young adolescent, whose father was persecuted by the Nazis and who was uprooted and separated from her older protective siblings. We see Lucienne P.'s parents through the eyes of their daughter and in her relationship to her son. In both instances—but much more so in Lucienne P.'s parents—we appreciate the adolescent survivor's struggle for identity—a struggle that was transmitted to the children. In both instances, the identification with the persecutor is counterbalanced by the equation of the child with the persecutor and the abandoning parent (Krystal 1968). Lucienne P.'s case, although not studied in depth, revealed the influence of the Holocaust on the third generation.

### THE INFLUENCE OF PARENTS PERSECUTED IN ADULTHOOD

When children witnessed the degradation of their parents, they lost trust and transferred their belief in parental omnipotence onto the Nazis, whom they put in the role of avenging, punitive parents.* This displacement was also evident in adults who were haunted, tortured, starved, degraded, and rendered helpless by their Nazi persecutors. Many adults behaved as if the traumata they experienced had been perpetrated by the parents of their childhood (Krystal 1968).

The shift from identification with parents to identification with the persecutors was supported by a defensive identification with the aggressor; both infiltrated the parental ego of survivors. Children were treated as if they were reincarnations of the Nazi oppressors. Children who were slated to replace offspring who had died in the Holocaust, were made to feel especially responsible for their failure literally to reproduce the dead, and hence were identified by their parents with the Nazis who had killed them. The resulting hatred of parents for children or their estrangement from one another was often counterbalanced by the child's and the parents' yearning for reconciliation. To help survivor-parents reunite with the loved ones they had lost, many survivors' children embraced religions and cults that not only promised reincarnation but also created the image of a good and holy parent, an image used to redeem the real parent.

Having escaped the ovens of Auschwitz, a Hungarian woman found herself without a family. Not only her parents and siblings were dead, but also her

* According to M. Schur's report on Gretchen B. (personal communication, 1956).

husband and children. When she remarried later in life, she hoped to restore her pre-Holocaust family. In marrying a man who had also lost his wife and children, she wanted to rebuild his family as well. Born to them late in life, the baby, Marvin K., was to be a child of hope, of resurrection, and of repudiation of Hitler's genocide. Paradoxically, the symbol of all good became the personification of evil. It was as if Hitler himself had been resurrected rather than the good children he had killed. The "bad" child was reminded daily that he did not come near the perfection of the deceased siblings he had never known. His father told him that he should have been killed at the age of three—the exact age at which the father's oldest child had been killed. His mother wanted to place him away from home because he was a "Hitler," and she could not cope with him.

Marvin did poorly in school, sought Gentile friends, and easily drifted into the drug culture. He hitchhiked into foreign countries, picking up casual friends and one-night stands. He periodically returned home, trying to start a better relationship with his parents. Once there, he provoked his parents until they screamed at him. He could always reconcile himself with his mother, but he never could really speak to his father.

Marvin came into analysis in his late adolescence. A large part of his analysis was concerned with the way he tried to disappoint and downgrade the analyst while at the same time making "dirt" of himself. Nobody seemed to want him, and he was forever looking for friends. Learned Jews, he felt, looked down on him; and his parents scorned his "low-class" Gentile companions. He was looking for someone, a father who could undo all his early sufferings and thus relieve him from having to become a redeemer himself, a task in which he continuously failed.

Marvin was forever testing his own ability to survive, but he wanted more than his own survival: the dead must come alive and be counted. His thoughts turned to Jesus Christ as a symbol of the goodness that he could find neither in his father nor in himself. However, East Indian lore was more acceptable to him because it did not require him to desert Jews and become a traitor to his parents. He joined a group of ascetic adherents to a "guru" who had died but continued to live in their thoughts. The guru represented eternal goodness and bestowed it upon his followers. Implied was a merging between the father and the followers, on the one hand, and the sibling-followers on the other. For Marvin, this philosophy was a means of merging rather than competing with the deceased siblings and of elevating fatherhood to a high spiritual level. The first signs of his feeling a need to rescue those who were abandoned revealed themselves when Marvin gave all he had to anyone in need. However, his high aspirations as a redeemer did not become apparent until Marvin understood that his "badness" and "stupidity" were the outcome of both his parents' and his own ambivalence about becoming better than his deceased siblings. He then became interested in teaching children through nonverbal communication.

Marvin did not stay in treatment beyond two years. He had to wander away, join the strictly moral group in another part of the country, and visit the guru's grave. However, his image of himself improved considerably. He was making his parents happy by working, going to school, and speaking kindly to them when he saw them. He wrote the analyst that his father had changed for the better. Perhaps he thought that he contributed to that change by reincarnating his own and his mother's dead children through his faith in a man whose thoughts lived after death.

Upon the analyst's request, Marvin came for a follow-up interview when he finished his studies and was continuing his chosen vocation. It became apparent in this interview that Marvin did not have his mother's approval to continue in treatment. She had been the first in the family to sanction his studies with the guru group, which had made him into a "good boy." Marvin seemed satisfied with his progress, but there was a melancholy thought haunting him: that he could not find a Jewish girl whom he could marry and who would have his children. The doubt of his parents whether they should have created him (a new Hitler), instead of mourning for the children who had perished, remained to cast a shadow over his life as a parent of Jewish children. The suggestion of the analyst that he could get help with this problem, tempted him to resume treatment. Instead, a few months later, he found a Jewish girl with whom to go steady.

The question of replacing loved ones killed in the Holocaust becomes a crucial conflict for many survivors and their children. Regardless of the age during which their traumatization occurred, survivor-parents introduce into their parenthood the usual identification and counteridentifications not only with their own living or deceased parents and siblings, but also with various people—some well known to them, some anonymous—who were part of their persecution experience. Through this extension of the usual type of identification to include persecutors and victims, they re-create the atmosphere of the Holocaust in their homes (see chapter 4). Many of their children, like Marvin, attempt to rescue them by creating a new past that extends into the present and the future.

Knowing one's persecutor as an individual—a guard in a camp, a man who barged into a house to arrest Jews, a neighbor who betrayed them, or a doctor who experimented with human beings—makes for a more clearly perceived experience than the memory of faceless, marching storm troopers or unseen, but imagined pursuers from whom one has to escape or hide. The younger the child, the more the reality of persecution was perceived through the eyes of one's parents or other caretakers. Harry R., for instance, looked at every separation from his father and brother as an undefined threat to his survival. Only once did he feel imperiled by a guard who aimed a gun at him; and this experience was perceived as factual, lacking the uncanny quality of his "visions." Joseph S. and Karl F. perceived the persecutors as people who separated them from their parents and siblings, and seemed more afraid of those who hid them than of the Nazis themselves. Mirelle G.'s father did not have a real concept of Nazis from whom his family had escaped. Primarily, he wanted to avoid conditions like those under which he had lived in Russia. Like Harry R. he transferred most of his fear of persecutors onto his degraded father, who had "abandoned" him. The distrust of strangers is often universal and cannot be pinpointed by special events. However, within this general atmosphere of doom, there stand out themes that are of special significance to the individual survivor-parent.

## The Choice of Crucial Themes in Survivors and Their Children

Memory for crucial dates and the anniversaries of special events influence survivor-parents' behavior toward their children. S. Axelrod et al. (1980) pointed out that children are frequently hospitalized at the same age as their parents had been when they were removed from home. It is sometimes difficult to get such parents to take the child home after he or she is released from the hospital. Another anniversary reaction pertains to the time when a child reaches the age at which a deceased child or sibling was killed. Each year that a child lives beyond the age of a deceased may be considered to be borrowed time. Each year of survival creates the illusion of an omnipotent child who lives on despite persecution. Perhaps one time he or she was lucky not to be selected for extermination, but the danger is not over: it can happen again. Needless to say, in some families this theme is overtly expressed, while in others it is only alluded to. An uneducated father may say, "I should have killed you when you were two years old"; a more refined parent may become insensitive to the child's physical needs and neglect his or her health, without being aware of death wishes toward the child.

A recurrent theme is the messianic task, assigned to the child who must justify his or her existence by great deeds. At the same time, the degradation the parents suffered, and their guilt over their inability to rescue Jews, is transmitted to the child, who begins to doubt the survivor-parents' morality in surviving. This doubt sometimes tempts survivors' children to side with Nazi "justice." They ask, "Are our parents guilty, and if they are what have they done to deserve such an extreme punishment?" (Kestenberg 1977, 1981a). Or, "Are our parents heroes because they survived against odds, or are they traitors who left others to die while they escaped?"

Beyond the general theme of survival and resurrection, guilt or heroism, certain parts of parents' experiences become dominant during specific developmental phases of their children—phases in which children are more accessible to what is being transmitted. This thesis is tentative because it is not yet properly documented. However, it has sufficient credibility to be put forth as a likely hypothesis.

Certain events in a parent's life are of much greater importance than others. Traumatic experiences become connected to early infantile memories and fantasies. Like screen memories, some stories are repeated to children, emphasizing a special theme which may be loss of liberty, abandonment, or torture. Escape, liberation, the influence of the displaced persons camp as a second edition of a concentration camp are also high on the list of themes; but these tend to be looked upon as signs of recovery from trauma. For instance, being chased, taken away, or shot at are repeated in dreams and fantasies or works of art within the framework of repetition compulsion (Freud 1920). Escape, shooting at the aggressors, and rescuing others are frequently considered signs of triumph over the persecutor. However, it is important to note which particular action is stressed in the stories and dreams recounted.

Normally, each parent regresses with a child and, through this adaptive regression, understands the child better and can guide him or her to solve the problem of a given phase. The parent, especially the father, is usually the first to progress and pave the way toward the resolution of a developmental conflict. Analyses of children of survivors indicate that their parents often tended to put the major burden on the child to progress from a phase that was especially meaningful to the parents within the framework of their Holocaust experience. Such parental behavior sometimes went beyond normal parental regression; it led the child into a special time and special circumstances that had been traumatic to the parents in the past. A brief inroad into the sequence of developmental tasks will clarify this thesis.

The parents of the average baby become concerned with the child's food intake. Parents who have survived starvation continue to worry about feeding their children as if it were a matter of life and death. They think about food with a greater than average intensity. One such mother reminded her daughter repeatedly that she had had to eat mice while in a concentration camp. The child's oral phase was prolonged and distorted; but beyond this, the communication with her mother, which is rooted in that phase (Kestenberg et al. 1971), was a continual subject of concern, with the child feeling that she— rather than her mother—must overcome the problem.

Parents who had been most affected by diarrhea, lack of toilet facilities, and curtailment of autonomy by their sadistic oppressors, may become more sadistic in the child's *anal-sadistic phase* than they were in earlier phases of the child's life. Marvin K.'s mother plied him with suppositories, restricted his movements, and plagued him with her insistence on limiting his autonomy in a pathological way. Marvin's answer was extreme sloppiness and returning home late. The ensuing arguments were used in part to solve the problems of cleanliness and independence and in part to solve the mother's fear of the return of the Holocaust.

In the *urethral phase* (Kestenberg et al. 1971), children are fascinated by floods and fires and so preoccupied with running that they frequently get lost. Practicing initiative, they habitually escape from their parents or hide from them. The escape is a triumph, but it also provokes fear because it connotes being alone and losing one's mother. A parent preoccupied with the hazard of fires, of escapes, and of being found, burdens the two-year-old with fears belonging to the parent's Holocaust past. An example of a fixation in the urethral phase is the case of a patient who came to analysis because frequent urination prevented her from functioning normally. She had to interrupt what she was doing to "run" to the bathroom. She did not connect this symptom with her dreams of escape, of facing electrified barriers, of shooting and fires. Neither did she connect it to her parents' escape from the ghetto into the woods where they joined the underground. Her urethral fixation was overladen with her parents' special experiences in the Holocaust.

In many cases the central issue in the parents' life is the loss of a child. This makes pregnancy a difficult time, and there is great concern with the survival of a healthy child. When the child reaches the *inner-genital phase* at the age of two and a half and three (Kestenberg 1975); when both sexes become preoccupied with pregnancy, birth, and death; when they test the animateness of their imaginary children—the issue of a parent's lost child receives new emphasis. At three, one tries to connect the present with the past and, in doing so, one goes beyond one's individual past to that of the parents. At three one asks questions about one's own and one's parents' earlier experiences (Kestenberg 1981a). It is at that point that one realizes which problems in one's parents' past must not be talked about.

The issue of life and death—as seen through the eyes of the parent-survivor—attaches itself to the child's concern with his or her own life as a growing individual and a future parent. Lucienne P.'s deprivation seems to have begun at the age of three. Her conflicts over motherhood were related to her early aspirations to be a mother. The problem of infertility loomed large in the life of her own mother, who had been amenorrheic when she left the camp in adolescence, and had had difficulty conceiving after Lucienne was born. Lucienne's father told her repeatedly that he should have killed her when she was born. Her relationship to her son was tinged with similar fantasies. These seem to have arisen in the third year of her life.

The wish to possess a parent is dominant in the *phallic-oedipal phase*, at which time the theme of life and death is linked with death wishes toward the other parent. In this context the repudiated bad wishes can be projected upon the Nazis. A parent who responds to an oedipal child's wishes, may revive the sado-masochistic relation to the persecutor or victim.

School requirements in *latency* can be burdened by a parent's fear of the teacher or of other persons as dangerous persecutors. Other parents make exaggerated demands that the child perform in school to prove his or her parents' intactness of intellect—despite starvation, lack of schooling, and blows on the head.

Regardless which theme is chosen, its elaboration in oedipal fantasies in *adolescence* can become an obstacle or an incentive to development of independence. Resolving the problems of a parent's individual past can become a hindrance in the development of autonomy, of one's own sense of reality and actuality, and of one's values and aspirations. Resolving problems creatively to relive the Holocaust and undo its effect—in works of art, in political action, through education, and in one's own parenthood—enriches the lives of survivors' children and helps them to see themselves as part of the past, the present, and the future. By bridging the gap in their parents' history, the children can help them to regain their self-esteem (Aleksandrowicz 1973; Klein 1973; Williams 1970). In each case we see a balance between unusual ego strength and a measure of pathology, both developed out of the stress imposed by being born under the shadow of the Holocaust.

The choice of strength or pathology is predicated on many variables. Specific ways to react to specific, phase-linked events such as starvation, anal degradation, child murder, or parent killing may serve to resolve parental conflict and to undo the effects of the regression parents were forced to suffer in the past. From the desire to cure parents and to progress in one's own development, symptoms may develop such as anorexia, obsessions, anxiety, and phobias; but from the same source, there arise solutions of a sublimatory nature that give survivors' children impetus to nurture others, to be active, creative, to join helping professions, and to be socially conscious. The wish to live in the parents' past and to undo the Holocaust may lead to pathology, but it may also lead to a desire to study history and to learn from this study how to prevent another Holocaust.

## Summary and Discussion

This chapter was based on the perusal of many analyses of children of survivors, some analyses of survivors, an occasional psychotherapy, and incidental results of a research on fathers (Kestenberg et al. 1981b). In all cases, the need to discover, to re-enact, or to live the parents' past was a major issue in the lives of survivors' children. This need is different from the usual curiosity of children about their parents. These children feel they have a mission to live in the past and to change it so that their parents' humiliation, disgrace, and guilt can be converted into victory over the oppressors, and the threat of genocide undone with a restitution of life and worth.

It is especially difficult to correlate the parents' ages during persecution with their children's current attitudes. Since separation is an important theme in most survivors' lives, it should not be necessarily linked to the parents' separation-individuation phase. Neither should one assume that symbiotic relationships abound whenever there is a separation problem. In addition, the epoch of traumatization could extend over several developmental phases, as in Harry R.'s case (pp. 86–87). The outcome also varies depending on whether a child was left on his or her own, with peers, with foster parents (Keilson 1979) or survived with a parent or a sibling. Harry, sheltered by his father and brother, became a dependent and phobic child; the Hampstead children who had come from Theresienstadt, seemed self-reliant and independent, at least at first (A. Freud and Dann 1951).

One must also keep in mind that later events can be condensed with earlier ones, especially since regression in the face of repeated trauma was common. This was evident in the case of Joseph S. (pp. 87–88), who linked his regressive bed-wetting at the age of eight with the training of his young son at an age when Joseph S. had first fled from the Nazis. This case also throws light on the intricacies of parents' interaction, whereby the child's behavior and fantasies serve the combined needs of father and mother.

There are numerous ways in which parents transmit their feelings to their children. It seems likely that the highlights of experiences in which survivor-parents live their past—such as torture, escape, confinement, or starvation—are easily transmitted to children in those phases where the themes of parental trauma coincide with a child's current developmental task. Some themes that are concerned with bodily functioning, begin to be transmitted at birth, and continue. Growing through nurture in the oral phase, exerting self-control and gaining autonomy in the anal phase, gaining initiative and freedom to move in the urethral phase, coming to terms with issues of procreation and life and death in the pre-oedipal—or inner-genital—phase, and identifying with the parent either as victim or as persecutor in the phallic-oedipal phase, are but a few cursory examples of the manner in which survival themes evolve in the development of survivors' children.

As anticipated, not all themes are present or dominant in each case; yet there is a common base—a *survival complex*—that is transmitted to children. Most, if not all, developmental phases are tinged with issues of survival. Perhaps this complex is as universal to human nature as Freud thought the Oedipus complex to be. Thus, it may become a source of either strength or pathology. We may not be able to detect it because it is latent in most human beings and becomes activated only under catastrophic conditions, threatening the perpetuation of a people.

Such an intense survival complex could not reveal itself in special survival themes without affecting psychic structure—a result that may, in turn, influence the second generation. Chapter 7 will give an account of a long analysis, which was the basis for a metapsychological assessment of the patient's psychic structure.

**5**

# *World Beyond Metaphor: Thoughts on the Transmission of Trauma*

WHETHER one focuses principally on the intrusion of actual Holocaust imagery or on the evolution of interests and capacities designed to explicate the parents' pain, one is still left with similar questions: How does what the parents endured or escaped make its way into the child's mind? Are the modes of transmission conscious and intentional, or do they occur through the unconscious channel? Can a general model for the transmission of trauma be constructed?

C. Barocas and H. Barocas have commented:

> The children of survivors show symptoms which would be expected if they actually lived through the Holocaust. The children present a picture of impaired object relations, low self-esteem, narcissistic vulnerability, negative identity formation, personality constriction and considerable affective impairment. They have to deal with the conflictual issue of intrusive images of their parents' suffering and the association between these images and ideas about their own vulnerability to death. They seem to share an anguished collective memory of the Holocaust in both their dreams and fantasies reflective of recurrent references to their parents' traumatic experiences. These children wake up at night with terrifying nightmares of the Nazi persecution, with dreams of barbed wire, gas chambers, firing squads, torture, mutilation, escaping from enemy forces and fears of extermination. The children come to feel that the Holocaust is the single most critical event that has effected their lives although it occurred before they were born. (1979, p. 331)

In approaching these most difficult questions, these authors have drawn not only on analytic experience with survivors and children of survivors but also on clinical research experience with caretakers and young children. The Clinic for the Development of Young Children and Parents at the Children's Hospital in Boston, has been studying early family development and the way in which caretaker conflict and content is transmitted to children. A model has been constructed out of an understanding of the ways in which what is of concern in the caretaking dyad either is or is not communicated to the child, and in which what is communicated to the child becomes or does not become a part of the child's internal reality. Here again, the complexities of the process give one pause. What a child is told may register less profoundly than the mannner in which one is treated. Certain affects and conflicts may have greater saliency for a child at one developmental point than at another. The impact of these very affects and conflicts is likely to be mediated by the presence and the processing of significant others, such as siblings, peers, grandparents, or friends. There appear to be so-called sensitive periods in which the developing child is particularly open to communications, both conscious and unconscious, from parents (and these periods may not be the same for mothers and fathers, for sons and daughters), from siblings, peers, and others.

Perhaps the greatest valency for the young child in a two-parent family, however, are those drive-related issues that cannot be contained in the adult-adult interaction between the parents, and that thus overflow onto the child. The parental protective envelope that optimally functions to shield the developing child from potentially harmful influences and forces, both intrapsychic and external, is forged by a *parentogenic alliance* between the spouses designed to provide a safe space for their own developmental failures, fetishes, and fantasies and a relatively safe space for the optimal development of their child or children. This safe space permits not only titration, expression, and containment of libidinal and aggressive impulses and their derivatives, whose direct application might prove deleterious and overstimulating to a child, but also a mourning and restitutive place where prior and current mortifications, hurts, and discontents can be healed and handled. What we are describing is an ideal. It is probably never achieved in absolute terms and, perhaps, never should be. The explanatory power of the model seems most apparent in situations of gross abuse, either sexual or physical, or of major impediments to the marital relationship (such as psychosis, divorce, or death). To assess its applicability to average expectable environments with less extreme provocations or actions is a more difficult task.

This parentogenic alliance and protective shield is as often observed in the breach as in the practice. We are continually impressed as psychoanalysts with the impingement of parental neurosis and pain upon our child and adult patients. Dorothy Burlingham (1951) and others who have reported on the simultaneous analyses of children and parents have gone even farther, citing the sharing of unconscious material between progenitors and offspring which seems to be transmitted in an uncanny and unspecified fashion. Most often this material is of a sexual and aggressive nature. Drive expression and conflictual overflow appear to be transmitted. Real events play a part, but even these are usually primarily drive-related. The work of certain family therapists has led to an expansion of these notions: many family members appear to be affected by real events that are thought to be unknown. These so-called family secrets are then found to be either pathogenic or otherwise deleterious. Bringing them out of the closet, so to speak, seems to be the first step in resolving certain forms of family pathology.

What of a situation in which the spouses are survivors of the Holocaust? The extremity of this experience is beyond debate. It appears that the environments created by survivors both in their marriages and in their subsequent development of families were, and are, as varied as the survivors themselves. Anna Ornstein (personal communication), among others, has called attention to the fact that post-Holocaust adjustment is by no means uniform among survivors. The quality of the adjustment is affected by critical variables, including: one's pre-war personality; age and capacity for adaptation at the time one's life was disrupted; the supports available during imprisonment, including one's capacity for fantasy; what one actually endured; whom one actually lost; and one's capacity to live a kind of dual existence—not only to exist in the camp, but simultaneously to be grounded in one's prewar existence. This last capacity may be particularly significant and has been observed in children of survivors seen in an analytic setting.

Post-Holocaust marriages (and, in those rare circumstances where both marital partners survived together or apart, pre-Holocaust marriages) provided an opportunity for survivors to create or re-create a safe space in which to share the exigencies of the present and the anguish of the past. But what kind of safe space must be created to contain and heal life in Auschwitz? What are the conditions that facilitate therapeutic sharing? Does it matter if the survivor-spouse is husband or wife? Does it matter what the relative capacity of each marital partner is to bear and endure not only one's own but the other's grief, mortification, or exultation in having survived? What happens to basic trust when one's world—at least the world of one's childhood, one's parents, one's past—has ceased to exist? Though the answers to these questions will contain significant individual variation, they must be considered in approaching the issues of the nature both of the adult-adult relationship in a marriage between survivors and of the parentogenic alliance. Furthermore—and this may be a primary factor—survivors often have an intense and overwhelming wish to create something new. To replace, to refute, to undo and go on may become the overriding motif in a marriage of survivors. The survival of the species is at stake.

It is one thing to pose these questions; another, to answer them. Some information pertinent to the answers is available. It seems that first marriages of survivors, those not burdened by murdered spouses and murdered children, lend themselves more easily to the creation of a shared space where what they have endured can be shared and processed in a way that least traumatically impinges upon the development of their children. It may be surprising to find that marriages in which both partners are survivors, or at least refugees and survivors, seem to facilitate sharing. Should not a double burden more seriously compromise the parentogenic alliance than a single one? Logically, yes; but empirically, no: for a nonsurvivor-spouse often displays complex and confounded motivations for his or her object choice. Survivor-fathers (husbands) seem to be more impaired in the establishment of safe spaces than are survivor-mothers (wives). Was the European-Jewish masculine identity more disturbed than the European-Jewish feminine identity by the experience of subjugation, humiliation, and genocide? The very making of these generalizations is potentially misleading. They arise from small numbers of cases, and almost always the idiographic outweighs the nomothetic. Particularly in regard to the gender differences of the survivors, gender difference appears to disappear when both adults are survivors. Then the woman's capacity for intimacy often allows her to help her husband into a safe space. The wife who is not herself a survivor, may not be able to exercise this "feminine" quality. These impressions suggest that there is some kind of spectrum (perhaps normal distribution) of the ability to create a safe space in the one-to-one adult relationship. Within the framework of the existence or the nonexistence of a safe space in the marriage, it then becomes possible to formulate the following hypothesis: the more constricted the shared safe space between the spouses, the less the opportunity for healing and containment within the relationship and the more the child (or children) of survivors is asked to serve as a special kind of self-object whose job is to share, undo, ameliorate, and restitute.

Having stated the hypothesis and some of the theory that underlies it, we shall now advance a clinical approach designed to shed light on this question of how trauma is transmitted. Our method has involved the careful examination of material from the analyses and analytically oriented psychotherapies of both survivors and their children. Some of these cases are our own; others we have been privileged to hear from colleagues and associates. We shall present here material from the psychotherapy and the analysis of a survivor and then from the analysis of a child of survivors.

# World Beyond Metaphor

A SURVIVOR—RUTH N.

Ruth N. was forty-one years old when at the urging of her internist, she entered psychotherapy for chronic depression. She was married and the mother of two adolescent sons. Her husband, from whom she felt emotionally estranged, was required to travel extensively in his work, but she never accompanied him. Her own traveling to Europe to visit surviving uncles always engendered considerable anxiety. She felt that it would be unsafe to travel with her husband, who frequently needed to go to the very countries she visited. "Better alone," she stated, and then added that she did not clearly understand the meaning of this sentiment. In referring Ruth N., her internist reported to the analyst that she was a very courageous woman who had undergone several serious medical illnesses with great fortitude. He also stated that she was a survivor of the Holocaust, having been hidden in a Catholic school in Belgium from the time she was three until she was seven.

Mrs. N. presented herself as an attractive, petite, French-looking woman who appeared older than her stated age. There was an air of agitation about her, and she would occasionally wring her hands. She stared at the analyst intently and stated that she was glad that he had not asked her to lie down on the couch as she had to study him carefully. In fact, he could not ask her to lie down because he was seeing her at his hospital office, which had no couch. He was seeing her there because she did not drive, would not take public transportation, and had not told her husband that she was going to an analyst. Similar complications arose in regard to the fee. Because her husband was not to know about her analysis, she would have to pay the analyst out of her grocery money.

Throughout the first meeting, Mrs. N. seemed frightened and distressed. She said that her marriage was unsatisfactory. Her husband was perfectly decent, but she did not want to share anything of herself with him. Her children were prospering, she thought, but were doing so somehow in spite of her, not because of her. There was an immediate problem in that she was planning to journey to Europe to see her uncle, and as usual her husband could not understand why she did not want him to accompany her. Gentle probing then revealed that Mrs. N. and her husband did very little together. They did not share the same bed and in fact barely shared the same house.

Over the next eight weeks, Mrs. N. told more of herself. With sad but restrained affect, she spoke of a recurrent dream about not being able to feed her youngest child when he was an infant—and then of another dream about being on a bus that would not stop when she was ready to get off. She was afraid that her children were lost in this latter dream. Then, with great shame, Mrs. N. related that when her youngest son was very small, she would often not bathe him and occasionally would forget to feed him. He did not starve, she stated. Mrs. N. was very concerned about the fate of the Iranian Jews and anguished about Cambodia. She was making contributions to an international relief fund, also from her grocery money. Her family was beginning to complain that she had them all on a diet, and she said that she could not pay for her treatment until some time in the future. Mrs. N. stated that she thought that she could trust her analyst. She noted that he crossed his sevens like a European, and confessed that she had come to see him because his last name is the same as a name in her extended family. She hoped he would understand.

Then one day Mrs. N. began to talk about her family of origin and her life in Europe. She described in exquisite detail her father, whom she had not seen since she was two years old, and his imprisonment in Paris. She also told of her mother's flight to Belgium with her. There was a memory of her mother telling her to come in from the balcony and to be quiet—for God's sake, be quiet! Then another memory of her mother feeding her. She was sitting in what might be a high chair. Her mother seemed to be forcing food into her mouth. She could not eat so much. What was the hurry? Mrs. N. said that she hardly ate anything now—a statement consistent with her extreme thinness.

Mrs. N. then moved on to life in the convent. Her name was changed so that she would pass for Catholic. She had many illnesses and was sometimes taken to the hospital by the nuns, who said that she was a great bother. Mrs. N. then brought in pictures of her father in Paris and her mother in Belgium. She also showed her analyst certificates of deportation and a death certificate issued by a committee to certify the deaths of foreign-born Jews deported from France. It stated that her father had died in Auschwitz. Mrs. N. said that her parents were actually from Poland but had met and married in France. That is why there was this particular record available of the transport on which her father left France.

Although Mrs. N. was visibly shaken as she shared these pictures, documents, and almost photographlike memories of her earlier life, her analyst was struck by the fact that she did not weep—particularly as he could barely restrain his own tears. At one session Mrs. N. was describing life at the convent: the day that the mother superior told Mrs. N. that her mother could no longer visit her as she had broken her leg. Mrs. N. described herself as feeling very alone. There was no place where she could run, no one to comfort her. The analyst stated to Mrs. N. that there was apparently no longer a place where her mother could run either. Mrs. N. stared at him and then let out an anguished cry. Her control and restraint, so conspicuous during the previous sessions, was gone. "What did they do with people who could not walk to the trains?" she cried. "Shoot them right there?" Mrs. N. walked everywhere. She never got on train, bus, or trolley.

The analyst's statement about her mother seemed to initiate a new phase in his work with Mrs. N. It was as if he had entered her affective Holocaust world. There began a long and rewarding journey in which they were to discover that Mrs. N. inhabited a double world. She simultaneously lived in Boston in the 1970s and in Belgium both with and without her mother in the 1940s. The work of her treatment centered on finding the connections between these two worlds and ways of organizing and separating what belonged to one and what belonged to the other. Analyst and patient were able to understand both her reluctance to share with her American-born husband experiences and feelings that she thought he would regard as crazy, and how some of these seemed to emerge in caretaking functions with her children which mirrored some of her most painful memories of her time with her mother. Moreover, the fact that her younger son had been named for her mother and in some ways was particularly subject to some of these dynamic currents also began to make sense. Mrs. N. arranged for him to be evaluated, and he was eager to embark on treatment.

Over three years Mrs. N. experienced considerable improvement. Particularly striking was the feeling that the double world of Belgium and Boston which she experienced so vividly began to recede. At the time when the treatment ended, which was necessitated by a move the family was making to another state, Mrs. N. reported that she felt as though she could now live in one place and one time and that her chances for survival, as both wife and parent, would benefit from her living fully in the here-and-now. Follow-up reports from Ruth and her family suggest that her improvement was indeed sustained.

Ruth's affective Holocaust world had, and had not, been previously shared with another person. It was not relegated to the safe space of her marriage. In fact, there was no such safe space—a lack that was due in some measure to the existence of her double world. Parts of that world were shared with her children, particularly her younger son who was expected to be a girl and was named for her mother. Very small parts of it were shared with her European uncles. Like many survivors, Ruth did not have much family left, and those who were, were far removed in time and space. Ruth's younger son was significantly affected by his mother's trauma. His therapist discovered him to be very concerned with themes of reproduction, reincarnation and redemption and closely resembling the survivor's-child profile constructed by Judith Kestenberg (see chapter 7). The boy also possessed, however, a strong masculine identification and had enjoyed an ongoing and sustaining relationship with his father.

Ruth's therapy and then analysis sheds light on the way in which parental trauma can be unmetabolized, unintegrated, and unbound. In such a situation and with such an affective charge, it seems incontrovertible that overflow will occur. That this overflow should find maximal expression in the area of caretaking—that area maximally involved in Ruth's own history—is likewise not surprising. Experience with other survivor-parents lends strong presumptive evidence to the notion that unbound, unintegrated, and unshared trauma is most likely to overflow. The very acts of caretaking, as well as the affective climate, then become the medium for the message. Without intervention, a relatively stable chain of transmission can occur. We are seeing not only survivors' children but also their grandchildren in whom there are manifestations of such a legacy.

But how does this phenomenon look and feel if observed from the other side, from the vantage point of the child?

A SURVIVOR'S SON—DAVID P.

David P., a thirty-year-old Jewish biochemist, entered treatment for help with feelings of depression, trouble in his relationships with women, and lack of spontaneity. A previous psychotherapy had focused on his separation difficulties from his parents and from his religious tradition. When it ended, his therapist had suggested that Mr. P. seek analysis. The Holocaust was not on the list of the patient's chief complaints, although the evaluating analyst related that Mr. P.'s parents were both survivors of the Second World War.

In the preliminary sessions before analytic work, there was a significant amount of difficulty in planning schedule, time, and financial arrangements. There seemed to be sudden changes in Mr. P.'s time commitments and in his means. Just as these arrangements were almost settled, an interruption occurred because of Mr. P.'s sudden and unexpected need to make a work-related trip. When the analyst inquired about this development, Mr. P. at first made excuses. Shortly thereafter he mentioned that he didn't like to be pinned down. It was better to be able to move, to keep people guessing, and not to have one's mobility impaired; and then he added that it made him very nervous to be embarking on a venture that should probably not be suddenly interrupted. In passing, he stated, "It's harder for them to catch you if they don't know where you are." When asked what he meant, Mr. P. said that he always noted the exits when entering buildings and always parked his car in a space from which he could readily escape.

At the beginning of the second analytic hour, Mr. P. stated that he liked coming to the analyst's office. Parking was easy, as was the getaway. He also stated that he liked the looks of the office and of the analyst as well. "You know, in ten years I'm going to become exactly like you," he stated. This statement proved to be the first of many that seemed to be related to a wish to disidentify from what he thought he was and what he thought his parental legacy entailed, and to a parallel aspiration to become someone bigger, stronger, and more free. That he had not been able to admire his father nor aspire to become like him, and that his father was impaired in his ability to celebrate, mirror, and admire him, was to emerge in stark relief as the analysis progressed.

Mr. P. spoke after some time of his family and their background. He had been born in the United States shortly after his parents had emigrated from Europe. Two older siblings were born following the end of the war before the family journeyed to the United States. His father had been an affluent lawyer in Eastern Europe before the war and had escaped the Nazis and made his way to Russia. He was captured and interned in Siberia. David P. knew nothing more of his father's experience during the war; this, he said, was because of a language barrier. He could not understand his father's Yiddish or Polish, and his father could not understand David's English. That David's linguistic abilities were pronounced had not solved this impasse; and toward the end of the analysis, Mr. P. finally conceded that it was fitting and proper that he and his Dad did not communicate. They both wanted it that way. He had an insight in relation to the occasion when one of his brothers told him that they (his brother and he) could not communicate, and that such difficulty was not fitting and proper.

David felt that his father communicated with his mother and maybe talked to his brothers. His father certainly got mad at the older boys and would sometimes beat them. He never beat David, however. David thought that the fact that he would begin crying as soon as his father got mad at one of the older boys might be the reason that he was spared. Then again, he observed, he gave his father no cause for anger. They hardly did anything together. Several memories then emerged of his father's incompetence in David's early years: getting lost on the subway, not being able to do things. Only much later did Mr. P. sadly say that he had not even known the warmth of his father's wrath.

The analyst further learned that Mr. P.'s father had been ill for many years with a progressively debilitating illness. Multiple surgeries had dispensed limited reprieves, but a definite downhill course was evident. An early attempt on the analyst's part to make some clarifying statement about one of these historical facts was dismissed by Mr. P. rather angrily as "dead wrong." Later Mr. P. responded to other statements of the analyst with the same phrase. The analyst was "dead wrong" in his understanding of Mr. P. and his background. At about the same time, Mr. P. had a dream in which the analyst appeared as a ritual slaughterer, and associated to his being four years old at the taking of a family photograph: he had struggled desperately to get out of his father's lap, out of his clutches. This was followed by an association to an automobile accident at about the same time: he had run into the street, while his mother watched with horror from the apartment window.

Two themes declared themselves early on and were to characterize the transference: the analyst was the potential destroyer of Mr. P.'s vivacity, spontaneity, and chance for a normal life; and the analyst was dead. He could not and would not respond to Mr. P. And there was more, much more—including the fact that if he could become his analyst, all would be better—but these were the initial themes. The last was re-echoed in an association toward the end of the eighth month of the analysis. The analyst's quietness, which sometimes distressed Mr. P., had another meaning. He associated to a short story about a Lithuanian rabbi who showed his love by being silent.

Mr. P. developed these two central themes of the transference over subsequent months and years. As he related many details about his life both personally and professionally, he gave example after example of his inability to establish empathic links with others. He could not "read" them or vice versa and would get terribly wounded and distressed over a misunderstanding. Simultaneously, it became clear that a recurrent theme in his dealings with older colleagues was to challenge them in such a way as to provoke anger. As he was speaking about one of these episodes, he mentioned that he had gotten a rise out of Professor J., a senior faculty member. When he was asked about this, it turned out that Professor J. was of European extraction, and a whole series of such incidents came to Mr. P.'s mind, which he described in exquisite detail.

Then Mr. P. had the notion that the analyst, by insisting on analyzing everything, would ruin even the fun that he, Mr. P., had with the harmless activity of challenging others. Shortly thereafter, Mr. P. returned to the notion that the analyst was dead wrong, and that maybe he was dead as Mr. P. could never get a rise out of him no matter how hard he tried. A dream of smoking pot in a temple followed, and the horrified rabbi by association became his father. It was a happy dream because he got a response, but then he realized with horror that he had attended the funeral of that particular rabbi, that he was dead. Once again Mr. P.'s thoughts turned to his father, and he recounted his impression of his father as a sad, silent, distant man who went to work, came home, and never had anything to do with him.

The preoccupation with the analyst's inability to respond now became paramount. The analyst was seen as strong, big, and sexually exciting. Mr. P. was not troubled by these sexual feelings. They were perfectly safe because by definition the analyst could not give in, would not accept the invitation. Masturbatory patterns and fantasies were now brought in and discussed in graphic detail. These were mostly homosexual. Mr. P. wore short shorts to the sessions and began a concentrated body-building program—swimming, jogging, modern dance—all at one time. Still he could get no rise from the already "dead" analyst. When this was not enough, Mr. P. began going to gay bars and had a brief homosexual relationship with a European-born lawyer. It ended rather quickly as he found it far from physically acceptable. When these activities were discussed in the analysis, Mr. P. said angrily that the analyst did not "turn him on"; he was too fat or too thin or whatever. Mr. P. had a dream about buying his father a Jacuzzi whirlpool bath to heal his tired and stricken body, but the bath contained hidden knives that did their devilish deeds cutting off his legs and penis. At the end of the dream, his father extended an amputated limb to David, either inviting him to come in or begging for assistance. The analyst pointed out Mr. P.'s rage both at himself, the analyst, and at the father for not responding, and also that Mr. P. experienced them both as castrated or deserving of castration. Was Mr. P. to be the castrator? Mr. P. wept and stated, "My father could not respond. He was already dead."

At about this time, another crisis in his father's health occurred. There was more surgery, but it looked as if the end were near. Mr. P.'s mother told him for the first time that his father had been previously married, and that his first family had been lost during the Holocaust. Mr. P. described himself as both stunned and not surprised. As he continued to explore his simultaneous patricidal and "patriphilic" wishes, he strove to be able to tell his dying father, now over eighty, that he loved him. In the analysis, he simultaneously experienced the therapist as analyzing all spontaneity out of him—a crime punishable by death—as not responding to him in a way that he could use, and as having a beautiful swimmer's body of the sort that he could develop. The thought entered Mr. P.'s mind that the analyst was a responsive good father to his children, and that his family's constellation resembled Mr. P.'s.

Mr. P.'s father died during the summer interruption following the third year of the analysis. Mr. P. wrote that he felt liberated—that his father's suffering had ended, and that his whole family had been released from their chains. He became mildly hypomanic and preoccupied with certain medical-legal issues surrounding the rights of physicians to terminate lives and the safeguards that protected patients. Major issues about killing and being killed surfaced and were worked on for some time. Mr. P. contemplated a career change to law or to medicine. New and important material about his mother's wartime activities emerged. Images of her as murderess, castrator, and inadequate protector were dredged up and appeared in dream material. He now knew more of her wartime activities as a partisan and of her role as protector of her brothers. There was no clear mourning for his father. Rather, Mr. P. felt that he had always mourned his father—and that his father had always been in mourning.

There was a change in the transference or—perhaps better stated—in the alliance. Mr. P. felt that the analyst was trying to help him—that he had empathy for him and could help him to learn to develop empathy for others. Mr. P. called this quality sweetness. He thought the analyst shared some of this sweetness with him. They talked together of a world beyond metaphor, in which many things that would have been fantasies alone for others had been literal components of Mr. P.'s parents' past and, in some less distinct way, of his growing up: lost children, murder, bottomless grief, and longing. Memories of having been called a little Hitler or worse than Hitler then emerged. Mr. P. said, "What does empathy mean in a world beyond metaphor? There are no boundaries, and I think there have to be for empathy to exist." He was haunted by a sense of knowing more about the past than he was conscious of. "When knowledge comes, memory comes too; little by little knowledge and memory are one and the same thing," the philosopher Gustav Meyrink has said.* The questions asked in the analysis were, Whose memory? Whose knowledge? And, How might one person's knowledge and another person's memory become one and the same thing?

Mr. P. began to piece together the tapestry of his father's hurt and of his father's hunger. He had a dream in which he was driving away from the synagogue in a car given to him by his father, but the car was without a door: without "a-dor-ing" he could not drive. The final two years of the analysis dealt with these issues.

* Quoted in Friedländer 1979, p. 20.

# World Beyond Metaphor

This patient's life occupied the last thirty years of his father's existence—the time in America. The family living in a metropolitan area with a large Jewish population managed to effect a new beginning. A business was developed and prospered. Mr. P.'s mother had family left; his father had none. His mother was energetic and alive, although her energy was consumed as the caretaker and protector of her husband. Mr. P. described the marriage as a treaty. There was no love or passion there, he stated—but rather a pact to go on, to start again, and to repopulate the earth with Jewish children. Following her husband's death, Mr. P.'s mother seemed to reflower. She came to life with both her sons and with everybody else. Upon returning from a gynecologist's appointment, she startled David by saying, "I'm beautiful inside," and smiling in a decidedly happy fashion. This was in sharp contrast to Mr. P.'s memory of her earlier methodical working and the funeral-parlor, anhedonic ambience of his home.

Both parents were true to the pact to go on. They worked, reproduced, and lived. Only the father could do no more. He sat in darkness, Mr. P. said. "He would stare ahead. It was so hard to get him to laugh. I guess he must have liked me when I was little and cute. He must have. Maybe that's why I try to be so cute now, although its far from appropriate." His father was silent, but he valiantly went through the motions. He tried. When he would hold onto David, not exactly in an embrace, the boy felt an irresistible urge to flee—as though to stay too close, to be held, was to become one of the living dead. In the last year of his father's life, when Mr. P. had the conscious information that his father had had a previous family in Poland, and that they had been lost, he began to feel that he could have reached his father had he been a girl like one of the lost daughters. He saw his desire to wear his hair long and curly in this light and some of the sexual imagery as also being influenced by the wish to be a girl like one of the dead daughters.

But still, the overwhelming sexual image, which was repeated again and again, of wanting to make a man writhe—of taking his pelvis in his hands and giving him indescribable pleasure—did not involve David's being one of the girls, the little lost girls. It distinctly seemed to him that he was a boy giving pleasure to a man, or maybe it was a man giving pleasure to a boy: "two live ones," Mr. P. said, "bringing out the life, him in him and him in him."

These two themes—of needing to draw away lest he become one of the living dead and, conversely, of wishing to infuse life into his father, to make him writhe with pleasure, with life—L'Chaim—came together under the rubric of sweetness. Mr. P. felt that his father's sweetness remained in Europe with the ashes of his loved ones; what sweetness remained after Poland was frozen out in Siberia; what remained after Siberia, was invested in his two older brothers and his mother. "By the time I arrived, he was all dried up. There was no more to give." Furthermore, he believed that his mother who might have given him something—not exactly sweetness but something akin to it—was wholly occupied with the care and protection of her ailing, mourning, then dying husband.

At first the analyst was seen as the blighter: to be analytical about everything was to be one of the living dead, devoid of spontaneity and feeling. Then he was seen as the already dead, one from whom or out of whom one could not get a rise. Over time, however (although it was already present in the second session), he became the one who could admire and mirror, who could be idealized without the need to flee or disidentify, who could and would impart some sweetness—which Mr. P. defined as empathy, not being wholly eaten up by one's own grief. At this point, Mr. P. no longer felt the need to flee the analysis, to disidentify, to get a rise out of the analyst that was either libidinal or aggressive, or to become him:

Somehow I feel that I get this sweetness from you. I can't exactly say how. I just feel it. That you like me not because I am seductive or cute or give you an erection or even make you writhe with pleasure. But because you have taken the time to listen to me and to try and understand me and to confront me when necessary with what I do and why. It's as if you say it's O.K. to be me. I don't have to be anybody else. It's even good to be me, all things considered. Not that I really have any other choice. Somehow it's all of that and more that I call sweetness.

Mr. P.'s father could not be a father to David. His paternal sweetness was gone. Not all survivor-fathers are like this, but Mr. P.'s father was. With the sweetness, this elusive masculine empathy, went his libidinal and aggressive availability—those factors critical to the development of masculine-core gender identity and to the modulation of aggressive drive and fantasy. He could not mirror, admire, or protect his last son, nor could he be idealized or idealizing. His mourning, his sadness, his darkness, and his depression—his hurt—made contact with him seem hurtful.

In other publications about father hunger (Herzog 1980, 1981)—what a boy experiences when he lacks a libidinally and aggressively available male parent to act as a mentor for his developing identity and drive organization—we have examined situations in which the father is either actually or psychologically absent. Mr. P.'s situation was different: his father was very much present and yet unavailable. Mr. P. felt his father's hurt as infectious. Complicated processes of projection and introjection were obviously at work. They, too, involved a melding of aggressive and libidinal forces. To get close to the father, to make restitution to him, and simultaneously to address and redress his own father hunger were seen by Mr. P. as to be swallowed up by his father's hurt and thus to become one of the living dead. He needed someone new. A new masculine self-object? A new father? But the techniques that Mr. P. had at hand served him poorly in the pursuit of this object. The analysis, perhaps, served him better. It served to explicate the father hurt and the father hunger.

Up until the last month, new memories emerged: "I once wandered off and then returned and asked my father for a dime. I knew it was the wrong man I had walked up to when he replied"—then tears. Or: "It was hard to have fun when he wouldn't or couldn't—but who would have fun if his wife and children had been murdered."

A dream in the fourth year involved a man embracing him. Both the man and he were wearing striped swimming trunks, but they were not identical. He suspected that the man was the analyst. They could swim together, pool their talents—a sweet thought. Mr. P. then associated to the many colored stripes of the bathing suit—Joseph and his coat of many colors. Then the stripes reminded him of a convict's garb—his father as a prisoner of the Nazis, in Siberia, of his grief; it should not be woven into something as beautiful and as revealing as those bathing trunks. David then moved from Joseph to Jacob: Joseph was the child of Jacob's old age; he was given a special role, a gift; Joseph the survivor—his father, the survivor; he, David, the child of survivors. He then thought of the analysis as a gift; the trunks had been emptied of the pain of the past, and somehow these "ruinboy—no, rainbow-like" trunks had been fashioned. He wondered if the analyst, in letting him feel for him, the analyst, and helping him feel for his father, had taught him how to feel. The analyst stated that a coat of many colors had many stripes, as did trunks. In the dream, their trunks were different, each from the other. Their work, their swim had involved learning about the patient's various components, where they came from, how they fit together, how he regarded them, that his stripes formed a cohesive and functional whole. Mr. P. said, "Yes, and I have learned something from you. It doesn't have to be ruin boy. It can be rainbow." "There are elements of both," the analyst said. "This dream is beautiful inside," Mr. P. said, quoting his mother. "I admire it as I admire our work."

His thoughts then turned to an older dream in which "chemo-analysis"—not chemotherapy—had been the treatment of choice for a slowly malignant tumor. Then he turned to a still earlier dream, also of tumors (the lost children), within an ambivalent host. In that dream, RNA, messenger RNA—that is, memory—had been the treatment. The analysis had begun by going after knowledge and memory and tried to sort out the question of whose knowledge and whose memory and how his father's and mother's experiences might have affected his own: what they could or could not eradicate, integrate, shield him from; what he could not, would not, or should not notice, absorb, know, or remember. By the "chemo-analysis" dream, the thought was no longer how to eradicate the tumor but how to understand and tolerate and integrate it. By the swimming suit dream, something else emerged. Not only had father hurt and father hunger been remembered and "chemo-analyzed," but also he was swimming with a distinct but closely linked helper, instead of swimming alone. Mr. P. said that he felt that the car of still another dream now had its door. He was not without "a-dor-ing," and he could now drive himself and, he hoped, other passengers like a wife and children of his own. He said he felt more whole. "My second liberation," Mr. P. said as the analysis came to an end. "My father's pain can be laid to rest. I understand my longing for him. I am still sad for him, but I am hopeful for me. I neither have to get away from his-my hurt nor be ruled by his-my hunger. I can live. L'Chaim."

As Mr. P. mastered his father hurt and his father hunger, he began to be able to focus more on the nature of his relationship with his mother. Interesting and important transformations occurred as actual memories appeared to take on new affective shadings. The world beyond metaphor had originally been used to describe the feeling that Mr. P. had reported that his mother would actually kill him for a childhood misdemeanor. This was Mr. P.'s feeling even before he learned that his mother had had to "kill" herself during the war. Later the same memory took on a different meaning. Mr. P. felt that not knowing what his mother might do, and knowing that his father would do nothing, had felt deadly. The metaphoric nature of his fear seemed to return. Mr. P. felt that he experienced something of what his parents had endured and something of what they had done in these chilling affective experiences of his childhood. The feeling of being held too close and not being held closely enough also seemed to him to become a metaphor: he was held too close to his parents' Holocaust past and not tightly enough in the world of his actual childhood reality. He, too, had had a double reality. He had lived in Poland and in America; although, unlike Ruth, he had never really lived in Europe nor did he know that he lived there in some aspect of his innermost being. In the fifth year of the analysis, he no longer felt the need to titrate the analytic activity. "I realize now that the Gestapo is not likely to find me here or anywhere else," he said. "They are not on the prowl here or even in Europe."

# World Beyond Metaphor

## *Discussion and Conclusion*

Mr. P.'s analysis did not clearly and concisely reveal the intricacies of his parents' relationship. What the analyst learned was through the eyes of a little boy as involved in oedipal and other distortions with his parents as is any other child. Nor did the analyst have the privilege of meeting Mr. P.'s parents and seeing for himself. It is for this reason that it was decided to present Ruth N's material as well as David P.'s, although they are in no way dynamically related. Mrs. N. could not have been David's mother, nor could David have been Mrs. N.'s son. The relationship is at the most that Mrs. N. is a survivor-mother and that Mr. P. is the child of survivors.

By juxtaposing these two cases, however, it may become clearer how trauma is transmitted. Mr. P. was the heir to his father's agony and longed for what his father could no longer give him. His mother's more active ability to cope and go on was not lost on him but was compromised by the cross-gender question and his own conflicted wish to be the lost daughter and thus the redeemer and reverser of his father's pain. His psychological career, which began as an attempt to understand and reverse death, became a well-sublimated endeavor focusing on the origins of life. It seemed that Mr. P.'s father could not be saved or revived even by his wife. His grief and despair surmounted any and all efforts to console or confine it to a safe space within the marriage. It could neither be confined nor neutralized, at least not by a new family of three sons. David was the last child. He had to be the lost daughter, but he could not be the lost daughter. Efforts to understand the origins of this impossible dilemma allowed him to escape from the time tunnel. Although he and Mrs. N. in some sense occupied differing points in that tunnel originally, they came eventually to occupy the same place—life in the here-and-now.

Elie Wiesel has repeatedly stated that survivors of the Holocaust live in a nightmare world that can never be understood. Although his opinion has its stark and bitter truth, we believe that the nightmare can be dispelled; that, through words, analysis can penetrate the shadowy inner world of the patient, which operates in metaphor, and, by illuminating it, diminish pain, and heal. Furthermore, analysis can demonstrate how the tragedy of one generation may be transmitted to the next, and then break the chain of suffering. Then survivors, children of survivors, and their children can remember but not relive, and concentrate on the difficult task of mere being.

# 6

# *A Daughter of Silence*

IN DISCUSSING the second generation of survivors of the Holocaust, we can make a general division between those whose parents spoke of it, of their personal Holocaust, and those whose parents were completely silent on the subject. This chapter deals with two examples of the latter—an Israeli child brought in for therapeutic consultation and an Israeli patient in analysis.

The following illustrates the observation that all children act out a scenario of which they have no knowledge, a scenario that is not theirs but, in fact, belongs to the history of their families, and especially of those that have survived the Holocaust. The details are late psychic signs of man-made disasters.

### MICHAL M.—A "LOST" AND "ABSENT" GIRL

Michal M. was a thin, pretty, dark-haired seven-year-old who arrived at the consultation room with her mother close at hand. The mother related some details of the family history. The father, originally from Poland, had gone to Israel as a young child. The mother immigrated to Israel from Argentina shortly before their marriage. Michal was their third child. Recently she had had disturbances of memory and cognition, amnesias and "absences." The latter, which most worried those around her, occurred at school primarily but also at home. Michal's mother described the child as "waking" from such an absence in a "lost state" and exhibiting what the analyst saw as dissociative phenomena.

The discussion with the mother lasted an hour. Michal was present the entire time. She looked serious but not frightened or depressed. The analyst asked Mrs. M. to leave her and the patient alone, and Michal and the analyst initiated their relationship through the "squiggle game," working, drawing, and talking for an hour. Toward the end of the session, in response to a question from the analyst, Michal answered that she would not want to be "an electric fence in the Warsaw Ghetto, they put the soldier's children there and if they touch the fence and electrocute themselves, they will die."

Several diagnostic hypotheses to this response could have been attached:

perhaps anxiety is related to aggression; and so on. But the analyst was troubled by Michal's words, feeling that their meaning lay beyond their specific diagnostic value. Michal seemed to demand that attention be given to thoughts beyond her conscious knowledge. These thoughts held a prospect so frightening that she may have preferred to be "absent" rather than cognizant of her surroundings and these thoughts.

The analyst decided to check this hypothesis in terms of the history of the family. The next session was held with Michal's mother present. The father, though invited, did not come. The analyst asked Mrs. M. if there was a story circulating in the family about the Holocaust. She answered that her husband's whole family had been killed, but added that they never talked about it at home. The analyst then cited Michal's statement from the first session and asked her mother for help in understanding it. The mother turned pale, appeared shocked, and said, "My husband was in the Warsaw ghetto as a child and later in a concentration camp. But we have never spoken about this with the children. How does she know? My husband always says that he arrived in Israel as a child and there are never any further questions about his background."

In the course of several therapeutic sessions, Michal, her mother, and the analyst worked through the connection between Michal's "absences" and her father's history. The father refused to join in but allowed his wife to tell Michal everything she, the mother, knew. The symptoms disappeared.

R. D. Laing and A. Esterson (1964) have presented many family monographs as clinical examples demonstrating how psychotic symptoms in children are an echo of their parents' "discourse." The things that a child "hears" in a family determine his or her delirious, hallucinatory, or autistic speech—or, in Michal's case, her "absence." These things also strengthen the archaic validity of the superego, which becomes threatening. Only the family can free the child from imprisonment. Michal achieved freedom through speaking about a previously taboo subject.

Michal's parents had behaved as if nothing had ever occurred in their lives. Alfred Lorenzer (1968) has written:

We believe that the defense syndrome of pseudo or super normality based on a split in the ego may also be relevant for the phenomenon of symptom-free intervals and may provide an explanation for the late decompensations in consequence of extreme emotional traumatization, after a prolonged intermediate phase of apparent health. (P. 317)

Today we may add that this apparent health may remain but that the children will decompensate through the mechanisms of identification and projective identification that relate parents to children during the latter's development. The children present symptoms that at first seem dissociated from their family history. Because the law of the family is "all or nothing," the only choices are either a total keeping-up or a total breaking-down of defenses, either pseudo-normality or psychotic confusion. The child finds an intermediate area of expression in his or her symptoms.

The more intolerable the reality, the more inaccessible is the internal situation and the stronger are the defenses of a split in the ego. (In Michal's case, her father was unable to talk to the analyst.) Then the child's reaction is more extreme on the continuum toward psychosis. The child has a feeling of the self not corresponding to its reality, and this feeling has a psychotic quality. Only through "decoding" which experiences belong to her and which to her father could Michal achieve a sense of "true self."

LIORA N.

"The fathers have eaten a sour grape, and the children's teeth are set on edge" (Jeremiah 31:29). It is likely that individuals of a generation whose tension tolerance was impaired in infancy by the failure of their war-stressed mothers and fathers to function as adequate protective shields (Khan 1963, p. 299) also incorporated the reality of war into their oedipal fantasies. The following clinical history and psychoanalytic process of a patient named Liora N. demonstrates this hypothesis. It took five years to understand the connection between current events and her parents' history as survivors of the Holocaust—in contrast to Michal's case, where a similar connection was achieved within a few weeks.

Liora's parents had immigrated to Israel from Europe in 1945 at the end of the Second War World. She was born in 1949, and her sister five years later in 1954. When she was twenty years old, after her release from the Israeli army, she had had an operation to straighten her "crossed eyes" and then plastic surgery on her nose. Then she had her first sexual relationship with a man. She did not want to acknowledge the existence of any experiences of hers prior to these. Her life and memories started from the age of twenty.

When I first saw her, she was extremely thin. Though twenty-five years old, she looked like an adolescent, walking with shoulders slouched over her chest as if to cover herself up. She was then a teacher of special education, having completed a B.A. in psychology and special education.

Liora was referred for analysis by the headmistress of the institution where she worked. The headmistress had noticed that Liora was isolated and could not relate to other members of the staff. Entering psychoanalysis was a condition for her retaining her job, and Liora accepted it almost unthinkingly. The hope that it would help her to find a husband also motivated her to undertake analysis, as she was conscious of a difficulty in relating to men.

At the beginning of the first diagnostic interview, Liora immediately threw herself on the couch. The act gave one the "impression" that she was prepared for psychoanalysis in a counterphobic way, "as if she knew what to expect."

She had the impression that her parents' house was full of secrets that her mother tried to hide. For example, her mother seemed to be arranging war compensation surreptitiously, but Liora knew nothing about what had happened to her parents during the war. When her parents wanted to hide something from her, they spoke in a foreign language. Liora found it difficult to understand these "secrets" and acccepted them as truths hidden from her. Therefore, she thought that what she was told in Hebrew was a distortion of the truth.

Throughout her life, Liora had been frustrated by those people most important to her. They did not provide adequate verbal answers to her questions. It was evident to the analyst that Liora had poor motor coordination. These factors suggested that the physical arrangements of the therapy—patient supine, motionless, lacking visual contact with the analyst—would activate childhood frustrations related to nonverbal aspects of communication. It seemed likely that this would lead to certain problems that, in fact, did appear later on in therapy.

It became clear that Liora's home was not only full of "secrets," but that words did not correspond with actions. People said one thing but did another. As a result, Liora did not value verbal interpretation. It was hard for her to believe that words and their content could provide her with meaningful information. Nevertheless, she was curious and listened expectantly to the analyst. For a long time, she would absorb the affective message of interpretations (tone of voice, its rhythm, melody and pitch) and not their content. In her childhood, the behavior accompanying grown-ups' speech had expressed the truth and therefore demanded attention. So through the nonverbal aspects of the analyst's interpretations, Liora returned, in transference, to her childhood relationships.

At the beginning of her analysis, Liora's relationship with her father, though intellectual, was good. They cooperated with one another because "he understands what's going on." He was an accountant who had begun to study for his profession when Liora was eight years old. During the therapy, she described her father as being helpless in the face of her mother's demands. "I don't want to be like him, nor like Mum. I'm so closed. I should have chosen another profession, office work with papers rather than work with people in a place where they expect me to give."

Liora did not like her mother: "Mother doesn't understand anything, including analysis, so I won't tell her that I come here." Later on: "She's impervious, doesn't hear what people say to her." Liora wanted neither to resemble her mother nor to identify with her. Mrs. N. could only feed Liora. In fact, Liora was very fat until her tenth year but, from then on, began to lose weight. Until recently, her mother had owned a shop, a fact that embarrassed Liora. Mrs. N. had worked as a seamstress when Liora was young, and used to leave her with a nursemaid or take her to a day nursery. Liora had not liked going to the nursery. When she started school, she was a good pupil. Her first-grade teacher gave her the opportunity to do new and different things. Liora admired her and, under her influence, stopped sucking her thumb. At the age of twelve, Liora began fighting with her mother. Liora started to menstruate at fourteen.

Liora sometimes felt that she "doesn't exist" and was afraid to remain alone as she required the presence of others to prove her existence. For Liora, every separation from an object was a hardship. This difficulty arises often in analysis with real separations (weekends, holidays), with fantasy separations, and in daily life in the fear of remaining alone and the inability to do so. Liora was continually searching for an object with which she could achieve physical but not emotional closeness.

During the first and second sessions, Liora displayed a certain model in communicating—that is, evacuation. She "evacuated" things with which her ego could not cope, things that caused pain. She was in continual need for external "containers" for this evacuation and searched for indiscriminate objects on which to project her pain. When she could not find an external object, she used her own body—vomiting, headaches, hoarse voice, and so on.

During the second session, she said, "Last time, I felt very good. I spoke and I emptied myself. Now two weeks have passed and I am full up all over again. Will I have to empty myself like this for the rest of my life?"

Liora's behavior during the first year in analysis and in daily life indicated a frightened personality defending itself against anxiety by using negation. At first the analytic atmosphere was anxious and tense, owing to her opposing desires to attack and to run away out of fear that she would be harmed.

A dream she described after being in analysis four times a week for six months exemplifies these feelings: "They are tying someone up in iron chains, covering all his body as if they are torturing him. They are rocking him and he wants to escape but they won't let him move. There are bad feel-

# A Daughter of Silence

ings but, on the other hand, it doesn't hurt. They don't free him; they are holding him down." These associations referred to the analysis that restricted her movement, causing suffering. She lay on the couch while the analyst was free. Nevertheless, she held on to the analyst as an object that could defend her from the "dangers" in the environment and within her. The therapist was frightening, threatening, and causing her suffering, yet serving her as a defending object.

Liora was always either overtly or covertly "on guard" for all external stimuli, also those external stimuli as they appeared in the psychoanalytic framework. This state of mind created confusion. She was blocked by so much excitement that she found it difficult to accept or respond to situations and felt totally frustrated. She avoided talking about interpersonal relationships and fantasies in analysis, as they caused attacks of anxiety. "I'm scared of being led on too much. I see this becomes harder and harder each session because each session new things come up and I don't want to say everything, but maybe it's for the best."

The first dream appeared in the twenty-sixth session, or after about seven weeks of analysis: "I am walking on a cage of lions and feel very heroic." She felt that she had begun to walk on all those threatening, wild, brutal, frightening, and uncontrolled things closed inside herself. She expected her heroism to be admired. It was not clear then what lions meant to Liora but, on the basis of additional material that arose a year later, it seemed she perceived them as a symbol of strength and perhaps also of voracity and greediness.

Liora could not cope efficiently with dangers by assessing their degree of seriousness, as she found it difficult to control those perceptions that caused anxiety. Thus, she had sexual intercourse with every young man she met without examining him or her desires. Through this activity, she avoided thinking—and also satisfied her need to be with someone; but it reduced her vitality and produced continual feelings of tiredness and depression but no satisfying experiences. When her feelings changed as a result of the analyst's interpretations and analytic confrontation, when she felt that the analyst could "contain" her suffering and had faith in her, she reported:

At the end of the week, I was less tired, and also at work, and I even related well to the children, I got closer to them, I was warmer. This is a result of the therapy, a feeling of "no worries." I told you at our first meeting that life was a burden for me, something lacking continuity. To get up in the morning—the continuation of the previous day. No, it used to cut. Now it's not like that. I wake easily in the mornings. It seems to me that instead of thinking why, how and analyzing every little thing every day, I do that here, not alone. And so a lot of energy that I previously used for this is left for me to live.

*125*

Other important fears were expressed during the first years of therapy. Liora was frightened of going mad. She also feared that the interpretations would bring her to feel, think of, and speak about repressed fantasies which were associated with primary processes.

Liora's experiences of separation, loss and abandonment in both reality and fantasy were the central themes of her analysis. What follows is the development of this theme from the beginning of her analysis until it was understood and perhaps validated by her real history.

The question of acting out is central, as Liora's acting out was rooted in her experiences of abandonment that brought about revivals of primitive memory. Memory caused painful emotional reactions: frustration, anger, anxiety, guilt, and depression; and Liora's weak, childish ego could not cope with such emotions.

From the beginning of analysis, Liora displayed a great need for an external object that would contain her pain and anxiety about separation. In the transferential present, in which there is a reactivation of past experiences, the analyst becomes an object into which the patient pours out her unendurable feelings and lives them anew. In Liora's case, all of the analyst's normal absences—for weekends, holidays, or unexpected reasons—led to the analyst's representation as an object whose absence is intolerable and may lead to disintegration. Every separation seemed to arouse memories of distant, dramatic events of abandoment.

The second dream in analysis occurred before a holiday during which she would miss two sessions. Liora opened this session with a question: "Are you going? Because I wear a suit when I go out, but not at home. Now, of course, you'll interpret this in terms of my fear of separation and my fear that you will leave me. That was a joke." The analyst replied that indeed there seemed to be a connection between this first break in the sessions and Liora's fear that the analyst would not wait for her or would leave the house when she arrived and leave her alone. Her response: "That's right. This will be the first time. Can you imagine, it seems such a long time from Thursday to Monday. We'll see how it will pass, though I'm not so inflexible." This session continued with associations whose content expressed resistance and a desire to revolt. In response to this interpretation, she said: "A good interpretation; it's also true. But how does it help me?" And after another interpretation, she presented her dream, introducing it by explaining that one of her friends, the head of a psychiatric ward, left work for two days to study: "The ward falls apart and the patients go wild. She's responsible. How can she leave? Even though I understand it logically."

Sometimes when the analyst works in a manner that dissatisfies the patient, it is "as if [the analyst] does not exist" and becomes an unwanted object that causes suffering and should be removed. Real and imagined absences of the analyst arouse aggressive and destructive fantasies in the patient, who subsequently fears the analyst's vengeance. Therefore, separations in analysis cause the patient to act out: one searches for a replacement for the analyst on whom one can unload one's frightening and unbearable feelings. The dream can act as a container that helps to free heightened tension. But with Liora, this replacement process involved a concrete acting out that lasted a long time, during which she initiated temporary sexual relations promiscuously. It seemed that the psychoanalytic situation was frustrating for her. She perceived emotional relations in terms of physical contact; and as this need was frustrated, she searched for its satisfaction outside of analysis.

The acting out was also expressed in late and early arrivals and frequent requests to change the time of the session. As she felt progress in therapy, she acted out even more. Liora refused to believe that she felt better, that she was more easily understood and relayed clearer messages. She was afraid that her improvement would result in termination of the therapy.

Sometimes the object that contained her suffering was her body—suffering exhibited, as previously noted, in vomiting, heartburn, headaches, and hoarseness. At some point in her life, a drive to die had coexisted with Liora's healthy self and her strong drive to live. Patient and analyst saw this in an important memory that had been hidden throughout Liora's life but appeared in the first year of analysis. The somatic symptoms—for example, Liora's headaches—were the focus of this death drive. At the time, her ego could not accommodate strong feelings—neither hate, love, excitement, fear, nor separation. Each of these feelings was isolated as a "foreign body" and focused in a particular organ of her body, which reacted by cramping and a tendency to destroy itself by deviation from its appropriate physiological activities.

The third dream in analysis illustrates how the continuing development of the theme of separation was facilitated by working through dreams. Liora mentioned that her aunt, a survivor of the Holocaust and married to another survivor, was an incessant grumbler. Years later, Liora found out that this aunt had been married during the war but had lost both her husband and child in the Holocaust. Often, when Liora got angry at home, her mother compared her to this Aunt Shula, which hurt Liora. She defined her aunt as a paranoid personality and told many stories about her. Liora had stopped visiting Aunt Shula a year earlier as she was afraid to meet with "madness, not knowing how to cope with it." Liora related the dream in the following way:

"The aunt got fat, blew up, and came over to our place completely mad. She wore a hat, impossible to speak with her, in her world, nothing moves her. Danced, climbed up the stairs. And I don't remember any other details of the dream."

In that first year, through the dreams and associations, she opened up and worked through the theme of separation. Her great fear that she would be deserted suddenly was expressed when she said she could be trapped and then she would really fall to pieces. Now she had begun to tell everything, but was the analyst faithful enough? Before the first summer vacation at the end of the first year of therapy, Liora felt that everyone was going on holiday while she was left alone to cope with all her frightening fantasies. The analyst, who helped her to organize and limit these fantasies, would not be with her. "To be alone" as far as she was concerned was not to exist.

In the second year, material on masturbation appeared. When she was alone, the temptation to masturbate increased, and the fantasies aroused while masturbating frightened her. Each time she was left alone, she felt great anger. She felt as if she were being killed. Therefore, the masturbation was accompanied by frightening, aggressive, and destructive fantasies through which Liora lost the meaning of the autoerotic satisfaction. She also lost the fantasies related to the good object present in her loneliness and fears, those fantasies that should help her wait for the object (another man). When masturbating, she had omnipotent fantasies involving her defeat of the object: "I don't need you." So in a fantasy, she would attack the object that she needed (parents, man, analyst).

During the third year of analysis, Liora began to solve aloud the problems of yielding and separation. It was hard for her to make decisions, as every choice involves a compromise. She could not cope with this, wanting everything with an unrealistic appetite that would never allow anyone to satisfy her. She began to ask why she could not consider her feelings at the termination of a relationship or the conclusion of a stage in her studies or work in terms of the enriching life experiences she had been through. Why couldn't she benefit from these experiences, learn from her achievements, and use them later on? She continued to weave the network of questions: If she was raised in a good, satisfying family ("I was never denied anything"), and not in a bad, frustrating family (like those of some of her pupils), apparently her greed, dissatisfaction, and aggression derived from the bad within her and not the bad in her environment. "My sister grew up in the same family and she's altogether different." When Liora was nervous, her mother said, "You're mad, you'll be the death of me, you're just like your Aunt Shula." Telling the analyst, Liora added, "And perhaps she's right?" This type of question arose as Liora gained insight that reached verbal expression: "Up until now, I approached everything from a distance; now, perhaps, I'm too involved."

During this period, in which the analytic framework represented at once both the peak of frustration and the peak of satisfaction, she dealt with the jealousy aroused by her best friend's wedding. She also had to cope with the frustrations evoked by the marriage of some of the men she had seen in the past, and the birth of a baby to her cousin: "They have everything I want and I'm still so far from that." She cried a lot and was angry that the analyst was not more active. Liora asked why she was not being helped in a more concrete fashion. She asked to be raised as a daughter from the beginning, with all the accompanying physical care: "I come here, I know everything well, like a second home." Still, she was able to cope in daily life and analysis.

Things reached a climax in the third year when the analyst had to leave for two months. Liora reacted with both anger and fear. She felt frustration, tension, death anxiety, and those feelings of disintegration that had been dominant at the beginning of analysis. These reactions surprised her. She was angry at and bothered by her inability to cope with frustration in her strengthened state. She asked to know what else was "behind all this."

Liora's cousin had given birth to a girl. This was her first child, and Liora noted that her cousin was unsure of how to care for the poor infant who could not yet look after herself. Liora was constantly troubled by this situation, which always evoked thoughts of one of her pupils. From the time the analyst told Liora about her coming two-month absence, she repeatedly mentioned this pupil who suffered from motor problems. The child had spent five months in an institution and was then adopted. "The poor kid; what they did to her!" Liora then asked, "Why am I obsessed by this child? I identify with her as if something like this happened to me. But I was never in any institution." Liora remained perturbed and thought that it was important that someone teach her cousin how to care for the baby. She decided to ask an aunt (her mother's brother's wife) to advise her cousin. This aunt had served Liora as a "good mother" throughout her life—Liora had always been able to talk to her and approach her for advice. The aunt was surprised by Liora's interest and told her that her mother had also found it difficult to cope when she, Liora, was born—so difficult that mother and child had spent a week at a rest home for mothers and their infants. This news was of great interest to Liora, and she subsequently asked many questions, not all of which her aunt was prepared to answer. The aunt was not willing to add details about Liora's life as a young child. However, she did reveal one of the *secrets* of the family.

Liora's sister had been born in a taxi on the way to the hospital, and her father had performed the delivery. This had happened because her mother had not wanted to waken her husband when she felt the contractions. Liora took the revelation very seriously. Her mother had not only not known how to care for Liora but had also been unable to protect her unborn sister. How could she not insist on her rights with her father, and why did her father allow this state of affairs to exist? Why didn't he support her more? And, apart from all this, the *secrets* at home were not a product of her imagination!

The next day, she returned to her aunt and pressed her to divulge more information. The aunt agreed and told her of the difficult times when Liora was born. Her father had been sick and was hospitalized for a whole year. Her mother had to provide for the family singlehandedly. In the aftermath of Israel's War of Independence, when the financial situation worsened, her mother had been forced to place Liora in an institution for a while. At this point, the aunt stopped and asked Liora to keep these things a secret as she should not have divulged them. But Liora continued searching because now she knew two more secrets: her father's illness and her own institutionalization.

After working through this material with the analyst, Liora approached her parents with the *true* story. Her mother said: "Who told you these things? You're crazy." And her father, according to Liora, maintained a guilty silence. They then told her the following: When her mother was in her fifth month of pregnancy, her father got sick and was hospitalized. He returned home when Liora was five months old. They all lived in one room and, for reasons that are not clear, did not rent an additional room. As it was forbidden to allow the infant to sleep in the same room as the sick father, they placed Liora in a WIZO* institution for five months. Then, when she was ten months old, Liora contracted food poisoning, diarrhea, and vomiting and was hospitalized for a month. Only then did she return home.

Her parents found it difficult to speak about all this and apologized profusely, claiming to have visited her every day at the institution. This discovery made things easier for Liora: "Until now, I thought I was crazy; now at least I have reasons." Now her worrying about and identification with her cousin's baby and the adopted pupil were more understandable. "Now many things are clearer. Apparently I was alone a lot in the instutition . . . and the business of secrets bothered me. This feeling I had all the years that they hid things and that I was paranoid seems strange, as if it all happened to someone else."

In abnormal development—like Liora's institutionalization for six months

---

* Women's International Zionist Organization, which provides social services.

during her first year of life—the prohibitions, the frustrations, and the resulting lack of emotional contact causes greed, jealousy, and guilt. Liora's curiosity could have led to regression, pathology, and compulsive acts instead of becoming a positive motivation toward development and independence. The analysis allowed Liora to open a channel directed inward, to make conscious her fantasies, her conflicts, and their roots. This process is known as *insight*. Therefore, the analysis served as a sublimation of the drive to curiosity and permitted a search for the secrets of the ego. According to the book of Genesis, our first sin was to know: "and the eyes of them both were opened, and they knew that they were naked."

Later in analysis, Liora undertook a comprehensive "research project" of her stay in the institution. She went there, requested her file, and met the caretaker who had supposedly been most attached to her. She collected all the details, so that she was able to paint a complete picture of her five months there. She did the same with the hospital where she had been for a month before her return home. The information she discovered justified her state and enabled her to integrate logically the reality of her past and to demystify her childhood. This contact with the reality of the past enabled Liora to feel more real (to feel that she existed) and allowed a clearer and more logical understanding of the present.

Before the analyst left for her two-month journey, Liora stated what she had learned. She had learned to honor refusal and to expect that others would respect her refusal. She could identify with and assimilate an object that can say no, that can limit and honor itself, and whose actions relate to words and its words to feelings: "In this place, I learned that a word is a word. Now I try to hear the content of the spoken word and don't just look at the movements." The analysis allowed her to re-create the image of a good mother who takes care of her. Liora could begin to sense her continuation with the past, emotionally to work through guilt associated with her mother, and to feel that despite all her parents' failures, they had some positive qualities. Likewise, she could view her father more realistically, including the negative aspects of his character. She began to allow herself to enjoy things, through introspection to discover from within, and to discover the extent to which feelings within her had been forced upon her by others. By withdrawal to apathy, she had submissively defended against these things. She began to sense her body and was able to enjoy it. She straightened her posture and looked more feminine. She made sure to dress well, enjoyed going out, and began to look for a better apartment. Patient and analyst revised things they had worked through in the past, remembering, for example, the time Liora asked to be accepted, but not unconditionally, "so that you won't fall into my trap," as there were things that only "seem[ed] to be but they [weren't] the truth." Liora had been afraid that the analyst would behave in what "seemed to be the truth" and therefore not help her to arrive at the truth. She then moved on to the theme of acts that seem to be love but are not love (what she had experienced for a time with many different men). During that phase of the analysis (the first year), she related this theme to her mother and to what she didn't say, that she didn't know what love is: "Mom would buy ice cream, and later we would find out that there was no money for bread."

When Liora had started analysis, she expressed, among other things, the hope that the exposure of her secrets would help her, and that someone would hold on to her. After a long time, she succeeded in finding out that analysis could be also an emotional experience that would help her to know and to be herself.

After these discoveries, Liora continued to research her family history. She began to question (1) why her parents did not have children during the first five years of their marriage, and (2) whether the fact that they had placed her in an institution was an act of deprivation or of salvation. A. Lorenzer's thesis is, "Victims are thrown down to the level of primary traumatization and the structures built up in the earliest mother-child relationship are annihilated." He also quotes Klaus Hoppe's opinion "that in extreme traumatization, basic trust is destroyed" (Lorenzer 1968, p. 318).

This opinion is exemplifed by those parents who tend to defend against the anxiety resulting from their poverty and illness by resorting to the regressive pattern laid down during the war. If we accept this hypothesis, we may suggest that Liora's parents led her to experience what they experienced during the war. One of the common means of persecution involves scattering social groups, especially families; one is thereby pushed out of one's social background and placed in a situation of loneliness. Thus, we may interpret Liora's placement in an institution as an act of deprivation.

However, during the Second World War, parents placed their children in foster homes in an effort to save their lives. These parents could not serve as a protective shield either physically or psychologically. Liora's parents explained that, in the difficult period after the War of Independence, many parents, in cases of poverty and illness, handed their children over to WIZO. We know that, when extreme stress is shared by a whole group, it is not felt as an individual injury.

Let us consider the effort invested by survivors of the Holocaust who reorganized their lives in Israel in the hope that their children would not suffer a future of war and persecution. Yet they also unconsciously led their own children to experience the deprivation and destitution that they, the parents, had experienced during the war.

Can we explain this repetition-compulsion in terms of the unconscious seeking a revival of traumatic events in consonance with the repetition compulsion? And are these compulsions likely to be set in motion by some present stress?

Liora began to question whether her mother's behavior and personality had been affected by the Second World War. Her mother was afraid to venture out into the street alone. She hoarded things. She dressed sloppily and closed herself in the toilet, blocking up the keyhole with a towel. Then there were the secrets in the house. "What did the war do to our parents, and what is it continuing to do to us?" Liora started rummaging through photograph albums and cupboards. She found a photograph of her mother taken in 1939. She was wearing shorts, laughing, and looking pretty—"so different." Liora brought this photograph, and others taken after the war in Israel, to analysis. There was an enormous difference between the one extreme of easy-going happiness and the other extreme of tension and depression.

In the fourth year of analysis, Liora had her first meaningful relationship with a man, which lasted about a year. He was the twenty-nine-year-old son of aging parents, survivors of the Holocaust. He had immigrated to Israel from Russia at the age of nine. When she began to research his past, Liora made her discoveries not directly through him, as he did not know everything, but rather through his cousin's wife. His father was injured in the head in a concentration camp and now, when nervous, had murderous and uncontrollable outbursts.

During the fifth year of analysis, the subject of the Holocaust remained associated with events in Liora's environment. For example, one September, after the holidays, when analysis was resumed, she said that she had sneaked into the discussion of the Holocaust at the psychoanalytical congress in Jerusalem. "Because I am the result of this and so is David [her boyfriend]. He experienced the same thing with his parents. If I didn't know what happened to him, I wouldn't stay with him." But, later, the fact that he was of the second generation was one of her reasons for leaving him: "What sort of children will we produce, having parents like us and grandparents like our parents?" Liora was more conscious of her own disturbances and those of David and other friends. By working through her feelings, Liora developed a "theory" of the personality of children of survivors of the Holocaust and noted the common phobias, the suspiciousness of people, the tendency to somatization, and the moods and guilt of the children of survivors of the Holocaust. It is interesting to compare Liora's conclusions with those of investigators, who have maintained that the following symptoms are the same as those found in the concentration camp syndrome: difficulty finding one's identity; weak social ties; psychosomatic disorders; generally depressed mood, inclined to apathy; aggression turned on the self; and tendencies to self-reproach, self-punishment, and various neurotic rituals.

The subject again arose when the 1978 television series "Holocaust" was screened. Liora was most affected by the part when the young girl—reacting to the way her mother continued living as usual—"ignoring reality, left the house and was raped": within a minute, the world had changed, things had become meaningless. Now Liora understood the dramatic changes in her mother evidenced in the photograph.

Several reality factors influenced the sessions after the Passover vacation: (1) the terrorist attack in Nahariya, a town on the coast near the Lebanese border (this was the first time in six years that she had mentioned this sort of event in analysis); (2) the week of Remembrance Day for the Holocaust; and (3) the fact that Liora had not been in a session for two weeks.

Liora immediately referred to the attack on Nahariya: "If I lived in Nahariya, I would have a gun in my home." She said that she had been to the Museum of Heroism (the Scaffold) in Acco (connected with the struggle against the British). Afterward she described dreams related to an escape: again, she was expressing fear of madness and disintegration. But at the same time, Liora mentioned that she had had a good time with her present boyfriend, Chaim. She spoke at length about his service in the army and how "the army tried to break such a sensitive young man."

Then she spoke of the difficulties of returning to school, of the children, of the fact that she must teach them about the Holocaust. It was the first year that she would do so, and she asked if there were any books that explain the facts of the Holocaust at a level suitable for children: "Can children in the first grade absorb this sort of thing?" It seemed that she wanted to be taught about the Holocaust as if she were a child, as that was all she could absorb at this stage, and this was suggested to her by the analyst.

Both Chaim and David [the previous boyfriend] have parents who survived the Holocaust. David's parents didn't tell him anything while Chaim's parents told him everything—they were incapable of making a *selection*. And my parents, maybe they are making a big deal about nothing.

But she heard things indirectly and illogically which confused her. "There must be a reason in the war. I know they were in the ghetto. That's all. It doesn't really bother me—we hardly ever speak, all the family together."

# A Daughter of Silence

At the next session, she said that this was the first year she had watched all the television programs about the Holocaust, about the terrible ways people can die.

I was shocked how people can speak of these things, with the same feelings of vengeance even today. They are exaggerating. In class, while teaching, I also exaggerated the severity of things, but I emphasized the revolt. I brought a book, a story about a girl, the heroine, who moves from place to place hiding. Her mother was killed, her father sent to a concentration camp. The girl flees from every place. She hides as soon as she feels that her pursuers are getting close to her. She even met her father in the camp—I cried when I read this—but then she leaves and prefers to be alone—to be alone is safer.

Then, on Remembrance Day, Liora bothered her father all day by telephoning him continually, saying, "You didn't suffer anything during the Holocaust," in an effort to get him to tell her something. Her father then said that he and his family had been forced out of their homes and had wandered from place to place.

A week later, she brought a dream to analysis: "Chaim and I are on our way to a school, crawling through barbed-wire fences on our backs, then on our stomachs—which is easier—trying to see the barbed wire. In the end I crawl on my stomach." The associations related to the dream revolved around her parents' home—a crazy, dirty house where things were hoarded, and only eating took place. She returned to a story she had read to her class, and spoke about the concentration camps as related to barbed-wire fences.

Suddenly she shouted, "I wasn't in the Holocaust or any place like that! Why do I feel persecuted? Why do I flee? These things don't belong to me, they are theirs, they should keep it in their museum."

Several weeks were spent on the material she had "evacuated" and wished to freeze in a museum, locked up and distant from her, a part of the personal-family history that she wished were otherwise. Patient and analyst tried to reconstruct in correct dimensions what was hers and what related to other people. Her identification with the subject was worked out, with its projected and introjected parts that did not permit her to differentiate between what related to her, to her parents, and to an entire generation. At the same time, an attempt was made to separate external and internal objects that related to the subject, the "good" and the "bad" in them. At the height of "working through," Liora brought the analyst a present—the poem entitled "Everyone Has a Name" by Zelda, an Israeli poet, that serves as the final epigraph to this book.

Through this poem, Liora continued to work out her identity; and it became for both her and the analyst a confirmation of her name and her place in the world. Liora traveled a long way in search of herself through the discovery of family secrets, and learned to distinguish between masochistic suffering and the suffering that comes from one's knowledge of the past, which belongs to and is a part of oneself. In her search, Liora uncovered the history of a generation. For her, it was a bridge with the past that permitted her to feel alive and to experience the present as a logical reality. This permitted her introjective identification and the ability to assimilate herself as a human being with a name and a continuous existence and as one who is mortal.

# 7

# A Metapsychological
# Assessment Based on an
# Analysis of a Survivor's Child

BEYOND THE INDIVIDUALITY and the universality of themes in the analyses of survivors' children, one can detect in them certain combinations of structural elements, a complex that can be defined in a metapsychological profile. The following history of a long analysis of an adult daughter of a survivor will serve as a source for such a profile, which may be used as a model for comparisons with other cases.

In Rachel M.'s case one can see a telescoping of problems that beset survivors' children—problems that become both illness and a source of ego strength. Only through a daily analysis of many years was it possible to unravel the subtle nuances by means of which the attitudes of the survivor-father were transmitted to the child, reinforced by the mother, and expressed in a multitude of ways in childhood and adulthood. Only through a differential investigation of her drive development and her ego and superego attitudes was it possible to determine the influence of the father's experiences on the development of the patient's psychic structure. To do so, one had to ask oneself continually how development would have proceeded without this influence—a question difficult to answer with any degree of certainty. Long phases of analysis investigated defenses and underlying wishes and the genetic antecedents of conflicts without any reference to the Holocaust. Other phases focused primarily on the father's life during the Second World War; and still others, on the mother's feelings about the father's past. Before the influence of the Holocaust could be established, Rachel M. appeared sicker than she was. Once the various layers underlying particular problems were uncovered—layers that included the patient's attitudes and fantasies about the Holocaust—what had appeared bizarre became understandable. After a long time it became clear that the Holocaust in general and the father's fate during the war in particular, as well as the mother's and Rachel's school's reaction to these events, acted as organizers of the patient's development (see the Prelude to this volume).

Rachel sought analysis, in transition from her adolescence into adulthood, because the majority of her bodily functions were disturbed, and her performance fell below her ambition. She was isolated from people and had difficulty talking. She ate very little, sometimes to the point of starvation, and she retained stool. She was amenorrheic and could not sleep at night. She lagged behind in her work, behaving in a "stupid" or "crazy" way, laughing when she was criticized, and unable to explain her errors.

To make the account more comprehensible, it seems advisable to abstract from the analysis the history of Rachel's father. He had been hiding during the war. Sheltered by a peasant who made room for Jews in a dilapidated, dark barn, several times he was almost caught by storm troopers, but his ingenuity always helped him to escape detection. He had been a practicing physician before the war; for some time during the war, he passed for a Gentile working as an orderly in a rural hospital. There he had to refrain from going to the bathroom or risk capture. His immediate family could not be found after the war and Rachel had been named after his mother to whom he had been very attached. Rachel's mother was very sympathetic to the father's plight and both parents were family-oriented, solicitous, and proud of their children's achievement.

Rachel's history, as told to her by her parents and remembered by her, reveals that she had been bottle-fed and had acquired one brother at twenty months and a sister at the age of six years. The daughter of Orthodox parents, she attended a Brooklyn Yeshiva school where she saw films of the Holocaust and was assigned readings of accounts of the heroic Hanna Sennesh and of Elie Wiesel's works. She had been nagged to eat and to study and was brought up in a Spartan way. Her father laid stress on will power. When she ate a snack at a friend's house before a meal, he told her sternly that it was a weakness to give in to appetites. She and her siblings had been given laxatives and enemas. Yet once when she was in a taxi with her parents, she asked that it stop so she could go to the bathroom, but was denied with the excuse that waiting would help her develop self-control. She learned early to suppress all urges of aggression. Rachel began systematically to exert will power over her bodily needs when she reached adolescence. Analysis revealed that this was a virtue that, in her mind, would prepare her to withstand Nazi tortures. Indeed, neither did she feel hunger pangs nor was she aware of a need to defecate: this she accomplished by ignoring the signals of an empty stomach or a full rectum. In her fantasies she could inflict upon herself any punishment the Nazis had invented. Isolating herself from social life, she went into "hiding" as her father had. Fearing that she would be abandoned and delivered to the Nazis as her grandmother Rosa-Margit had been, she gave no one a chance to come close to her. The rare friends she made, she rejected before they could abandon her. Identifying with her father's ability to outwit the Nazi persecutor, Rachel invented devious ways of taking revenge on her own "persecutors." If her art teacher criticized her, she would spill paints and drop brushes. She emulated the courage of a Jewish slave-worker who sabotaged German munition factories.

Both father and mother taught Rachel to be suspicious of others and to look out only for herself lest someone would exploit and enslave her. She was to beware particularly of non-Jews. Once when Rachel volunteered to help a Gentile friend move to a new apartment, her father admonished her that she should mind her own business instead of assisting someone else. Furthermore, she should not be friends with Gentiles. Withdrawn and afraid of rejection, suspicious of kin and strangers, Rachel thought of herself as the daughter of Jephtha about to be sacrificed for the glory of a victorious father-king. The worthlessness of her individual existence was conveyed to her in a number of nonverbal messages. When she was sick, she was not taken to the doctor; when she fell and hurt herself, the father's first thought was whether she had ripped her clothing.

Rachel's father told her a few anecdotes about his war experiences, but she learned more about them from listening to his talks with his friends. When she asked him questions, he did not refuse to answer but would display an attitude conveying the question "Why should we talk about it?" Rachel got the feeling that she must not know about the Holocaust and she was unable to read about it. As most other children of survivors, she asked herself how her father had been able to escape while others perished. On the other hand, she felt that he had gone through enough hardships and it was up to her to restore his family to him.

Much of Rachel's fantasies and acting out concerned the mysterious coming and going of the father long before she was born, in World War II and after. She consciously felt that hers was a mission to vindicate the Holocaust through great deeds, especially regarding the survival of the afflicted. An extensive analysis of Rachel's silence in analysis and outside of it yielded the following information. Speaking of her accident proneness, Rachel expressed a doubt whether her father wanted her to live or to die, and then concluded, "Me, I should be a sacrifice—atone for the sins." Like her father, she habitually turned frightening ideas into jokes. This time she added longingly, "I'll be on an altar and go up to heaven." When she spoke about concentration camps and was asked since when she knew what concentration camp victims looked like, she said: "I always knew. I don't remember not knowing." She pondered the question why she would have wanted to be there: "It has something to do with being a martyr and, second, then I'd have done something," and "I was furious I could not do anything. I guess I thought I could be in the past and do something."

During the next session Rachel defended her right not to tell: "I don't see why I have to tell. It happened to him." The analyst suggested that she find the obstacle to her talking and improving, and Rachel responded, "First, if you don't talk, you're protected from people. If people don't know who you are, they can't be hurt. And also to be strong. When people . . . speak they need other people." She continued to say that her father spoke only about trivia. The prohibition was against "revealing what is inside." She laughed as the following "funny" thought came to her: "Sometimes I feel like I have memories I should not talk about—it's not me—it's him." She dreamed about cannibals cooking her analyst and herself in a pot, and she began to talk about death: "Dead people don't eat and talk. They sleep. . . . If I was alive I'd be speaking. This thought is not from my father, from me. Then he'd probably want me to speak." Then she pondered, "Maybe he wasn't supposed to be alive. If he wasn't supposed to, then none of us should be. If none of my family is alive, how come I am alive?" She then spoke of a relative who had died after the war: "It's natural he shouldn't be alive because his was a natural death. It was not natural for my grandmother, Rosa-Margit." She repeatedly asserted that people who had died during Nazi persecution must be revived through descendants: "If you're named after someone you are supposed to be living for her" (meaning her grandmother). An illuminating thought came to her: "It's time. We don't really live for ourselves . . . either for people who died or as an answer to German and Jewish people. They tried to destroy Jews but we are still living. If you live, you take up the responsibility. . . ." The question evolved whether she should be sacrificed and die as a redeemer or live as a reincarnation of the dead, revived through her and in her.

When she became conscious of her need to revive the father's dead mother, Rachel revealed through acting out that her mission had enlarged. She sought ways of delivering from persecution not only his whole family but also the whole Jewish population. Throughout this period of analysis, she had repeated nightmares, mostly about the Nazis. Everything that happened reminded her of the Holocaust. Her little nephew buried a turtle, and she thought how Jewish people were buried in holes. Father had said that knowledge lived forever and it worried her that she could not concentrate on her studies. She thought of becoming a great doctor like her father, but the Nazi doctors' experiments came to her mind. She sided with the Orthodox Jews against dissections, because one needed one's body to live again. These thoughts were connected with transference ideas about killing the analyst who looked inside of her. In her quest for messianic deeds, she was disturbed by her identification with the persecutors and her competition with them. She revived the Jews and the Nazis as well.

Once she was able to break her silence and talk about her rescue mission, ideas came forth that had a strange reality value. They could be best understood in terms of the "time tunnel" that Rachel had seen on a television show in her childhood: present-day people were able to descend into this tunnel and change the course of history. At the same time, the structure of the time tunnel was her own body which harbored the people of the past. Rachel lived in a double reality. She was Rachel and Rosa-Margit, her grandmother who had been killed by the Nazis. This was accomplished *not by identification* with the grandmother but by a more far-reaching mechanism: *a simultaneous double existence* similar to a hysterical double identity. She lived in a double reality: in the current world of study, going to school, and painting, as well as in the past of her grandmother which she reconstructed from scattered bits of information and from books and films she had forgotten. Her messianic idea, developed early in life, had been transmitted in a complex way by the mother who used her as a conduit of her own rescue dreams, and by the father who wanted her to do what he himself had not been able to accomplish. The messages were complex in another way as well. Study and intellectual achievement were the most important means, qualifying Rachel for her mission. Yet perhaps more important was her *body*, a machine devoid of emotion, which both parents clearly saw as a *vehicle of omnipotence*. Spiritual survival was not enough; a physical resurrection of the dead was the Messiah's task. The steeling of the body to resist assault upon it was a condition for one's own survival and for the rescue of others.

Rachel remembered that in her childhood she had believed in spirits and was afraid of robbers who could enter her room. Once she thought that the would-be robber was her father, checking up on her. She had fantasies of little people invading her body. They most probably represented sperms, given to her by her father to re-create six million Jews. These oedipal fantasies were tinged with oral-anal and anal-sadistic representations. Rachel had difficulty tolerating the unconscious wishes she acted out. She would repudiate them as crazy or funny and would project them onto her analyst in transference, with fleeting thoughts of their coming from the analyst's mind. She would indicate that she fabricated thoughts to please the analyst, who she thought was, like her father, preoccupied with the Holocaust. The fantasies about her body were concrete and need-related. When she ate, she fed Rosa-Margit as well as the grandmother's deceased children, her father's siblings. In addition, she had to feed six million starved Jews. However, a double task was imposed on her: to eat in order to feed, and not to eat to steel her body. Rachel experienced these peculiar injunctions in her early childhood and linked them with the reality of that time. For instance, she knew that her mother, when pregnant, fed the child inside of her. She also remembered vaguely hearing that the doctor had advised her mother to watch her weight during her pregnancies. At the same time she was given innumerable hints that a diet was advisable, and that weighing too much made women undesirable. It seems likely that Rachel was weaned just before the birth of the next sibling, when she was twenty months old, and that toilet training had begun before that time. Her envy of her baby brother, who was fed and diapered by the mother, flourished during Rachel's rapprochement phase. At that time eating, defecating, and separating from the mother was connected with her being replaced by a baby. Her anger was suppressed, and reaction formations were formed in the face of a constant reminder that she was older and therefore more responsible than the younger children for the happiness of her parents, especially of the father "who suffered enough." From the start, Rachel felt that her father valued her more than he did the others, and had chosen her to lead the family toward excellence. He became an ally when Rachel felt deprived by her mother, and helped her to separate. As an extension of the mother, he also participated in Rachel's bodily care and taught her to control her bodily functions.

Carrying with her what seemed to be an anal-sadistic predisposition, Rachel interpreted pregnancy and birth in terms of eating and defecating. The inner-genital phase, in which a child wants to have a baby and be maternal, was distorted by anal representation of babies as newly born and dead; the phallic phase was also tinged by oral-anal representation of a penis that could be broken and thrown out. Unable to compete with her father and her siblings for her mother's favors, Rachel—at the height of her Oedipus complex—offered herself to the father as a companion who could fulfill his ideal of intellectual achievement and practical rescue ability, superior to those of the mother. In this way she became his "boy"; to reproduce the children of Israel for him, she needed to be a girl.

Rachel's latency was permeated by her school life which seemed an extension of her Orthodox father's teachings about Judaism. Stories about the Bible and the Holocaust intertwined in her mind. All through her adolescence she suffered from asceticism and a need to sacrifice herself for others. Her identification with her father's mother intensified, partially as a defense against wanting to be close to her own mother. She veered between wooing her mother away from the father and degrading her mother to show that she understood her father better than her mother did. She identified with the father's austerity and tried to outdo him intellectually. She would regress to a baby state in which she yearned to be fed and taken to the toilet by the mother. Then she would rebel against her dependent wishes and resist eating and going to the toilet for a while.

In line with her age and phase when her mother was first pregnant, Rachel looked upon her intestines as a tunnel, containing Rosa-Margit. She looked upon herself as a reincarnation of Rosa-Margit, to be sure—but she also kept her inside, as mother had done with her invisible baby brother.

During her analysis, Rachel became conscious of her need to starve herself as a magic means. When she starved herself, she also starved others inside of her. As she became the intestinal mother of all Jews, she felt burdened by all the people who had invaded her body; and she had to ration food in order not to make them too fat and burst. She knew that some of the survivors had been overfed after liberation and had died. She imprisoned those she rescued in the concentration camp she had created in her intestines, and—constipated—she kept them there for days, not letting them escape. When she did evacuate, she did it very thoroughly. Perhaps she was letting them escape at last, all of them, not only the few who had survived, escaping like her father. She said that, when they left, she was no longer in charge of them, and they died. Feeling her freedom for a short time, she would soon reincorporate them, or else she felt like dying with them, depleted and empty. In an ambivalent way—corresponding to her fixation in the anal-sadistic phase—she not only loved them, but also hated them in identification with their Nazi oppressors. She incorporated them but feared that they would escape as ghosts (spiritual beings) who evanesce and cannot be seen as they depart. The ghosts were represented by feces which also signified dead children. Her death wishes against her siblings were connected with her ideas about relatives who had died in the Holocaust.

Along with her Holocaust life, Rachel had the usual fantasies about being pregnant and having a penis inside, and she reacted with oral envy and anal revengefulness to the birth of her siblings. All these reactions to the past and the current struggles with colleagues, teachers, and family did not have an independent existence. Everything had to be analyzed from at least two points of view; and the Holocaust fantasies, because of their concreteness, were more entrenched than others. When Rachel began to think of having children, she reported that she had been afraid of holding a baby because she might drop it. She immediately linked this feeling to her anger at her siblings when they were babies, and felt a sense of relief. However, she was frightened by the association of Nazis flinging babies to their deaths—so terrifying and concrete an image that she had to repress it almost as soon as it passed through her mind.

Rachel trained herself to ignore or deny bodily signals, and she also ignored signal affects. For that reason, she was periodically overwhelmed by needs and frustrations. She did not allow herself to cry except in the privacy of her room. A feeling of being rejected or unloved would overwhelm her after a long period of denial. In public, she would often laugh inappropriately, especially when she was reprimanded. Laughter was not only a reversal of affect but also the expression of a fiendish enjoyment of hurting anyone who frustrated her. She forbade herself to react immediately to setbacks, and she had to pretend that she was not hurt lest the frustrator might triumph over her. Although she plotted revenge for a long time, she would see to it that it came when the frustrator could not expect it and was not able to connect it with what he had done to her. When Rachel had positive feelings, she was afraid that they would mount too high, and that she would become a slave to someone she loved. Paradoxically, she would give vent to affection when she was already rejected. The rejection was often provoked by her tendency to interrupt the expression of feelings and to become a "robot" or a "stone." She interrupted the rise of her genital sensations to be ready for any interruptions imposed by the Nazis who were out to humiliate her. Feelings were dangerous because they made her vulnerable to attack. Being inanimate or dead, she could not be hurt or killed. Rachel described how her mother systematically shielded the father from any intensity of feeling, and how her father cautioned her, Rachel, against getting excited over anything that did not give her immediate benefit. Once she was able to make a request, her mother would ignore it, and her father would laugh. It was shameful to have feelings, and impractical, because they interfered with alertness in pursuing one's self-interest. All wishes had to be subordinated to the principal aim to survive.

Many of the features seen in analyses of other children of survivors, revealed themselves in Rachel's analysis. Some that have not been discussed in this report will be mentioned in the metapsychological assessment of her psychic structure that can, perhaps, serve as a model, albeit incomplete, of a survivor's-child profile.

# A Metapsychological Assessment

## Rachel M.'s Metapsychological Assessment*

REASONS FOR REFERRAL

Rachel was referred for treatment for depression with curtailment of physical and mental functions, at times life endangering.

POSSIBLE CONTRIBUTING CIRCUMSTANCES

The father-survivor seemed to suffer from a masked depression and guilt in relation to the loss of his immediate family. To justify his survival, he seemed to groom his eldest daughter—named after his mother—to become outstanding. His failure to rescue his family was not only a source of guilt but also a narcissistic trauma. He did not complain about the injuries he had suffered, and he steadfastly worked to elevate himself in the community, helping many sick, indigent people and contributing to just causes. In this effort he was aided by his socially conscious wife. Both seemed to rear Rachel to become a heroic resister of such tortures as starvation, sleeplessness, and curtailment of freedom to use the bathroom. As a physician, the father remained emotionally aloof from his patients and likewise warned Rachel against emotional involvement, encouraging hard work and achievement. He looked down on his wife who seemed to be his shadow and was extremely protective of him. The mother would deny her children's needs and adhere to routine and convenience without recognition of their hurt feelings. Minor religious rituals were more important than the children's needs. She looked upon the father as a hero and supported him in his endeavor to make Rachel into a healer of the world's ills. She had been a nurse before she married and she went out of her way to be helpful to people who needed her; and that, too—Rachel thought—took precedence over the needs of her children. There is evidence that the mother was attentive to her children when they were babies, and instilled into them a feeling of family sharing and family loyalty, amounting to "one for all and all for one." She supported the father's rearing of the children, especially of Rachel, for survival and would periodically institute rescue operations, which took the form of cleaning a child's room, giving a lot of food, or buying a surprise present. To compete with her

---

* Modeled after Anna Freud's 1966 child profile. The use of a child's, rather than an adult's, profile is due to the author's long experience with the former and to the greater facility of abstracting its features from complex material. It is also better suited than the adult profile to cases in which regression is predominant.

mother, Rachel had to sacrifice her life for her father's needs; to compete with her father, she had to be a victim whom her mother could rescue and a hero whom she worshiped.

PSYCHIC STRUCTURE

*Drive Development.* Rachel's yearnings for being mother's baby, rather than the exemplary older daughter, were overshadowed by sado-masochistic, oral, and anal wishes. The oral fantasies of food as creator of babies, of rescuing people, and making them grow were subordinated to the main theme of her body as an independent control mechanism, magic and omnipotent by virtue of its ability to hold, withhold, and release, to become numb and dead and free of urgency at will. The themes transmitted by both parents were carried by double-bind messages to eat and not to eat, to defecate and to be free of bathroom needs, to suffer and be indifferent, to become a heroine of the Holocaust and be ignorant of Holocaust history, to achieve and gain recognition and to fail, especially when family needs were in conflict with work requirements. Messages that she be Jewish in a religious sense, but not too Zionist, and that she should do Jewish community work, but only if she had some time left from work, overwhelmed Rachel and made her live in a world of noncommunication.

It seemed that all of her drives were overshadowed by and mixed with the urgency of survival in the face of impending death. When she denied her needs and her frustrations, she would come close to feeling neither dead nor alive; she could casually refer to herself as dead or talk about her own communing with the dead. At the same time she developed a system of counting which relied on symmetry and attested to the existence of things and their adherence to a certain order. When she starved herself, she would periodically rescue herself in order to survive. Failing this, she provoked others, especially the analyst, to take responsibility for her survival. All of this acting out had a life-endangering, concrete quality.

The average individual seeks pleasure in drive satisfaction rather than in a triumph of survival. Aggression is ordinarily experienced as a reaction to frustration, which one perceives as unpleasant. Signal affects such as anxiety and anger are used to evoke defenses against danger. For Rachel, all appetites and corresponding wishes were concretely linked with survival. To ensure it, pleasure had to be given up. When good feelings began to develop, they had to be interrupted and/or stifled. Aggression had the raw quality of being immediately linked with death. The body-linked, concrete quality of her drives was enhanced by her inexperience with fulfilling such needs as hunger or sleepiness. Suppressing the acknowledgment of, and the reaction to, body signals prevented her from knowing how to cope with needs, affects, and wishes in an appropriate manner. Once an awareness of a need broke through Rachel's special stimulus barrier, it had the effect of a trauma.

Rachel's narcissistic grandiosity was evident in her handling of her body and in her fantasies that prompted it. She was trying to conquer bodily needs without having to get sick and die. There was ample evidence of primary narcissism when she felt beautiful, could adorn herself, feel desirable, and smile. Her basic trust in the durability of her body, and her conviction that she could function in a superior way, were overlaid by masochistic positions. She would distort her body image to fit the look of Nazi victims. Her secondary narcissism enhanced the grandiose idea that she could withstand tortures and deprivations and rescue others, so that the world would know that a Jew was capable of great deeds. Her father nurtured these ideas and provided the supplies for her narcissistic self-aggrandizement. When he and her mother left or rejected her, her self-esteem would lower and turn her aggression against them on herself. These narcissistic and masochistic representations invaded her ego ideal and the punitive functions of the superego in a concrete fashion.

Rachel's relation to objects had an uneven quality. She could withdraw into an auto-erotic state, devoid of thoughts; and when she recovered, she became preoccupied with rationing need satisfaction. The former brought her closer to her pre-oedipal, physically nurturing mother, and the latter had become part and parcel of her oedipal relationship to her father. She had a much more advanced relationship with her siblings for whom she cared in a loving and sensitive way. She was capable of forming lasting friendships with people who frequently could not give as much as Rachel did. Her relationship to men was disturbed by the unevenness of her functioning, and by her withdrawal when she anticipated rejection, and by her lack of understanding of signals given to her by others. In withdrawing, Rachel unconsciously wandered off into the world of her father's former life and fantasized that she was communing with people of the past within the confinement of her own body. At the same time she would spin out tales about her body that were related to her parents' treatment of it. The analysis of a picture she painted revealed that the image she had created symbolized her care of her grandmother in a maternal way. The grandmother died in this fantasy; yet, in the next fantasy, she was cured and alive again. As analysis progressed, the transformation of her death-rescue preoccupation led Rachel into the world of today where she sought and found real people with whom to associate. However, on the road toward this transformation, each object carried the stigma of either the damaged, dependent dead Jew or the triumphing, persecuting, cruel Nazi. In correspondence to her oral-anal-sadistic fixation, Rachel's relationships were primarily, but not consistently, sado-masochistic. The masochism was also related to her oedipal relationship to her father and to her failure to woo her mother in a phallic-oedipal way.

Rachel's aggressiveness found new overt outlets. Mostly she had turned her aggression against herself and indirectly tortured those who cared for her by becoming a visible indictment of their capacity to nourish and protect her. Her fantasies revealed oral and anal sadistic ideas toward those she loved, but had had to be converted into rescue fantasies before they could penetrate her consciousness. As indicated before, every aggressive impulse led her directly to the idea of being dead; overcoming of the aggression served survival or reincarnation of herself and her victims.

Sublimation, though abundant, was invaded by the special nature of the drives from which it emerged. Painting had to be rationed and understanding curtailed, especially in regard to the Holocaust. Rationing of need satisfactions was connected with flattening of affect and inhibition of function as well as with the use of inanimateness as response to pleasure and displeasure. The most characteristic all-encompassing internal conflict in the id which interfered with sublimation, was centered around life and death as opposite poles.

*The Ego.* Rachel's cognitive functions were of a high caliber, but they were invaded and distorted by defenses and fantasies of an archaic nature. As expected, survival was the principal theme, with its core in the body ego and with many ramifications into higher ego functions, adaptive and defensive. Adaptation to reality was characterized by the simultaneous living in her present and in the past of her father. It is not sufficient to speak of her identification with the father as he was in the past and as he was currently, nor to speak of an identification with the mother as rescuer of the father. The mechanism goes beyond identification.* I have called it "transposition"† into the

---

* This phrase emulates Dr. James Herzog's terminology: he speaks of his patient's feelings and thoughts as "beyond metaphor" (see chapter 5).

† The need to use a special term, *transposition*, becomes apparent when one hears the anguished cries of survivors' children who want to live in the past, and harbor the dead within themselves: they may well be equating the unknown past with the unknown insides of their bodies.

Marvin K. (see chapter 4) found solace in the world of Indian lore, in which his deceased guru dictates a book. Marvin had transposed the Nazi world into the guru's timeless realm where he could heal and unite rather than injure and abandon. The guru lived inside his disciples and made himself known to them. The goodness that Rachel sought in her parents, siblings, and friends, Marvin found in the guru and his followers.

Yoav C., a survivor's son whose ideas were reported by A. Lieblich (1978), asked the crucial question: "Why do I have to reexperience the Holocaust in my dreams?" He, like Rachel, acted as if he himself had been there, and the experience was his to relive. Perhaps he, too—like a

world of the past, similar—but not identical—to the spiritualist's journey into the world of the dead. Living in the past, Rachel was not only enacting the role of her grandmother but was also active on her own behalf, bringing order into the Holocaust chaos, providing for food and rationing it, letting people come in and out of confinement and watching over them, yet killing them as the Nazis had and then resurrecting them. Playing all roles in the historical drama into which she wandered, she was her own father, his mother, herself, people in ghettoes and camps, their persecutors and their rescuers.

A peculiar, yet complex, integration in the ego consisted of an adaptation to the Holocaust and to present-day reality, providing a contradictory and a unifying base to Rachel's identity. She was a painter, a magic healer who resuscitated the dead, a cheat who outwitted the Nazis and extorted money from them; and she cheated her superiors as the Nazis had cheated and as the Jews had cheated to escape their persecutors. She was a briber and a bribe taker, a traitor, a hero and a victim of the persecution. She was also a child who cried for her mother and hated her two siblings, and a mother to the siblings whom she thought she treated better than their own mother did. She was also a henchman of the Nazis who executed the children her father was not supposed to have. Throughout she was Rachel, the American college girl, an artist, and her grandmother Rosa-Margit as well.

Rachel's affect control was excessive. Using inhibition, reversal into its opposite and turning into inanimateness, she would rarely betray any modulation of feelings. She held back signals of needs and affective expressions until she could be alone, when she cried, giving vent to her injured feelings. Estranged from her affects, she would sometimes ask herself what the proper feeling should be. She explained her inappropriate giggling and her flat facial expression by insisting that no one must have the satisfaction of knowing that she had been hurt. When, on occasion, she would express positive feelings toward someone, her behavior was devoid of subtlety, and she sounded more like a demanding child than a loving adult.

One of the ego realms where fantasies and defenses met was the incorporation of the dead for whom her father should have mourned. Their repetitious killing and rescuing in fantasy did not lead to the decathexis of the incor-

---

patient of H. Z. Winnik (1968)—had nightmares identical with those of his father. However, Yoav took his experience in the Holocaust beyond dreams. He said that he feared being taken "again" to the gas chambers, although he knew—as Rachel did—that they did not exist any more. Just like Rachel, he wanted to use his strength and perfection to "comfort, to hide someone in me."

Helen Epstein expressed herself in a manner almost identical with Rachel's: "Hundreds of people lived through me, lives that had been cut short in the war. My two grandmothers, whose names were mine, lived through me. My parents, too, were living through me" (1979, p. 147).

porated objects. Although Rachel's total demeanor was that of a mournful person, we cannot properly speak here of mourning. Rachel borrowed her father's world and the objects of this world and took upon herself to resurrect them rather than give them up. She could not help her father complete his mourning, and she felt oppressed by his inability to mourn. Perhaps her great need to know about her father's past was related to her attempt to mourn real people rather than illusory shadows. At the same time, she was impressed by her father's reluctance to talk about his past. Hers, then, was a double task to live in the past and to forget the people she was supposed to liberate.

Rachel had many conflicts—internal, external, and internalized. The conflict between wanting to know and to weep, and not being allowed to know and show feelings, overwhelmed all others, bringing into play a vast complex of defenses. She used incorporation and projection abundantly, with denial and repression stepping in especially when the isolation between the present and the past threatened to break down. Defensive suspiciousness and identification with the aggressor were called upon to help Rachel survive the Holocaust in which she lived. Somatization and inhibition of function, rigidity and deanimation were defenses acquired long before verbal themes entered the realm of her body training. The defense complex was loaded and constantly in operation, often serving to combat the needs of the present and the frustrations of the past in a double sense—the past of her own babyhood and her life in the father's past.

Many of Rachel's defenses were directed against specific drives—oral, anal-sadistic, inner-genital, and phallic. Outstanding was the obsessive defense of counting to put order into the external chaos. At the same time Rachel had a total antagonism against drive activity that she could interrupt, inhibit, but not really control. She used primitive defense mechanisms, such as stiffening, regression to infantile states, and inhibition of function alongside the more advanced and more effective defenses that revealed the strength of her ego. The defense activity interfered with ego functions and was specifically directed against such overt functioning that would incite persecutors to effect her death. It is difficult to decide whether one can speak of Rachel's paranoid defense mechanisms or whether one should consider them adaptive reactions to the reality of the Holocaust in which she lived.

Although it is tempting to think of an ego split that made Rachel live in a double reality, it is more accurate to speak of a synthesis that made Rachel's complex functioning possible. The creativity involved in Rachel's double existence paved the way toward sublimations. Her conflict regarding knowing and not knowing led her to become a visionary artist who could see what is beyond the macroscopic reality of the present.

# A Metapsychological Assessment

*The Superego.* Rachel's ego ideal was not easily distinguishable from the punitive superego and from her narcissistic omnipotence. Dominant was the aspiration to be a redeemer—a great painter who would bring all Jews back in a magic way. This fused with the narcissistic overvaluation of what her body could endure without suffering, and with the need to be punished for the father's survival. With bodily manipulations and with excursions into the past, she hoped to make up for the father's "unlawful" escape from death: "unlawful" because most of his family had died, and "unlawful" because he did not pursue his ideals and was paid for helping patients. By providing the money for her education, for her nurturance and freedom from worry, he contradicted his injunctions that she must control herself and steel her body so that the Nazis could not make her suffer and die. Money from the father and from the Nazis coddled the Jews and made them weak. Yet money was also a proof that her father was smarter than the Germans, more influential and more capable of destruction. No sooner did Rachel feel destructive than she became afraid of punishment; she had to impose taboos upon herself lest she become a successor to Hitler. Superior to money was knowledge which— her physician father said—was "the only thing that remains with you throughout life." Knowledge and foresight could be used to sabotage the persecutors' war plans. Silence, disguising one's inner life and knowledge, assured that the Nazis would not know the extent of the sabotage. Silence was also imposed by the Nazis themselves, who hid their crimes from the world. It was also imposed by shame that forbade talk about Jewish degradation. Working for oppressors and sabotaging them was the most valuable aim in life. At the same time, Rachel needed to be a victim, sacrificed for the sins of her father in order to assure his survival. All these ideas became highly sexualized and aggressive in the context of the heightened narcissism of the Oedipus complex. To be a redeemer, to be a victim, to serve her father through the workings of her body were all intrinsically interwoven with Rachel's penal code which resembled the one the Nazis had imposed upon the Jews.

Rachel needed to be punished for fantasies of sex, especially with non-Jewish people. She had to become sexless through starvation, pregnant through constipation, deprived of progeny through loss of menstruation, and penisless through castration. She needed to be punished for eating when she was hungry, and had to train herself not to go to the bathroom. Intertwined with these needs was the double function of eating and defecating in terms of rescue, survival, and death. Living in the past involved also the personification of the Nazis who were aggressive jailers, but so stupid that they could be outwitted. Her devious tricks to destroy material entrusted to her were easily uncovered, and she was reprimanded and threatened with dismissal from school.

Being caught implied that she would be sent to a concentration camp and become a slave. One of her teachers recognized the source of her peculiar behavior and, without knowing her ancestry, told her in anger that the school was not a labor camp.

As indicated in the case described by M. Laufer (1973), self-idealization and idealization of parents were invaded by conflict. Rachel looked upon herself as a heroine, upon her father as a great man who had outwitted the Germans and rescued many people, and upon her mother as an aide who sacrificed herself for the father's lofty aims and aggrandized him at her own expense. At the same time she saw her parents, especially her father, as degraded. She had the fantasy that her father had performed experiments for the Nazis; she saw her mother as abdicating her maternal protective needs and her own intellectual achievement so that the children and herself could be sacrificed for the father. These conflicted assessments of the parents' attitudes invaded Rachel's ego ideal and her punitive tendencies, with a resulting *split in the superego* (see chapter 15). Whereas her ego could absorb and integrate diverging tendencies, the superego became fragmented* in more ways than one.

Rachel aspired to be a great painter, a benefactor of her father who deserved fame as a reward for his deprivations. At the same time she felt degraded and hid her status as a survivor's child from most people she knew. Nevertheless she found ways to provoke people to degrade her by treating her like a small child who had to be punished. The external degradation gave credibility to her feeling of persecution as a Jew in the time tunnel. It was also a just punishment for her desire to compete with her parents, especially her father who gave her signals that she must become famous, yet not better than he. She had to be degraded and killed because she failed to live up to the many details of her functioning, as proscribed by her father—rules erected in the service of survival. These were reinforced by the mother's frugality and periodic withholding of food and money. Even though the severe restriction of her body functions was meant to be a safeguard against sickness and death, in reality it had the effect of bringing Rachel close to death by starvation and by accident-proneness. As representative of her grandmother, she was supposed to be dead like her, or allowed to live only if she could rescue the dead.

Rachel credited her father with an enormous survivor guilt. She herself suffered from an excessive guilt for her wish to detach herself from her parents and live an independent life. To create her own family and be rid of the father's need of her as redeemer was paramount to killing the father—an act that the Nazis had not accomplished. On the surface she knew that she was

---

* The use of this term does not imply a psychotic process.

expected to be married and have children, that this was one of the tasks through which survivors and their children had to undo Hitler's genocide. Caught in the vise of this double bind, Rachel sometimes behaved like a loose girl who had to be reprimanded by her parents; at other times she was only interested in painting. The latter behavior was almost always respected, as long as it did not estrange her from the family. The message was that she should get married, but this should not interfere with her mission to rescue the dead. In transference, Rachel longed for the analyst to take a stand in one or another direction. The analyst was clearly allied with the goals of survival, health, and gratification as well as of achievement. To confront Rachel with the contradictory features of her superego was not enough. To help her understand the conflicting nature of the cues given to her by her parents, was not enough. Only when, at last, Rachel was told that she could not really live in the past, and that her time tunnel was unattainable, did she begin to seek real people to love and befriend without dragging them down with her into the dangers of the Holocaust. She would provoke the analyst by not going to work, by starving herself until she fainted, and by missing appointments. She wanted to hear a reaffirmation of her right to live and be cured. Only when she was told that analysis was not possible when the analyst had to worry about her, did she become more careful and punctual and begin to eat in a normal fashion. These injunctions had to be repeatedly checked, with the analyst having to assume the function of a caring nurturing parent. Although she knew that the time tunnel was a figment of her imagination, and that she was not in real danger of being run over by cars and starved, she needed external referents to verify her doubts about the feasibility of living in the past. This verification aided her in the restructuring of her fragmented superego and allowed her to transform her "mission impossible" into a desire to serve Jewish causes and investigate the effect of the Holocaust. Painting provided her with the opportunity to do something real. The concreteness of a touchable and visible creation would counterbalance the semi-concreteness of her fantasies which had begun early in life. Because of her superior intellect and her precocity as a child, she seemed to have engaged in thought processes underlying her rich fantasy life at a time when symbolization ordinarily begins and concrete thinking prevails over abstract. The archaic precursors of her superego were based on the concreteness of her punitive tendencies.

## THE DIAGNOSIS

It is difficult to fit Rachel and many other children of survivors into a diagnostic category. Because of her ability to empathize with both her parents and her siblings, excessive narcissistic deprivation in the first year of life, as described by H. Kohut (1971 and 1977), seemed highly unlikely. Neither was there a type of grandiosity associated with idealization and mirroring. The grandiosity concerned the theme of survival in face of adversity and did not have the infantile features of early illusions. There was considerable traumatization and vulnerability in the second year of life which increased Rachel's probable predisposition to obsessiveness. A repetition of trauma at the age of six undoubtedly contributed to her hysterical and phobic acting out. The birth of each sibling was traumatic in a double sense: it deprived her of her mother, and it brought about death wishes, which were imbued with fears of abandonment and torture, later tinged with Holocaust features. Rachel's increased narcissism and her narcissistic neediness as well as her masochistic leanings were closely connected to her continuous concern with death and survival. Under conditions of danger, narcissism heightens adaptively and counterbalances the giving in to the wish to find relief in death. Rachel acted as if she were in constant danger of being killed or of dying and was forever prepared to rescue herself and others. Her narcissistic grandiosity seemed in keeping with this internal reality. She did not suffer from delusions. Repression had to be lifted before her fantasy about the Holocaust came to the surface. Undoing and isolation had to be consistently analyzed to bring her grandiosity into consciousness. Underneath the concrete fantasies one could detect a tremendous strength and vitality that enhanced her creativity and fed into her lofty ego ideal.

It would be tempting to subsume her condition under the heading "borderline"; but her relationships were too solid, and her transference revealed a degree of constancy and fidelity of which a borderline ego is not capable. It was possible to analyze her with a minimum of parameters; once she was assured of the analyst's dedication to her survival, she entered into an excellent therapeutic alliance. The most disturbing feature in her psychic structure was the split in her superego which contrasted with a surprising cohesiveness of the ego. Both the transposition into the past and the fragmentation of her superego seemed ominous signs until her capacity to sublimate was freed and the analysis of her superego released the inhibitions that stood in the way of her functioning. An unusual patient, she remained an unusual young woman who could express herself in writing, in music, and in painting. Her narcissism was highly gratified when she became artistically successful, and perhaps by identification with the analyst, she became particularly concerned with the furthering of children's perceptual development. This constituted a sublimation of her involvement with the past of her forebears, a past she could not see and understand when she was a child. The complexity of her adaptation came to her in good stead when she began to organize her work in a superior, multifaceted way, and she became capable of discriminating between and coordinating the technical and the spiritual aspects of her art.

The peculiar features in Rachel's functioning cannot be simply explained on the basis of oral dependency, obsessiveness and hysterical symptoms, and acting out. Perhaps we are dealing here with a type of *transmitted traumatic neurosis* which results from problems, conflicts, and fantasies from a parent's traumatic past. The transmission continues throughout life, with exacerbation of certain pathogenic ideas in discrete phases of development. It cannot be construed as M. M. R. Khan's cumulative trauma (1963) where stress is produced by the insensitivity of the mother. No doubt, Rachel's mother, herself not a survivor, may have contributed to her daughter's affect disturbance; but far more important was her unconscious enhancement of Rachel's transposition into the Holocaust world.

## Discussion and Summary

A presentation of an analysis of a daughter of a survivor was used to examine how her psychic structure was influenced by the transmission of her father's traumatic Holocaust past.

A metapsychological assessment of the patient's id, ego, and superego revealed the following salient features:

Her drives were distinguished by an urgency of life and death tendencies. Many of the fantasies uncovered in analysis had a semi-concrete character. Aggression was turned against herself and punishment was acted out through provocations. Narcissistic aggrandizement alternated or operated simultaneously with self-degradation and pessimism. The relations to objects were of uneven quality, with anaclitic needs vying with oedipal attitudes.

Her affects were ambivalent—often primary feelings like emptiness, fullness, deadness, or excitement. Her ego attitudes and defenses were concerned with survival, not only in the present but also in the past and the future. She lived in a double reality, one current and the other transposed into the era of the Holocaust. This transposition is a mechanism beyond identification, as the descendant into the time tunnel of history is identifying with more than any one person, such as parent or deceased relative, but with the oppressed and the oppressors who were living at that time.

Defenses were many, some archaic and others advanced—with deanimation, regression, somatization, and denial alternating or operating along with reaction formations, regression, and identification with the aggressor. The defense complex interfered with everyday functioning in school and at home.

Rachel, like most other survivors' children whose cases were studied, exhibited an unusual capacity to integrate and to sublimate. The very same characteristics that underlay pathology, also were the source of sublimation. Going through life with the burden of a double reality, and maintaining the ideal of a messianic mission, put a particular strain on the ego—with a resulting precociousness and seriousness of purpose that counterbalanced its vulnerability. Although withdrawn and silent, oppressed by a prohibition against divulging Holocaust secrets, Rachel was observant and always knew more than could be expected of her. In her quest for the uncovery of what was hidden, she developed an eye for the composition of shapes, shadings, and colors. This was part and parcel of her seeing what is here in the present and examining the ways she had perceived the shadows and ghosts of the past in her early childhood.

Rachel's superego was fragmented. Archaic superego features were derived from the id's all-or-nothing principle; their punitiveness was modeled after Nazi excesses toward Jews. A split in the superego resulted from an incompatibility between Rachel's lofty ego ideal and her conviction that she did not deserve to live.

It was difficult to arrive at a diagnosis. The suggestion was made that Rachel suffered from a transmitted traumatic neurosis, initiated by her father and enhanced by the nonsurvivor mother.

It is proposed that Rachel's profile be used as a model for our understanding of a survivor's-child complex—not syndrome—as it reveals itself in analysis. Perhaps all children of survivors have traces of what is aggrandized in patients. The analogy is drawn from the Oedipus complex, common to all, but a source of pathology in some. Freud sought the source of the Oedipus complex far back in drama and myth. The historical impact of the Nazi Holocaust may have exaggerated the survivor's-child complex that may operate in generations to come. No doubt many questions remain unanswered. A few have been noted as guidelines for future research.

Of particular interest is the relationship between the nature of the drives, the affects, and the fantasies as they reveal themselves in analyses of survivors' children. The transition from need to drive, and from drive to feelings and wishes, deserves a study of its own. The effect of the emergency, created by the impact of forever-looming impending death, seems to be such that archaic feelings of distress and/or emptiness prevail and invade intimate functioning. The fantasies arising from states of emergency, created by external sources, seem to be closer to needs and drives and thus more concrete than

# A Metapsychological Assessment

are those arising from drives differentiated under peaceful conditions. The question has arisen whether this type of drive-affect-fantasies configuration creates in the psychoanalyst a sense of urgency by contagion.

The method of transposition into the parent's past must be differentiated further from identification with the parent's past. Its relationship to a bridging of history as a method of adaptation must be examined. Transposition has a certain relationship to mourning and is perhaps a substitute for it. It is possible that it serves the rescue of the love objects of parents, who themselves did not accept their death. As long as the survivor's child takes it upon himself or herself to descend into the past and to enact roles of parents, of deceased family members, and of Nazis as well as of others who lived at the time, the parents need not come to grips with the fact of the irreparable loss of their relatives (Klein 1973). When relieved of the rescue task, the survivor's child feels liberated. It is very likely that survivor parents are unable to complete the mourning process (A. and M. Mitscherlich 1970) because of the altered conditions in which they found themselves at the time they realized their loss. Judging by Rachel and other children of survivors, their depressive affect and their incorporation of the parents' lost objects can be considered only akin to mourning, but not as mourning itself. Mourning leads to an identification with the lost object and to its progressive decathexis (E. Furman 1974). Through these mechanisms, the psyche becomes reorganized. In contrast, the transposition into the past and the introjection—unknown to the patient—of many objects of the past do not lead to a decathexis of the objects, and the identification with unknown objects has a shadowy quality. Here we have to concern ourselves with the analyst's own mourning processes. One can help the patient to mourn, deny one's own sadness, or point out that mourning cannot be accomplished through transposition. Whether the analyst's therapeutic attitudes stem from countertransference, from empathy with the patient's suffering, or from a need to have reality reign, is open to question (Hoppe 1966). The analyst's own denial, inability to listen, or overinvolvement require a special study which has not been undertaken in our group.

Among many other topics worthy of mention, is the need to differentiate between situations where only one parent was a victim and others where both parents had been victims. There is little knowledge about the motivation of nonsurvivors to marry survivors. In some cases, as in Rachel's, the nonsurvivor mother seems to work hand in hand with her husband to impose upon the child the task of a redeemer and/or a sacrificial victim (see also Joseph S. and Karl F. in chapter 4, pages 87–89).

There is a great need to collect more data from analyses in order to differentiate the variables, among which the most important seem to be the type of persecution suffered and how old the victim was at the time. The question has arisen whether older children are more affected by their parents' Holocaust experience than are younger ones. This question raises the issue of family dynamics in relation to the respective ages of children.

Lastly, we should investigate the different impact that survivor-fathers, as compared with survivor-mothers, have upon children; further research on this question is needed (Danieli 1980). My own impression is that the image of a victimized mother is far less threatening than the image of a persecuted, helpless father. Mothers themselves seem to be less ashamed of the degradation they have suffered than fathers are, and are therefore in less need of being vindicated by their children. Perhaps bodily needs and the urgency to fulfill them is more emphasized by survivor-mothers, while the pull toward undoing the past is primarily exerted by survivor-fathers. The persecutory nature of restitution procedures (see chapter 3), which required the opening of wounds from the past and tested the credibility of the survivor, seemed to have a more detrimental effect on men than on women.

# PART III

# The Persecutors' Children

# Introduction

WHEN our group was founded in 1974, we knew that the study of children of Nazis was of equal importance to that of problems encountered by children of survivors. The few cases of Nazi children who had lived in the United States and could be analyzed here, gave us insufficient insight into the manner of transmission from Nazi parents to their children.

Some years later we were able to get in touch with German analysts who had formed a group headed by Lutz Rosenkötter for the study of survivors' children in Frankfurt. Time was not yet ripe for the organized study of Nazis' children; but some German analysts responded to a questionnaire regarding this topic, and a few were willing to share with our group what they had discovered. Our group in New York discussed the German cases (chapters 11 and 12) and sent the transcripts of our discussions to the participating German analysts. In the meantime, Erich Simenauer (1978) and Lutz Rosenkötter (1979) had written pioneering papers on the analyses of the second generation in Germany. Exchanging views with them as well as with other psychoanalysts, such as Martha Eicke, Rosemarie Berna, and Jacques Berna in Zurich, Lotte Kohler and Ingeborg Zimmermann in Munich, Peter Riebesser in Freiburg and Ilse Grubrich-Simitis in Frankfurt, enriched our understanding of the psychology of the second generation abroad.

The congress of German-speaking analysts in Bamberg (1980) concentrated on the question of the effect of the Second World War on today's world. From the congress emerged the paper of Erich Simenauer on the return of Nazi ideology (reprinted in chapter 8 in English) and a courageous, emotional account by Gisela Leyting (1980), who queried her contemporaries, students of analysis, regarding their childhood experiences during the war.

Many German analysts were children during the Nazi era: most came from families who disagreed with Hitler, but some had to deal with the contradictory messages of established superego values and the new ideals of the Nazi Reich. How many of the children who could not participate in the "glorious" activities of the Hitler Youth, were envious of their contemporaries who could? How many felt a conflict between the wish to march and sing and a nagging guilt that some neighbors and their children were excluded from the general feeling of grandeur and elation? How many objected when their Jewish friends were expelled from schools? How many asked their parents where their neighbors had gone, and did not get an answer? Although persecution was quite open, talking about it was dangerous. W. G. Niederland's (1980) book in which he presents histories of survivors who were refused compensation, suggested that the silence on both sides had the common feature that it was dangerous to speak. He described how crying or making a face when one was hit in a concentration camp was a crime that would prompt immediate execution. The conspiracy of silence in survivors, persecutors, and their children has many determinants; but, no doubt, it also has as its source the taboo on telling and denial instituted by the Nazis themselves and continued to this day by neo-Nazis.

Analysands as well as analysts also reflect the cultural trends of their time. Now that Germany has produced books for children explaining the persecution and encouraging people to describe their experiences during the war (Hans Peter Richter 1974; Winfried Bruckner et al. 1978; Franz Fuehman 1981), patients have begun to speak about, and act out, the Nazi past, and analysts to awake from their own latency period, to examine their counter attitudes to the patients' silence, and to speak out.

Can we speak of countertransference when analysts are shocked by the revelation of Nazi ideology in their patients? Can these analysts indeed analyze "objectively" and not convey to patients that their values are different? These and other crucial question are raised in the following chapters. After Simenauer's introduction on the return of persecution in today's analyses, there are vignettes presented by Rosenkötter (chapter 9) who, in agreement with Simenauer, points out disturbances in these patients' superegos. As elaborated in his previous paper on the subject (1979), Rosenkötter reiterates that Nazi mothers have had a more pathogenic effect on their offspring than have Nazi fathers. There follows an analysis of a patient who had been the daughter of a Nazi; and who later moved to another country with a different ideology (chapter 10). Eckstaedt's case history (chapter 11) deals with a man who grew up in Nazi Germany in early childhood, while Hardtmann reports one case thoroughly (chapter 12) but refers to five similar cases of children born to Nazi parents after the war was over. Yet, regardless of these factual differences and of the theoretical differences between the authors, the similarity of material and of views is striking. However, more material will be needed before one can venture the opinion that Nazis' children have a complex that can be defined in metapsychological terms (see chapter 7).

It is striking that, in almost all cases in this section, there is the predominant influence of a mother who imbued her child with omnipotence—a shared omnipotence that became a fruitful field for the adoption of the grandiose Nazi dogma. In Hardtmann's case, the ego ideal has become like a parasite eroding drives and endangering self-preservation. Under the façade of civilized cooperative behavior, the analyst is subjected to inhuman treatment at the hands of an inhuman patient. Patients treat their analysts as they have been treated by their parents (see Anna Freud's [1965] discussion of this attitude, which must be distinguished from transference). It stands to reason that an analyst who grew up under Nazi rule, would be vulnerable when faced by an individual behaving with the grandiosity and inhumanity of a Nazi. The suggested diagnostic categories of narcissistic neuroses (Kohut 1977) or cumulative trauma (Khan 1963) fade before the staggering fact that an analyst—treated like an inferior, inanimate being, and used by a patient—reacts with such defenses as silence, rationalization, or denial. Analyzing survivors and their children, we have been shocked by even such mild repetitions of man's inhumanity to man as attempts of these patients to victimize us or to cast us in the role of a persecutor. We who worked together became aware how much self-analysis was needed to keep our patients in treatment; and even then, we did not always succeed. The first analyses of Nazis' children in Germany were done mostly in isolation. European analysts who are working with Nazis' children are courageously looking within themselves and undergoing a new analysis, a self-analysis, as they conquer what can be generally subsumed under the heading of "countertransference," but requires a more precise definition and a closer scrutiny (Klaus Hoppe 1966; Yael Danieli 1981).*

Perhaps it will help to take a close look at the predominance of narcissistic grandiosity and lack of empathy in Nazi mothers. Is it conceivable that those mothers who were born two or more decades before Hitler came to power, were so highly traumatized themselves before the Holocaust that they had to traumatize their offspring in turn? The question must be left to analytic historians and sociologists. In discussing the matter with Dr. Hardtmann, this author suggested that narcissistically disturbed and needy women may have selectively found, in Hitler's grandiosity, an answer to their despair. His glorification of the German mother who produced German children may have been a way out for women who felt unloved, unappreciated, and downtrodden. Perhaps their children now come for treatment because they are suffering from the discrepancy between their mothers' and fathers' grandiose teachings and the officially accepted ethics of today's Germany. Inasmuch as

---

* One cannot be impersonal when viewing this kind of reaction to one's patient. Rather than conform to the generally impersonal style of this book, we have, therefore, retained the use of the pronoun "I" in sections where analysts speak of or allude to their "countertransference."

survivors' children have exhibited a similar attitude—for instance, that they can get away with anything (Laufer 1973), or that they can prevent future victimization by becoming Nazi oppressors (little Hitlers) themselves—they, too, have suffered from the conflict between "Might is right" and "Love thy neighbor as thyself." In the depth of their unconscious, these children received the message that it was better to be a Nazi than a Jew; and in this respect they may have shared the problems of Nazi children whose parents were supported by the State in the repudiation of Judeo-Christian morality.

As we compare the case histories in the first and the second parts of this book, we are struck by the similarities between the second generations of the oppressed and the oppressors (chapter 11), but we must proceed with caution and perceive the differences as well. This author has written elsewhere, that

children of survivors need to rid themselves of the invasion of their superego by the double image of the persecutor and his victim . . . that Nazis' children need to come to grips with their own conscience, with the guilt of moral self-degradation imposed upon them by their Nazi parents. The destiny of children of the persecuted and those of the persecutors is in their hands. They are not tied together by the Holocaust (Kestenberg 1977, reprint 1981a, p. 29).

Yet—while the survivor's child cannot get rid of the image of the persecutor—at least in two of the detailed analyses of Nazis' children, there is either none or only a scant reference to the persecuted. We may speculate that feelings about them are expressed in transference and hidden from the view of the analyst. In the dream of starved birds in chapter 11, are there two determinants—the reference to hunger in a prisoners' camp (perhaps an Allied prison for Nazi criminals), and that to the starved concentration camp inmates? Or, as suggested by Martin Bergmann in one of our discussions, are the Nazis' children preoccupied with their own hunger, their fear of bombs, their fathers' absence, degradation, or death, and only some are capable of dealing with the persecutor's guilt? Perhaps the guilt transferred from the parents of some is so devastating that they cannot face the past. Do they envy the victims, as is evident in the dream of a patient who wanted to redeem herself by being reborn as a rabbi (chapter 12)? Perhaps they experience themselves as their parents' Jews (chapter 12) and talk about the maternal lack of empathy for them, remaining silent about their substitutes, the Jews. The question asked in 1977—Did "the perpetration of infanticide on Jews only serve to deflect and deny the Nazis' wishes to kill their own children?" (Kestenberg 1977, reprint 1981a, p. 26)—still begs for an answer.

Such questions bring up the possibility that the greatest similarity between the second generation on both sides is their common conflict. Should they

# Introduction

have lived or died? Should they have been born or left unborn? The question of life and death looms large in the drive development of this new generation. Nazis' children may equate defeat with death and victory with life (chapters 11 and 12). Does this problem play as important a role in survivors' children? Do some groups of survivors' children equate living in peace with victory? Both—children of persecuted and of persecutors—live in a double reality; both may have a mission to rehabilitate their parents and undo the past. However, their missions are different. Nazi children must solve the problem of their parents' moral degradation; survivors' children's concern about their parents guilt is in great part an illusion. Perhaps what for survivors' children becomes a task of ego integration between past and present—as they live in both—for Nazis' children may be a split, much more difficult to analyze than is conflict. Both groups of patients seem to suffer from a split in the superego, especially because of the distortion of the ego ideal and because of a regression to archaic superego demands, resulting in a lack of progression into an independent ideal fitting present-day reality. Here we must appraise the borrowed grandiosity of the children of the persecuted against the grandiosity of the accepted, enjoyable Nazi superiority. We must further distinguish between the old-time illusion of Jewish superiority which involves intellect, study, and alliance with God and the Nazi superiority which involves power, conquest, and victory.

No doubt, there are, between patients on both sides, structural similarities and differences, which must be studied much further in joint conferences and in exchanges of views. Many more cases must be analyzed before the second generation fades from our view and the more complex problems of the third generation begin to occupy us. One insight however—discussed by Rosenkötter in chapter 9 and illustrated in chapter 10—emerges with great clarity.

One can develop a superego with new values and new ideals even though in early childhood one has been inculcated with such inhuman dogmas as "Jews are to be hunted as naturally as cats are hunted by dogs" (chapter 10). The teachings in schools, the examples of friends and their parents, the values of the community at large can influence structure formation, and the prevailing cultural mores may force the parents' immorality into hiding (see the case of a Nazi child, influenced by the teaching of the church, and her acquaintance and friendship with Jewish children and their families in chapter 10).

What emerges for us as psychoanalysts of the adult second generation on either side is a conviction that analysts are not completely neutral: they stand for something. Tolerant as they are of verbal expressions of drives and impartial when it comes to the solution of conflict, their superego, their reliability is clearly defined in terms of truth seeking and of acting on the basis of truth rather than in terms of denial that shields inhumanity. Allying themselves with patients for the sake of therapy, analysts cannot sacrifice their principles to allay guilt feelings or maintain "curative" illusions (Klaus Hoppe 1966). Perhaps their stand—moral though tolerant of wishes—should be re-examined in light of the parameters that have been used in analyses of the second generation. We need not stress where we stand when we analyze survivors and their children, but we must be careful not to enter into an alliance that would support the illusionary grandiosity of parents without making it impossible for the patients to reconcile themselves with them or forgive them. For this insight, we are grateful to the psychoanalysts who so generously and courageously discussed the feelings they had during the analyses of children of Nazis. We must also deal with our own stand on the issue of non-German bystanders who let the Holocaust happen, and on the issue of German parents who were afraid to talk openly to their children about the Nazi menace for fear of incrimination and cruel retaliation. By considering these parents and the messages they have given their children, we must become concerned with all our patients and the effect that the brutalities of the Third Reich had on the second generation as a whole. Encouragement to re-examine our own past comes from those in the young German generation who, like Gisela Leyting (1980), bring into the open the issues of how we are to handle our parents' "morality."

# 8

# *The Return of the Persecutor*

THE RECURRENCE of war and persecution in psychoanalyses, as it has been observed in Germany, is but one aspect of their recurrence—with varying degrees of intensity—on the sociopolitical level. Both of these phenomena possess the same characteristics as the return of the repressed. The underlying repetition compulsion in each is revealed in the polarity of remembering and repetition in life and in the psychoanalytic process (Loewald 1965).

It is striking that the persecutions of the Nazi regime, and the far-reaching psychic damage that they caused, were only recently explored in a systematic fashion. A "latency period"—to use an expression of Judith S. Kestenberg's (1979*a* and *b*)—was necessary to enable analysts to deal with the unthinkable horrors of this period. This latency period lasted until the 1960s. Other than individual publications, the problem of the psychic aftereffects of the Holocaust surfaced for the first time, as a topic of official scientific discussion, in 1965 at the twenty-fourth Congress of the International Psychoanalytical Association in Amsterdam. The discussion continued at the twenty-sixth congress in 1969 in Rome and at the twenty-seventh in 1971 in Vienna.

The title that was chosen—"Sequelae of Man-Made Disasters"—makes it clear that the psychoanalysts were concerned not with mere aftereffects but with sequelae—the pathological morbid state of these aftereffects, according to the *Oxford English Dictionary.* The papers in these congresses were concerned almost exclusively with the sequelae of the extreme persecution suffered by the victims. The consequences for the persecutors were hardly touched on; those for their offspring, not at all. One can understand the reluctance of psychoanalysts to deal with this problem, if one considers that the unimaginable global cruelty of the persecution blunted peoples' senses.

Persecution of Jews, in its various forms, was a continuous phenomenon of the two-thousand-year-old Christian epoch. One can grasp the effect of the sequelae upon the psychic processes of the persecutors only by seeing the basic distinction between historical anti-Semitism and the Nazi mentality within the framework of drive theory. The hate object of the traditional enmity toward Jews had to be *retained*, in order to ensure continued persecution, defamation, and spoilation, as befits the compulsion structure of *anal aggression*. By way of contrast, the uninhibited destructive, extermination strategy of the Nazis was rooted in the further regression to primary *oral destruction* and, thus, was perfectly suited to become a mass psychosis.

But these rational considerations can no more suffice to effect personality change than they do in the psychoanalytical process. It may be that—if, through historical data and personal anecdotes, abstract formulations can be transformed into concrete facts—an emotional experience approximating "reliving" can be attained.

In an apocryphal anecdote, which we owe to Friedrich Torberg (1978), a filthy rich American went to be treated at a Jewish-run sanatorium in Vienna after his treatment at home proved no longer possible. He suffered from a type of aggressive paranoid psychosis, in which stubborn silence led to catatonic retreat. At last, since nothing is too costly for a filthy rich American, the Austrian psychiatrist Julius von Wagner-Jauregg was called. A few minutes after his arrival, the patient went into a rage and Professor Wagner-Jauregg, who had to be protected from assault, left the scene of his futile visit. Now only one hope remained: Professor Freud. He arrived and was led into the sickroom. Inside all remained quiet. No raving. After ten minutes, the head physician risked opening the door a crack. Doctor and patient sat engaged in animated conversation. After a half-hour Freud emerged to the enthusiastic praise and congratulations of the assembled staff. One of them plucked up his courage and said, "We ought now make a confession to you. Prior to your arrival, Professor Wagner-Jauregg was here and was not able to make contact with the patient." Freud modestly shrugged this off, saying, "I ask you, what does a *goy* know of meshugge ['being crazy']?" Told of this, Wagner-Jauregg dismissed it with a wave of hand: "So what else is new? It takes one *meshuggener* to know another."

Set against this story is a concrete historical quotation involving the commandant of Auschwitz, Rudolf Höss. When Höss, in 1946, was apprehended by Fred Jackson and his colleagues in the Field Security Service, he admitted voluntarily and proudly that it had been his job to exterminate Jews and other subhumans, adding, in these words exactly, "My best accomplishment was ten thousand Jews a day" (Jackson 1980).

The perversion of ideals in the Third Reich ultimately led to the total dissociation of emotions from memories. It is especially this split that psychoanalysts encounter with the return of persecution in psychoanalyses. Repression, denial, and reversal into the opposite—though they played a large role in the defense mechanisms of the Nazi mentality and in the experiences of that time—are too simple an explanation of the defense, whose complex nature can be seen especially in its relationship to the process of mourning.

Concerning A. and M. Mitscherlich's thesis about the "Inability to Mourn" (1970), one should first recall Freud's observation that mourning is a great enigma for psychologists. Why it must be such a painful process and must, as such, give rise to resistance against it, we do *not* understand and cannot deduce from any hypothesis. In *On Transience* (1915, pp. 303–8), a year before he wrote *Mourning and Melancholia* (1916a), Freud gave his definition of mourning: "We only see that libido clings to its objects and will not renounce those that are lost even when a substitute lies ready to hand. Such then is mourning" (1915, pp. 306–7). The mourning terminates spontaneously. One must also remember that, two years earlier in *Totem and Taboo*, Freud had written that the function of mourning is "to detach the survivors' memories and hopes from the dead" (1912–13, p. 65).

We must consider some manifest sociopolitical aspects before examining the relevance of Freud's model to our theme. These aspects are seen in daily life, and their more precise counterparts are rediscovered in analysis. Among these is a multilayered, as well as multifarious, myth, to whose binding power broad segments of the people of West Germany attempt to cling.

The first manifestation of this myth is: "We did not know." We meet, in life and in analysis, people who were, for example, witnesses as neighbors in their apartment house were seized and deported; people who heard and saw their colleagues being picked up at work; lawyers who were present when their Jewish partners were forcibly removed from their offices; and German doctors who watched as Jewish doctors were arrested in hospitals in the dead of night, never to be seen again.

Helmut Dahmer's (1979) poignant remarks are, in this regard, relevant, though they have probably already faded from the memory of many readers. He labeled, with the words of the Jewish prophets, those who knew, heard, and were eyewitnesses: "They have eyes but they do not see; ears but they do not hear." The prophets were referring to the idols of ancient Israel. The parallel with the dangerous idols of modern German history lies in their common blindness: no one did any evil; everyone merely performed the highest duty, blindly to obey.

A second aspect of this myth of mass hypocrisy is: "We did not want this to happen." That may be, but it is also undeniable that the majority of the population sympathized with the Nazis and identified with the Hitler ideology. Consequently, psychoanalysts must confront patients early with their contradictory attitudes, whereby they exculpate Nazi sympathizers but condemn sympathizers of terrorists. This conflict is due to their own emotional participation in the deeds of the Third Reich.

Usually, these two aspects of the myth play the most prominent role in analyses; and, without exception, these myths urge the patients on, or put pressure on them, to work through the problem. These two aspects of the myth play a great role in the material of this writer's analyses, and, without exception, facilitate further elaboration. An unusual defense mechanism arose frequently in these analyses. In order to defend themselves against guilt feelings and in order to unburden the ego, these patients attempted to balance their own misdeeds, or their tolerance for those of others, against the hostile actions of enemies. Through utter disregard of logic they used exclusively wartime enemy actions as justification for all actions of Nazis and sympathizers; the equating of incompatible, unrelated deeds derives its origin from the primary process.

What is involved in this balancing is a primitive defense mechanism. It is a higher form of denial, but it is distinguished by an immense ego restriction. Furthermore, it has many features in common with the reversal into the opposite that Anna Freud (1946) extended from the area of drive theory to that of the ego's defense mechanisms.

Tolerance and exculpation of the misdeeds of the Nazi regime, its perpetrators, and sympathizers are motivated by a person's own sympathies for and partial identification with the Nazi ideology. The pathway to this tendency was eased by *historical* anti-Semitism. The Wagner-Jauregg anecdote is but a tamed—one might say, sublimated—example of Jew hatred and seems rather sophisticated. Besides, it provides an example of Jewish reactive aggression. It ought not be misunderstood and occasion nostalgic longing. The proper lesson about the thousands of years of Jew hatred can be learned from the history books. Only this intensive and extensive historical record makes it clear to subsequent generations that the traditional anti-Semitism of the Church and the princes, of government, and of society was what initially made all else possible. Anti-Semitism was indeed the lowest, albeit eminently effective, common denominator, which united all German nationals, regardless of the varying degree to which they agreed with the Nazis. That is why the Nazi ideology and all the Nazi measures integrated anti-Semitism as alpha and omega, even though for such completely heterogeneous goals as national greatness, military superiority, and world conquest. The intimate interweaving of the symptoms and observations of sociopolitical phenomena, as seen both in everyday life and in psychoanalyses, justifies this broad presentation of these phenomena; indeed, it demands it. Occasionally, insignificant peripheral symptoms allow one to uncover the most peculiar aftereffects, which can arise in daily life and recur in analysis. The word *Jew*, for instance, remains such a particular defamation that many Germans are barely able to utter it. Indeed, one might think that there were no Jews in the Federal Republic of Germany: in public pronouncements and private discussions, Jews have become "our Jewish co-citizens" or "colleagues" and, at best, the "racially persecuted."

This common behavior represents a regression to earlier levels of human development, and its extent testifies to the universality of the traumatization. Freud discussed in detail in *Totem and Taboo* (1912–13) why it was that primitive people could not mention the names of the dead—a phenomenon that the German psychologist Wilhelm Wundt had already noted. This regressive significance is obviously not shared, in Germany, by the adjective *Jewish*.

Another pertinent observation is of importance for psychoanalysts, for it touches upon our work in the area of psychosomatics. The authoritative work in this field in Germany stems from Viktor von Weizsaecker, the mentor of many German *Psychosomatiker*. As the historian Walther Wuttke-Groneberg revealed, Weizsaecker advocated that medicine must be transformed from a "pure preservation theory" to an "extermination doctrine" and an "extermination policy" (Wuttke-Groneberg 1979).

Yet vestiges of the *Lingua Tertii Imperii** are still to be found in great numbers uttered in public and on the analytic couch—barbaric encroachments upon the body of the venerable German language. Recently, highly placed politicians labeled a liberal German author a rat and a blowfly which, in light of the experience of the past, is tantamount to incitement to violence and destruction.

The diversified consequences of the collapse of the Third Reich cannot, therefore, be seen in isolation from the convictions of the majority of the people, from the internalizations that they effected and that now, in turn, have marked their basic beliefs and attitudes. These remain largely unalterable, mainly because the motives for their genesis have remained untouched in the unconscious. This conclusion accords with our understanding of metapsychology, but the preconscious defenses are carried out with the aid of mechanisms that are not so frequently recognized and that must be seen as specifically linked to postwar events.

To return once more to the problem of mourning. Where, for the majority of the population, lay the actual loss due to the total collapse of the Third Reich? We must distinguish between two main groups of people, avoiding

---

* Here is meant the perverted German language as perpetrated by official Nazidom.

schematization and keeping in mind that mixed and intermediate groups have their own autonomy as well. Phrased another way, as with all judgments of collectivities, the underlying phenomena that are described should be understood as the ones that predominate. Individuals who have struggled to achieve integrity are left out of account.

For the first group, the great loss lay in the military and political débâcle itself, in the destruction of the cities, in the misery and want, in hunger and cold, in families torn asunder, and in grief over the dead. These actual losses had to lead to a spontaneous mourning response, to a withdrawal of the libido from what was gone. The substitute of which Freud wrote (1915) lay ready at hand only when the alternative possibilities in the new reality could be recognized. They were perceived (*Wahrgenommen*) in the double sense of the word.* How this happened is well known. Every ounce of energy was spent on the economic recovery and the success of the Federal Republic which, taken in isolation, were stupendous. Cities were rebuilt, and new public institutions were created. The high price paid for this achievement is a matter for sociological system investigation which would be of equal interest, for ego psychological evaluations do not obviate the drive theory. On the contrary, they are implicitly embodied in Freud's (1915 and 1916a) remarks concerning mourning, according to which the libido does not want to relinquish its objects. By this, he must have meant that since the libido as a drive does not "want" anything it is expended through the efforts of the ego as a constituent part of the self.

The second group of people presents a quite different picture, and it is members of it who are most often met in analysis. These are usually the persecutors and perpetrators: the countless ones who were in some fashion accessory, as well as the standard-bearers of the perverted racist world view. What is revealed concerning this group, from a few in-depth analyses, is that no fundamental changes in their basic convictions have occurred. To be sure, some things have been repressed, much has been denied, and much more dismissed through projection. Naturally, the desire to forget through successful repression plays a role in this complicated process, which is familiar to psychoanalysts. Freud, who described this process in detail, commended, as the best brief formulation of it, Nietzsche's aphorism: " 'I did this,' says my Memory. 'I cannot have done this,' says my Pride and remains inexorable. In the end—Memory yields" (1901, p. 147n). Another role is played in their defenses by the fact that the deeper awareness of guilt was not a product of insight but was insisted on by others, the hated victorious Allies. With the aid of the defense mechanisms already mentioned, this circumstance strength-

---

* *Wahrgenommen* means "perceived" as well as "taken as true."

ened still further the resistance against any insight or led to obvious hypocrisy, which served just as poorly.

We have all found in our milieus analogous experiences that illustrate the extraordinary, subtle, evasive tactics of these people. The author Gottfried Benn is but one example of a public figure in Germany who has demonstrated this behavior. As is revealed in the recently available letter from him to P. W. Oelze (see Benn 1979–80) written after the Second World War, Benn, in his enthusiasm for the Third Reich, was neither ready nor able to deal with its culpability. In his world view he did not look for Nazi motives; it was all only a "mistake" on his side. He continued to adhere to aggressive all-inclusive condemnations of others, especially of the emigrants among his literary colleagues. In postwar Berlin, he was disturbed by the "Hawaii garbage" and the "Cossack bloodstain" in the midst of the racially pure and worthwhile population. This cultured and worldly German author did not note until the end of 1948, "the chicken-hearted" [doglike] cowardice with which the intellectuals accept political ideologies and relinquish to politicians—that is, to people of the lowest type—the creation of values." It causes much pain and sorrow to see many similar cases, often among important, intellectually creative individuals with whom people identify in their social attitudes; and it hurts to discover the same dark stains in their characters, once they expose themselves to public scrutiny.

In short, for those in the second group, their beloved objects—the Nazi ideology and the delusion of chosenness—continue to survive. No loss has occurred; at worst they were "robbed" by the enemy. The libido has not been required to relinquish its objects. This means that no loss, no demise has taken place—and thus, in turn, that no mourning work could be or needs to be performed. Substitutes were not acceptable. By incessant rationalization and the use of other multiple, convoluted, out-of-the-way defense strategies, a liberating result was achieved that led to a rehabilitation of the old Nazi *Weltanschauung*. Perpetrators became innocent victims. They felt doubly confirmed in their paranoia, for the war was lost—"as we all know"—due to treachery and sabotage, while the victorious Allies were incited and led by "World Jewry."

As it has emerged from our analyses that the same mechanisms operate in the psychic lives of the offspring, a general formulation has been settled on: the parents have passed on their views and attitudes to their children. The correctness of this formulation is beyond doubt. The behavior pattern of the parents created a family atmosphere that had to leave its mark on their children. The parents' character formation must certainly have proved crucial, as exemplified in the view of Rosenkötter (1979), that the identification with mothers who had an outlook of hardness and severity toward the weak had to

have unhealthy consequences. Children's thinking was channeled into particular paths, and the urge to imitate was evoked; this was reinforced by the premium of identificatory participation in supposedly high-minded enterprises
and ideals. An analysand recalled that for many years he had felt frustrated by
his father and mother and had reacted with withdrawal and hatred, because
in his childhood they had tried to forbid him to participate in the activities of
a National Socialist organization.

However, we cannot be satisfied with only this information. The supposedly automatically operating perpetuation of nazism was stabilized by individual and specific psychic processes. The return-of-the-persecutor mentality
in the next generation is linked to the transformations and fixations in the
structure of the superego and the ego ideal. This author (1978) has attempted
to describe these mechanisms in case histories of representatives of the generation born during the Hitler years.

The persistent influence of the ego ideal upon ego and superego is the motive force for the observed phenomena. From the seeming paradox of the
same youths who rebel against their fathers and everything they represent yet
continue to be prisoners of those same fathers' ideologies, it is possible to
conclude that these young people have abandoned only those identifications
with their fathers that were localized in their, the sons', egos. The original
ideal formations in the sons' superegos were never altered. If this distinction
in the localization and identification and internalization processes is not considered, then the fantasies, emotional states, and ideas of the rebellious students, for example, remain incomprehensible.

Freud wrote:

The past, the tradition of the race and of the people, lives on in the ideologies of the
superego and yields only slowly to the influences of the present and to new changes;
and so long as it operates through the superego it plays a powerful part in human life,
independently of economic conditions. (1932, p. 67)

Edmund Bergler (1952) proposed that the aggression of the superego toward the ego is alleviated if the ego submits to the demands of the ego ideal.
The present author believes that the perpetuation of the Nazi mentality is
virtually preordained in many psychoanalytic models: in the theory of affects,
in the structural theory itself, in the methodological approach, and, following
these, in the type of clinical experience that was demonstrated in a previous
paper (Simenauer 1979).

The problem remains why few relevant analyses are available. Complicated
countertransference phenomena play a role here. The analyst, faced with a
patient's undisguised fantasies of violence and extreme self-depreciation, may

find that his generally recognized and familiar psychoanalytic world threatens to collapse, especially when theoretical and technical adaptations are not available. This result is even more likely to occur if the analyst himself belongs to the racially persecuted group. As Rosenkötter wrote, "The analyst may feel himself so threatened by the fantasies of depreciation and destruction that he can no longer optimally mobilize his interpretive faculties" (1979, p. 1035).

Present-day reality, with its ubiquitous and latent aspect of violence, no longer permits the generational conflict to be understood and treated exclusively from the point of view of the oedipal conflict. The special character of this aggression requires that present-day reality, of which the analyst is himself a part, be interpreted. The particular difficulty in dealing with this type of material lies in part in its very nature but, above all, in the degrees of the specific resistance on the part of analyst and patient toward the ideology. Surely, the analyst must be disciplined to explore the material in his interpretations. The refusal to empathize plays a role here. Behind this refusal lurks the unrecalled anxiety of the past—that weak, primitive ego nuclei, in the process of formation, will be inundated by the archaic primary processes—with the consequent danger of psychosis. This primary psychological resistance of the psychic apparatus fuses with the external countertransferential actuality. This actuality is characterized by a repressive social structure that puts the analyst under its spell. In this manner the most powerful resistance is created in the analytic process.

Rosenkötter (1979) phrases it in this way: that psychoanalysts are not immune against the regressive changes to which are subject the ego and the superego in certain groups. The "group" can be the entire world around us and its leading conventions. Analysts and patients belong inescapably to the same social structure. Beyond the *neurotic* conflict, the human conflict is always present. Whether we like it or not, the analytic relationship is always a social relationship as well. A tacit understanding is always reached between analysand and analyst. Because of unconscious defenses, certain themes remain untouched and are not worked through; silence is inevitably practiced so as to let sleeping dogs lie. The analyst cannot but adjust in varying degrees to the social constraints of the surrounding world—to the "conspiracy of silence."

As the French statesman Léon Gambetta (1838–82) openly enjoined the defeated French people after the Franco-Prussian War, "Always think about it; never speak of it," so the German people are led spontaneously by their needs and by following the example of most of their leading public personalities in economic, political, and scientific life.

We live still in the midst of a great collective silence.

# 9

# The Formation of Ideals
# in the
# Succession of Generations

THE PROBLEMS observed by German psychoanalysts in their patients who are children of Nazis have cast new light upon the complex patterns into which historical events and individual pathology are woven. Freud postulated that the "process of civilization" demanded an increasing inhibition of immediate satisfaction of instinctual drives—particularly the renunciation or sublimation of asocial, aggressive impulses (1930a, p. 139). While he considered the "advance in intellectuality," or the strengthening of the "voice of intellect," the only way in which civilized man could survive (1937–39, p. 114), Freud always emphasized the precariousness of this increasing renunciation of instinctual gratification.

The development of civilization has not suppressed the aggressive inclination of man—as the continuous history of warfare makes evident. But the development of human culture has nonetheless shaped each individual. This "localization" of cultural forces upon the individual is considered, in psychoanalytic theory, to be the ego ideal that was formerly believed to coincide with the superego: today analysts view these two notions as separate but closely interconnected. The ego ideal can induce the superego to release its norms and prohibitions. The ego ideal originates first from identification with the primary objects and is later shaped by parental goals and values. During its evolution in childhood and adolescence, it can include further ideals of religion and ethics. The child analyst Peter Blos (1962) has shown that this later development takes place from latency through adolescence until early adulthood and enables an individual to sever his ties to the primary objects.

But this process of increasing internalization of values can be reversed—as we know by painful experience. In many people, the figure of a leader can

# Ideals in the Succession of Generations

take the place of the ego ideal; such a leader can seduce the masses into obedient bondage (Freud 1921). Faithful compliance (which is not the same as calculated obedience) to National Socialism was just such a corruption of the ego ideal in terms of the values acquired in the process of civilization. Hitler and his followers turned away from the common cultural ideals: the prohibition of murder and violence and the recognition of a justice valid for everyone. Instead, they glorified violence and the rule of their own group, of their "race" over others. The arrogance of declaring that certain groups are "unworthy to live," and the humiliation and annihilation of these groups, are clearly regressions in terms of the process of civilization.

The individual may awaken from the bondage imposed by such a leader as one does from intoxication; and such awakening is usually connected with intense shame. But when, after the war, a legal constitution was re-established in Germany, the necessary work of shame and mourning was often not accomplished (A. and M. Mitscherlich 1970). Instead, most people withdrew from working through their bondage and encouraged each other in a mutual denial of their past.

If we agree with Peter Blos's opinion that identification with intact, and not overtly contradictory, parental ego ideals is a prerequisite for the child's own ego-ideal formation and, thus, for the adult's resolution of infantile dependencies, we must expect to find, in many present-day young adults in Germany, traumatic sequelae due to the deficiency of parental ego ideals that were deficient because of regression, bondage, and denial. The following vignettes reflect typical examples of such patients observed over a period of two decades. While the personal data are veiled in order to protect the patients' identities, the crucial facts reveal a distinctive pattern of parent-child relationships which have resulted in deficient ego-ideal formation.

Kurt H., a civil servant who was born in 1933, suffered from a severe obsessive-compulsive neurosis. A typical obsessive fear of his was that he might have pushed a woman from a station platform down to the rails before an incoming train. He had developed numerous rituals of control and undoing to placate his rage as well as his guilt feelings.

Mr. H.'s maternal grandfather, to whom his mother was still very much attached, had been a guard in a jail. The grandfather had died before the patient was born, but his portrait was hanging on the wall of the family living room. It was a picture of a stern, bearded man; the frame was decorated with little swastika flags. From the time Kurt H. was a small boy of four or five, he had each night to stand erect before the picture, raise his right arm, and say, "Heil Hitler, Grandpa!" before he could say goodnight to his mother. Although it is only one tile in a pathogenic mosaic, this private version of a political mass ritual is characteristic of the way in which the pathology of this patient had been shaped.

Another patient, Werner C., born in 1935, had comparable childhood memories. He suffered from an obsessive fear that he might kill his three-year-old son, whom he consciously loved dearly. Mr. C. was the oldest son of a businessman who had not returned from the war. The father must have held traditional conservative views; Mr. C. had few memories of him. His mother came from a family of impoverished craftsmen. She had moved from another area to a southern German village, where she remained a stranger. In order to overcome her often depressed moods, she became a fanatical follower of Hitler and was active and locally prominent in the Nazi women's organization. Thus, she hoped to become important and cross the line that divided her from the village people. This participation in the grandeur of the "Führer" served to counteract her feelings of inferiority.

When Werner C. was little, her treatment of him was demanding and unempathic. After the birth of his brother, when Werner was three years old, he was forced to walk to kindergarten by himself. The way there, about two thirds of a mile, seemed endless to him. He felt isolated in kindergarten and often soiled himself and was sent home. On the long walk home, he almost died of shame, hoping that no one would see him. At home, his mother criticized him sarcastically, instead of offering the consolation he needed.

During the war, the mother used to listen to radio news with the three children she by then had. Whenever the news contained victories of the German armies—"special announcements" (Sondermeldungen)—she and the children sang the national anthem, their right arms raised. Here again, the transferral of a mass ritual into a private context betrays its pathological character. After the war, the mother became severely depressed. She was overheard saying, "Head off, that's what I deserve." She finally committed suicide by taking an overdose of sedatives.

The good maternal object with which Mr. C. needed to identify was deficient. In his analysis, many sadistic impulses and character traits had to be worked through. He had been unable to develop ego-syntonic controls over his unconscious aggression against his young son, who was as helpless as Werner C. had been at the age of three; he had to revert to obsessive defenses instead. His obsessive symptoms were overdetermined; they were also an equivalent of depression. His fears concerned not only his deeds but also their consequences, which to him would have meant social death: "After having committed such a crime, I would be unable to live among people; I would be either in prison or in an insane asylum." The identification with his depressed

# Ideals in the Succession of Generations

mother became evident here. In an analysis of five years' duration, he not only lost his symptoms but also improved his personal relationships and his social status.

Helmut E., born in 1939 to a high-ranking SS official, was fully identified with his father-aggressor. During the war, Mr. E. and his brother, who was three years his junior, lived with their parents in the style of a ruling élite—in hotels and county estates with servants and an abundance of material goods. The end of the war amounted to a catastrophe for this family. The father had to make his living from now on as a simple laborer—he had no other skills. The mother obtained a divorce. She succeeded in getting hold of the house the couple had owned and of the remaining fortune. The children were given in custody to the father, who soon remarried.

The father of Helmut E. tried to shape his son following Hitler's motto for the upbringing of German youth: "Hard as steel [Kruppstahl], tough as leather, quick as grayhounds." Helmut E. was brought up with many restrictions. He was frequently beaten and had to help support the family, from the time he was twelve, by working at a gas station. He had to deliver every cent he earned to his father; often he did not have enough money to pay the tram fare to get home from work. The mother controlled the boy's progress in school but otherwise remained detached.

Mr. E.'s younger brother suffered from a severe speech impairment and for that reason had to stay in foster homes and institutions from where he never returned home. Today he lives in a protected environment and is barely able to make a living for himself.

Mr. E. is now employed in a business firm. He is married to a good-natured, "soft" woman whose father died in a concentration camp where he was detained for sexual offenses. Until recently, Mr. E. was fully identified with Nazi ideals: toughness, aggressiveness, and an almost paranoid mistrust of others were part of his character armor. Only the choice of his partner gave evidence of his hope for a better way of life. Mrs. E., who had also chosen her partner for neurotic reasons, entered into a long and patient battle with him over values. She finally succeeded in "softening" him, which made him turn away from the ideals of hardness upheld by his parents. Only recently, he visited his brother, whom he had not seen since childhood, and was deeply moved by his fate. When he told his mother about this, she said, "But he did not look after me in all these years."

This case is particularly instructive because it demonstrates that the elimination of people who are weak results from an identification with pitiless parents and serves to stamp out infantile, helpless sides of the person's self. Mr. E. is now trying to find another value system. His character armor, which still

179

has preserved many features of the "master race," is hard to overcome. Cases like this tend to create countertransference problems in therapy or analysis.

Mr. E.'s psychic conflict intensified when the "Holocaust" movie was shown on German television. He became increasingly pale and silent as he watched it together with his wife. She seized the opportunity and said to him, "Now you understand why every day of our marriage in which you continue to hold up these ideas is one day too much." Mr. E. gradually developed more understanding of his wife's viewpoint and developed more distance from his parents' views.

Konrad D., born in 1938, teaches mathematics at a university; he is successful in his field. He grew up in a small German town where his father was a prominent Nazi official and, at the same time, a passionate hunter. In a vague, mystical way, the father saw a connection between his patriotism and his love for the German woods. He would have liked his son to be a wiry little hunter, but the son was a dreamy child who was more interested in intellectual and artistic pursuits. The father tried to make the little boy tough by giving him exaggerated tasks and challenges, but without success; and the father took revenge with sarcastic, humiliating remarks which undermined the child's self-esteem. The tensions between father and son increased after the father had been detained in a camp for former Nazi officials for a few years after the war. After his return, the father was more irascible and embittered than before. The boy's strivings for more independence were literally beaten down. Later, when the son was an adolescent, the father tried to win him over to his right-wing ideas and to his passion for hunting, but was unsuccessful. Instead, the patient developed into an intellectual with liberal views, and the father died without there ever having been an open argument or discussion between them.

When as a patient Konrad D. described how his father had beaten him as a child, the analyst asked how he felt now. Mr. D. smiled in a detached way that meant, "Well, my father obviously had some fascist inclinations." He was unable to overcome the intellectualizing defense that made him lose his capacity for indignation.

The following episode illustrates the same point. Konrad D. wanted to give the best mark (*summa cum laude*) for a doctoral thesis to a student whom he regarded highly. Another professor on the committee said he would not agree because he was opposed in principle to giving *summa cum laude*. Mr. D. felt helpless, unable to argue. When he reported this to his analyst, the latter said, "Your colleague has broken away from the generally accepted standard of evaluation. All theses are evaluated on a similar scale; only your

# Ideals in the Succession of Generations

colleague is deviating from it—to the student's disadvantage." Mr. D. replied, "You are right; he is incredibly arrogant." Only then could he feel some anger and become more capable of defending his views. Although he had withdrawn from his father's ideals, he had avoided a dispute with him, even in thought. Therefore, he was easily disoriented in questions of right or wrong and often unable to decide in cases of conflict.

Gerhard H., a teacher, was born shortly after the war. His father was a dentist, an honorable and well-to-do citizen, but often depressed and unable to enjoy life. It was disappointing for the boy to see how anxious and overeager his father was to adjust to others although he had a clear judgment in public matters. Gerhard H.'s reluctance to identify with his father made him shy away from adult life.

His late adolescence coincided with the student protest of the late 1960s. He adopted new models who did not stand for compromise, among them Herbert Marcuse and Sigmund Freud. Although his political activities in these years must have frightened his parents, there was no break with them. The father only kept warning his son, "You will be disappointed!" It turned out that this pessimism was based on the father's own experiences. In the Second World War, he had been an airplane pilot who went through many battles and fully identified with the patriotic, military side of Nazi ideology. As a young man, he had been a courageous soldier who loved the adventure of war. The insight that he both had been deceived and had deceived himself turned him into a resigned conformist.

Although his son, Mr. H., had not always escaped the dangers of succumbing to group influences, the ideals he had chosen for himself permitted him to mature without a break in his identity. One explanation for his capacity for development appears to be that his father had done some work of mourning for his lost ideals and had not crushed his son's self-esteem.

This case presents some typical features of the group of patients discussed in this chapter: a father who has lost his sense of personal integrity because he has fallen victim to faulty ideals; a mother who adheres to a philosophy of strength and rigor combined with contempt for the weak and dependent. The father, despite the fact that he had not been involved in serious crimes, could not convey to his son the self-esteem deriving from a harmony between the ego, superego, and ego ideal. Even more pathogenic was the influence of the mother, whose attitude toward supposedly "harmful" people paralleled her attitude toward her own children who failed to live up to her expectations.

Neither the case of Gerhard H. and his parents nor the other cases presented in this chapter give a precise description of a clear-cut psychopathology. It is impossible to conclude that a certain neurosis originated from a corrupt parental ego ideal; this ideal is not an etiological factor in itself but explains some part of the content and shape of the neurosis.

All of the descriptions in this chapter have been of male patients. Although similar conditions can be found in women, this author was unable to describe a pertinent case. Erich Simenauer has studied ego-ideal formation. While many of the observations arrived at in the present chapter concur with Simenauer's, this author was not able to find regular connections between Nazi bondage of the parents, student protest, and terrorism, although the fascination exerted by violence is a theme that may occupy the unconscious of several generations.

The impossibility of adopting an intact parental ego ideal may lead to certain structural defects, sometimes combined with other neurotic symptoms. Typical complaints are an unusual proneness to shame and a defective capacity to hold onto certain values and act in accordance with them although the patient does not doubt their validity. This constellation may occur particularly in patients whose parents maintain their inhumane ideals overtly or secretly in order to justify themselves. The adolescent children of such parents can either share their right-wing ideals and, thus, openly oppose present-day society; or they may break with their parents, who, in their rigor, cannot bear to be questioned; or they may leave the matter open and go on living with conflicting ideals.

The dream of Volker M., a patient with such a conflict, reflects the helplessness of a superego/ego ideal that has no access to an ego-determined action, because the ego is much more influenced by the id than by the superego. In Mr. M.'s dream, the patient is a terrorist who has invaded a department store; at the same time, he is an impartial observer of the scene. On the first floor of the building, the terrorist and a policeman, both of whom are armed, fight a life-or-death battle. On a floor above are three blindfolded judges, erect and immobile like statues, unable to see what is happening and unable to interfere. Mr. M. awoke in fear. He had no conscious sympathies for terrorism.

And, as this dream suggests, the relationship between history and individual pathology is, in fact, a dynamic process. As Freud pointed out over half a century ago:

... the two processes ... cultural development of the group and ... cultural development of the individual are, as it were, always interlocked. For that reason, some of the manifestations and properties of the superego can be more easily detected in its behavior in the cultural community than in the separate individual. (1930a, p. 142)

**10**

# *Child of Persecutors*

CHILDREN of those who participated in the Holocaust as persecutors have a legacy that must have affected their lives and development in many ways. We know very little about this group, for there has been nearly a total lack of published case material—even though it is likely that many children of persecutors must have found their way into analytic or psychotherapeutic treatment.

With this paucity of clinical material, the patient whose analysis will be discussed can hardly be classified as typical. It should also be noted that this patient had one important life experience that made her differ from her cohorts: she had emigrated to another European country during her latency and no longer lived in a community of people with similar past experiences that might support repressions or make certain memories free of guilt or shame. Instead, she lived in a country whose articulated values held the Nazi past in unspeakable contempt. (In passing, it might be noted that she became an expert at discerning distinctions between articulated values and disguised Nazi-like attitudes among the people in her new homeland.) She had made many Jewish friends and consciously sought out a Jewish analyst for reasons that became a part of her analysis. Much material that demonstrates drive conflicts is omitted from the following case history in order to highlight the effects that the special circumstances of her relationship to the persecutor had on her development.

When she began treatment, Frieda T. was twenty-six years old and single; she had been born in Europe just before the Second World War. Her father had died before she was born; and, when she was three, her mother had remarried. Her stepfather, whom she revered, was an officer in the German army and was killed in combat when she was nearly five. During the analysis, she discovered that he had been an SS officer and that other members of her family had participated in the extermination of Jews. Therefore, the problems raised by paternal loss were complicated by her need to keep repressed her knowledge of these facts, to maintain her idealized images, and to defend herself against (as well as to gratify) the fantasies engendered by this combination of circumstances.

Frieda T.'s symptoms on entering analysis were periods of anxiety and depression. In addition, she was unable to sustain a long relationship with a man, and recognized that she invariably provoked a situation that would allow her to leave him. She was a tall, slim, attractive woman, with a bright, engaging manner, and never had difficulty in attracting men to her. She was anesthetic during intercourse. Her last complaint was her inability to get along with her mother, who lived in a small town a few kilometers away. She found herself always irritated with her mother and with the latter's attempts to dominate her life. Her mother's attempts had become particularly evident in recent years as the mother was showing signs of becoming dependent on her.

The mother's marriage to Frieda T.'s biological father is shrouded in some mystery, for the mother said she had never loved this man, a well-to-do farmer who had a violent temper and was terribly jealous. The mother said that she had become pregnant immediately after the marriage; and six weeks afterward her new husband died of peritonitis following an appendectomy. The mother said that friends urged her to have an abortion, but she elected to go through with the pregnancy. She herself had been an only daughter and had lost her father when she was three, living thereafter alone with her mother. Frieda T. was often cared for, while her mother worked, by her paternal grandmother who lived on a nearby farm.

When Frieda T. was three, her mother married again, this time much higher on the social ladder—to a member of the country's officers corps and a graduate of an élite military academy. This gave the family a social standing far superior to the comfortable farming background of the patient's real father. The Second World War was going on, and the stepfather's activities were idealized by his stepdaughter, who knew of his élite position even among other officers, and that he was the bravest of the brave. Shortly after her second marriage, Frieda T.'s mother again became pregnant and delivered a baby boy, M. The patient had some memories suggesting jealousy of the special attention given M. in the house, but she recalled no conscious jealous feelings. It is not clear how much time the stepfather spent at home, since he was in active combat: but from various associations the analyst had the impression that she had long periods of contact with him. When he was away fighting, there were repeated rumors of his death, which turned out to be unfounded. However, when Frieda T. was nearly five, a fellow officer reported seeing the stepfather mortally wounded in a farmhouse, just before an enemy advance.

As the Russians advanced, the family moved, under primitive circumstances, toward the interior of Germany. Now Frieda T. began to feel that they must be criminals to have to move in such a manner. When the war was over, they were put in a displaced persons camp. In the camp the mother was an organizer and teacher and generally had little time for her daughter. The mother was never warm with her but always clearly respected her and expected Spartan virtues of her. Frieda T. became self-sufficient, and both she and the mother devoted their time to coddling M., who remained passive and dependent as a young man. The mother never remarried, despite several opportunities in the DP camp. In the camp, Frieda T. began to steal—an "exciting" pastime that she abandoned only two days before analysis, so she would not have to discuss it. The first object she remembered stealing was a tiny baby doll from her mother's classroom, then some of M.'s chocolate, then flowers, and later coins and objects. Before the analysis, her mother found out about the stealing. Her only comment was, "Don't tell your brother."

When Frieda T. was ten, a religious organization helped them emigrate to another continental country where they settled in a rural town. Although the family's position was eased, they continued to "live like DPs": that is, several families of the same ethnic background, without men, shared a dwelling, with each family occupying one room. Late in the analysis the patient revealed that she had slept in the same bed with her mother until she was sixteen. This practice had long since ceased to have any semblance of necessity—if it ever had; and Frieda T. rather fearfully ended it herself.

Frieda T. did not know the language of her new country but was so determined not to be laughed at as a foreigner that within several years she had mastered the language without any trace of an accent. This was a tribute not only to her talent but also to her pride, which burned fiercely and constantly and could transform the smallest issue into a source of combat. The mother was insistent that she maintain contacts with her ethnic subgroup; and Frieda T. would, until recently, recognize only her own ethnic or religious holidays, ignoring those particular to her new country. At the center of the family group was a handful of memorabilia of the stepfather: his briefcase, his wartime letters (which Frieda T. had never been permitted to see), and his picture, looking handsome and dashing in his uniform. The stepfather's birthday was celebrated annually. In spite of this effort to maintain the past, some aspects of it were notably missing: for example, certain ethnic events relating to the Second World War were remembered annually, but the patient had no grasp of where they fit into the history of the war. In fact, her knowledge of the war, which had been a part of the daily fabric of her first six years and shaped her life thereafter, was almost nonexistent. She was aware neither of the sides on which many nations had fought nor of the chronology of events;

and she claimed to have totally forgotten every German word. Hearing German spoken often gave her a headache.

Frieda T.'s first personal contact with Jews came after she arrived in her new country. In her public school she had Jewish children as classmates. She became very close with some of the poor, more Orthodox Jewish girls and was invited into their homes. The Friday night ritual, with the entire family gathered around the table, its warmth, the family-centeredness, and the reliability of the fathers, impressed her deeply. She said she had always loved the Old Testament with its unseen God more than the God of the New Testament, who walked on this earth as a man. At one point in her adolescence, she wanted very much to become Jewish. She said her knowledge of what had happened to Jews in Europe was acquired through mass media considerably after the war, and she was deeply shocked. Her mother assured her that she, too, had known nothing of what was going on. Yet there was a persistent memory of playing in a basement with an abandoned swimming pool filled with stagnant water and tunnels nearby. She and her playmates felt that the pool was filled with the bodies of dead Jews, and that the tunnels were where they had hidden.

Frieda T. lived at home during university training and then left for her professional work. Although she functioned excellently in her professional status, the symptoms and interpersonal difficulties noted earlier became more prominent. She wanted to be close to men, but in her first pre-analytic interview reported with delight that "I break men's backs." By this she meant escapades in which she would seduce a man and allow him to spend the night in bed with her without any form of direct gratification, or in some other way render him frustrated and impotent. She had no other sexual activity, and masturbation was denied. Later she would share stories of her adventures with a girl friend, D., who was similarly inclined toward men. They would exchange stories in an amiable sort of competition as to whose conduct with men would be the most outrageous. Frieda T. also managed to become "adopted" by D.'s father, who was the last and least important of a lifelong series of fathers of girl friends whom she shared. When D. decided to go into analysis, Frieda T. decided that she needed analysis for herself.

## Course of Analysis

Two interviews with the patient before using the couch were in marked contrast to her behavior once on it. Sitting up, she had been bright, open, lively, and mildly seductive. During the first few sessions she was anxious and subdued. She felt at a disadvantage lying down, and warned that she was going to make a battle out of analysis, as she did with most people of authority in her life. She said that the only way she would cooperate would be if the analyst punished or threatened her. She knew that she was starting to feel angry, and that looking at her anger was like looking at a "dangerous wild beast under glass."

Frieda T. was true to her word; within days of the beginning of the analysis, she was deep in battle with the analyst, doing everything within her means, both inside and outside the sessions, to defeat the analysis and to provoke the analyst into kicking her out or attacking her. She flouted and railed against the basic analytic rule, to speak what comes into the mind without censoring. She would tell little of her daily life and often deliberately omitted vital components from the little information she did convey, thus making it almost incomprehensible. If the analyst asked a question about any information she had revealed, that was a signal to her that he was interested: she would thereupon change the subject. There were long periods of silence, often terminated by her walking out of the sessions early, in fury. Almost all of the analyst's comments to her provoked anger. Characteristically, she would stride into the office, go to the desk and pick up an ashtray, take it to the couch, and smoke defiantly during the session. She kept careful track of the time, so that it was always she who would terminate a session by butting out her cigarette and remaining absolutely silent for the last five to fifteen minutes. Her behavior often seemed like a parody of a wartime movie stereotype of an arrogant German prisoner contemptuously defying his interrogator. The truth of this transference would, however, only come much later in the analysis. She volunteered for dream experiments, where she would tell the experimenter dreams she refused to talk about in therapy; she also had a few sessions of hypnotherapy and psychodrama, allegedly "to dilute the analysis." There was always the open invitation to apply some form of coercion that would stop her from being provocative.

With the steady maintenance of analytic attitudes toward these potentially disruptive provocations, the significance of her behavior became clearer. These activities had many layers of meaning for her, and the entire analysis might be thought of as uncovering the determinants of the behavior we have described. She could not tolerate any deviation from the schedule without going into a fury. If the analyst was one minute late, if the session was canceled for a holiday, she would become angry. The weekends were difficult times for her: on Friday, she raged because her analyst was leaving and might never come back; on Monday, she was not reassured by his presence, only angry that he had put her through so much torment. It became absolutely clear that for her a man was always in the process of leaving. He was really defined that way in her mind: "man" means "one-who-leaves." Above all else, she had to defend herself against being caught helplessly dependent upon such a creature when he made his inevitable exit.

Circumstances particular to her analysis permitted the emergence of a double transference: one to the institution tht helped sponsor her analysis; another to her analyst whom she saw as taking her on as part of "a package deal." This split represented the biological father, whom she had never seen but whom she felt watched benevolently over her, and her stepfather who had to accept her "in the package" with her mother. Miss T.'s language about conflicts of loyalty between them was sprinkled with words like "allegiance" and "traitor."

Miss T. told the analyst that at the age of fourteen, she had suddenly begun to write in a beautiful script like her real father. This was her nicest legacy from him. At this point in the analytic session, she suddenly remembered the Lord's Prayer, the first lines of which concerned her, but which she would not say. When the analyst said them for her, "Our Father, Who art in Heaven," Miss T. appeared deeply moved. That evening she was worried that she had not turned off the gas range, and thought she was going to die during the night.

What followed were dreams that clearly indicated the wish to die and rejoin her father in heaven. During this period, the patient became preoccupied with suicidal thoughts that frightened her. Dreams, slips, and associations made it evident that she was preoccupied with a fantasy of intercourse with "her heavenly father." More religious motifs came into analysis although she had previously denied any training in religious matters. It was close to Easter, and Miss T. found herself drawn to church on Palm Sunday. On the Thursday before Good Friday, she volunteered for an experiment in which a group of volunteers had blood drawn; the blood was made radioactive and then returned to them. The doctor in charge called out another person's name and beckoned to Miss T. She allowed the other volunteer's blood to be returned to her, and then told the doctor that he had probably made a mistake. Fortunately the blood type matched hers, and there was no damage; but Miss T. was frightened that she could have allowed such a thing to happen when she was all too aware of the dangerous consequences of mixing blood of different types in one person. In relation to this mistake, the patient said that she had an incredible thought that she was ashamed to say because it might indicate that she was psychotic: perhaps she was identifying with Christ in trying to be killed on Good Friday. She then recalled a line from the Apostles' Creed:

# Child of Persecutors

"He ascended into heaven, and sitteth at the right hand of God, the Father Almighty." The analyst agreed that to identify with Christ would mean just that to her: to die and be with her father. This sequence of events and associations were among the earliest of many indications that identification with Christ and the Holy Family had formed an important part of her childhood fantasies. As each layer of her fantasies was uncovered, the repressions around her religious education lifted: she would vividly recall more of the stories and pictures of her Sunday School education in the DP camp, whereas previously she had said she had no religious education, much less belief.

Much material came up in which she spoke of her mother as the "black widow spider who kills men after copulating." At the same time, she identified her mother with the Virgin Mary whose Immaculate Conception from the Heavenly Father had created Christ. Her mother had made it clear to her that a man was necessary only to fertilize and provide the best genetic material; beyond that, he had little role in a woman's life. Through a dream in which a woman associated with her mother was a madam in a brothel, a new aspect of the mother's activities while in the DP camp was uncovered. Her affairs with the black marketeers had caused the more staid women in the camp to call her by a name meaning "loose." In connection with this recollection, the patient revealed her belief that the Virgin Mary and Mary Magdalene were the same.

Before the analyst's summer vacation in the first year of treatment, Frieda T.'s rage was intense. She dreamed of three dogs, two of whom were buried (father and stepfather), and the third (analyst) was about to be. In the last session, she was fearful she would cry, a weakness not permitted by her ethnic group. Upon the analyst's return, material revealed by the patient in subsequent sessions permitted the interpretation that she was attempting to provoke him to make a sadistic sexual attack upon her.

With this interpretation emerged the first material, albeit distorted, concerning her stepfather's connection with the Nazi cause: she had a belief that, even though he wore a German uniform, he had not been a Nazi but had fought against the Nazis with guerrillas, and had died a martyr to the anti-Nazi cause. Nevertheless, she noted that she was reminded of her stepfather by a deluded man who thought he was in communication with Hitler; and she wondered how her theory could be true, since her mother received a West German pension for her stepfather.

It should be noted here that, in spite of the obvious progression in the flow of material, her overtly uncooperative behavior continued throughout the analysis, although it lessened as time went on. Still, from time to time she would think up something unique to obstruct the analysis and to frustrate the analyst. Shortly after the new material about her stepfather emerged, she had a flare-up of anti-analytic behavior even though she knew it was, like many things she did, "against the rules." She got a sense of excitement from breaking rules and felt that there was nothing wrong with doing so, as long as she was not caught. The analyst's interpretation at this time was that she felt she did not have to obey analytic rules, or many other rules of life, because she had suffered enough. Her suffering, particularly her not having been given a father, made her feel "unique"—and thus, uniquely exempt from obeying rules. The patient's response to this interpretation was typical: she gave material from her history that confirmed the interpretation and at the same time increased her anger and her provocative obstructionism. The interpretation of herself as an exceptional character had to be worked through repeatedly in numerous settings over the next few months.

Miss T. reported a dream in which the key element was a frieze of the Roman soldiers casting dice for the robe of the dead Christ, this being the subject of a tapestry that she loved. The idea of getting something from the leaving (dying) man before his departure was confirmed in her acting out and in her transference wishes. Her intense wish to have a baby frightened one part of her, since there were repeated occasions (generally before the analyst's departure) when nothing on earth, including her own estimate of the situation, could get her to use contraceptive methods.

In conjunction with a raise in the analyst's fee, Frieda T. felt that he was cheating her; although she had withheld from him her true income. She revealed a fantasy of the analyst having been an infantryman in the Second World War and engaging in bloody hand-to-hand combat with her—the enemy whom he, as a Jew, would have reason to hate. In the midst of this fantasy, she reported being afraid to lie down, feeling nauseated, and having had a sticking sensation in her throat for the past month.

Miss T. began the next session with the following dream:

I was driving along the route here and passed a radar trap. I felt anxiety and excitement, as I knew I was going too fast, and wondered if I would be caught. A police car spotted me, and a trooper in jodhpurs with a stripe down them, and black leather boots, motioned me to pull over.

The activity in the manifest dream was what she would actually do while going past a speed trap on the way to analysis. She recognized that this was what she did within the analysis as well—provoke the analyst to see what she could get away with. At first she said that she had no association or memory of the black boots, but was startled to recall, in amazing and precise detail, her stepfather's black shining boots, both inside and out. She used to love

# Child of Persecutors

them and to touch them as they were lying on the floor. She then spoke of her love for uniforms, even the sanitation workers' uniform. She then recalled a modern poem in which the poet imagines herself a Jewess and her father an SS man taking her to a concentration camp. The remainder of the dream led to material that involved the wish to orally incorporate the analyst's penis. The patient's affective response to this material was striking. She lost her flip tone and became markedly anxious, and then began seriously to describe in detail her destructiveness toward men, an attitude that she had always glorified and thought of as defensive. Now she decided that this was not so.

When the analyst informed her of his midwinter vacation, Frieda T. was furious for several weeks. Then, almost casually, she announced that she had learned several days before from her mother that her stepfather had been an SS officer. She was not noticeably upset about this news: her mother had explained that all officers above a certain rank had to join. However, in the next few weeks she began to struggle with fantasies of killing off her analyst. In the next to last session before his vacation, she sat up in an effort to control some unspecified feelings, at least one element of which, she hinted, was tears. She said, however, "In a battle, you don't show the enemy how weak you are. You always make him think you are stronger than you really are." It seemed apparent that part of the genesis of her sadistic, oral incorporative fantasies was her wish to achieve identification with her stepfather, so that she was the one who did the terrible things to others, both sexually and by desertion. The analyst disclosed this interpretation in part to her. Miss T. then recalled a childhood book written for the children of soldiers at the front, which related in patriotic terms what was going on and how children should behave. She still had this book among her possessions. In the last session before the analyst's vacation, the transference was made dramatically evident when she said, in connection with controlling her feelings about his going away, "You have to see I do it for your benefit. If someone goes away and he doesn't want to, you make it worse for him." This was said in complete seriousness about the present situation but could have had reference only to the situation of her stepfather leaving for the front and ideas she had gotten from her childhood book. She ended by saying, "Anyway, if anyone really wanted to leave you, you'd hate him so much, you wouldn't want to show him your feelings."

Following this and some events that brought up more thoughts of her mother as the "black widow spider," she reported the following dream:

I was alone in a room with a dangerous, homicidal man, whom I kept unconscious by depressing an aneurysm on the side of his temples; but my hands were bloody like Lady Macbeth's. I ran away.

In connection with this dream, Miss T. reiterated a previously expressed idea that analysis was incompatible with marriage, and so she might have to terminate. The analyst suggested to her that she was using this idea as an excuse to run away from something that made her feel she had blood on her hands. She began to muse about Lady Macbeth, and to ruminate over whether she had actually killed Duncan or had been an accessory. The analyst recalled that, early in the analysis, Miss T. had remarked in a general way that she felt that she had been an accessory, along with everyone in Germany, for the murder of Jews, and now asked her if the blood on her hands did not in some way refer to memories or fantasies about this murder or her stepfather's part in it. She then recalled that the man in the dream was someone she had read about as having been committed to a mental hospital for trying to kill his family with a gas oven. She recalled another dream in which the contents of her fish tank had been replaced with blue powder on the bottom, which stuck to the hand like the blood in the other dream. There were stone slabs on the bottom of the fish tank, and nothing was alive in it. The analyst pointed out the similarity to gas chambers, and the patient said that it could not be: she had had no knowledge of what went on, and her mother had told her that she (the mother) had no knowledge of it either.

Over the next few months, the image of the fish tank was to appear repeatedly in Miss T.'s dreams. In some, dead fish would be littered on the bottom; in others, fish were dead and put into the tank, where they swelled and were resuscitated. It became apparent there was a second level of meaning in which the tanks were a representation of her vagina and uterus—her ambivalent fantasies toward whatever was inserted or growing there.

Over the following weeks, the patient's associations were interspersed with ideas of being in battle with her analyst and of wanting to run him down in her car, which she "drove like a tank." A very old fantasy of being a criminal, of killing someone and getting away with it, popped up again, but now with guilt, not pleasure. She went back to her stepfather's being an SS man and, this time, recognized that he must have been one voluntarily; but now she explained to herself that he could only have done this because of something bad in her. At this point, the analyst told her that she had assumed the burden of her stepfather's guilt and had been punishing herself by treating herself as a criminal and sometimes acting like one. This interpretation of shared guilt was incomplete, since she also identified with him as a source of gratification and defense. The patient's response was that if he was a confirmed Nazi, she could not love him but would hate him so much she would want to kill him.

# Child of Persecutors

After the preceding material concerning her identification with her step-father was elaborated, Miss T. reported having an orgasm for the first time in her life.

At this time in the analysis, a crisis in the Middle East was deepening, and Miss T. began to worry that her analyst's involvement might lead him to leave her and die. As a consequence, she experienced an increase in ideas about stealing something or becoming pregnant. On the Friday before the 1967 Arab-Israeli war broke out, she arrived late and deeply anxious. She said that she had a dream the previous night which she felt might refer to something that had happened in reality. In the manifest dream, she was a child riding in a car with a man. He said something pro-Nazi to a doctor, and she inadvertently revealed this to a trooper with a black uniform, who was following in a car. The man was summarily taken away.

Miss T.'s only thought about this dream was that perhaps, as a child, she had once informed on someone. There were no other associations, except for the pervasive conviction that the dream pertained to something that had happened in reality.

On Monday, the day the Arab-Israeli war began, she was late for her session. She said that she was afraid to tell the analyst what she had learned by questioning her mother over the weekend, because he would hate her. At last she began, "You are my enemy." Her mother had told her that the Arabs were simply about to finish what Hitler had unfortunately not been able to complete. When Miss T. had reminded her mother that Christ was a Jew, her mother had replied that Christ had been an Arab. Furthermore, she learned that her real father had been a member of a right-wing nationalist group that had terrorized Jews before the Nazis came. He had been jailed for desecrating synagogues. He had died before the Germans arrived and allowed his group free rein, but his work was carried on by his brother, whose group was responsible for the extermination of the Jews in their town. She lamented the lack of guilt on the part of those people who had participated in these events. Only she, Frieda T., who had been just two or three years old at the time, felt guilty. Now she felt that she had "guilty secrets" from all her Jewish friends. The analyst suggested that this was an old feeling and must have been a part of the sense she had of being a criminal fleeing in Germany—because of things she had seen or heard. Furthermore, she had taken this guilt on her shoulders.

Miss T.'s guilt continued unabated: if she were still there and had not made new friends, she would have been one of those people, sharing their attitude and actions. The analyst pointed out that, as a very small child, she undoubtedly did share her community's attitudes, and that this was one of the main sources of her personal feelings of guilt. During the next week or so, she remembered that the word *Jew* was an abstraction that meant to her the same thing as "to hate." It seemed as natural that Gentiles should do things to Jews as that dogs should attack cats. She had great difficulty in discussing anything touching on this subject and was silent much of the time. Finally, she hit upon the felicitous euphemism "cowboys and Indians" to describe the state of affairs. From this phrase it was possible to reconstruct that her frequent memory of play near the swimming pool, in which she thought Jewish bodies had been thrown, and in the nearby tunnels, where she felt Jews had hidden, was probably a version of "Cowboys and Indians," with the Jews being the Indians.

She then reported a series of dreams about Jews and the current Israeli war; and in them, her ambivalence was in marked contrast to her conscious strongly pro-Israeli sympathies.* All this was new material to her. She had blinded herself for years to the virulence of her mother's anti-Semitism. Long ago she had heard her mother's statement, "We knew nothing," as an injunction to repress or deny, although Miss T. needed no external force to add to her motives for repression. How much else had to be repressed, or isolated, or denied, has been mentioned earlier in respect to her lack both of historical knowledge and of memory of the German language.

There was another marked change in her attitude toward the analysis. She seemed more human, no longer bristling at the slightest provocation. She refrained from smoking in the sessions, which had gone on almost uninterruptedly in the manner described earlier. In the next month, for the first time, she celebrated a national holiday of the adopted country in which she had lived for sixteen years.

The analysis continued beyond this point, but neither the new material nor the working through are pertinent to the issues in this book.

## Conclusion

This case material has been presented in a manner that highlights the defenses this patient used against her knowledge of her family's participation in Nazi activities. Repression, denial, isolation, and reversal were the primary

---

* When her ambivalence to Israel was pointed out, she responded sarcastically, "I am neutral in thought, word, and deed." This reference to the words of a U.S. State Department spokesman about the conflict was meant to convey her observation that other very respectable people had shown ambivalence about the fate of Israel's Jews.

defensive modes. But for these mental mechanisms to operate, a sense of guilt is needed to motivate defenses. Thus, a most interesting problem this patient presents is: Why did she develop the idea that sadistic treatment of Jews was something to feel guilty about? She described a milieu in which none of these activities would be a source of guilt any more than a dog feels guilt when it tears, or aims to tear, apart a cat, or than the cowboys in children's games feel guilt when they destroy Indians. She spoke perceptively when she said that, but for events, she could have become like them: killers without guilt. Certainly the usual moral identifications would hardly tend toward guilt over anti-Semitic feelings; instead, insofar as she identified with her mother, her stepfather, or her true father, she would become the Black Shirt or "black widow" who deals sadistically with others. It would be instructive, therefore, to consider some of the forces that interfered with the transmission of unconflicted anti-Semitic attitudes.

First of all, Germany lost the war, and she lost her fathers. As a child, Frieda T.'s world was so shattered that parental omnipotence as a source of security, and therefore of loving identification, could not be maintained. She began to think in the primitive logic of the loser: there must be something wrong/criminal in me or my tribe that would cause such a calamity to befall us. That she was "rescued" by a church organization made the religious teachings of the displaced persons camp (run by the sect) of a high order of interest to her. During the analysis, she would recall with great clarity the page and the illustration of each heretofore forgotten religious lesson. It is of interest that these teachings had to be repressed in order for her to maintain her major identifications.

But Christian religious teachings can themselves be a powerful source of anti-Semitism. Moreover, cataclysms have befallen other groups, whose defeated values have nonetheless been perpetuated and further idealized—as, for example, the post-Civil War Southern attitudes toward Blacks.

Miss T.'s mother was unable to sustain or idealize Nazi values, although she tried and had succeeded more than the patient understood before her analysis. Her mother failed to transmit the belief that killing Jews was justified, because—from the time Miss T. was five years old—she had lived in a social climate that regarded her mother's anti-Semitic attitudes as literally unspeakable. In the postwar world, even covert forms of anti-Semitism were seen as shameful. By not being able to say explicitly until June 1967 that she favored the extermination of Jews, her mother could not effectively counteract postwar articulated social attitudes in which anti-Semitism was inevitably linked to Nazi atrocities and strongly condemned.

The unconscious memories of, and identification with, the Nazi figures were complexly intertwined in symptoms that were evoked by Miss T.'s current conflicts over libidinal and aggressive drives. These identifications appeared also as character traits that, at the beginning of the analysis, were ego-syntonic. One can speculate that, under continuous social endorsement, the identification with the anti-Semitic attitudes and other ruthless traits of both parents would have come into full play.

If these possibilities existed for this patient, one can only wonder what the psychological balance of forces might be in those who did not experience parental loss, did not emigrate, and had no possibility of relationship with Jews as friends. For while there is much in this case to be hopeful about in the remarkable potential of the human spirit to rise above circumstance, there is much to convince us that the dark forces that caused the Holocaust are transmitted to a new generation by identifications that have a profound influence on each child's development and taming of primitive drives. The total social climate and prevalent conscious group attitudes may play a significant role in determining whether these identifications will remain largely unconscious and a source of conflict, or will be permitted to come into the open as desirable qualities in a totalitarian society with values like those of the Nazis. It would appear that no generation or society can afford to be complacent about the problem, for although identifications may vary, the potentially destructive drives that must be modified by development are common to us all.

# 11

# *A Victim of the Other Side*

SHOULD MY PATIENT ever read this, I ask him to forgive me for publicly presenting intimate aspects of our working relationship and the life experience he entrusted to me. The unavoidable distortion that ensues in transferring this experience from an intimate to a public, theoretical context must be distressing and offending. In the hope that our common, painful efforts might contribute to understanding and peace everywhere, I felt the insights gained from this case should be made available for publication.

## *Introduction*

In connection with research on the psychoanalyses of patients whose parents were Holocaust survivors, Judith Kestenberg and her colleagues in the Group for the Psychoanalytic Study of the Effect of the Holocaust on the Second Generation noted an unusual reaction on the part of analysts who reported cases. Hardly any of these analysts were able to associate, with the historical events of the Second World War, certain anxieties and material verbalized or acted out. Fragments of memories, dreams, and fantasies presented by their patients were obviously related to the experiences of their parents under the Hitler regime, but could not be adequately understood by the analysts in the therapeutic situation.

As an example of this phenomenon, Kestenberg (1979a) referred to the analysis of a boy whose mother had been imprisoned by the Nazis. The boy told the analyst, in the first session, that he was afraid of getting stuck in a tunnel where he would suffocate from gas. Kestenberg described with astonishment the failure of the young analyst and her supervisor to connect the child's fears with the mother's past. Moreover, this material of the first session was never referred to by either patient or analyst for the duration of the treatment. The analyst's non-interpretation in such cases needs to be examined within the framework of countertransference problems.

Only by admitting that I had countertransference difficulties similar to those pointed out by Kestenberg, am I able to present the case reported in this chapter. It is the analysis of Dietrich L., a thirty-four-year-old man whose parents had been avowed Nazis. This fact was clear to me all along, for Mr. L.'s father had worked as a government legal official in Vienna just before the Second World War, while the family stayed behind in a German town far away. Also, his mother had belonged to the *Deutsche Christen* ("German Christians"), which was a front for persecutors of the *Bekennende Kirche* ("Professing Church"), a group that opposed the Third Reich. Dietrich L. never told me directly that his parents were Nazis, nor did I ask—this being unconsciously a taboo subject and part of my countertransference reaction.

It is important to give some information concerning my own personal background, in order to make my countertransference more intelligible. I had just turned four when the war broke out, and experienced the sharp contrast between war and peace. My parents neither belonged to nor sympathized with the Nazi party—perhaps the reason that many of Mr. L.'s attitudes and ideals, which reflected the political atmosphere of that time, were incomprehensible to me. An example of such attitudes is conveyed in the following statement that Hitler made in 1939 to his commander-in-chief and generals a few days before the war began:

I shall present propagandistic grounds for starting the war [with Poland]; whether they are believable is irrelevant. The victor will not be asked later whether or not he told the truth. In starting and carrying on the war, what is important is not what is right, but victory. (Quoted in Gebhardt 1976)

Although I was well aware of similar idiosyncrasies in my patient's behavior from the start, I was unable for a long time to deal with them and the feelings they aroused in me, at least not to the extent required by the analytic situation (see chapter 8).

## The Patient's Background

My initial encounter with Mr. L. took place at the university psychiatric hospital where I was then working. He had a powerful body and his dynamic movements lent him a certain vitality; but at rest, sitting in a chair, in clothing that a farm boy in earlier times might have worn, he made a shy, pale, and helpless impression. The youthful face and boyish haircut underlined this bashful self-consciousness. I did not notice at the time that this hair style had gone out of fashion thirty years before. The reason he gave for seeking analysis was an earlier serious depression which had lasted several months. He talked as if the depression had been imposed on him from outside; it had been triggered by the fact that for the first time in his life a vocational goal he had set for himself had been denied him by others. He felt annoyed and insulted. I realized later that this depression, while real enough, had been less the cause of his seeking treatment than his interest in pursuing a new vocational goal. The depth of his reaction aroused my sympathy and perhaps also the feeling that he really should not have to undergo such a depression again. So I became involved; without my realizing it, the preverbal contact was stronger than the verbal one. Mr. L. related his life history in brief outline form, and some of it struck me as strange: he had failed twice in grade school and later had not been able to pass even relatively easy examinations. In spite of this and in spite of the fact that he seemed to be very tense, his expression revealed an appealing warmth and openness. The man seemed so stable and impressive that I failed to recognize his naïveté, his need for support, and his tendency to cling. I sensed his hopefulness and an unexpressed yearning to change himself, and so agreed to an analysis.

The patient had been trained as a business consultant, and was married and starting a family.

He mentioned casually that he would like to become a psychiatrist. Because at that point I underestimated the degree to which he identified in a most concrete way with someone he considered to be in a more highly regarded profession than his own, I did not take his casual remark seriously. By identifying with that person's profession, he sought to take on his or her vitality and ability to work creatively. Although this concrete identification was recognized as inadequate and pathological, it seemed that the healthy side of Mr. L.'s motivation would provide a basis for his development in analysis.

From the information the patient provided in this initial interview, the following biographical framework could be reconstructed. Dietrich L. was born a few days before the outbreak of the Second World War. A son at that time in Germany was a potential soldier and would carry on the family name; and young Dietrich's blond hair and blue eyes further fulfilled the Aryan ideal. He must have been his mother's crown prince. His brother, one year younger than he, had been less successful, had not even finished school, and probably had not received as much encouragement as Dietrich L., who seemed to have been his mother's favorite. She supported all his plans and activities, hardly imposing any restrictions on him.

Shortly after Dietrich L.'s birth, when general recruitment had just begun, his father volunteered for service at the front. He not only fought as a soldier, but also took on the duties of a judge in court-martial cases. After 1945 he was a prisoner-of-war for several years, and thus Dietrich L. was eight years old when his father finally came home.

## The Analysis

After a few minutes of silence, Mr. L. began the first session of his analysis by holding up his hands and saying to me: "These are my hands, they are the hands of my father. My father has blood on his hands." Not receiving a reply, the patient proceeded to say that his father had been awarded the Knight's Cross, first and second class, and had been decorated for hand-to-hand combat. Mr. L. explained that this type of ribbon was awarded to those who had seen the whites of the enemies' eyes five times. His statements sounded like a declaration, and I was so impressed I failed to notice that I was also deeply shocked. I was involved inwardly with the macabre way in which the patient had equated his own hands with those of his father. The concreteness and the confusion of this gesture disturbed me, and I began to have doubts about his ability to think logically. By involving myself in theoretical reflections about this form of defense, I avoided my initial shock. I said nothing, even though I then felt that a response on my part might have helped to clarify the emotional side of Mr. L.'s statement. He himself said nothing further about the matter. It is possible that an intervention in the first hour would have been premature. I hoped that he would come back to this important scene at a later time—at a point when he himself would find it easier to return to it within the framework of our working alliance. I also consoled myself with the thought that Mr. L. would certainly think of the guilt suggested by the bloody hands—a thought that had occurred to me immediately. This proved to be a false expectation. I never forgot the scene; my patient, however, retained no memory of it. Only later did I realize that this scene had constituted a threat. My reaction to his opening words—the fact that I had avoided confronting the patient by not putting into words the emotional experience—was to determine the whole constellation of transference in his analysis. Without meaning to, I had become passively involved in a situation in which I actively witnessed his potential violence. The patient experienced this as an initial victory: he had subtly induced me to take part in his defense mechanisms.

Two factors were presented in this initial scene: the patient was like his father, and the father had been capable of taking human life. At the time this analysis began, many years after the lost war, no one in Germany boasted about his war medals, certainly not about the kind Mr. L.'s father had attained. But Mr. L. apparently identified himself with the victorious father of the war period and thus with the murderous element in him. He had revealed to me the supposedly admirable but also threatening greatness of the father, and that conflict with him or his conflict with his father could end in only one tragic way: it would cost someone his life. In other words, the patient was afraid of being murdered or of becoming a murderer himself. This dramatic beginning of the transference relationship contradicted my expectations as an analyst: the patient began with an immediate challenge to fight in an unusually direct and threatening way—it was almost an assault. Normally an analyst expects to be needed by a patient to help him through the stages of perception, experience, and presentation to an understanding of himself. Here, however, I was suddenly confronted with the demand that I take a stand. What occurred was a reaction: survival. I held my breath and was at a loss for words, a reaction similar to the reflex of one who, confronted with an expression of insanity, plays dead in order to ensure one's own psychic survival. In this extreme situation I found myself suddenly disarmed and without analytical tools. Erich Simenauer has commented on similar difficulties:

The analyst, faced with a patient's undisguised fantasies of violence and extreme self-depreciation, may find that his generally recognized and familiar psychoanalytic world threatens to collapse, especially when theoretical and technical adaptations are not available. (1981, p. 16)

As the analysis got under way, Mr. L. began to boast about the glorious aspects of his childhood. Since neither the admiration he expected nor an interpretation of his boastfulness was forthcoming, the patient repeated the performance with even more vigor. For fear of undermining the trust that normally exists between analyst and patient, I listened without questioning as he described the world of his childhood. In this world there were luxurious furnishings, many works of art, numerous servants, as well as the family's scholarly tradition and its connections with European aristocracy. The family's abundant possessions included a large collection of antique arms and armor, which had never frightened him although he had intimidated others with it. This residence constituted a kingdom or enclave in its own right. Those who lived there were not dependent on commercial exchange or the services of the outside world. They took pride in this autarchic independence, failing to realize how isolated they were. Scorn from others only fed their pride. Beyond recounting old memories, Mr. L. was trying to bring to life—in an almost concrete way—the flavor of an epoch of over thirty years ago. Yet he was not able to associate freely. The concrete descriptions of his childhood, which had an almost eidetic character, stood like isolated islands next to one another. He had not yet developed an adequate method of communicating with himself and others.

Allying myself with the help-seeking part of the patient, I not only perceived his repetitious attempts to impress me as defenses against criticism, but also as an appeal for help to make sense out of the petrified world of his childhood. He needed me to help him grasp the affective meaning of these association-particles, to bring them back to life, to internalize them, and to put into perspective the idealized pretensions and lack of human relatedness that characterized the family and dominated his formative years. This rump of a family, which had no father at its head, was guided by the demands of war and the hope that Hitler would be victorious. The patient related how one Christmas Eve the grandfather, followed by all the children, had stomped into the room decorated with the Nativity scene, singing:

"Bei Austerlitz da hat es gedonnert und geblitzt
Die Preussen haben ihr Blut geschwitzt. . . ."
("At Austerlitz stormed thunder and lightning,
The Prussians sweated their blood. . . .")

It seemed to me that, with this soldier's song, the grandfather was trampling not only on the Nativity scene, but also on the children's feelings. However, instead of crying, the children laughed proudly and triumphantly, pleased to be making so much noise and trampling on the normal feelings of others. Since the patient expected help in defining and evaluating reality, I confronted him with the inappropriateness of his grandfather's behavior. I spoke out more and more to aid him in the creation of a firm basis for the new norms and the new values he was developing.

In sharp contrast to his noble birth and family tradition, Dietrich L. had been a failure in school from the start. Twice in grade school he had had to repeat a year, and later failed his school graduation examinations. He also failed to pass the simplest tests when he attempted to pursue the career of a professional soldier. In analysis he realized that his failure in the army had been due to a psychological block he experienced when he had to hold a rifle and put his finger on the trigger. Only after he had left his family and experienced failure in his army career did he manage, in a sudden and almost mad burst of intellectual effort, to pass school graduation exams without external help. He then went on to become a successful business consultant; he had studied first in economics. During the first year of analysis, while working on the gradual diminution of his overt grandiosity, he was writing his dissertation.

All of Mr. L.'s associations sounded like statements of fact. He expected to have everything he said to be taken at face value. It is likely that his mother had handed him a great many categorical truths without explaining their meanings. He treated me as he must have been treated by his mother. Two recollections, most probably screen memories, illustrate his difficulty in relating to his mother and to others and reveal the source of the disruption of his emotional and intellectual growth. One of the incidents that must have distressed him greatly, and was never forgotten, goes back to the time when he was eighteen months old and his brother still an infant. His mother laid him down on her bed and left him in the care of a housekeeper. In identification with his rejecting mother, he "laid the incident down" before me in a detached manner. At the same time, he was making a concealed accusation that his mother had treated him badly. He described another incident from the time he was a small child and was standing on his mother's lap just about to put his arms around her. At this moment his mother seized him under his arms and swung him down beside her on the ground. This type of behavior on the mother's part revealed her overall attitude toward him which, in its cumulative effect, constituted a trauma.

Mr. L. adapted himself very subtly to the analytic setting, so that ostensibly everything seemed in order. For instance, he never came too late, and he paid for the analysis himself and always on time. He seemed to have associations—the statements of fact already described. He also reacted to interpretations. Yet these cooperative attitudes were integrated into a defensive strategy Mr. L. called "turbulences," expressed in tension and small "fights" with me.

While writing his dissertation, he felt an urge for the first time to develop a project step by step, although his impatience caused him difficulties. He showed some independence: he began to study medicine while holding down a full-time job. Pleased with this progress, I was all the more surprised that his success seemed to mean nothing to him. He called his success an obeisant prostration to society. My function, I began to see, was that of a flunky who is not supposed to ask questions; I was simply the host in a parasitical relationship.

Much time elapsed before insights gained in analysis resulted in real changes. For a long time, however, by adapting superficially to my expectations, Mr. L. led me to believe that he was changing, while actually he seemed to be engaging me in a subtle power play. For instance, I had questioned the fact that the only shoes he owned were a pair of clumsy wooden clogs. I thought that he was learning to stand on his own two feet when, after a year of analysis, he decided to exchange the clogs for sturdy, elastic leather shoes. Then I discovered that these actually had belonged to his father, who discarded his shoes at the first signs of wear. In a way this was a progressive step, in that he was identifying with his father, but at the same time it was a kind of trick: the patient enjoyed having found a solution different from the one that I had expected. I sensed that he needed such silent tricks in order to protect his autonomy. Much later, when this power play was no longer necessary, he did purchase his first pair of leather shoes, which gave him blisters but also the experience of standing on his own two feet.

The development of real autonomy had been retarded by the patient's grandiose fantasies, to which his childhood experiences had contributed. No boundaries had been set up to limit his needs and drives. On the contrary, young Dietrich had received active help in denying and distorting reality. No one educated him to recognize and respect the fact that certain activities were dangerous. When he burned some of his neighbor's things, instead of being punished he was given money to pay for the damage in case the neighbor complained. When he was digging trenches in the garden and a tunnel under the property line, he was probably identifying with his father, who dug trenches to undermine enemy lines. He was never scolded for such invasions of other people's rights. In analysis he remembered how proud he had been that his underground invasion of a neighbor's garden went unnoticed. He expected me to approve of his reckless behavior, while I expected self-criticism. He did not seem to be capable of this, for no one in the family had ever criticized him. Someone—perhaps the housekeeper or another servant—must have told him when he did something wrong, but someone else must have advised him that he could ignore the standards of such lowly people. Nevertheless, the servants' values must have made an impression on him, for although he remembered nothing of his relationship to the housekeeper, he frequently visited this modest and spontaneous woman after he started in analysis.

The educational ideals of his family environment, as well as those taken over from the Third Reich, had distorted Mr. L.'s emotional life. These educational maxims decreed, for instance, that a child must be inured to hardship at an early age, in order to develop strong powers of resistance, both physical and mental. Feelings were considered effeminate and were to be completely suppressed: one did not feel the cold; one did not succumb to a natural urge and rush to the toilet; a boy certainly did not cry or give way to fear but showed courage and strength. He had to achieve an early mastery of his motor activity so that he could reach his goals despite emotional hindrances. Sympathy and pity only hindered the hero. An aggressive attitude was seen as a virtue, and a premium was put on courage and valor.

The patient had a conflict: he was unsure whether he should give spontaneous expression to feelings or deny them with heroic stoicism. He did not know whether he should develop guilt feelings and allow himself to cry. I had the impression that he wanted me to tell him that his ideals were not realistic and to restrict his excessive behavior, so that he would no longer feel compelled to be the valorous hero who climbs up to the housetop and over the roof. As a boy he had been consoled for bad school marks with money from his grandfather, who had apparently been similarly unsuccessful in his school days. Although the grandfather took on the role of the father, he did not do so in the sense that he represented the paternal principle with a sensible No. His attitude of "We don't need anybody" gave his grandson a false sense of autonomy. The mother was upset that even in grade school her son did so badly; their common efforts to do the homework did not help. However, when one teacher, about whom Dietrich L. was most enthusiastic, succeeded in teaching him something, the mother dismissed her. Only the mother was allowed to love and help him. She was unable to tolerate bad marks. She scratched them out with a sharp knife and substituted better ones. No one in her family could do badly; the teachers were at fault. So two value systems developed side by side: one at school, the other at home.

Although the father was away during the first eight years of his son's life, the boy sensed his presence. The patient remembered seeing his father for the first time when he was fifteen months old and the father had come home for the brother's christening. This first encounter had not left a very deep impression on him, he said. He also remembered experiencing his father's presence in many indirect ways. He described, for instance, the strange changes in his mother's mood when the daily letter from his father arrived. The letters must have suggested a relationship between father and mother that he could not comprehend. On the other hand, at mealtimes the mother would set him at his father's place, with his napkin in the father's napkin ring. Young Dietrich also sensed that this place did not really belong to him, and that he might have to give it up one day.

Although he suffered a decisive physical separation from his mother with his younger brother's birth and the substitute care he, Dietrich, received from the housekeeper, his mother maintained an intimate secret tie with him. The following scene illustrates the nature of this tie. In front of the family house stood a chestnut tree. He liked to climb this tree, move out along the branches, and then suddenly separate the twigs from one another, appearing directly in front of his mother's second-floor window. This madcap behavior did not result in physical contact with his mother, but it succeeded in bringing a smile to her face and a light to her eyes. His mother must have approved of this dangerous game, or her son would not have repeated it so often. Her smile at such moments must have been especially important for his self-affirmation. Unfortunately this also meant the affirmation and finally internalization of those ideals that encouraged ambitious and bold exploits. Courage and physical agility were not enough in themselves but valuable in excess. His mother herself displayed an agility and a daredevil behavior that he admired.

His mother's expectations and approval were of utmost importance to him. External failure, which would have been unbearable for both of them, had to be avoided at all costs. He was convinced that physical and intellectual prowess were innate characteristics, a sign of the elect that one either had or had not—and thus felt obligated to perform extraordinary feats. Courage turned to recklessness. Any form of training that required prolonged or serious effort was looked down upon. He had been nominated to the Olympic team, for instance, but declined the nomination as if there were no further need to prove his athletic superiority. He also told me that he had matched the record for the one-thousand meter race. Later I found out this was the record for women—a fact he had not thought worth mentioning.

The bond between mother and son entered the transference relationship, becoming visible in an incident analogous to that of the chestnut tree scene. One day I was looking out of the third-floor window just before my patient was due to arrive. By the side of the road, at least twenty yards from the window, stood a chestnut tree. Mr. L. came on his bicycle, and we saw each other just before he passed the chestnut tree. A second later he skidded on the wet road but did not fall. I expected that during the hour he would mention what had just happened. Since he did not, I did. He was not aware that, when he caught my eye, he had been thrown off balance and had almost fallen. He surprised me by claiming that I had looked uncertain. He had suppressed his disappointment that I had not smiled in a certain way, and projected his feeling of uncertainty onto me. He went on to say that from my point of view it must have looked as if he were coming out of the chestnut tree: that is, he could see himself only as he imagined he would have looked from my point of view, assuming that I experienced the same feelings as his mother did. Through this episode I realized for the first time the extent to which he held fast to his mother's ideals in order to maintain symbiotic omnipotence, and I sensed how greatly he was frustrated in his attempt to separate himself from her. The patient had a false self: himself as seen through the eyes of his mother as her partner in the pursuit of mutual ambitious ideals.

After I had succeeded in showing him the complex nature of his relationship to me and his mother, he was overcome with hatred for his mother's wishes and ideals, which were "like cold lights . . . held out far ahead of me so that I could never reach them." At times his hatred took on grotesque proportions. Observing his mother's behavior toward her grandchildren, he decided that she was insincere and unnatural, and tried to expose her in front of the family. At the same time he was totally desperate. He hated himself for having given way to the temptation inherent in his symbiotic union with her—having been seduced at a period in his life when he had not yet developed the ability to resist.

The patient suspected that he had needed his father and yet was frightened of his father's return and of the changes that would then take place in the family. On the day before his father returned, Dietrich fell from the chestnut tree for the first time; thus he acted out the fall from his father's place in a most concrete way, for he was unable to bear all the happy and sad feelings connected with the latter's return. Dietrich L. had always denied these emotions, and so all of his subsequent relationships remained emotionally shallow, while the relationship between mother and son continued to grow in its unshakable symbiotic omnipotence.

The boy's fear of his father increased when he found out that the latter had conducted kangaroo courts and ordered deserters to be shot. He remembered hearing about three people whom his father had sentenced to death: one was a parson; another, a student; and the third he could not identify. Both he and I came to understand that he was afraid the third person could have been himself. The mother's scorn for the father, who had failed to return victorious from the war, was shared by the son. He told me for instance how ridiculous it was that his father sometimes suddenly had to find a toilet just before an important appointment. Mr. L.'s contempt did not prevent him from experiencing the very same symptom in the course of the analysis and suffering from severe diarrhea when changes in his emotional world and scale of values were imminent. He had been misused by the family and made to serve as its representative in its continual derision of the loser-father, who in many ways personified the collapse of the promised grandeur of the Third Reich. The family had been incapable either of mourning its loss or receiving the returned father with compassion; and the mother had failed to help her child integrate the new image of his father.

Up to this point I have described the most significant and formative aspects in the patient's childhood. His contacts with his mother, father, and grandfather were the most important. His brother and cousins might have been playmates, except that Dietrich L. hardly ever played games. Instead, he roamed about the house, garden, and countryside. He took great pride in knowing how to deal with other children. He followed a certain ritual: he would take them by surprise, "beat them up," and take over as their leader.

In his relationship to girls, Dietrich L. followed a maxim of his father's: "There are two kinds of girls: the kind one takes and the kind one marries." Following this rule, Mr. L. had had satisfactory sexual relationships at an early age. In analysis, he mentioned by name only one of his girl friends. He remembered that his passionate feelings for her had confused him, but only now did he recognize that she had indeed been his first girl friend. When, after a long period of friendship, she was ready for a sexual relationship, he discovered that he was impotent for the first time. The friendship was broken off immediately. Twenty years later he was able to understand how this break had come about. The girl had expressed a desire he could not satisfy, because satisfying her desire would have meant making her a gift. He identified himself with the Führer; and a Führer does not give gifts: he gives orders.

During the first years of analysis, the patient succeeded in drawing me into his egocentric world. Slowly I began to understand that he regarded me as his admirer. Much later he told me with conviction: "You are only my audience." I came to realize that my interventions were much too careful and delicate, giving too much attention to multidimensional and subtle meanings. He could not understand me and needed something much more concrete, immediate, and direct. We both realized that we were having trouble communicating. Often, with simple nonverbal gestures, he tried to show me what he was all about. He would throw his fist into the hollow of his other hand, saying: "That's me—there. Don't you understand?" and this gesture made me feel uncomfortable and increasingly irritated. More and more he complained that he was able to express himself only indirectly. The gesture with his fist revealed the inner dynamics of his drive and thought processes. Every wish demanded its *immediate* satisfaction, and every idea its *immediate* realization. He had no understanding of psychodynamic processes. When his hands became sweaty during the analytic hour, he drew on his knowledge of the behavioral sciences, and declared that his perspiration reflex was similar to that of a monkey: sweaty hands make climbing easier; one even spits into one's hands in order to get a better grip on a shovel. The patient overlooked the fact that in both cases, the monkey's and his own, fear and flight were involved. He knew of no conscious fear. Much later I understood this more fully. He sweated blood as did the Prussians in the soldier's refrain his grandfather had sung, and this sweat represented the blood on his father's and his own hands in the initial scene of the analysis.

The patient's repetitious, monotonous, and—as I thought—reproachful la-

# A Victim of the Other Side

ment that if he "only had feelings, . . ." became very annoying. Since he was, in fact, hardly capable of allowing himself to have any emotions, his statement was correct. Yet somehow his lament seemed shallow. His later complaint, which replaced the first, seemed more genuine: that he was lacking "a certain something." Although this "something" was intangible, his repetition of this simple statement seemed to be demanding something concrete from me, as if I could manufacture it at will.

It was only well into the analysis that I realized how retarded was the patient's emotional growth, and also how little he had changed in spite of the intensity and duration of the analysis. He had not made any friends. His relationship to his wife and children as well as his behavior at work seemed unchanged. He had married a woman whose personality was similar to his own. She pursued the same ideals and, like him, tried to achieve the impossible at the expense of the many children Mr. L. had fathered during the analysis. She took on "male" activities, although she was urgently needed as a mother; she resembled the patient in that she had no definite gender identity. As a pair they mutually reinforced each other's avoidance of sexual difference and the accompanying maturational process that this difference induces.

In my countertransference during the beginning phase of the analysis, I had felt that the patient was putting me under a great deal of pressure. Although he cooperated in a superficial way, he seemed to have a private goal that I could not understand. How difficult it was to communicate with him is exemplified in the following excerpt from his analysis. For the first six months of analysis, the patient always had an erection when he stood up to say goodbye to me. When I finally talked to him about this, he had no idea why it should warrant any attention. It was for him a perfectly natural and familiar reaction that he experienced, for example, when he picked up his crying children in the middle of the night. He felt no emotional excitement with such erections. I understood this reaction to be a concrete, somatic precursor of an affect that had not yet gained access to his psyche. His reaction was similar to that of a baby who automatically has an erection while his mother is bathing him or changing his diapers. Since this phenomenon was ego-syntonic, I was not able to apply traditional psychoanalytic techniques in working with the transference. For him, psychic change meant physical change; for example, he often went hungry in order to become a man with a strong sense of will.

In his essay "On Symbiotic Omnipotence" (1969), M. Masud R. Khan described how angry he had become with a patient who had not changed at all during his analysis. He realized that the symbiotic omnipotence of this patient and of other such patients could not be treated with the usual technique we apply to neuroses. To work through the transference of symbiotic omnipotence, he had to limit the "acting in" transference and take an active oppositional stance. Only then could his patients understand the ego-syntonic nature of their acting out behavior. Instead of analyzing unconscious fantasies, he analyzed their formation, and that was only possible when the patients' fantastic intentions and manipulations could be translated into verbal descriptions.

Mr. L.'s behavior and my response to it bore a striking similarity to what M. Masud R. Khan has described about his patients and himself. The persistence of the symbiotic omnipotent state prevented Mr. L. from developing mature ego functions. Part of his immaturity, however, was the result of pseudo-debility, which he cleverly employed as a kind of defense mechanism to conceal his grandiosity. He needed me to be unambiguous and to draw the line, for he was not used to being given a clear Yes or No. For a long time I was unaware of the pseudo-debility; slowly, my feeling of being misused and misled grew ever greater. Outside the analysis, the patient continued his irresponsible behavior: in an unreflecting and uncontrolled manner, he continued to act out his ideas in reality in a way that I considered indiscriminate and that threatened the security of his family. For instance, he made thirty mistakes on a single page of a letter he wrote for his employer. I recognized that this was due to his pseudo-debility; for he was in fact capable of writing faultless letters and passing difficult examinations without help.

Mr. L. had built up and preserved his delusions of grandeur by every possible means. His behavior reflected that of the contemporary demon as prescribed by Hitler. I had been working on the diminution of Mr. L.'s grandiosity for some years before a decisive breakthrough occurred that enabled him to take up an independent search for principles and values, to reflect and mourn. I had been irritated by the fact that Mr. L. neglected his professional duties and spent hours every day reading psychoanalytic literature. Impatience had prevented him from completing his medical studies; and he had taken a short course in nonmedical, mystical therapy and opened a practice in order, like myself, to carry on "psychotherapy." He spoke about a woman patient who had talked about her troubles and then looked at him, and said he saw in her face and felt in himself a "transference." For a long time I was in doubt about whether to confront him with the alternatives of giving up either the analysis with me or his own practice—an unusual step in an analysis. When I did confront him, I discovered my countertransference reaction: that is, I had feelings of doubt and responsibility that should have been the patient's. I was able to show him how this reaction had set in motion an action on my part to confront him with a choice. Mr. L. immediately decided in

A Victim of the Other Side

favor of his analysis. What I had not foreseen, however, was that this decision would plunge him into a psychotic episode. At its onset, I introduced a parameter by asking the patient to sit up. Since his attachment to me was firm and dependable, the psychotic episode lasted only two weeks and could be kept under control. He lay down on his own when he felt better and could understand me again. At that point he said that he was taking on the responsibility for the analysis.

Unusual contents came to light during the psychotic period of minimal ego control. His comment that I was a mere audience, which I have already mentioned, was the first unusual statement that he made after I gave him the ultimatum. He expressed his dismay and could not understand why I had become "disloyal." He said expressly that I had been pregnant with him, and wondered how I could drop him like this. Although startled, I recognized what I had long suspected—transference in the form of a symbiotic omnipotence. He was panic-stricken at the feeling that his penis was part of him but "loose in his vagina." He was terrified that at any moment I might seize it for myself. In spite of the impression of power he conveyed, he had never understood how insecure his sexual identity was, and how threatened and threatening he felt in his relationship to me. He seemed possessed by the polarity between power and helplessness. Up to that point, he had known no fears. Now they were elementary, concrete, and overpowering. His only salvation lay in combat. He was so caught up in some of his fantasies that he did not know whether they were present reality, memories, or products of his imagination. Suddenly he saw the room in which he was sitting as a battleground. He felt that he was hiding behind the curtain with a rifle. Then he wanted to crawl along the wall under the "cover" of another curtain to cut off my only avenue of escape through the window. He imagined a comrade outside the house who would shoot me if I managed to get away from him. Had he been a child, one would have called this scenario a game. Yet a child would have had a different attitude toward the game than did the patient. In an earlier session he had told a story in which his father's orderly had saved the father's life during the war by throwing himself in front of the man, and had lost an arm as a result. I now pointed out to him that in his "hand-to-hand combat" with me he was identifying with his father and imagining that the orderly was outside to protect him: at a later point of the crisis, it was understood that this episode represented a war between the analyst and the patient. The psychotic phase waned in a short time, but the insight gained from it became the most authentic part of the analytic work. Had I understood the meaning of the initial scene (in which he raised his hands, saying "These are my hands . . ."), I would not have been so surprised by the occurrence of the psychotic episode.

After this difficult but beneficial ordeal, the patient was no longer so dependent on concrete, immediate experiences. For the first time, he was able to relate preconscious fantasies and to realize that he had dreams. At first his dreams would disappear when he woke up or their remnants were transformed into what seemed to be forced fantasies. He would begin with a remembered fragment, gradually turning it into an elaborate fabrication of the moment. This was probably due to the ease with which the patient could glide into another reality.

Past dream content merged with present fantasy content, and he was not able to tell the difference, apparently lacking an internal sense of time. This peculiarity became more blatant in his delusional suspension of time—as if no time had passed since the Second World War. He described his elaborate war delusion as though it were currently taking place, and as if he had been aware of existing in this other world for ages. In his delusion the whole of southern Germany was under his command. Between distant mountain ranges he had dug trenches where not only soldiers sat but helmets were mounted on movable poles to deceive the enemy. There he shifted whole divisions from place to place. Escape plans for him alone were to guarantee his survival.

Thus, I discovered that the patient lived, at least in part, in a world of delusions. Kestenberg calls this psychopathological phenomenon, which appears sometimes in victims of the Holocaust and their children, a "pseudo-psychosis" (see chapter 7). With his delusions of war and victory, this patient denied the truth about the past and denied that Germany was a loser. In this he was faithfully continuing the glaring denial of his whole family who, because of their rigid ideal, refused to see that the Second World War had ended with defeat and the father a failure. The patient lived two lives in one with one part of the ego consciously insisting on reanimating the past. There ensued a distortion of reality that operated before the psychotic episode revealed its extent. Mr. L., for instance, bought himself a house far away from his place of work, claiming that this house was far from the airport and that the range of hills in between provided some security in case of attack. If this strategically important airport should be captured in a war, it would be impossible to reach him with certain tactical weapons. Not until I discovered my countertransference in which I denied the patient's "double life," was I able to help him to recognize the division of his life into two realities; he began to understand that, to him, war was simply either victory or defeat. Defeat meant death: he was afraid to put this thought into words, and in analysis he had to work his way toward the recognition of the victory = life and defeat = death polarity over and over again. When I seemed to him victorious, he literally went out of his mind. Five years after the beginning of the analysis, I reminded him of the "raised hands" scene he had enacted in the first session. Although he could not remember it, he accepted my recapitulation of it and immediately recognized the threat it contained. It came as a shock to him when he realized that, by the standards of present-day reality in which there was no war, death by killing would be looked upon as murder.

The patient was now capable of more painful insights, his psyche no longer fettered. He realized that he would have to change all the values he had believed in. The development of a new moral system took some time. He had been brought up according to the "norms" of a double morality, and rigorous clarity was needed to reevaluate them. He often accused me of putting him on the defensive, especially when I confronted him with present-day reality and tried to help him be honest with himself. He found me aggressive and stubbornly resisted the transformation of newly acquired insights into real development. Instead of changing himself, he passed what he considered to be my restrictions on to his children in a stern and inflexible manner. He also converted the process of internalizing insights into functional disturbances, suffering from digestive problems and violent diarrhea. These symptoms, which had been familiar to both of us in the course of the analysis, now became more understandable. At such times he felt that it was all too much for him, and he reacted in an anal way and let everything drop. In summary, this phase was characterized by his confrontation with limits and restrictions, with his anal obstinacy and passivity, and with his search for a new moral system.

DREAMS

The first dream he had in the course of analysis was composed of three scenes:

1. The analyst had a baby. During the day, when patients come, the baby is not there. Only on Wednesday afternoons, when the analyst is free, does she attend to the baby. [The patient explained that he did not like any of this.]
2. He is in a prison camp. There are many barracks and, far away, barbed wire around the whole area. He does not know why he is a prisoner and in this camp. With great effort he decides to flee. It seems to him as though he has succeeded in escaping into the woods, but then something happens. It was as though he wakes up in his dream and discovers that he has only moved up one hut in a whole line of barracks. So he is still in the same camp among the same hungry figures, lying awake on a cot.
3. He sees a garbage dump heaped up with empty cans and packing materials, the refuse of a well-to-do civilization. Under a tree in front of this mountain of garbage stand two other garbage containers. The leaves of the tree are all eaten away, and on

the branches perch many emaciated birds that are hardly able to stand. On one twig sits a fat young bird which seems to be the only one alive. Next to it sits an emaciated mother bird, whose head is almost completely engulfed in the open beak of the fat young one.

From this series of dreams fresh hope could be drawn for the further progress of the patient. In the first dream, the patient saw himself; he wanted to be my baby. For the first time, he allowed himself to give expression to this wish. He enjoyed feeling secure with me and sought continuity in our being together, even on Wednesday, when we had no hour. At the same time, the feeling of being left or put aside, which he had experienced as a child, became more alive. The patient also saw in the baby his brother, of whom he was jealous and on whom he took revenge by depicting him as abandoned in the dream.

When the patient reported the dream of the prison camp, I took the opportunity to ask what he knew of his father's past. He asked his parents about the war and the Third Reich, as he had done before when he began his analysis. Once more, his questions evoked the same strange reaction of utter silence, known to him from his childhood. They left him in despair. The few stereotypical stories about war experiences that he had been told again and again were like isolated islands, incomprehensible and not intended as empathic answers to the pressing questions of a small child. With his dreams the patient had now attempted to comprehend by trying for the first time in his life to identify with his father's fate. Through his dream and his understanding of it, he was able to experience how he basically felt himself, deep down, to be starving, imprisoned, and isolated. He shuddered when he said that this dream could also represent the self-punishment for his arrogant and grandiose presumptions about himself. This physical shudder, which occurred often after his psychotic episode, was his way of bringing about a psychic experience by initiating it through body sensations. When he became more capable of expressing mature affects, his reactions went beyond a physiological reflex to include psychic representation.

In the third dream, he recognized himself in the fat young bird that takes the head of the mother in its beak. He saw in the bird a greedy creature that had not only eaten away the leaves and everything in those mountains of cans, but had also sucked the vitality out of his mother as well. The bird had completely consumed its own world. He himself pointed out the bird's inability to become independent, since despite his intake of food he did not have enough strength to be creative and to relate in a vital and personal way to people or things. His interpretation was in keeping with my own countertransference feelings: the patient had taken from me again and again—he might even take my soul. Through oral incorporation, he hoped to gain that "certain something" he lacked.

In his childhood, Dietrich L. had been prevented from developing the natural potentials of his psyche. He had been duped with a false system of values and with an ambiguous morality that led him to believe in the pseudo self-sufficient, grandiose world of his mother. The lack of the "certain something" must have referred to his lack of general vitality. After working through the dream material, the patient felt for the first time guilt and shame in relation to the analyst. He saw that he had been searching for something to consume. In the feelings of guilt or shame that had started with a physical shudder, this "something" came to life in him for the first time.

THE TALE OF WITZELSPITZEL

These dreams introduced the last phase of treatment. The patient took more initiative and was able to reconstruct an important part of his own history. By chance he found in a second-hand bookstore a fairy tale collection that he knew from his childhood. Although it did not even cost a fourth of what he paid for an analytic hour, he found it hard to persuade himself to buy it. He had the idea that the book was his and should be given to him. He told the tale of *Witzelspitzel*, written by Clemens Brentano (1778–1842), as follows:

Once upon a time a king loved a young nobleman, Witzelspitzel, and showered presents upon him because he was clever and well-behaved and served the king with great skill. This aroused the envy of the other young courtiers. Because the king wanted to possess the countries bordering on his own, he wished to have as his queen the lady to whom all of these lands belonged. In order to please her, he had to be her first suitor on a certain day when she was going to church. He deliberated about how he could arrange this. The courtiers suggested that Witzelspitzel should steal the horse of the giant Labelang: this would ensure that the king arrived first. Witzelspitzel was ordered to steal the horse, and everyone thought that the giant would kill him. With great cunning Witzelspitzel was able to dupe the animals guarding the stall, steal the horse, and bring it to the king. The king was indeed the first to reach the lady and they married immediately. The courtiers, who were then even more envious of Witzelspitzel, convinced the king that the precious garments of the giant would also suit him very well. Witzelspitzel should fetch them. The king was taken with this idea and gave Witzelspitzel the order. But this time he had to take something not just from the barn but from the giant's own chamber. The animals who guarded the giant were tricked by Witzelspitzel in such a clever way that they themselves brought about their own deaths. Witzelspitzel brought the garments to the king. The royal family was struck dumb with admiration, and kissed and embraced the young hero. But his enemies were beside themselves with anger because he had once again escaped the giant. Now they suggested to the king that the palace of the giant would also suit him well. And the king, who was rather childish and who wanted to have everything, turned again to Witzelspitzel, promising him a reward. This time Witzelspitzel killed all the inhabitants of the castle in a most cruel way. He killed the giant's wife, her child, and finally the giant himself and then brought the key of the castle to the king. As a reward he asked for the princess and the castle itself, which were given to him.

In light of the discoveries made in the patient's analysis, and extending them to the understanding of the patient's milieu, the following interpretation of his favorite story suggests itself:

None of the characters is open about his goals; all motives remain hidden. The hero has three assets—good manners, cleverness, and skill—all of which he devotes to the fulfillment of the king's wishes. His own wishes remain a secret until the end of the story. The king loves him for his "devotion," which makes the aristocrats envious. Since they cannot bear their envy, they want to destroy the good relationship that Witzelspitzel has with the king, even if it means Witzelspitzel has to die in the process. The king, in turn, wants the princess only in order to extend his kingdom. He conceals this motive and delegates all the risk taking to the hero. His greed, together with his lack of initiative, cause him to push the hero into the most foolhardy exploits. So the king knows no measure and has no consideration for other people, not even for the beloved boy who is to take up the fight with the giant for him. The boy is enthusiastic and willing to exhibit his prowess in order to receive more love and, finally, the reward. Confronted by an almost impossible challenge, he extends his powers to include cunning and deceit. In the process he becomes indifferent to the lives of other people. Although the hero has capabilities of his own, he uses them not as *he* sees fit but as a delegate wanting to remain the royal favorite. In the end he becomes like the king himself, taking the other man's goods. Finally he allows the king to give him what he himself had stolen for the king.

Having a wish and fulfilling that wish are split between two people, neither taking the responsibility for his action and each achieving his goal without guilt feelings. Underlying all of this there is a latent homosexual wish for identification with and passive enthronement through the mighty figure he serves. The king misuses the boy's love by exploiting him for his own great ends. Hence, the hero's courage is transmuted into daredeviltry. The reciprocal achievement of aims hides the initial abuse. Witzelspitzel can enjoy the fulfillment of latent homosexual wishes and grandiose fantasies by living gloriously in the castle the king gives him, without having to think about the fact that it was he himself who used violence in obtaining the castle in the first place. At the end of the story, therefore, we can see what Witzelspitzel has been hoping for and working toward all along: he knows immediately

# A Victim of the Other Side

what his reward is to be. Yet we can also see how the king's greed and his inability to provide a model of discipline, justice, and moderation lie at the bottom of all the destructiveness.

This tale had often been read to my patient and it was his favorite. Now he was shocked to discover in it the greed, envy, brutality, and perversion of human relationships. During the months that followed, he was confounded again and again when he recognized the barbarous impulses he harbored.

During the latter part of the analysis, elements of the oedipal constellation, with its concomitant tolerance of the third person, appeared. Just before the end, a number of symptoms flickered up for the last time. The questions that came up again clearly in the terminal phase were: Who had won and who had lost? Who was a hero and who a victim? Who lived and who had been murdered?

A year after the analysis was over, I found lying on my doorstep a bouquet of flowers with a greeting and Mr. L.'s address. It was like a letter from the front, but not like those that his father had written: it was the former patient's first real gift.

## Conclusion

The following factors were instrumental in shaping this patient's personality and his fateful development: the predominating presence of his narcissistic mother, the absence of the soldier-father, and the historical background against which these parents were clearly defined. Without knowledge of the historical background, it would have been difficult to understand the severe psychopathology of this patient, especially the occasional tragi-grotesque incidents that occurred during the analysis. On the other hand, his particular fate embodied the traits of the Third Reich and its means of achieving grandeur which involved de-individualization, destructurization of society, and primitive aggressiveness. It behooves us to examine how the development of this patient's object relationships and the ideology of National Socialism were interwoven.

### THE ROLE OF NAZI IDEOLOGY IN THE PATIENT'S FAMILY

It is difficult to judge whether the first year of Dietrich L.'s life was satisfactory. The mother must have felt that her sturdy, blond, blue-eyed baby boy, corresponding to the Aryan ideal and therefore belonging to a special race, enhanced her own narcissistic worth. Her preoccupation with his nutrition and continuing physical growth were in keeping with National Socialist principles for rearing children—that is, with the promotion of physical growth together with psychological toughening—that led to the avoidance and suppression of all tender feelings. Such concerns made up the main themes of the patient's bird dream. Nevertheless, even if the mother's care was biased in this way, it seems to have stood him in fairly good stead during the first year. The patient's hypermnestic ("remembering with unusual clarity") description of the sudden unpleasant change in his world when his mother laid him on the bed and left him, suggests that he had experienced the previous period as satisfactory.

Dietrich L. was thirteen months old, a vulnerable age in respect to separation-individuation tasks (Mahler et al. 1975), when his development was complicated by his brother's birth. This forced his separation from his mother, causing him to feel insecure and narcissistically injured. Since his father was not present, the pre-oedipal triangulation could not take place (Abelin 1971), which would have been necessary for a successful separation.

When this little boy felt deserted by his mother, he consoled himself with the fact that he could function as a substitute for his absent father, and from this he got a new sense of importance. He was told that he could sit in the place of his father at the dinner table, and his mother ascribed to him qualities of heroism and courage, which rightly belonged to his father. Normally courage and heroism are associated with such qualities as boldness, intrepidity, intelligence, and intellectual as well as physical skills. In Hitler's regime, however, these qualities were taken out of the social context of fairness and respect for the other, and physical assault on the helpless was accepted as a measure of heroism. The demands of the superego were distorted, vice becoming idealized in lieu of virtue (Kestenberg 1977, 1981a). Apparently Mr. L.'s mother not only furthered "virtuous" vices in her child but even insisted upon them. As a small child, he sensed the nature of her expectations. Later, they were reinforced by rewards. Inasmuch as the mother expected qualities in the child more suitable to the father, while neglecting the former's specific talents and needs, idolization took place.

Khan (1979) defines *idolization*, in contrast to *idealization*, as an overcathexis of an external actual object. An ideal is abstract and can never be attained; an idol is concrete and can be realized. This idolization is then sustained by painfully achieved ego attitudes and ego functions as well as by id investments.

Idolization therefore entails a mental exploitation of instinctual components and primitive psychic processes in the relationship to an external actual object, in this case

# A Victim of the Other Side

the infant-child. . . . In this climate of mother-child relationship, the child very early on begins to sense that what the mother cathects and invests in is at once something very special in him and yet not him as a whole person. The child learns to tolerate this dissociation in his experience of self and gradually turns the mother into his accomplice in maintaining this special created-object. The next step in this developmental schema is that the child internalizes this idolized self that was the mother's created-thing. This, in my clinical material, usually happens around the oedipal phase when these mothers suddenly become self-conscious about their intensive attachment to and investment in their child and withdraw abruptly. Hence these children seem to experience a belated separation trauma at a stage where their ego can register it more acutely. They register this as panic and threat of annihilation and especially as abandonment (unconsciously). (Pp. 12–13)

That the mother idolized her son as her hero, using him for the narcissistic completion of her self, prevented the development of a mature object relationship. This was particularly evident in the boy's constant repetition of the chestnut tree scene. Satisfactions based on approval—for instance, through his mother putting her arms around him and giving him the satisfaction of her physical presence—were impossible. His inordinate efforts, therefore, never attained completion: he had to do it again and again. The deep and unbridgeable gap in their relationship was represented in the chasm between the high chestnut tree and the window. It seemed as if the two people, mother and child, were standing eye to eye, as though they were physically near to one another. Yet is was only in the face of this dangerous abyss that the patient was able to harvest what he needed for his psychological growth: the glow and smile on his mother's face. He fulfilled his side of this unspoken agreement, which guaranteed his sense of greatness. He was unable to refer to this openly, for it would have meant breaking a tacit agreement. This explains his silence in respect to third parties and his inability to communicate with himself or to associate in the analysis.

The mother's behavior toward him seemed to the patient like an enthronement: she spoiled him and set him up on an unrealistically high pedestal. If the father had been physically present, perhaps some of the patient's fantasies of grandeur that fed his grandiose self would have been corrected. Kohut (1971) has called attention to the pathological persistence of infantile grandiosity in personality structure. The phantom presence of the father caused an exaggerated idealization of the Father-Imago, instead of its normal de-idealization. Furthermore, the absence of the father as a guide in mastering reality probably resulted in a distortion of the patient's hopes and thoughts about the future to come after the final victory. The emotional toughness to which he had been trained would not allow him to recognize the fear lurking behind these hopes, a fear equated with a weakness and a hindrance to their realization. The idealization of extreme behavior, present in stories about the father's daring escapades, encouraged this child to act out dangerous stunts that were way beyond his age.

The maintenance of his grandiose self prevented a normal development of ego functions, and was also of decisive importance in the development of drives. Especially in the anal phase, this meant a limitless expansiveness of aggression which remained ego-syntonic. Anal obstinacy added a defiant streak which insisted on satisfaction, come what may. Whenever he was denied something he could not obtain by cheating or stealing, the patient became very upset. His bad temper became apparent when he drove his clenched fist into the hollow of his hand, a sign that he could not tolerate frustration. Any desire had to be satisfied immediately so that the distance between experiencing a want and its satisfaction was practically obliterated. As a result, there was no room for the accompanying affects that usually elevate a drive to the level of a psychic experience. He had never known the experience of waiting, hoping, fantasizing about surrogate satisfactions, exercising patience, and enjoying full satisfaction. He was not capable of weighing possibilities, of modulating or varying his feelings. Premature satisfactions or rewards prevented the cultivation of his feelings. As a result, the satisfaction of his drives remained physical, crassly elementary, and overpowering. His thoughts suffered from his inability to form more realistic and stable representations and symbols. He had to rely on concreteness and on false abstractions (see chapter 15). Shame, guilt, and a sense of social consciousness could not develop normally. On the contrary, invasion and expansive behavior—as well as an unscrupulous attitude toward other people, their feelings, their possessions—were rewarded rather than punished.

The life style of Dietrich L.'s family did not further the development of genuine autonomy. The family lived in an enclave, nursing the glorious feeling of being special, thus reflecting the values of the German Reich at that time. The subjective grandeur of this ideology contained the insane certainty that the impossible could be achieved. Within this framework one felt not only independent and privileged, but lived according to one's own laws, in the illusion of self-sufficiency. It was an almost paranoid system according to which people outside it were either enemies or worthy only of scorn. One's greatness was exaggerated further through the degradation of others. Lies and forgeries could be used to support such a mentality; they constituted an alternative truth in the service of this hoped-for better reality. Guilt or shame were thus expendable, and the traditional ethical and moral values dispensed with. Beneath the state of ecstasy lurked a sense of emptiness and dreariness. As in

# A Victim of the Other Side

Beckett's *Waiting for Godot*, the family lived in a state of suspense, waiting for the final victory that never came, while they became inwardly lifeless.

Under normal circumstances the father could have provided an integrative function and endowed the family life with meaning, with a sense of the present and the future. The father, however, was at the battlefront, and the grandfather's traditional emotional and social values had been irreverently perverted. He encouraged taking advantage of others and seemed to have followed Hitler's 1933 suggestion that the Lord's Prayer be converted into a prayer for present-day hopes. Thus, he could desecrate the Nativity scene by singing a German militaristic song. Identifying with the grandfather, Mr. L. supported the corrupt conqueror world of the Third Reich.

Mr. L. was not able to identify with his real father, but identified rather with the phantom-victor-father who was the narcissistic ideal of the entire family. This was a masculine identity mediated primarily by the mother. The patient, however, just like his favorite character Witzelspitzel, yearned to be made great by a passive enthronement through the father, his majesty. The homoerotic attitude reflected the patient's diffuse sexual identity. He experienced his masculinity as something that could be taken away, as something "loose" in him.

Behind the personal heroism of the phantom-father loomed a bigger contemporary idea: the victory of Hitler and the establishment of the Thousand Year Reich. Thus, Dietrich L. developed his Führer's qualities and imposed his will on other children. The patient said that his mother carried the "cold lights" in front of him to egg him on. He did not dare fail; it was a constant unconscious obsession and an utterly existential matter. Just as it was not permissible to feel anxiety while striving to achieve an illusion, the possibility that the goal might *not* be reached was unthinkable, for this would have involved disgrace. The means for achieving the goal was combat. To lose in combat meant not just disgrace, but the end of the promised greatness and therefore also the downfall of the self: it meant death. For Mr. L., being defeated in war meant being murdered, a horrifying possibility that he, in his delusion of victory, managed to deny. The role assigned to and accepted by him of prospective victor was actually a double role of victor and loser. Thus, in adult life Mr. L. suffered under the constant fear of having to kill or being killed. He had to be a victor in order not to be a nothing.

The existential character of this patient's identification with the victor is evident in the Third Reich's assumption of hereditary greatness: "Either one had it or one did not." This ideology manipulated those who wanted to belong to the select into compulsively undertaking extreme and foolish actions that required an exaggeration and perversion of drive tendencies. The promised reward was always just beyond, luring them on.

Within this atmosphere, Dietrich L. identified with an ideology, not with a real person. The return of his father from war and imprisonment meant for the boy, therefore, not only another abandonment by his mother but also a confrontation with reality. His father was not a victor and not at all the figure with whom the son had identified. The narcissistic anger due to the boy's disappointment developed into hatred of the father and an unconscious undermining of his own self-respect.

Hannah Arendt wrote on ideology: "An ideology which has to persuade and mobilize the masses cannot choose its victims haphazardly. The fact that a myth and a falsification is believed is more important than the fact that it is a falsification" (1958, p. 7). In order to establish the situation in which an ideology can flourish, the longing for regression must be stimulated in the masses—regression to the immature symbiotic state of grandiose omnipotence. Children are even more vulnerable than regressed adults. The children in the second generation, therefore, whose mothers transmitted the ideology through the early object relationship, were not only influenced but cumulatively traumatized.

In a paper on "Antisemitism and Nazism" (1962) Martin Wangh traced the allegiance of Hitler's followers (expressed in Nazi terminology as "devotion to the Führer"—a matter of belief and unconditional loyalty) to a psychic splitting-off of hatred. In Wangh's view, these followers were like their Führer, in that they reacted to fear and guilt with massive defense mechanisms. According to Wangh, the willingness of a large group to leave the verbalization of hatred and the responsibility for persecution to the Führer, must have had its roots in early experiences of a particular kind. One can recognize in the childhood history presented here a continuation of such a pathology into the next generation.

The splitting mechanisms, described by Wangh, are apparent in the fairy tale of Witzelspitzel, which is an excellent representation of the absurd social interactions that prevailed in the Third Reich. In it a reciprocal exploitative form of bondage guarantees both parties fulfillment while allowing each to escape responsibility for his actions. The incorporative identification with the other in the service of self-completion prevents genuine satisfaction, on the one hand, and the development of guilt and shame, on the other. This form of relationship, which Khan calls symbiotic omnipotence, allows the exploited aggressor, acting on behalf of another, to demand the fulfillment of his own drive-wishes through the exploitation of another victim.

Mr. L. also needed another person in order to establish again and again the omnipotent symbiotic object-relationship that has already been described. The other person was essential for his self-completion. This was perhaps one reason for his choice of career. Not only did his clients need him; he also needed them for his self-vitalization and enhancement. In ego-psychological terms, this patient could be described as having poorly developed self- and object-representations. He was dependent on splitting mechanisms and on the establishment of a false-self and its concomitant false-object.

The patient was right in looking upon the analysis as a path leading toward his real self, but for a long time his habitual form of life continued; transference merely brought about a continuation of the already existing symbiotic omnipotence. As to the scene with which the analysis began, I now see in it his attempt to involve me as an accomplice or false-object in a reconstruction of the archaic symbiotic interaction. He was to be my hero. Thus, when the patient extended his hands toward me, I was supposed to seize them so as to become his leader, for they were hands that were prepared to shed blood. He expected me to take pride in his self-sacrifice, through which he sought his right to exist.

THE ANALYST'S COUNTERTRANSFERENCE

To return to the countertransference difficulties mentioned in the beginning of this case study, and in particular to my apparently inexplicable tendency to remain silent for so long, it seems that there were four reasons for my behavior.

First, little is known thus far about the psychological structure of such a patient, so that for a long time I had no theoretical ideas on which to rely, and my general policy was to remain silent in a critical and unclear situation.

Second, I was shocked by the absolute either-or quality of the patient's acted-in transference and by the pressure I felt Dietrich L. was putting on me to act out with him an archaic mother-child relationship. One of the two was to be sacrificed; the other was to become the murderer. I wanted neither to be sacrificed nor to feel that I was a murderer who, by manipulating him, would deprive him of his real self.

Third, in order fully to understand the patient's transference, I needed, even if only for short moments, to feel what it was like to be part of his mother-child interaction. I would have had to identify in part with the psychotic delusion of grandeur and the insane ecstasy. I would have had to experience his inner alienation and falseness. It is likely that I refused to go far enough with such an empathic identification. (See chapter 8.)

Fourth, as a German, with a background very different from the patient's, I nevertheless had to carry a burden of immense guilt and shame in connection with the Third Reich. I would have had to identify myself, however briefly, with "the other side," with National Socialism. This is a much too difficult, and perhaps also threatening, task for someone who lived through those years of barbarism and insanity, and whose psychic survival and sense of self-worth depend on an identity that abhors them. It was impossible for me to set aside my condemnation. I could, at best, try both to mellow and to demonstrate my disapproval through silence.

My silence was clearly a result of countertransference difficulties. The question, however, is: What would have been a more adequate reaction? It could be that silence was necessary, at least in the beginning, in order for the pathological symbiotic form of transference to develop, and in order for the patient to feel safe with me and not be overwhelmed by anxieties from the start.

COMPARISON WITH CHILDREN OF SURVIVORS

If we proceed to compare the findings in this case history of a child of avowed Nazis with those reported in the research on children of the persecuted, we discover some remarkable similarities. Like the children of some of the surviving Jewish parents, Dietrich L. was given the feeling that he belonged to a chosen people, except that, in his case, this did not occur within the framework of a genuine tradition, but instead was embedded in the Nazi ideology and craving for admiration and power. The patient's parents denied their unbearable disappointment over the loss of promised grandeur, and, not unlike the persecuted parents, zealously passed on to their child the task of vindicating them.

As in the case of some of the Jewish children, the oral and anal-sadistic phases of development were emphasized by the parents, so that, through the modalities of oral incorporation and anal-sadistic offensive maneuvers, the child could obtain a superior position in the object relationship (chapter 8). Due to the intense trauma of persecution and merciless declaration of their worthlessness, some Jewish victims suffered from conflicts based on simultaneous identification with both the persecuted and the persecutors, and transmitted these conflicts to their children. In a similar way, Dietrich L. was caught up in his double role as victor and vanquished, and so resembled those children of Jewish survivors who identified with the aggressor as well as with the victim. On both sides it was a matter of life and death. In the case of the children of the persecuted, fear of death was an existential reaction to extreme danger that their people had actually experienced. Mr. L. as a victor anticipated death from the retaliation of the persecuted (Kestenberg 1977, 1981a). Neither set of parents could come to terms with the past and they carried it over to the present. Both sets conveyed, to their children, the past as present-day reality. The Jewish parents could not come to terms with the intensity of the trauma they had suffered. Dietrich L.'s parents could not come to terms with the collapse of the Third Reich. Mr. L.'s parents were unable to reintegrate their superegos, because parts of each had previously split off, to be delegated to the Führer. Furthermore, they did not genuinely mourn their misfortune (M. and A. Mitscherlich 1970).

Because the past was still alive for both sets of parents, they were unable to talk with their children in a way that would have helped them to understand the past. The children on both sides, while suffering from lack of verbal communication with their parents, were nevertheless given an important mission via nonverbal channels. Jewish children were to rehabilitate their parents and restore to them their lost dignity. Dietrich L. was to undo the loss of the war and attain victory.

The children of both persecutor and persecuted felt called upon to repair the fatal events in the histories of their parents (Prelude and chapter 3). Since they were burdened with a task stemming from a past reality that was incomprehensible to them, they could only act out what had been engraved, but not integrated, in their parents' memories. Thus, a second reality was actualized in the present reality of these children, but they had no insight into its points of reference. The result was the suspension of time, which—together with the persistence of symbiotic omnipotence—allowed the illusion that the parents' past fate could still be changed. This meant, however, that battle and persecution had to be carried out continuously and endlessly. The ego distortion caused by the second reality, and by the simultaneous contradictory identifications with perpetrator and victim, resulted in insufficient means for adequate repression and reality testing.

Kestenberg has called the overlapping time schemes a "time tunnel"; the phenomenon of an artificially actualized second reality, a "pseudo-delusion"; and the process of shunting a piece of the parent's past into the present, a "transposition." She speaks of an integration of the past and the present in the ego of survivors' children and of the ego strength generated by the task before them. In Mr. L., ego distortion resulted from his efforts to make room for a second reality.

The second generation's elemental fear of victimization appears later. It can appear in the individual's development as a form of castration anxiety. It continues to generate distrust and an artificially forced autonomy which, in both types of patients, may take the form of physical efforts to strengthen the will through fasting, suppression of feelings, and other forms of self-control. Perhaps another similarity in the second generation of both sides lies in their inability to form friendships other than a relationship with the immediate partner who is needed for self completion.

Mr. L. sought "great rewards" as he pursued a mission, and thus was able to retain a sense of hope, a hope that allowed him to exercise his generative function and establish a large family. In reality, this was a misdirected hope and did not give a good foundation to his family. It took an enormous psychoanalytic effort to help him reintegrate his family. Although survivors had their hopes more profoundly shaken, and their very survival through procreation attacked, they, too, were able to build families.

Because of these similarities, the technical parameters employed are similar or identical in both sets of patients. Also in both it was essential to react to pertinent associations by linking them with their parents' past during the Third Reich. In both, countertransference analysis was much more important than in other cases.

Mr. L. differed from the children of the persecuted in that his parents were not traumatized by a serious threat to their physical integrity; at worst his father would have died a hero's death. Mr. L. also differed from most survivors' children because of his symbiotic transference, which defied recognition by me. For a long time it looked as if the patient were adapting to me and to the conditions of analysis; yet it was actually I who adapted to him and his inner reality. The purpose of his pseudo adaptation was exploitation: that is, the establishment of a parasitic grandiose self on the shoulders of the host. Thus was blurred the fact that I and the patient had very different value systems and attitudes, and that I, orienting myself by my own values, tended to reproach him. The misconception that we shared a similar inner reality sometimes led to a sense of helpless despair in both of us. I became aware of the fact that his true-self was still much too weak and insecure to recognize and give up his false-self. The suffering due to the necessity of this false-self had the quality of urgent distress.

There are many more differences between the second generations on each side. The most pronounced similarity lies in the charging of this generation with the task of repairing the parents' past. This feature can be conceived of as a cumulative trauma (Khan 1974, Grubrich-Simitis 1979). Breuer and Freud (1893) linked this phenomenon of cumulative trauma with hysterical neurosis (see also chapter 14), and a quotation from them illustrates what is common to children of the persecutors and children of survivors:

Observations such as these seem to us to establish an analogy between the pathogenesis of common hysteria and that of traumatic neuroses, and to justify an extension of

the concept of traumatic hysteria. . . . In the case of common hysteria it not infrequently happens that instead of a single, major trauma, we find a number of partial
traumas forming a group of provoking causes. These have only been able to exercise a
traumatic effect by summation and they belong together in so far as they are in part
components of a single story of suffering. (Pp. 5–6)

The children of both persecutors and survivors suffer from cumulative
trauma. In 1962 Wangh pointed out that Christianity and Judaism represent
a cultural unity, and that persecution of the Jews as carried out under Hitler
ultimately threatened the very existence of Christianity itself. Similarly, the
second generation of both sides together form an essential unity. The destruction of the one side inevitably led to the victimization and downfall of the
other side.

# 12

# The Shadows of the Past

WHEN in 1914, the poet Hugo von Hofmannsthal and the composer Richard Strauss were working on the text of *Woman without a Shadow*, they differed about a short scene in which, for dinner, the dyer's wife gives her husband roast fish, which symbolizes unborn children. Strauss thus criticized Hofmannsthal's ideas:

One gets the impression that the husband would eat this fish; an act that would be considered without taste. Please reconsider this; maybe you should omit the phrase, "The heavenly aroma of frying fish and oil" in order to avoid misunderstanding.

Hofmannsthal replied:

Frankly, I consider your objections to the eating of fish too precise. The fish are not the children themselves, they have only a symbolic meaning. I can't imagine that anybody could take offense—most nursery rhymes are similar. I don't see any reason to change it. (Strauss and Hofmannsthal 1978)

Considering the matter further, Strauss became even more disgusted than he had been originally. He reasoned that, if the fish symbolized unborn children, the impression would be relayed on stage that the children had been fried by the mother and eaten by the father.

Ernst Kris (1952) maintained that illusion in art invites us to a unique experience. During a performance we may allow ourselves to be pleased by what is ordinarily not pleasing—that is, by something originating in unconscious conflicts. Through his questions, Strauss revealed his tensions and fears which were aroused by the idea of infanticide. To him, the play suddenly became serious and literal. He revolted against a symbol that disgusted him. Hofmannsthal's reply was realistic, uncomprehending, and even patronizing. For him, the esthetic aspect of art prevailed. Nevertheless, Hofmannsthal's diaries and other works (1959) revealed that he, too, was involved in a personal generational conflict. The longer he dealt with the material for *Woman without a Shadow*, the more he distanced himself from the folk theater he had originally planned. Germany and Austria were then in the throes of the First

# The Shadows of the Past

World War; another generation of young men was forced to murder itself. Hofmannsthal himself increasingly avoided his family and friends after his father died in 1915. One day after his favorite son committed suicide, Hofmannsthal himself died. What children meant to him is revealed in his diaries: "These unborn children are the improved mirror-images of their parents. Parents gain self-realization by gaining their children." When his narcissistic mirror shattered, Hofmannsthal shattered as well. He had placed great hope in his son's career as a poet. Perhaps he expected his son—in his "unborn" poetry—to achieve what he, the father, could not attain. Was his son capable of fulfilling his father's great expectations? Could he and should he have taken a different path without incurring the hate of his father?

When we talk of ogres, as Hofmannsthal did, we think of fairy tales and child's fantasies. However, not only children but also parents can be afflicted by a "mental cannibalism" toward their children—a parasitic relationship in which, under certain circumstances, parents expand at the expense of their children and cause their destruction. There is also an internal cannibalism within the psychic apparatus in which one set of functions triumphs over another, sucks it dry, empties, and destroys it. This cannibalism is illustrated in Hofmannsthal's *Woman without a Shadow* where the empress needs the dyer's wife's shadow to save her husband from petrification and thus to humanize him. Yet she decides to refuse what she desires most—that is, to relinquish her and her husband's personal happiness—for the good of the dyer's family. Strauss referred to the empress's decision as "something unnatural," because she seemed so "obsessed by the concept of her own humanity that she considered only the sorrow of the dyer and his wife and has forgotten the emperor totally." The solution of the empress's conflict lies in a sacrifice of her instinctual drive and the humanity of her libidinal object in favor of her ego ideal. The fulfillment of the latter's demands takes absolute precedence over the other aspects of her self. Her loyalty to her parents—represented by the dyers—triumphs over the healthy drive for self-preservation.

The arguments between Strauss and Hofmannsthal form the introduction to this chapter because they foreshadow the conflicts arising in the second generation, born after the Second World War. Nazi ideology intrudes into the psyche of children of Nazis. In today's analyses we are faced with the question whether the adherence of loyalty to Nazi parents erodes the young Germans' self-preservation, or whether the latter save their psychic structure from erosion by gaining insight into their parents' malfunctioning, and separate from it. The theme of *Woman without a Shadow* was suggested by a patient, born of Nazi parents some years after the end of the Second World War.

# THE PERSECUTORS' CHILDREN

## Data from Analyses of Children of Nazis

The effect of the Nazi period on the second generation, born after 1945, was evident in five patients in whose dreams and fantasies Nazi uniforms and Nazi emblems appeared. These patients experienced themselves as the "Jews" of their parents' generation, as the persecuted and the hunted. Born and raised in postwar Germany, they had had no personal experience with Nazis. However, since puberty, they had been interested in the subject of National Socialism. When they questioned their parents about their Nazi past, the children were met by a silence that could be felt even when parents gave answers. Cold and reserved, the parents sounded like history teachers in school. They did not refer to their own participation in the Nazi party, even though they had been active or passive members of the organization and ideological disciples of the Nazi system. Some parents had gained a great deal from the changes instituted by the Third Reich. The concealment of the Nazi past went so far that some people erased traces of their former existence and changed names as well as residences and careers. However, despite the effort to hide, evidence of the Nazi era was preserved in boots, insignia, pictures, mementoes and especially in such mental traits as arrogant feelings of superiority, racism, dislike of foreigners and such jokes as the one a patient heard in 1979 from her father: "Germany these days has to build artificial cinder-tracks (*Kunstaschenbahnen*) because Jews are not burned any more."

Dreams of "fascism"* were occasioned by day residues. One patient was advised by her feminist friends to put her newborn child up for adoption because it was a "boy." That night she dreamed that the Gestapo are looking for a child who is seeking shelter in an apartment in which members of the National Socialist women's confederation lived; these women turn the child over to the Gestapo. The patient realized that the child in the dreams represented her own son. She looked upon herself as an accomplice to his destruction; and only years later, in her analysis, did she recognize herself in the unfortunate child of the dream. This and the other patients discussed here were conscious antifascists. They feared the resurrection of German fascism and made an effort to prevent it. However, when during their analyses, dreams of uniforms and emblems emerged, they reacted as their parents had. They refused to think about them and acted as if they were "foreign bodies" rather than their own thoughts. They put the analyst in the position of the child that they themselves had been: the child whose parents will not answer his

---

* Even though fascism is abhorred, it seems to be a universal euphemism for "Nazism." (Ed.)

questions. Upon receiving this interpretation, they suggested that they would talk about their parents. Listening to them, one could see that, when they talked about their parents, they were talking about themselves and their experiences. They felt oppressed, destroyed, obliterated, and demoralized by the behavior of their parents who had committed "soul murder" (Shengold 1979; Niederland 1980) on them.

These children of Nazis resembled the victims of persecution described by William G. Niederland (1980). They suffered from insomnia and nightmares; their concentration was impaired, and other ego functions were disturbed; they were irritable, depressive, and excitable; they lacked initiative and lived in constant fear because they were not able correctly to evaluate themselves and the world around them. They experienced themselves as "strangers in their own house," in their bodies and souls: they felt like "skin and shells" without a nucleus of the self, and they suffered from psychosomatic disorders.

They tended to build illusions about themselves and about others and approached analysis with unrealistic expectations that often included a wish for the reversal of something that had passed. What sort of experience did these patients have with their parents?

TRANSFERENCE MANIFESTATIONS

During the initial stages of transference, I felt as if I was being totally ignored. Punctual and reliable, these patients were formally polite, their facial expressions and gestures rigidly immobile like those of dolls. Only their eyes showed signs of life—the sad eyes of children. My intense countertransference indicated how aggressive they were. They rejected no interpretation, but neither did they accept any. It was like speaking to a brick wall. One patient said to me later that, in the beginning of the analysis, she had felt as if she were in a "steel submarine."

I as analyst must have seemed threatening, since the patients had to shield themselves against any intrusion. However, they did not consciously perceive it at the time and believed that they were ideal patients. When their dreams had aggressive and destructive contents, they could not relate them to me or to themselves. They viewed me as an institution—"the analysis"—that needed to be consulted due to difficulties. Treating me as if I were dead or made of stone, they were able to come to treatment. This type of transference helped them to defend against their extreme fear of helplessness, of being defeated and wide open to attack.

One of the punctual patients, Elsa B., showed up one day five minutes before the end of the session and continued her associations from the previous session, behaving as if she had not been late at all. I was so amazed that I began to doubt my own perceptions, checked my watch for accuracy, and wondered whether I had mistaken the time scheduled for the appointment. When I pointed out Miss B.'s tardiness, she acknowledged it with an aggressive undertone. She had been delayed against her will and felt a helpless rage, which she defended against by behaving as if nothing had happened. By confronting her with her lateness, I destroyed her illusion, and her anger directed itself against me. Could I expect her to have empathy with me? Could I expect her to understand how I felt while waiting for her for forty-five minutes?

Miss B. remarked in passing that I should have been able to see for myself why she had come late. In transference she had included me in the following illusion: if I knew why Miss B. had been late, then Miss B. wouldn't have to tell me. I reacted with a feeling of disorientation which showed me that the patient's and my own orientation were on a different plane, the patient's being illusionary. When I confronted her with this difference in our respective attitudes, Miss B. behaved like someone unwilling to be awakened from sleep: she became irritable, unmotivated, and moody. The question arose whether she used illusions to defend herself, and, if so, against what?

Some time later when the patient became ill and was left alone, she gave shelter to two cats and indulged in their "tenderness." She spoke of a feeling of being bound to persons close to her by a system of pipes. One day when a friend visited her, she became upset because he disliked cats and "belittled" them, referring to them as "only cats." She began to scream, "He should love them! He should love them!" To her the cats did not have an individual existence but were an extension of her grandiose self. She was connected with them by an "inner channel"; she gave them souls and thus protected herself from the pain of loss and from apathy. The disillusionment implicit in the friend's statement that cats are but cats was extremely painful, because it represented her disillusionment with her mother, who had been indifferent to her and did not listen to her. Miss B. had to endow her mother with a soul in order to escape the narcissistic injury of being an unloved child, a child used as a narcissistic extension of the mother instead of being loved and valued for her own individuality. She used the system of invisible channels (pipes) to give her mother a soul, a soul to love her. When the illusion of being loved shattered, she felt "alone" as never before.

She looked upon the lack of mother-love as a weakness in herself. The illusion of being loved made her feel strong and shielded her from a harsh reality. The illusory mother-love guaranteed her mental survival, restored her trust, and gave her security. She behaved like a wanderer who reaches a dangerous

# The Shadows of the Past

precipice and yet feels secure because the abyss before him is hidden by fog. When the fog subsides, the wanderer is shocked. The illusion of safety is lost. Miss B. expected the analyst to share and safeguard her illusions and accept them as reality. She did not expect the shock that occurred when her "fog" lifted.

The more such patients were mistreated by their parents, the more they needed their illusions, and the more they defended them, especially when they preconsciously perceived that a breakdown was inevitable. Another patient whose mother had been extremely unreliable during her early childhood and had left her for weeks in a relative's home, assured me that she had a boundless feeling of security. She went on to say that she must accept the fact that, despite all evidence to the contrary, her mother had been reliable. After this session her preconscious suspicion that her mother had actually embezzled her money, was confirmed. The truth was that she had been abused by her mother since birth and was robbed and "disemboweled" to satisfy her mother's needs. Another patient required several years of analysis before he was capable of seeing his mother realistically. Influenced by the account of a trial of a criminal abuser of juveniles who killed boys by removing their intestines (Moor 1972), this patient feared that he, too, was capable of seducing and slaughtering and disemboweling boys. In this he identified with his mother who had exploited him to such a degree that legal action had to be taken to protect the patient from her.

All these patients suffered from real traumas, usually a sequence of traumas (Keilson et al. 1979), which could be traced as far back as infancy and could be reconstructed from acting out of the original trauma. These patients let the analyst feel how they had felt as children, helpless, dependent, demoralized, ill, and misused for alien purposes. At the same time—and herein lay the unsolvable discrepancy—they did not believe that what they perceived was reality. They denied whatever had been done to them.

At first, without knowing it, I was endowed with the role of participant in these scenes of denied abuse. Especially during sessions where I felt confused by a patient's associations, I began to think about their impact on me, about what they were doing to me. This gave me hope that my feelings would adjust appropriately to these patients' communications. In some technical aspects these sessions reminded me of D. W. Winnicott's (1971) scribble therapy. Though I did not scribble with the patients, they initiated something, I reacted to it, and they completed the "drawing." For example, in one session, Miss B. spoke so quietly that I could not hear her. She continued on this tack despite two requests that she speak louder. When I intervened the third time, saying, "Your words are flowing past my ears," Miss B. began to talk normally and suddenly remembered a dream from the previous night: she is holding a baby in her arms and has enormous breasts from which copious amounts of milk are streaming; but the milk never reaches the baby's mouth.

When I explained that I had not heard anything that Miss B. had previously said she was amazed. Even though her words had been copious, I received nothing from Miss B. I was the baby whom the milk never reached. Is the mother in the dream object-related, responsive to the needs of the child, or is the nursing a narcissistic triumph of her huge breasts? The patient's mother had chided her repeatedly because she did not suck properly and only nibbled on the breast—a reproach that evoked guilt feelings. Was the mother incapable of adjusting to a baby? Did the patient as a baby feel as I had during the session—helpless, annoyed, and forced to repeat senseless efforts that led nowhere? If I found it painful, for a helpless child it would have been excruciating.

Several sessions later, Miss B. was extremely tired because she had worked very long hours. Nevertheless she did come to the session. She talked about her fear that if she attended a convention with her colleagues, she would not be able to leave when she wanted to. She had been complaining of extreme insomnia. During the night she had been plagued by lack of sleep, and during the day she was almost too tired to work. In recent days her sleep rhythm had deteriorated completely. As she continued in this session, I had the distinct impression that the patient was "getting something out of the session," something like breast feeding. Toward the end of her hour, she became increasingly tired and resisted fatigue like a small child. When I commented on this, she became silent and then suddenly said in a tone of voice I had never heard her use before, "These sessions are not for sleeping." The incongruence between the patient's babylike regressive state and the strong, adult tone of voice caused me to chuckle quietly. When I told her about it she was reminded of her mother's tone of voice and of being chided for falling asleep during nursing.

Miss B.'s mother insisted that her daughter always be alert while in her presence. She was not able to give her daughter a space where she could approach others or retreat into herself. The mother forced her daughter to subordinate even such an elementary need as sleep to her own needs. The patient left the session convinced that she would be able to attend the convention without fear of having to act according to the wishes of her colleagues. She slept deeply the following night. In the next session she asked what I would have done if she had really fallen asleep. I answered that I would have awakened Miss B. at the scheduled end of the session, in order to tell her that I did not share her regressive state, but neither did I simply subordinate my needs to hers. This statement gave the patient a sense of trust and a security that she was never able to experience with her mother, and she seemed relieved.

Her mother had used Miss B. as if she had been an extension of herself, as a self-object. At the beginning of her analysis, Miss B. related the following fairy tale about Godfather Death:

A young boy received Death as his godfather. He grew up to become a famous physician because Death always gave him the gift of a correct diagnosis. If Death stood at the foot of the bed, the patient died; if he stood at the head of the bed, the patient recovered. Twice the physician outwitted Death by having the bed turned around so that his wife (a princess) and her father (the king) recovered despite Death's decree that they die. Death then took the physician by his hand and led him into a subterranean cavern where many candles were lit. These were the lights of life. Some were being lit; others were on the brink of going out. Death showed the physician his own candle that was about to be extinguished. The physician begged death to give him a new candle, but the moment he received it, this candle too was extinguished, and the physician died.

Miss B., a physician herself, experienced each patient's death as a personal blow. Dying patients would point out to her that she herself was afraid of death. Miss B.'s family enforced a taboo on death, even stronger than the taboo on sexuality. It was forbidden to talk about illness, old age, or death. One was not allowed to take final leave and mourn. Both parents looked upon the children as extensions of themselves and thought it was the children's duty to produce children of their own.

There were many ways to build illusions around a never-doubted core of immortality. For a relative to die of old age was considered the doctor's fault. Conversely, for a relative to have survived the war was a merit and a source of pride. Death was a narcissistic injury, a defeat; it did not lead to mourning.

DREAMS

During early childhood, Elsa B. and similar patients never really experienced a situation where life or death was an issue. Nevertheless, they gave the impression of people who had been confronted by death early in life. In dreams, which patients themselves referred to as "fascism dreams," there were violence, helplessness, extinction, annihilation, and a triumph of the stronger over the weak. Elsa B.'s dream sequences illustrate this point.

*First Dream*

She sees a man and a woman in uniform fighting each other and a similar group of women, also fighting. She walks past my office with her boy friend. He suggests that they spend the night in my garden in sleeping bags, but Miss B. refuses. He goes in alone and meets two cripples who fight each other and attack him also. The police arrive and kill everybody except the boy friend, who is left shackled on the ground. He could, however, free himself, but does not.

At first Miss B. experienced this dream entirely from the point of view of an observer of an entirely alien event. This had been the attitude of her godfather. After her real father returned from the war, he gave the following advice to his children: "It is best to remain an observer of the stage of life." However, he himself, as an observer, was magically attached to suffering. When the patient, at the age of five, was stricken with osteomyelitis and confined to bed for a long time, her father spent a lot of time with her. Long after she recovered, he told friends and relatives that she still suffered. (She was loved by her "godfather," as Jesus was loved by His father in His suffering.) Her father was weak and lacked self-confidence—he could not even drive a car for fear of collision—and needed his daughter's weakness to secure a sense of personal strength. He did not like children; they were too loud, too boisterous, too driven. Miss B.'s superego represented her father as the police who maintain law and order in her dream, a police with whom she was fully identified. When I pointed out to her that the police in her dream kill many people, she replied with an unmistakable tone of satisfaction that this was the only way to re-establish order.

Miss B. had an unempathic relationship not only with her father but also with her mother. As a result of early frustrations, she was incapable of tolerating tension. She could neither tolerate nor resolve the conflicts between her ego ideal and her actual self. On the day before the dream, she had an inconsequential argument with her boy friend which had scared and paralyzed both. Neither had been able to perceive their own flaws and weaknesses. Miss B. could not forgive him. Like the "woman without a shadow," she sacrificed her instinctual drives as well as her object relation to her ego–ideal. She could no longer sleep with her boy friend. Miss B.'s parents could not cope with conflicts; they silenced them to death and gave the appearance of an extraordinary uniformity, as if they always agreed on everything.

Miss B.'s dream contains conflicts between men and women, between women and between children and older generations. When I first began working with Miss B., I noticed that she used the words *race* and *opposite sex* interchangeably, and conjectured that her race hatred was directed against men. This assumption proved to be false. Miss B. unconsciously knew only two races, independent of sex: a strong race and a weak one. The powerful white race was white and therefore always in the right; the inferior race was dark or black and therefore wrong. Her childhood fantasy was of a "flawless white" mother. Her father had no color; he stood in the shadow of the mother, his maleness denied. When her mother was pregnant, the five-year-old pictured the baby as the child of her mother and a black soldier of the occupying armies. When Elsa B. was very young, she was blinded by her mother's narcissism and ideas of grandeur and could not evaluate whether they were genuine or a fraud. She clung to the external attributes of her motherly, feminine figure. To her mother, however, Elsa B. was merely a demonstration object of motherhood which placed her, the mother, above the father. In their joint madness, their *folie d deux*, Miss B. was called upon, from time to time, to compensate for the mother's missing phallus and give her the gift of a second youth. Fusing with her mother, she projected all evil onto what was outside their symbiotic unity. Although separated externally, they maintained an illusion of internal unity. This relationship collapsed when the younger brother was born. By supplying the mother with a real phallus, he was instrumental in devaluating Elsa B. She became superfluous and a burden. Her mother treated her as if she were a sick and malfunctioning limb which needed to be amputated and replaced by a prosthesis.

There was no place and no reason for sorrow. While Elsa B. took a nosedive from the heaven of her illusion into hell, her mother denied even the existence of a problem and maintained the illusion of unity by behaving as if the brother was also her daughter's child. All were to be united and identical. Floating on clouds, unreachable and inviolate like a madonna, the mother ignored the abyss that had opened between her daughter and herself. Miss B. thought that she meant nothing to her mother as a separate individual, that she was replaceable and expendable, depending on her mother's needs. Her own tender feelings toward the baby brother were nipped in the bud. When in her school years she became acquainted with the "slaughter of the innocents" in Bethlehem, she cried so much that she had to be removed from the classroom. In her analysis she quickly recognized her aggressive feelings toward her brother, but not until the end of it did she realize that she herself had been the murdered "innocent." She said that she had seen death twice wearing the visages of her father and mother: when her father humiliated her, enjoying her weakness, and her mother destroyed her suddenly by extinguishing her into a "nothing." This idea about death occupied her mind in the next dream.

## Second Dream

She is celebrating an ecumenical service with her parents and has an extraordinarily exalted and festive feeling. At the end of the service she joins a group that descends into a crypt from where there is no way out. She ascends again and wants to leave the church by the front entrance, where she encounters a marching column of soldiers wearing black boots. Afraid, she re-enters the church. There is no escape. Even the "madonna of the protective mantle" (*Schutzmantelmadonna*) offers no protection.

The madonna represents Miss B.'s mother and brother who look down upon her and her father. This is the "virgin mother" who has hurt her husband's male pride. Yet she is able to ward off all evil within the walled confines of the church. However, those who are afraid of their own destructive impulses cannot gain access to her.

The black-boot symbolism plays an important part in the dreams of all five patients. Boots are an expression of a weak maleness, injured male pride, but also of male vanity. A boot seems to give the foot (= penis) a dashing shape and to make it hard, handsome, and supple. It protects the foot–penis from contact with dirt emitted from the female genitals, represented by a cloaca— a reaction formation against pure white womanhood. These boots are expressive not only of male weakness but also of male superiority and vanity. They divide humanity into boot-wearers and non-boot-wearers, the latter being inferior.

While the mother fell in love narcissistically with her boy child (= phallus) and degraded her husband, this weak man took revenge on his daughter, crushing her with "boots" and letting her feel how powerless and weak she was. Miss B.'s parents were of different faiths: her father, Catholic; and her mother, Protestant. Her mother raised her, however, in a strict Catholic dogma, "more Catholic than the Pope"; for the Catholic Church was the embodiment of the female principle, the victory of mother and son against the father. Miss B. experienced male and female narcissism, masculine and feminine ego ideals, shaped by her parents, as irreconcilable. Although they seemed unified, her parents included her, from birth on, into their feuds, from which the "madonna of the protective mantle" invariably emerged the victor.

Even before her analysis, Miss B. realized how much she hated her mother. When she aborted a child, she experienced it as aborting her mother. The abortion was at the end of a period of extreme self-neglect, during which she confessed her "sins" to her mother as one would to a priest. The priest-mother was always ready to forgive her generously and take the burden of guilt upon herself. The lower the daughter sank, the higher the mother towered over her. The more criminal she felt "out of a sense of guilt" (Freud 1916a; Alexander and Staub 1929), the less possible it was for her to mourn and allow others to mourn as well. During the analysis she projected her guilt feelings about the abortion by saying:

It was a common practice in my circles to undergo an abortion! Perhaps I was not pregnant; I did not even wait for a medical confirmation before I underwent the abortion. It is the doctors' fault; they are the ones who aborted the child. It was only a bunch of cells anyway.

Thus she defended against her helplessness and sadness. She had robbed herself of something that might have brought her happiness—a child. Because she could not mourn, she had to fear pregnancy. She saw the fetus as cells growing together and becoming cancerlike and, hence, threatening. At first she let me feel the mourning, which she could not experience herself. When she said, "It was only a bunch of cells," she added, "I believe you are sad." When I confirmed this, Miss B. broke into tears.

One can only mourn something that one has loved and valued. Miss B. realized that she missed her parents more than they missed her. When she stayed away for some time, her mother did not notice it. She was not sad that her daughter was gone, and did not want to mourn for her when she could separate from her, the mother. Earlier when her brother was born, Miss B. had felt that the mother should have mourned losing her as a valuable object.

Another patient, whose father had volunteered to join the SS occupation forces (*Einsatzkommando*) and revealed the persistence of his Nazi feelings in the joke about cinders and Jews, dreamed of the examiner in a forthcoming test as wearing a Nazi uniform. Despite the fact that this patient was well prepared for the test, she was afraid of a second and final failure. She recalled that once, during her latency, she had wet her bed and stained the mattress. According to her father these stains could be never removed. Her father, she said, recognized only the existence of those who committed an irreparable crime. The crime of bed wetting allowed her to be someone rather than dust and ashes.

*Third Dream.* Miss B.'s third "fascism dream" was the last dream of her analysis:

She is eavesdropping on a man and woman, wearing uniforms. They consult with each other on how to accomplish a return of fascism. Hidden under a chair, she sees only the tips of their boots, and she manages to escape unnoticed. On a path she meets other refugees who are recaptured by the Nazis. The path ends in a concentration camp that resembles a soccer stadium. She escapes, crosses a river, and meets Nazis again in front of my office. She cannot escape.

Children are the natural survivors of their parents. Their weakness is also their strength. With the discovery of birth and conception comes the discovery of mortality. Miss B. really met death in front of my office when, with the curiosity of a child, she tried to intrude into my private life and found out about a death in my family. Fearing that I would stop her analysis as punishment, Miss B. did not discuss this discovery with me. At last Miss B. expressed sympathy for me but, at first, used the false tone of her father, conveying a false sympathy. Then there followed an attempt to act as if nothing had happened. She thought that she might have misunderstood something. Realizing that I, too, was human and could incur a loss, she became disillusioned and devaluated me as a person and as a representative of analysis. Miss B. acted as if I had promised to protect her from death but could not keep that promise. Her dream contained the river of death. On each of its shores the same things happened. Death was inescapable.

In Miss B.'s life there was no room for death, no room for sickness. Sorrow was weakness and mourning was weakness. Since childhood when she was taken ill with osteomyelitis, at the age of five, she remembered only two ways out:

1. Through self-denial one could reach comfort in illusions. She began to fantasize that she was a fairy and could dance, float, and fly.
2. Through the slogan "War, not sorrow," she could become an enemy of the whole world. She dreamed that the sun explodes and destroys everything with its poisonous rays. When things were catastrophic for her, others had to suffer.

She complained, "Why me? Why not the others?" In a dream, she is floating in pink clouds in Noah's Ark with her parents and is suddenly placed on top of a high mountain; a difficult descent to the valleys "where people live" awaits her. The mountain symbolizes the monstrous abruptness with which her mother discarded unpleasant things, automatically expelling and throwing them away or cutting them off through amputation. The descent was tedious. Miss B. not only had to "shrink" into health, as she came down to earth (Kohut 1971), but she also had to accept herself as she really was. It was a question of survival whether she could love herself with all her flaws showing, for all to see. Toward the end of the analysis she repeatedly dreamed of sailing the seven seas with her parents and being unable to dock in a harbor. To land would mean to make friends with the world and its people without harboring illusions. That meant declaring war on and alienating herself from her mother, because she never protected her daughter enough. Coming down to earth with me implied that I had not fulfilled Miss B.'s childhood dreams, and she had to give them up.

During the last stages of her analysis, when she became more independent of her mother, the latter became paranoid. She referred to Miss B. as a "poisonous snake," indicating from time to time that she was afraid to be poisoned by her daughter. In response, Miss B. dreamed that she split into a baby and a snake. The mother repeated now what she did when, as a child, her daughter began to separate from her. She protested against her daughter's growing autonomy. Due to her increased maturity and a better functioning of her ego, Miss B. was no longer really threatened by her mother's behavior, but was frightened when she recognized how sick her mother was. She recognized that the mother's holding on to the illusory symbiotic relationship with the daughter also served as a protection against her destructive wishes toward her daughter (Lichtenstein 1964).

Miss B. had rejected her instinctual, libidinal drives quite early. Her ego ideal embodied the concept of a lack of personal needs. The identity that was forced upon her by her mother—the "pure white woman" = the woman without drives—was the ideal identity that her mother herself was incapable of attaining. The mother had sacrificed her daughter at the altar of this ego ideal. Miss B. had been used and misused by her mother. She was to be an "improved mirror image" (Kohut 1977) of her mother. During her analysis, Miss B.'s grandmother died, and Miss B. was able to mourn for her. She realized how attached she had been to her and how she was able to counterbalance her frustration with her mother by her trust in her grandmother.

### Fourth Dream

Miss B. is dead and is reborn as a rabbi. She is on a ship, fleeing from the Nazis, wants to get to the United States, but lands in Israel and speaks up from there as a voice of warning.

The dream is associated with a feeling of relief; she recognizes in the rabbi her true image and understands why she always feels persecuted. The dream symbolizes for her a new beginning that will make all that happened undone. She returns to the womb and is reborn.

This dream occurred in a phase of analysis when Miss B. was becoming increasingly aware of her hatred against strangers, her "race hatred," her hate of her younger brother and of Jews. The dream was occasioned by her treatment of a Jewish patient, who was mentally confused and accused the Americans of being responsible for his severe physical ailments. Miss B. did not contradict him, although she knew that the accusation was absurd. It came to her mind, though, that she would have interrupted and would have castigated a German, equally sick patient who would have complained that the Jews were responsible for his sickness. This association led her to the understanding of her latent race hatred. She was plagued by intense self-reproaches and guilt feelings, which she tried to resolve in the dream by becoming the victim herself.

## Conclusion

The ego ideal of the patients who were children of Nazis has its counterpart in the ego ideal of such obedient servants of the Third Reich as Rudolf Höss, the commandant of Auschwitz (Broszat 1963). In his memoirs he wrote that his father had originally selected him to become a priest, a vocation that he pursued with vigor until puberty and gave up only after the death of his father. Yet he continued to feel guilty about the disavowal of priesthood. During a prison term in the 1920s, he suffered from nightmares and felt persecuted, beaten, shot at, and pushed into an abyss. He could no longer find "the way to God" and believed that God had left him because he had left God. For him, the demand for absolute obedience was connected to the principle of unconditional submission to an alien self. When he joined the SS, he traded the order of priesthood, in which submission and obedience were expected, for the new order of Nazism.

When the ego ideal contains childish fantasies of grandeur and omnipotence, the real self seems ugly and crippled in comparison. The tension, caused by a discrepancy between the ideal self and the ego ideal, is lessened by an illusionary connection with another self that contains some of the yearned-for ideal qualities. Sometimes the self comes nearer to the ego ideal; usually, however, the delusions of grandeur produce painful inner tensions and set in motion projective and illusionary defense mechanisms that serve as a bridge over the chasm between the actual self and the ego ideal. Yet this conflict only *seems* to operate between the psychic structures; it originates in an interaction with an object in which one misuses the other as a self-object in an attempt to free oneself from painful inner tensions. Once internalized, the conflict can be re-externalized and experienced subjectively as cure—a temporary healing.

The parents of my five patients who were children of Nazis, were all faithful followers of Hitler. They had not been forced to join the party. They unconsciously searched for an idol to whose rules they could submit. Their illusionary view of the world was built by an inner compulsion which the toppling of the Nazi state did not change. At the dissolution of Third Reich in 1945, some of these parents renounced nazism in favor of a new religion; others embraced new ideologies. They retained a perverted pleasure in what is usually not pleasing: in submitting to others or in having them submit, in letting themselves be abused or in actively abusing others.

Hitler's own past was intertwined with the past of his parents. He was born under the shadow of death. Three siblings died before his birth; when he was ten years old, his brother died, and his mother died of breast cancer when he was eighteen. He was a product of a society in which "the fittest survived." There is no mourning in such a society and no place for motherliness (Rosenkötter 1979). Instead, it has physical motherhood and a false motherliness, an "as if" nurturing.

Hitler saw a special purpose in raising healthy bodies and considered it an evil to keep healthy children from the nation. He expressed his aggression against his sick mother in the following words: "A putrid body is not compensated for by a radiant soul" (Toland 1976, p. 453).

In their view of cancer, my five patients betrayed their fear of parasitic relationships, condensed in their concept of pregnancy. This fear mirrored Hitler's fantasies that he revealed in his statement that, if one opens up a tumor, a Jew pops out. Hitler also referred to the Jew as a stranger who awakens the jealousy of those who see in him a foreign object in their own body (p. 340). One can speculate that this idea has something to do with the birth of Hitler's younger brother when he was five years old.

In comparing the German people with an organism plagued by a malignant tumor, Hitler betrayed his equation of Germans with his mother. By adopting the German people and giving them his name *Hitlerdeutschland*, he accepted his mother at the expense of his father and saved her in the "final solution" of a malignant sickness (cancer = pregnancy = Jew) and made her aesthetically acceptable again. In his restitutive fantasy, he made her into a new human being, a being without shame and guilt, a perfect being without a conscience:

Only when an epoch ceases to be haunted by the shadows of its own consciousness of guilt, will it achieve the inner calm and outward strength brutally and recklessly to prune off the wild shoots and tear out the weeds. (P. 30)

The illusion that the Final Solution—that is, the total extermination of Jews—restores German beauty and health, maintains the belief that the symbol is identical with what is symbolized. It transpires not only in the analyses of patients but also in the ideological, religious, and political statements of Nazi Germany's world-wide sickness, as Freud envisaged it prophetically in 1937.

The confusion between the thing and its symbol characterizes regressions to very early infantile states. The "shadows of the past" discussed in this chapter refer to the effects parents have on children whom they misuse as extensions of themselves and rob of individuality. As aggrandizements of their parents, these patients were not separable from them. As individuals they were expendable. The psychic structures that these patients developed under the influence of their primary objects were, in part, narcissistic, unreachable, and unrealistic ego ideals, precipitations of the joint delusions of omnipotence; and, in part, harsh, cruel, and destructive superego punitive functions. When Hitler realized his defeat, he wanted to destroy the German people. Similarly, these patients' parents became raving persecutors when the patients removed themselves from their all-powerful control—a removal that the parents equated with defeat. As a result, these patients' consciences were not their friends and their guardians but, rather, their persecutors. Due to their immaturity, these patients could not protect themselves from the invasion of their own inner structures by their narcissistically disturbed primary objects. They could only protect themselves from perceiving how they had been misused by building illusionary ego ideals. They constantly had to fight for their survival; yet their independence meant the destruction of their parents. During their separation-individuation phases (Mahler and Furer 1968) and during later stages of development, these patients feared their persecutors, and thus was engendered a conflict between their instinctual drives and the demands of their ego ideal. Although they developed neurotic symptoms, unlike neurotics they had no sense of time; past, present, and future had become confused. Thus, they built their future as if it were the past. Inflexible as they were, any differences they perceived intellectually were only external: from within all things were uniform. They moved not in a completely "psychotic universe" (Grubrich-Simitis 1979) but in an illusionary "as if" universe. The evil that they combatted and placed in the external world was within themselves, in their "unborn children."

The plight of these patients is best illustrated in Hitler's well-expressed need to project all evil onto the outside. When, in 1939, Hermann Rauschning (1973) asked him whether the removal of Jews from Germany would rid the world of this No. 1 enemy, he replied: "We would have to invent them; one needs a visible enemy, one in plain sight. The Jew is always within us, but it is simpler to fight him in bodily form than as an invisible evil." (Rauschning 1939, p. 223).

# PART IV

## Theoretical and
## Clinical Aspects

**13**

# Recurrent Problems in the Treatment of Survivors and Their Children

IT IS NOW commonly accepted that Adolf Hitler and Nazi Germany waged two wars simultaneously. One was a war of conquest aimed at world domination; the other was a war of extermination primarily directed against Jews, but also against other minorities. It has been noted that as Nazi hopes for conquest faded, persecution of Jews became more savage and systematic. Despairing of victory against Russia, Germany declared war against the United States in December 1941 and one month later initiated the Final Solution calling for the total extermination of all European Jews. As the war continued, the campaign against the Jews became increasingly important to Hitler. A race developed with the aim of implementing the Final Solution before the ultimate defeat of Germany. If Hitler would not be remembered in world history as a conqueror, he would at least be gratefully acknowledged as the exterminator of the Jews. Violent anti-Semitism, as distinguished from merely social and professional discrimination, has always shown paranoid features; but the anti-Semitism professed and practiced by Hitler and his henchmen transcended anything Jews had experienced throughout millennia rich in persecutions.

The paranoid aspects of Hitler's anti-Semitism demanded that the survivors of the Holocaust come to terms with a new psychotic reality. H. Krystal and W. G. Niederland have stated:

Considering the nature and extent of the events of the past, it would be less accurate to say that this type of patient (the survivor) has a constitutionally determined schizophrenia than to say that he grew up in a psychotic world, and therefore he acted appropriately to this eerie reality. (1971, p. 335)

This nightmare period in European history, with all its fiendish details, is resurrected now in another context, as the investigator is immersed in the psychological problems presented by survivor-families and their children.

247

The procedures used in studying the clinical material derived from the treatment of survivors of the Holocaust and their children have been summarized in the introduction of this volume (see Prelude). The learning process and experience that illuminated the special problems presented by this group of patients will be recapitulated in this chapter in a condensed form from the case material offered by a group of therapists. A certain amount of controversy has been generated in connection with a method that relies upon clinical vignettes; and, indeed, by its very nature a vignette can often take a problem out of context and distort the total picture presented by a patient. Such abbreviated material often raises questions and can defy attempts at logical organization. On the other hand, fuller and more detailed case histories have been presented elsewhere in this volume. While recognizing the shortcomings of vignettes, this method seemed the most appropriate for a discussion of the technical problems encountered in therapeutic work with survivors and their children, as it allows a comprehensive view of a larger group of patients than would otherwise have been possible within the confines of a single chapter.

## The Inner Readiness of the Therapist to Treat Survivors and Their Children

It would seem axiomatic and self-evident that the treatment of concentration camp survivors and their children is bound to evoke strong emotion in the therapist. Such emotion has been commented upon frequently and has been most sensitively described by Ilse Grubrich-Simitis (1979).* It is therefore not irrelevant to point out that the group of investigators who participated in this study consists of survivors, refugees who—escaping the Holocaust—came to the United States, and a few American Jews; the majority are refugees. The reporters who came as guests to present case material were gen-

---

* One therapist opened his remarks with the following statement: "I found it very difficult to prepare myself for this meeting from the aspect of your focus. I think it has already been most valuable to me because I think it has brought up some points that I have minimized and that certainly were slighted in my personal analysis. My sleep in the last two or three weeks has been disturbed, signalling to me that something was obviously troubling me. It was not difficult to find that giving this presentation was making me anxious. One morning when I awoke much earlier than I usually do it occurred to me that to say that I have four cases to present is incorrect; what I need to do is to bring in the fifth case, which is myself."

erally younger colleagues and American-born. Every member of the group was therefore confronted with the necessity of reliving some portion of an unmastered past. Resistances were experienced both individually and as a group. Some of these resistances were of the usual type that might occur in any group—loss of interest, failure to attend meetings, difficulty in following through on assignments. Certain other resistances deserve special comment. Among psychoanalysts, anxiety may often manifest itself by premature closure and by a tendency toward too early theorizing. In this study two polarized tendencies were noted: a persistent emphasis on the role of the Holocaust as a causative agent in the pathology of the patient; and the very opposite, an ignoring of that role.

One surprising lesson came from the discovery that the initial anamnesis frequently contained the information that the patient was either a survivor or a child of a survivor, and the fact was never mentioned again. It was later learned that this failure to mention the Holocaust represented, from the point of view of the patient, a transfer of the pact of silence that prevailed in the home to the therapeutic situation, and from that of the therapist, an unconscious and understandable aversion to being engulfed in Holocaust memories. It was observed that after the presentation of a case and discussion of the problems involved, Holocaust material began to emerge in the dreams and memories of the patients, suggesting that they were waiting for a signal from the therapist to speak about these matters. The reaction to an interpretation as permission to speak has been demonstrated by V. H. Rosen (1955)—a contribution that indicates that some patients, not necessarily survivors, need to wait for such a signal.

It is customary in psychoanalysis to subsume such reactions under the term *countertransference*. However, the term does not seem altogether appropriate to describe the responses considered here. Countertransference refers to a response evoked in the therapist by the analysand—which is based on the patient's standing unconsciously for an object in the therapist's past who had prompted similar reactions. The patient may also represent an aspect of the therapist's self-representation which is currently repressed and projected onto the patient. The behavior of some patients may also evoke powerful defenses on the part of analysts, making it necessary for the latter to ward off intense instinctual impulses. What happened in the extermination camps goes beyond the repressed instinctual wishes of the therapist. The therapist must experience in an attenuated form the trauma endured by the patient. Goethe, in an oft-quoted aphorism, said that he never heard of a crime that he could not imagine himself committing; but he spoke more than a century before the extermination camps. While it does happen that hearing about concentration camps may evoke sadistic or masochistic wishes, this is rarely the important point. What is typical is the evocation, first, of disbelief and, then, of mourning that such organized cruelty was indeed possible in our time.

## Holocaust-Induced Pathology and Personal Pathology

One question that had to be grappled with constantly, because it appeared so persistently, was: How much of the pathology one sees is to be attributed to the Holocaust experience of the parents and how much to other incidental or personal sources? Judith S. Kestenberg (chapter 7) showed how every phase of psychosexual development can become invaded by the Holocaust memories of the parents.

A. Freedman (1978) described the case of a survivor, where it was felt that all the conditions necessary to account for the pathology seen in the patient were present before the Holocaust. The patient was a man who became a ghetto fighter and later developed an unusual perversion, which involved finding sexual release in a barber chair. He would select a barber, seeking one with preferably Aryan features, and ask for repeated shavings, allegedly in order to obtain a smoother tonsorial result. The patient carefully watched the growing impatience and agitation of the barber; and when it reached near boiling point, he concluded his clandestine masturbatory activities with an ejaculation and left the shop on friendly terms. In his heterosexual relationships, he pushed his finger far into his partner's throat and ejaculated when she gagged or became angry. As a youth, the patient had attended a Polish military school, where as the only Jewish student, he was subject to sadistic mistreatment by his teachers and developed sadistic retaliatory fantasies.

War came when the patient was in his late teens. His mother and grandmother were killed, and he and his father were separated. Speaking flawless Polish, he was able to "pass" as a Pole and was protected. Eventually he became a hero of the Warsaw ghetto, where he killed a number of German soldiers. This period was the only one in his life when he was free of anxiety. In his perversion he seemed to enact a double role: that of a victim, and that of the master of the situation. The therapist felt that all the conditions necessary for the psychopathology shown by the patient antedated the Holocaust. He stressed that the war permitted the patient to express sadistic impulses without guilt, and allowed him to be symptom-free during this period, only to develop his perverse symptoms after surviving the Holocaust.

H. P. Blum (1978)—in a published discussion of the case which was later elaborated during a conference with the therapist and the investigators—felt that an alternative view was possible, and that the barber in the perversion represented more than the Polish officers at the military school. He could have stood for the father from an earlier period and the Nazis at a later time. Blum felt that the horrors of the Warsaw ghetto, where four hundred thousand Jews lost their lives, was an organizing factor which fixated the perversion, and that it might not have appeared in adult life under ordinary circumstances. Blum believed that the perversion could be seen as part of a survivor syndrome. Although many in our group agreed with Blum that the symptom could be better explained by the patient's Holocaust experiences, the issue could not be resolved at a clinical level.

In another discussion of a published case (I. Schieffer 1978) the same question, how much of the pathology should be attributed to a pre-Holocaust traumatic past and how much to the concentration camp experiences, was examined by our group with the author.

The patient, called Lilli in Schieffer's book, was an attractive, young, married nurse who by the age of eleven had been an inmate of Theresienstadt, Auschwitz, and Bergen-Belsen. At Auschwitz she was separated from the closest person to her, her grandmother, who blessed her with the Hebrew "shma" before they were forcibly separated. She survived four years of incarceration.

Her pre-Holocaust history was also traumatic. When she was six her mother had died of cancer. Her parents had separated when she was three. Her father fled, leaving Lilli behind with her grandmother.

Marriage and motherhood could not eradicate Lilli's chronic depression. She kept hearing children's screams and suffered from hypnogogic hallucinations of burning human flesh. She was also haunted by survivor's guilt. She, therefore, presented in a striking way the two types of traumata in rapid succession.

Lilli had no difficulty in conceiving, but pregnancy was difficult because she equated the fetus with mother's cancer. The patient's depression turned into a dangerous melancholia triggered by Adolph Eichmann's capture. Eichmann was equated both with the father who escaped, and, in the transference, with the analyst. Lilli incorporated Eichmann into her superego as a sadistic attacker who killed her beloved grandmother.

It was evident that all the traumatic events were activated at the same time, resulting in a pathological gestalt. The analyst felt that were it not for the concentration camp, the patient could have compensated by the formation of a grandiose self, which she indeed developed before incarceration. The case shows how a therapist confronted with ordinary traumas of life and Holocaust traumas in the same patient, must have the flexibility to address both, often in rapid succession. Therapist commitment either to the concept of early trauma as the all-decisive cause of pathology or to Holocaust trauma as the only relevant one, would cause difficulties in the necessary therapeutic flexibility. Had the Holocaust not intervened, the depressive constellation behind the grandiose self would have emerged in the course of psychoanalytic treatment. But because of the trauma of the Holocaust the patient began her treatment already in a dangerous and highly vulnerable state which necessitated hospitalization.

Internalization of Hitler and Eichmann are not unusual among survivors and their children. A child of survivors commented: "I have the mind of a Hitler and the soul of Eichmann." A similar mechanism often appears in transference when many children of survivors see any psychoanalyst with a foreign accent as German and are disappointed when he turns out to be of more "benign origin," such as Swiss or Swedish. They are even more disappointed when the psychoanalyst is a Jew. In a few cases this may become the cause for leaving treatment.

Franz M., the thirty-one-year-old son of two survivors, was treated in psychoanalytically oriented psychotherapy for a period of six years, after he had made a suicidal attempt by slashing his wrists and been admitted to a state hospital. An earlier attempt by drinking iodine was prompted by global feelings of inadequacy, followed by a surge of elation and increased psychomotor activity that finally led to decompensation. He compared himself with biblical characters (Cain, Joseph, Moses), developed insomnia, stopped eating, and at one point smeared his body with sperm to anoint himself. He became delusional, believing that he was Jesus Christ. His past history revealed that he was a twin and regarded his twin brother as more aggressive and more successful. The conflict between the twins became so intense that they could not be invited to their parents' house at the same time. Significant in his personal history was the fact that he used to accompany his father to the racetrack, an activity that had to be concealed from the mother.

Mr. M. recalled most vividly that when his mother was taken from the ghetto, she told him that she was all dressed up in a long gown which she had worn throughout her internment in the concentration camp. She used to tear the gown into little strips to use as toilet tissue. She repeatedly pointed out with pride that through the years of confinement she had neither soiled nor prostituted herself. She also emphasized that the same prostitutes serviced both men and women. She was asked to be a leader of her group but refused that, too. She also told her son that she had been taken to the gas ovens three times, but each time the machinery failed. On one occasion the mother told Franz M. that the experience of being in the ovens was not as horrifying as was his mental illness—a typical statement, which many children of survivors hear. In a similar vein, Mr. M. recalled that during his frequent and intense fights with his brother, his mother would call him "little Hitler." One month before his discharge from his fourth hospitalization, following an examination of a penile lesion by a male physician, the patient made a suicidal attempt with a massive dose of medication that his father had covertly obtained for him outside the hospital. At one point, three years after he began psychotherapy, he cut his penis with a razor blade. When his mother took a vacation during his sixth year of treatment, he drew closer to his father. The father's collusion evokes indignation. Howevet, if we assume that the deluded father and the son developed a transference psychosis, the hospital may have been equated with a concentration camp, and their behavior becomes intelligible. Upon the approach of his mother's return, which coincided with the therapist's vacation, Mr. M. underwent a massive decompensation marked by a delusion that the therapist was intending to molest him, and confided this to his father. The father responded by sabotaging the treatment, and the patient dropped out.

Several sources of pathology were discernible in this case: the mother was not apparently able to handle the twins adequately; the father was seductive and allied with Franz M. against the mother, and later against the therapist; and there were the Holocaust experiences of the mother as conveyed to her son and worked over by him. Psychosis blurs the distinction between self and object representations; therefore the patient was unable to convey to the therapist whether the central place occupied by the gown was his own, or his mother's distortion. Had further treatment been possible, a major aim would have been to re-establish the boundary between Franz M. and his mother. The case illustrates another striking mechanism: the Holocaust, with its multiple meanings, became condensed by the patient into the narrow channel of maintaining cleanliness at all costs and under the most adverse conditions. The patient's destructive gambling was considered significant: it could represent an identification with the father, who was also a gambler, or an unconscious identification with the father as a victim. It is likely that only a deeper and more thorough psychoanalytic investigation could have decided between the two interpretations, or whether the symptom was overdetermined.

## Eruption of the Unmastered Past

Krystal and Niederland (1971) have commented on the fact that the only genuine disturbance in reality testing shown by many survivors consists in reacting as though they were still living under the domination of the Nazis. A child of a survivor described a shopping trip taken with her mother. The two were in a car when they were stopped by a policeman, who accused them of passing a red light. The officer demanded to see the mother's driver's license and also asked her to turn off the motor. In sudden panic the mother bit the hand of the policeman, then stepped on the gas and attempted to escape. A chase ensued. Her car was soon surrounded by policemen, but she apparently conducted herself in such a manner that she evoked sympathy and was charged with no more than a minor traffic violation. The sudden eruption of Holocaust memories and the equally sudden and amazing recovery are characteristic of many survivors. The comment of the patient who told this story in treatment was: "In our home there are no small dangers, only catastrophies." It is obvious that the past erupted when the mother saw the man in uniform. Even under conditions prevailing in the most democratic societies, we know that the anxieties that motorists experience when stopped by a figure representing authority are far beyond the actual danger; in this instance, the anxiety was so great that it overruled the capacity of the ego to test reality. It should be added that these unexpected eruptions of the traumatic past should be differentiated from the chronic and more or less constant state of anxiety, such as expecting the Gestapo when there is a knock on the door.

## The Double Registry of the Holocaust Trauma

An American-born woman, Sara R., sought analysis because of anxiety attacks, insomnia, ulcers, and frigidity. She was a daughter of partisan fighters who had operated behind enemy lines. Unlike many concentration camp survivors, these parents, proud of their active resistance, believed in telling the children everything.

At the end of the first year of analysis, the patient reported a dream in which she is lying on the couch coughing: the therapist places a hand on the patient's forehead to soothe her; then the therapist is lying on the couch with her shoes off; Sara R. remarks that the therapist's feet have no odor. The dream revealed the patient's guilt and awe toward her parents and also relief at being with someone who was not associated with the dread past. Miss R. again spoke of how the parents related their experiences to their children:

For a few days they stayed in the sewers; then they left, but returned several times. I would not have made it. They were up to their shoulders in excrement and there were rats all around them. I have these vivid images in my mind. I see my parents walking through the filth in the pitch dark. I want to shake these pictures out of my head. My mother tells how she jumped out of the train on her birthday. She was then younger than I am now.

Miss R.'s past history featured prominently prolonged sadistic mistreatment by her brother. He was a bright and ambitious boy who showed unusually cruel behavior toward his sister. He used to beat her and twist her arms behind her back until she would scream in pain. He also held her by the feet and swung her in a game of mounting excitement and fear until both were exhausted, and then he would throw her on the bed. At other times he would put her head between his knees and squeeze, or would pin her to the floor, sit on her abdomen, hold her arms outstretched, and jump up and down. On a few occasions he put her outside in the snow without shoes. Sometimes he put her on his knees and fondled her genitals.

Sara R. complained continually to her mother, never mentioning the molesting; but the mother always brushed her aside, telling her to stop provoking her brother and not to be a "cry baby." The patient said over and over again, "Nobody believed me. I was even afraid for my life. I used to stand by the window waiting for my parents to come back. I was terrified that something would happen to them, and then I would be left in the hands of my brother. I was sure he would kill me." Gradually she developed the conviction that her brother wanted to eliminate her: "When I was little I felt my brother sincerely wanted me out of the way. He sincerely wanted to kill me. But I couldn't accept it. I wanted him to love me." For many months, each time the subject of the brother would come up, Miss R. would almost immediately become emotional and begin to sob. "Why did he treat me that way? Why was he so cruel to me? Why didn't my parents stop him? Why didn't they believe me when I said he was so bad to me?" As she repeated her story countless times, she would make a long, loud, shrill wailing noise. The patient is the only informant, but there seemed no reason to doubt her veracity about the facts. What surrounds these facts—the emotions, distortions and fantasies—were gradually being reconstructed in the analysis.

In this case neither patient nor therapist saw the sadistic treatment of Miss

R. by her brother as a re-enactment of Holocaust sadism, with the covert encouragement of the mother. The therapist had ultimately to make this connection in the form of a reconstruction if Miss R. was to free herself psychically from these reminiscences and traumatic memories. Here the images of the parents were hypercathected in terms of the Warsaw ghetto experiences and emerged vividly, while the connection between the brother and the Nazi tormenters was repressed. We reinterviewed the psychoanalyst after the termination of the analysis. The interpretation was not made. The analysis ended when the patient was able to forgive the brother and the parents.

## The Oedipus Complex in Children of Survivors

Freud regarded the Oedipus complex as the nucleus of the neuroses. Subsequent psychoanalytic investigation brought out earlier determinants of pathology, but even today most psychoanalysts believe that the Oedipus complex works over and transforms the earlier pathology. Kestenberg (chapter 7), in describing the analysis of Rachel M, stressed early phases of the patient's development but did not focus on her oedipal phase. It would be possible, however, to look upon Rachel's pathology as a regressive expression of oedipal conflicts. At any rate, apart from this one case, there are other instances where the oedipal pathology takes on a special depressive coloring.

A young woman, Hannah V., who was the child of two survivor-parents, sought treatment because of a crumbling marriage. The couple had engaged in a *ménage à trois*, in which Mrs. V. was gradually reduced to the role of spectator, which left her enraged and depressed. She lost all interest in sexual relations, but was nonetheless promiscuous, particularly under circumstances when she felt sorry for the man. She had a recurrent dream in which she is in heaven, completely alone, as both her father and mother are united with their prewar families. In the Holocaust, her father, a religious businessman, had lost his wife and their four children; her mother had lost her husband and one daughter but had managed to save an infant daughter. After the war, following the second marriage for both parents, two male children were still-born. Another sister died in infancy when Hannah V. was three years old. However, a younger sister survived. After the still-birth deaths of his sons, the father had a psychotic episode in which he danced on the graves of his still-born children. After recovering from the episode, he found work as a caretaker of a cemetery, where Mrs. V. often visited him. She commented, "My father's love was buried in Auschwitz."

The father developed an idiosyncratic Sabbath ceremony. He would dress in white and remain uncommunicative throughout the day. The patient assumed that he was communicating with his dead sons whose names he had forgotten. At Sabbath's end he would resume his everyday personality, speak with his family, and play cards as if nothing unusual had occurred. The patient said that she wished to be employed by a burial society—a position not open to women according to traditional Jewish custom. When her father was dying, she rushed to his bedside from another country to be with him. She felt that he died more serenely than he had lived, released at last. After his death, she went to the morgue, stayed the night, and joined the men in reading the Psalms.

Mrs. V. was jealous of her father's relationship to her half-sister, feeling that he preferred this daughter of her mother's first marriage. Significantly, her jealousy was fueled by the fact that the two were not blood relatives and therefore could engage in a relationship without the dreaded incest taboo. It is evident from the clinical material that her oedipal attachment to her father was not only intense, but that it also continued after his death.

As the treatment proceeded, Mrs. V.'s marriage broke up, and the therapist became her main, and perhaps her only, love object. However, she could not endure the deepening transference tie, and left treatment. After one year she called her thearpist and said she wished to resume; but by that time he no longer had any free time. An important lesson to be learned from this case is that a certain amount of "acting out" must be tolerated in the treatment of some children of survivors, including the leaving and refinding of the therapist, if a patient is to develop slowly and perhaps painfully a sense of object constancy in the treatment process.

## *Superego Problems in the Treatment of Children of Survivors*

All human institutions known to us—including some that in their very essence, are hardly benign, such as wars, prisons, and slavery—have had some moral code by which they were governed. The absence of any such code was a unique feature of the extermination camps. It is therefore not surprising that the normal development of the superego was often affected in the survivors of concentration and death camps and in their children. This problem is dealt with more comprehensively and in greater detail in chapter 15, but here we will cite an abbreviated case history to indicate how one analyst coped with this problem.

When Ruth W. was twenty-one years old, she began analysis with complaints of anxiety, indecision about whether to marry her fiancé, and work and study inhibitions. She had been born in Poland and was a victim of Nazi persecution in the Warsaw ghetto and later in a concentration camp. Her sister, six years younger and her only sibling, was killed by the Nazis. Miss W. was separated from her father until liberated. During this period of incarceration, she lived in the same camp with her mother, an aunt, and a female cousin. About two years prior to beginning analysis Miss W.'s mother had a mastectomy for a carcinoma of the breast, thus reviving the daughter's anxieties about death and separation, which she had experienced between the ages of six and eleven in the camp. In the analysis Miss W. was found to be intelligent and perceptive, with a good ability for introspection which, however, she did not always exercise.

Soon it became evident that she tended to act out her conflicts, particularly sexual ones. Indeed, her sexual indiscretions played a role in the patient's decision to seek analysis for herself. She had reported that, several months previously, she had had intercourse with three different men in the course of forty-eight hours. It would not be far-fetched to speculate that her life in the horrors of a Nazi concentration camp—where human life was regarded as cheap by the persecutors, and the threat of death for the victims was ever present—had some decisive effects on her psychic structure. The undermining of mature superego functions and the reactivation of living patterns determined largely by the pleasure principle, with inability to postpone gratification, had become a way of life spawned by dire necessity and the urge for survival. Even after liberation it was not easy to reverse this pattern, which presented a most difficult resistance in the analysis. The patient found it hard to conceive of the future and to delay any gratification of her wishes. Her descriptions pointed to certain distortions in her mother's superego, with which Miss W. tended to identify. The mother had encouraged Ruth W. to get extra food in the camp by devious means, and also engaged in shoplifting since liberation and tried to have her influence the analyst to falsify his records in order to obtain a larger award from German reparations.

Miss W.'s occasional enuresis, which had started at the age of eleven, was revealed not only as a masturbatory equivalent but as an expression of a fantasied phallus. In some dreams she presented herself as standing and urinating like a man. A wealth of material, which emerged through dreams, fantasies, and overt behavior, made it possible to interpret pregenital wishes, penis envy, latent homoerotic longings, and yearning for oral gratification. Further associations confirmed these interpretations, but little change took place in the actual behavior of the patient. She exercised such poor judgment in her sexual activities and choice of partners that it became a matter of grave concern in the analytic work. Further efforts at clarification did nothing to alter the risk of impregnation, venereal disease, or other dangers. Reluctantly, the analyst decided that, if the analysis was to proceed, it was necessary to forbid such acting out. Although she became violently angry about the prohibition, Miss W. complied; at the same time she viewed it as a method of infantilizing her, and reacted in kind. Regression in the form of not going to work, urinary urgency, and loss of bladder control, often at or near the analyst's office, occurred regularly. Bed-wetting began to occur more frequently. Retrospectively, the analyst could see that much of the previous acting out had been used by the patient in order to resist the development of the transference neurosis.

The changing quality of Miss W.'s involvement in the analysis made it possible to elicit further dynamics in her development and intrapsychic conflicts. Her promiscuity represented a search for an object who could gratify her sexually, as she was frigid during intercourse ordinarily. Her behavior was also a defense against her fear of acting out homosexually. Her masculine identification represented a compromise between the wish for a penis and a defense against her fears of penetration and childbirth. She recalled that when her mother was on the delivery table giving birth to her sister, there was an air raid. The entire staff fled to the shelter area, leaving her mother strapped to the table. Further dangers in being a woman were exemplified by her mother's mastectomy and hysterectomy; the latter occurred during the analysis. The symbolic castration as well as the actual threat of death were evident in both events.

Continuing ego analysis and identification with the analyst made it possible for Ruth W. to see that she was no longer a helpless child, that the dangers of Nazi sadism were over, and that she could exercise control over her infantile wishes. About one year before termination, she met a young professional man who proposed marriage. With him she refrained from foreplay, only to be left frustrated during coitus. Gradually, however, she became able to experience clitoral orgasm in sexual intercourse. At this time a dream was analyzed that ordinarily would have been accompanied by her wetting the bed but, in this instance, was not. The occasion was the prelude to a discussion of the possibility of termination of the analysis, and therapist and patient agreed on a date for the end of treatment.

This case illustrates how a malfunctioning superego exposes the patient to severe anxiety states. This point has been stressed in the psychoanalytic literature, especially by E. Jacobson (1964). In this instance, the analyst attempted interpretations aimed at developing insight without employing parameters for some time, but without success. The prohibition against promiscuity could have been only a temporary parameter; but the report of the analyst makes clear that, in his opinion, making the unconscious conscious and the resolution of the intrapsychic conflict played only subsidiary roles. The main emphasis was on identification with the analyst, the building of a new and better-functioning superego, which then facilitated better reality testing. Apparently the patient developed enough love for the analyst to be able to give up her promiscuity for his sake. This may indicate that the promiscuity was taken over from the world of the concentration camp and was not a real reflection of the patient's basic developmental arrest. This phenomenon has been observed in many cases where children of survivors make more rapid progress than one could expect in instances where there has been a clearly nuclear intrapsychic conflict or developmental arrest.

## Recurrent Problems of Technique

Every psychoanalytic endeavor raises questions and issues involving technique. Many of these ubiquitous and recurrent problems are particularly sensitive and delicate when they are encountered in the treatment of survivors and their children. Some examples can be subsumed under the following categories:

### PROBLEMS OF TIMING

Earlier we presented a clinical vignette (pages 16–18) describing a man who had been in a concentration camp as an adolescent and developed, years later, severe fantasies of jealousy about his wife. In one of his early sessions, he told of a series of dreams he had had during his childhood, soon after the death of his father. He searched for a word to describe some frightening figures with demonic qualities appearing in his dreams. The analyst suggested in Hebrew the word for "the angel of Death," in an effort to help the patient to express himself; the patient smiled in recognition and commented in surprise at the analyst's guessing what he meant. Shortly after, the patient developed coryzal symptoms, attributed to allergies, which prevented him from lying on the couch. The analyst offered a tentative interpretation in the form of a question, connecting the symptoms with the patient's report of having cried incessantly for days after having been separated from his mother on their arrival at Auschwitz, never to see her alive again. Although the symptom cleared after the interpretation, the patient had an intense negative reaction to the analyst's comment, accusing him of jumping to conclusions and also of listening too much and saying too little. The treatment came to an abrupt end soon after, following the discussion of a dream that the patient used in a deceptive way to test the analyst. With the benefit of hindsight, it was possible to see that the interpretations were probably correct and even effective, but premature. The paranoid core in the patient's character structure and his tendency to be mistrustful and suspicious, should have been more carefully respected. His need not to be understood too quickly, to deal with anxiety and fear of being penetrated, mobilized an intense resistance and created insurmountable obstacles and irreparable damage in the therapeutic relationship.

The technical problems in this case can be usefully compared with the report (see chapter 5) where missing interpretations based on Holocaust experiences were offered later in the treatment, after initial defenses had been dealt with, and thus provided a propitious atmosphere for interventions.

PROBLEMS OF ANONYMITY

Freud, in his papers on technique, made it a cardinal rule that personal data from the life of the analyst should not be allowed to enter the analytic work, because knowledge of such facts can interfere with the flowering and full development of a transference neurosis based on the fantasies of the analysand. This otherwise useful dictum, when rigidly employed, can become a source of difficulty in the treatment of children of survivors. An excellent example has been provided by Kestenberg (see chapter 4) in her report of the case of Marvin K. It will be recalled that the patient interrupted treatment when he joined a guru's group; but even before that happened, he was alienated by the refusal of the analyst to supply him with astrological data related to her birth. In retrospect, one can see that, in his own fashion, Marvin K. was testing his compatibility with his analyst. The analyst, in her otherwise correct refusal to supply this data, appeared to have frustrated the patient's attempt to build a bridge between himself and his therapist. When Marvin K. found the guru, he attempted to integrate guru and therapist by trying to persuade the latter to join the group. Marvin K. finally concluded that she refused to do so out of loyalty to her own guru, Sigmund Freud. Psychologically, Marvin K. was not sufficiently individuated to be able to tolerate divergences without losing the analyst as a good object.

The therapist herself was in conflict. She debated whether she should analyze the cult as an attempt by Marvin K. to find a father and a subsitution for his dead family. She also thought that Marvin K. needed an external representative to reinforce his wavering superego, and was concerned that her interpretation might be taken as a rejection of his new-found goodness. In retrospect, it seems that Marvin K. had found a corrective emotional experience in life that was more powerful than the insight therapy offered him. The therapist was caught in a dilemma; she could neither give Marvin K. her full blessing as his parents had done, nor did she feel justified in analyzing away his new-found family.

Another example illustrates the problem of the anonymity of the analyst (see pages 12–13). The patient was a survivor, as was the analyst. The treatment was marked by a striking absence of interest on the part of the patient in anything pertaining to the life of the analyst. Throughout the treatment, the patient made no reference to the fact that his analyst might be a refugee, a survivor, or even Jewish. The analyst himself maintained total anonymity throughout the treatment, which lasted for two years, and was reasonably successful, although there was some question whether it was terminated prematurely. Ostensibly the patient ended treatment because he had to seek employment outside of the city where the analyst practiced. Further questioning of the analyst revealed that the patient was still within commuting distance and could have continued treatment, perhaps in a modified form, while working at his new job. The possibility remains that, had the analyst drawn attention to the absence of fantasies and his own lack of interest—particularly to questions involving his relationship to the Holocaust—a deeper and more meaningful analytic relationship might have been possible.

H. Klein (1968), working in Israel, noted that when survivor-patients learned that the therapist had also been a victim, their paranoid projections onto him or her diminished. Here the evidence is not clear, because one does not know what interfered with the projection onto the therapist. Anonymity not only encourages projections but also offers the patient a chance to work them out. Yet another problem of technique is highlighted: the value of preserving anonymity in instances where projection is found to play a major role.

THE VALUE OF METAPHOR IN INTERPRETATIONS

The significance of metaphor in the communication between patient and therapist may have a special relevance for the understanding of the special group of patients who are children of Holocaust survivors. It has been said of survivors themselves (see chapter 5) that, during the Holocaust, they lived in a world beyond, or even before, metaphor. Terence Des Pres (1976) has written movingly of a life in extremity where behavior has no meaning in a symbolic or a psychological sense. One task of a survivor's child may then be to seek some symbolic realization of a parent's experience, and the child's symptoms may express metaphorical attempts at such a re-creation and restitution of the parent's symbolic processes.

A young, married professional man, John Z., came to treatment because of an unusual symptom. He had suffered from myopia since boyhood, a condition that frequently becomes associated with some degenerative process in the vitreous humor of the eyes and the precipitation of opacities, or "floaters," which he had noticed about two years before seeking help. Most people get used to "floaters" and adapt to their presence, though conceding they might be unpleasant or mildly annoying at times. Despite the assurance of ophthalmologists who said that he suffered from no ocular disease that would impair visual acuity, Mr. Z. was in a great state of anxiety and depression when seen, cried frequently at home, and despaired about his career, which once had seemed promising. Even though he regarded his plight as part of a "reality" situation, he was sufficiently psychologically minded to recognize his response as inappropriate and hoped his mood would yield to a better understanding of himself.

John Z. was the elder of two, with a sister four years his junior. His mother had died during his last year at professional school. He mentioned, almost in passing, that his father had been born in Poland and had suffered incarceration in a concentration camp before being liberated. The father's family had all perished in death camps, and only one of his brothers survived. He rarely spoke of his experiences during the Holocaust, and Mr. Z. asked few questions. The father worked at a routine job, was reluctant to seek advancement, and preferred to "keep a low profile." The patient felt that his father saw the world as an inimical place where the fewer "waves" one created, the better off one was. Mr. Z. now has an energetic and optimistic father-in-law to whom he is particularly devoted, and whom he uses as a confidante when he feels at his most downtrodden and desperate.

John Z. was a pleasant young man who quickly developed a strong therapeutic alliance and a positive transference with passive and dependent features. He had a remarkable ability to describe the sizes and shapes of his "floaters" and drew them for his therapist. When he was sufficiently free to speak of his life in general, he lamented that he was imprisoned by his symptoms, and that nothing but a bleak landscape of despair faced him. Gradually it appeared that the theme of his lamentations sounded like those he had attributed to his father who had been mourning his lost family. Some of the patient's diatribes against the "foreign" bodies in his eyes seemed to possess the ring of metaphor. At the end of about one year, he brought up the first of several dreams whose manifest content dealt with Holocaust experiences. After some preparatory remarks, he was told that he was responding to the "floaters" in his eyes as if he had incorporated his father's persecutors and the murderers of his father's family, who were now in the process of persecuting him. Mr. Z. was initially startled, but the change in the clinical picture was almost immediate and dramatic. During the next several months, he indicated that his eyes no longer troubled him as before, although the "floaters" were still visible. His life and work continued to go well, and he considered termination.

The ubiquitous foreground character of metaphor drew J. A. Arlow's (1979) attention to its role as a derivative of the basic, persistent unconscious fantasy life of the patient. Metaphor may be seen as an outcropping of unconscious fantasy, whether it is creative and even when it may be stale and banal. The use of metaphor may be greater at points of intense transference, helps to ward off anxiety, and may reveal the nature of character structure. Sometimes large segments of an analysis center about the understanding of leading metaphors. A seminal point in our experience is that variations on the themes clustering around a metaphor regularly lead to the discovery of an unconscious fantasy that is usually connected with some trauma. Although many psychoanalytic writers have urged that more attention be paid to the concept that analytic work is essentially a metaphorical enterprise, some have been wary and defensive about its use as an explanatory idea in psychoanalysis. On balance, it appears that metaphor constitutes a unique way by which what was previously unknown may be reorganized and reconceptualized in a novel way. This concept is applicable to all analytic work; but especially in work with patients whose lives have been influenced by such central, starkly tragic, and overwhelming experiences as those of the Holocaust, a sensitively attuned and careful attention to the role of metaphor may be crucial in the refinement of the therapist's technical skills.

## Conclusion

This chapter has shown that treatment of survivors and their children makes extraordinary emotional demands on the therapist. The temptation to act as a savior for a patient who suffered so much is great indeed. When the therapist yields to this pressure, the transference neurosis that must result in the equation therapist=Nazi guard does not develop. This makes treatment easier for both patient and therapist, but a phase of negative transference essential for future cure is bypassed.

The evidence also suggests that only few survivors and not many children of survivors could tolerate the rigors of the classical psychoanalytic technique, particularly the anonymity of the therapist. This should not be interpreted to mean that they all fall diagnostically into the borderline psychotic category, but the Holocaust trauma has adversely affected the structure of the ego. One might say in general that the Holocaust trauma was a trauma to the superego, ego, and id. The fact that the camps were instituted by a government representing parental authority offended the superego. That the cruelty witnessed went beyond ordinary wishes of the id shook both the id and the ego. Time and again it was noted that the awareness that the parents were helpless pawns in the hands of a malevolent destiny destroyed idealization of the parents at too early a time in the life of the child. For that reason, children of partisans or ghetto fighters faced an easier task psychologically, because they could continue to idealize their parents. However, even in these instances, children were at times overawed and overwhelmed by their parents' past.

A most important insight is the recognition that children of survivors often do not get to live their own lives. They feel obliged to undo the trauma endured by their parents; or else they rebel against this task vigorously, feeling that it has been imposed upon them arbitrarily. If there is one generalization that can be made about therapy with survivors, it is that the therapist must assist the patient to work through a mourning process that was cut short when one loss succeeded another with unbearable rapidity. At the same time, the daily threat to one's life made mourning impossible. An equivalent generalization in the treatment of children of survivors is that they must be helped to finish the interrupted work of separation and individuation from their parents. The Holocaust trauma is probably transmitted with devastating effect to the child precisely because the parents could not assist in the process of separation.

Dr. Margaret Mahler generously reviewed many of the cases discussed in this chapter. From the special vantage point she and her co-workers have developed (Mahler, et al. 1968 and 1975)—while it was not always possible to reconstruct the separation-individuation phases of children of survivors—almost universally it was seen that there was a failure to take advantage of the "second chance" that adolescence under favorable conditions offers (Blos 1967).

There appears to be a special mechanism that has interfered with an optimum degree of individuation in these cases. The trauma encourages the survivor to see the child as the reincarnation of the evil he or she has suffered. Clinical records abound with statements such as, "What Hitler did not succeed in doing to us, you will succeed in doing." Conversely, it seems that those survivors who were successful in fostering, or at least in permitting, the process of separation-individuation in their children could also prevent, or at least reduce, the transmission of the trauma. Doubtless, such parents do exist, but their children are less likely to be encountered in a clinical situation. Whether a similar mechanism also operates in other situations of massive trauma, or whether it is unique to the Holocaust, is a subject worthy of further exploration.

**14**

# Hysterical Features among Children of Survivors

## Introduction

It has been stated repeatedly that, in one way or another, the children of survivors tend to be preoccupied with the suffering of their parents. To many people's surprise and pain, children who were often conceived in order to reaffirm life, have shown signs that the past suffering of their parents plays an important part in their own existence, and that their concern with the horrible events preceding their own birth is expressed by a tendency to repeat the suffering themselves. This wish tends to be repressed, since the parents have placed much stress on survival and the new life; and the tendency to repeat the past is clearly contrary to the view consciously shared with their parents that it should never happen again. However, when some malfunction brings one of these children to the attention of professionals, the analyst is apt to be confronted by symptoms that can only be explained when one understands that year after year the patient has attempted to relive aspects of the persecution of his or her parents and relatives. This has been a painful discovery for all concerned. At the Psychoanalytic Congress in Jerusalem (1977), Erich Gumbel stated that it was particularly difficult for those living in Israel to recognize that the second generation was still experiencing the past, and that the founding of the Jewish state could not wholly undo the effects of the persecution. He thinks that therapists and analysts have suffered a 'narcissistic blow,' which they share with everyone whose basic sense of values was affronted by the Holocaust, and which they must recognize within themselves. It is equally difficult to accept Emmanuel DeWind's (1968) references to a "hate addiction" among survivors which leads ex-prisoners to what he called "the most serious problem which is that they so often direct their aggression onto their children, thus fulfilling the Biblical saying that the sins of the fathers shall be visited upon the children unto the third and fourth generation" (p. 304).

This is not to say that all survivors are sick and have damaged their children, but many children of survivors do need help and understanding; and as the cases unfold, the wish to experience the persecution expresses itself in many forms, most of which do not reveal the underlying motive. For instance, it was detected in the artistic creations of one who was unaware that he was expressing his longing to share in the deaths of his relatives so as to have a place in the minds of his parents and be loved as he felt that only "they," his relatives, were loved. These fantasies were apparently present despite an outwardly close and intricate tie to the family, which had no connection with these creative efforts; and the patient's intense outpourings of emotion stood in sharp contrast to the drabness of his daily existence. As in so many other cases, concern about the choice of a career had brought him into treatment. Inasmuch as his artistic creations expressed feelings that were dissociated from the rest of his personality, they took the place of a symptom; and it had to be assumed that he could not improve his life without integrating into the rest of his personality the fantasies they expressed.

Sylvia Axelrod et al. (1980), whose experience with thirty hospitalized children of survivors led to similar conclusions, described patients who have staged real persecutions or have repeated, within the hospital setting, being locked up as their parents had been; thus, they were alternately preparing for the Holocaust and testing whether they could be freed. In each case, the nature of the underlying motive was unconscious, but it became a familiar part of the picture to those observers who had become sensitive to such fantasies. It is as if these patients needed to abolish the time difference between themselves and their parents, and, in order not to suffer from the sense of exclusion, had to relive, often on anniversaries, the latter's fate in order to go on with their own lives. "Their story becomes more real to me than my own life, at times," said one child of survivors who, for that reason, could not afford to become too immersed in their story. She also said, in describing events that preceded the time of her birth, "We lived . . . ," instead of "My parents lived. . . ." Nevertheless, she was not aware how many of her actions were determined by the wish to take part in the trauma suffered by her parents.

Once it has been established that the need to repeat the fate of the parents dominates one part of the lives of the neurotic and psychotic children of survivors who seek treatment, it is important to assess the mechanisms by which this need is both integrated and dissociated within the rest of the personality. No attempt is made here to attribute one single mode of psychic functioning to a population whose members are almost as varied as is society at large, having in common only the fact that their parents survived the Holocaust, were in constant danger during it, and incurred important losses of objects as well as narcissistic losses. However, the fate of the parents favored certain adjustment mechanisms that entered into their relationships with their children; and the study of hysteria is particularly relevant for some of the problems which confront the analyst who is trying to understand them. For example, those who have studied the effects of the Holocaust on the survivors, have often referred to a period of latency. The traumatic impact of the degrading and cruel treatment by the Nazis has often been delayed, so that at first the survivors seemed less damaged by what they had undergone than they actually were. This observation turns out to be compatible with what was observed about traumatic hysteria: "After the physical trauma, the life-endangering shock, there exists a period of latency, of incubation (Charcot) or of 'elaboration' (Freud), that leads one to think of something different from a purely causal physiological sequence" (Laplanche 1970, p. 130). Martin Wangh refers to the relationship between the trauma and its long-term effect as "permanent character changes through stress." He goes on to assert:

At the time of the traumatic impact, through a defensive depersonalization and derealization, clear apperception of external stimuli is greatly reduced and hence the potential for the emergence of internal repressed ideation, consonant with the present sado-masochistic stimuli, increases. At such a time, the percepts of the cruel external reality that have not been entirely warded off by the defense, form an amalgam with the emergent percepts of the past, thus obtaining a lasting energic cathexis as great as that of a traumatic experience in childhood. Once the traumatic situation is over, an effort usually only partially successful is made to forget, to rerepress. (1968b, p. 320)

As a further elucidation for this process, Wangh suggests that the process of defensive depersonalization and derealization is akin to the "hypnoid state" first postulated by Freud and Breuer (as quoted in Wangh 1968b, p. 320). If, then, the trauma is defended against by means of a process known to be productive of hysteria, it is permissible to hypothesize that hysterical mechanisms lend themselves to the mastery of the trauma suffered by the survivors.

To postulate that this mode of defense leads to the mastery and subsequent transmission of the trauma requires considerable justification, but it can be demonstrated that there are striking similarities between the traits and conditions favoring hysteria and those under which children of survivors were brought up. This understanding is particularly important in those cases in which the dissociations are so severe that they attain psychotic proportions, since hysterical psychosis is a diagnostic entity that has fallen into relative disuse, and the proper assessment may not be made.

## The Uncertain Status of Both Hysteria and of the Pathology Afflicting Children of Survivors

Axelrod and her co-workers (1980) remarked on the fact that many of the survivors' children who came to their attention presented atypical pictures, and a number had defied categorization. Judith Kestenberg has stressed repeatedly (and has incorporated her conviction in her diagnostic profile in chapter 7) that even though some of the patients were at times psychotic, many did not suffer from the fragmentation seen in schizophrenia and displayed ego strength not usually associated with psychotic episodes. While they seemed at times confused, their boundaries conformed to their own boundaries and to those of their internalized objects; however, they did not seem to be living their own lives during the psychotic episodes. Many of them did not settle into a state of chronic psychosis, so that often its episodic, encapsulated character suggested a dramatic re-enactment in an "altered state of consciousness" rather than a state of fragmentation compatible with schizophrenia or the chronicity of manic-depressive psychosis. In this, what they suffered seemed to resemble the description of hysterical psychosis: "A type of transient psychotic state [which] can be differentiated from other psychogenic psychoses. It is usually sudden in onset, short-lived . . . and has no long-term sinister prognosis of psychotic deterioration" (Blacker and Tupin 1977, p. 117). There is a relatively rapid reconstitution of ego functions both in hysterical psychosis and in the psychotic episodes suffered by some of the children of survivors.

In the survivor children, the onset was at times triggered by their having reached an age that was crucial in the history of their parents' persecution.

It may thus be true that the puzzle represented by some of these patients mirrors the uncertain status of the disorder from which they suffer, and that a further exploration of hysteria will be helpful for the assessment and treatment of these particular cases. Unfortunately "the unrewarding areas of psychiatry attract the interest of neither the practitioners nor theoreticians. Hysterical psychosis is one of these, and as such has been neglected by research workers" (Gisela Pankow 1974, p. 408). This situation is to the detriment of those patients whose degree of pathology may be overestimated because of a more damaging diagnostic label.

At the present time, when the tendency is to consider neurosis and psychosis as two distinct categories, and when we try to find a *fixation point* by which one can judge whether the main difficulties are oedipal or pre-oedipal, it is frustrating to approach hysteria where no differentiation has been made between neurosis and psychosis. Nor is it at all clear how the oral fixations so often mentioned in the cases of hysteria interact with the observation that the hysteric has failed to detach the libido from the oedipal object. This lack of clarity has undoubtedly contributed to the decline of hysteria as a diagnostic category at the present time. Yet, in a strange way, these patients reflect this uncertainty: "They are not as sick as they look" is one of the frequent observations that has been made about them; and what distinguishes them from other severely traumatized patients is precisely the remarkable ego strength in the presence of extended pathology (see chapter 7).

Indeed, we may be forced to accept the elusiveness of this neurosis, which ranges from the most advanced (fixation at the oedipal level) to outright psychosis. In this context it may be helpful to recall the pathology of Anna O. (Breuer and Freud 1893, pp. 21–47) and compare it with her subsequent career. The severity of the one stands in sharp contrast to the adaptiveness of the other; and the tendency to suggest that those whom Freud treated were not hysteric because of their psychotic or borderline features, may reflect the wish to redefine the term rather than to make a renewed effort to understand its complexity.

In the case of those patients who fall into the realm of hysterical psychosis, only a proper diagnosis will lead to appropriate treatment. The problem of proper diagnosis is not nearly as crucial in the case of neurosis.

Despite the uncertainty about hysteria, the literature on the subject is abundant; and within the last three years alone, there have been two books attempting to give an overview on the subject. The Paris Congress in 1973 devoted to the subject yielded many interesting articles integrating what is known about the dynamics with more recent ways of conceptualizing psychosexual development. As we review some of the salient points methodically, the parallels between the experiences of children of survivors and those of hysterics become unmistakable, so that it seems as if in many essential points the descriptions of hysterics in general fit the cases that are known to us.

## The Reality of the Trauma

Ever since the time when Freud abandoned his theory attributing the cause of hysteria to childhood seduction, there has been a tendency among psychoanalysts to consider events in outer reality as being the concern only of sociologists. But this tendency has never detracted from the effort to find in treatment memories of the event that caused the pathological defensive reaction within the ego. Psychoanalysis emphasizes the reaction of the ego in response to what happened to it. In the case of the survivors' children, the trauma of the Second World War has the same role as that attributed to seduction in hysteria. The complicated interaction between inner and outer reality was never stated, as when André Green wrote:

What comes into play is not a seduction which is put into action, rather it is a matter of the minimal signs, indicative of such a desire, which are recognized by the girl, as the jealous person recognizes the seductive behavior of his lover toward his rival. What comes into play is the function of the misapprehension of the desire of the girl who wishes to be seduced. Perception serves repression in this case. External reality furnishes exoneration to the interdiction which weighs on internal reality. Fantasy is nourished by the kernel of reality, as in delirium, but the role of perception is to [obscure] the fantasy while having induced it. (1973)

Inasmuch as there is evidence that the often-unspoken reality of the trauma that the parents have suffered, and the anxieties it has generated, are communicated to the children in the same way as the seduction described by Green, this reality can be said to have the same function in the fantasy life of the children. This is true even though the reality of the trauma pertains to the life experiences of the parents and not to those of the children.

What is transmitted is at first as mysterious as adult sexuality when it impinges upon the child's consciousness and is assimilated in that realm where perceptions merge with fantasy. Only later can one sort out one's reactions as a child and distinguish between the life experiences of the parents and one's own fantasies. If Dora's fantasies concerning Mr. K. (Freud 1905) were of utmost importance for understanding her difficulties, the memory of Mr. K.'s advances was crucial for the pathological outcome, since she was subjected to a seductive climate that stimulated her beyond her capacity for discharge. Psychoanalysis has always taken into account the events that have triggered the fantasies underlying pathology. It has therefore had to stay on a fine line between inner and outer reality, somewhere between solipsism and sociology. Axelrod and her co-workers report on the hazard of emphasizing one aspect at the expense of the other with reference to survivor children:

We believe that some discordant diagnoses and concomitant treatments arise by reason of the unusual degree to which intrapsychic or endogenous factors are associated and confused with subcultural familial factors. Focusing on one set of factors to the exclusion of the other leads to poor results. (Axelrod et al. 1980, p. 8)

# Hysterical Features among Children of Survivors

Even though we are faced with the transmission of events that have actually taken place and are not exclusively part of the parents' fantasy life, many concrete details are simply not known and therefore bear the stamp of a reinterpretation by the parents. The anxieties of the parents in regard to survival and loss generated by those events can reinforce the child's anxieties in ways that are familiar to us.

## The Genesis of the Trauma

Eric Brenman's description of the hysterogenic mother so fits what has been written about women who have survived the Holocaust that he could almost be describing them and the conditions under which they tried to raise their children right after the war:

The mother is overwhelmed by anxiety, unconsciously conveying that the infant's anxieties are really catastrophic. 2. At the same time, she will provide a panacea to lull the baby and try to make it believe all is perfectly well. She provides a model for identification which is unreal, the prototype of the "successful hysteric." 3. She encourages negation of psychic truth. 4. She provides external love of an idealizing type, with excessive indulgence of the physical needs, devotion, excessive sensuous stimulation, encouraging greedy dependency and hypersexuality. 5. By these means she avoids psychic catastrophe. . . . We have an attack on psychic reality and an external mother forming an unreal relationship. Here we can see a *modus vivendi* established together with a defense against catastrophic anxieties of survival. (1973)

Brenman adds that the same relationship could exist between an average mother and a difficult baby. It also applies to the average woman who is trying to nurture a child in peacetime while being plagued by memories of war, death, destruction, starvation, and loss. John Bruggeman says:

I think that many concentration camp mothers used their first-born child after the war as a peace-child or as a substitute for the dead member of the family; sometimes as a reparation child for the reunification of the estranged family . . . by treating the child's fears and griefs as trivial and commanding it to enjoy itself because the war is over. (Bruggeman, unpublished manuscript, 1977)

The anxieties remained unspoken, and the patient in treatment later communicated only very indirectly his own belief and that of his parents that the truth is unbearable.

M. Masud Khan concurs with the view that the attack on psychic reality is essential to the etiology of hysteria, along with the overstimulation leading to a precocious body ego and sexualization of anxiety: "The body needs were satisfied but the ego needs were neither recognized nor facilitated" (1974b, p. 154). The trauma, according to him, is in the mother's inability to satisfy the psychic needs of the child and in the child's attempt at self-cure by exploiting body experiences and thus establishing the basic model for reacting to stress and conflict. Khan suggests that

hysteria is not so much an illness as the technique to remain *blank*, as if absent from oneself, with symptoms which are substitutes permitting the camouflage of this absence. In their childhood, hysterics become conscious early in life of the subjective mood of the mother, a mood which intrudes into her function as a caretaker. Under those circumstances, the child sexualizes a relation to the partial object in order to refuse this intrusion provoked by the emotionality of the mother and a relation which is too close for the capacities of the budding ego to face. (1974b, p. 156)

He, too, suggests the exclusion of an important part of the child's experience from the rest of the child's psychic organization, but adds that the missing part is replaced by excessive sexualization of the relationship. This part is repressed in later years as well and manifests itself as the return of the repressed in neurosis and psychosis. The two-phrase process—the exclusion of the mother's affective relationship to the child as well as the replacement of the missing component by a sexualized relationship that is later repressed— makes the fixation point in hysteria difficult to establish and causes it to look like more serious pathology, such as the "false self" or other schizoid phenomena. However, the intervening variable, which is the sexualization of the relationship to the object, allows development to continue and reach the oedipal phase, even if in what Gisela Pankow (1974) calls a truncated form.

Despite many advances in psychoanalysis, the process of sexualization remains mysterious; but it is also clear that through it, the relationship to the object is maintained and quantities of energy can be absorbed that otherwise would contaminate the ego to a paralyzing degree. If the ego is strong enough to sexualize the trauma, it can be contained.

This sexualizing of the trauma was brought home through the case in which the survivor syndrome was, as it were, absorbed into a sexual perversion, which was treated and described by Abraham Freedman (1978). The man, who had suffered greatly during the war, came into treatment because of a perversion that he was unable to control. As a result of psychoanalysis, he was greatly improved and left the treatment satisfied. The question that arose when this case was presented for study centered on the issue of the interpretations that, following the patient's associations, hardly ever touched on his experiences with the Germans. The content of the analysis dealt mainly with his earlier childhood in which the Poles or his father were imbued with the sadistic imagery incorporated into his scenario. It is as if the experiences that came later had been absorbed into an earlier structure, and reinforced it. We shall never be able to know what would have been the outcome if interpretations centering on the Holocaust experience had become more important in his analysis; but the potential for absorbing a trauma through sexualization was once more demonstrated through this patient's great improvement by means of insights geared at understanding the earlier trauma.

In this case, the patient's sexuality was used exclusively in the way described by Joyce McDougall (1970)—that is, to repair faults in one's sense of identity. As in all perversion, the patient attempted to create through the perverse scenario something that did not exist—as, for example, a man who at will "becomes" a woman while still retaining his phallic potency, or a fetishist who creates an illusory penis for a woman from an article of clothing. Through the act of creation such a patient can deny his anxieties about loss and castration on the one hand, and on the other avoid outright psychosis in which a large part of reality is relinquished. In this way, the patient avoids working through the Holocaust experience, since the anxieties associated with it are absorbed into those prompting the perverse scenario.

The neurotic, on the other hand, has acquired the right to experience his body as a unit, but at the cost of sexuality as an instrument of pleasure (McDougall 1970). Thus, sexualization of the trauma in hysteria allows a further refinement in the process of defense and the possibility that a greater segment of the personality escapes, at least in part, the pathogenic conflict. This factor contributes to the general view that hysteria, which centers on the repression of the conflict of the oedipal phase, retains to the greatest extent a means of containing the pathology.

In her attempt to link psychopathology to interactions within the family, Gisela Pankow states:

I wish to propose the following hypothesis concerning the correlation between family structure and the body image in hysterical psychosis: for a girl to develop her own world of sexual desire, i.e. unconscious genital desire, it is not only necessary that the father take his normal place in the family—which the father of the schizophrenic does not do—but he must also accept his sexual and genital role and the prohibition thus implied with regard to his children. (1974, p. 412)

Again, Pankow's comparison between the father of the schizophrenic and the father of the hysteric makes clear that the difference is crucial and that the pathological sexualization of the relationship allows an important step in development to take place.

275

Khan's observation (1974b) that the mother's inability to contain her anxieties—with her tendency to replace some of the flaws in her ability to care for her child by an emphasis on physical contact—contributes to hysteria is also relevant to the histories that emerge in the treatment of children of survivors. The parents wanted to reaffirm life through the birth of these children. It is remarkable in this context how many of those who have come to the attention of mental health workers were born in 1946, very often in displaced persons camps, or have siblings who were born before the parents found a permanent home. This fact suggests that the parents of our patients attempted, through the birth of a baby, to renew life after their release from the concentration camp. But their fears about survival were often greater than their ability to master them; and when they often engaged their children in a struggle with death, it was on a level that escaped conscious control and formed that core of anxiety that was recognized as inappropriate and therefore dissociated. In addition to their fears concerning physical care, their decision to have children before they had renewed their own lives caused them to inflict on their children unstable marriages, separations, and hostilities, which repeated some of the elements of their own lives. The attempt to compensate for some of these deprivations through denial and excessive physical care or abuse led to the sexualization of the parent-child relationship which caused fixation at that level.

Axelrod and her co-workers write:

Parents have difficulty in responding with adequate affect or setting limits, they are overanxious and overprotective and have difficulties with separation. They tend to overvalue their children, expecting them to accomplish enough in life to justify the parents' survival. (1980, p. 2)

Parents' anxiety and overprotectiveness can also take the form of encouraging the child to remain a dependent so that fulfilling his or needs can justify their existence in their own eyes. This causes some aspects of the relationship between parent and child to become unreal and makes it difficult for the survivors to respond appropriately to their children's suffering due to physical displacement from country to country, economic uncertainty, marital discord, and—most important—the overwhelming anxieties and depressions that formed their early environment. Since the parents of the children who later came for treatment tended to emphasize the positive aspects of their children's lives, the children, too, shared the former's fantasy that they, the children, had been lucky to be born under such favorable circumstances. The alternative between abuse and spoiling reinforced the fantasy that the parents were not to blame and that nothing of a traumatic nature was occurring in the lives of the children. Experiences were therefore repressed and replaced by a wishful fantasy. In most cases, the total abolishment of inner life—as occurs in schizophrenia—was avoided; instead, the child tended to adjust with the demand that he live out an existence fundamentally alien to his genuine feelings—as happens with the hysteric (Krohn 1978, p. 136)—but not out of touch with external reality.

Through his well-being, the child can prove to the parent that he is innocent of the suffering of his objects, either because they were never lost or because he had no hand in their fate. In this two-phased attempt to help the parents cope with the pain and guilt concerning the loss of their objects, the children can participate in the denial of that loss through an identification that constitutes a miraculous restitution of the lost object. The child participating in restitution of the lost objects alleviates the guilt concerning the death as well as the implied oedipal victory over the object, and follows the logic that since the object is resurrected in the child, no crime has been committed and guilt is unnecessary. Of course, the object must remain intact and happy and is called upon to play the parental role, or it must remain the needy child gratifying the parents' wish to retain a nurturing role. Ilse Grubrich-Simitis says: "They clung to their old objects and reprojected them onto their offspring. Lost parents became children. [Since] the fact that [the child] survived them seems to bring forth a statement of guilt, it signified somehow collaboration with the executioner; whereas only death through persecution is the clear distancing from the persecutor. In unconscious mental processes there is apparently a tendency toward a judgment which is quite without foundation and which idealizes the death of the victim and is suspicious of those who survived" (1979, p. 1016).

In many cases, then, this dilemma was resolved by the failure of a parent to take the rightful place in the oedipal triangle and by parental encouraging of the identification of the child with the lost object.

This process was particularly well illustrated in the case of Peter Y., whose parents had turned away from religion with the firm belief that it had lost its meaning for them. However, they gave their children a thorough religious education, so that Mr. Y. eventually insisted forcefully that his parents adhere to the ritual; this they did as if they were children who were being trained rather than adults who had gained certain experiences. It was Peter Y. who assumed the role of the lost rabbi in the family and punished the parents for their transgression.

In another example from an analysis, Naomi T. had been asked to change a certain session for the convenience of the analyst, but said that she could not. The following week, she requested an extra session in the same time that she had earlier refused, and was granted it. The night before this session, she had the following dream, which involves a woman about whom Miss T. had dreamed before and who was living with her uncle and had a shower for which one needs a screwdriver.

Miss T. is living in a commune next door, and there is a lot of borrowing back and forth. She goes into this woman's house to take a shower. The woman comes home and thinks that perhaps her mother or father are in the house [later the patient said, "Funny, first I made her into an orphan"]; and when she finds out that they are not there, Miss T. gets worried and wants to rush lest the woman think that she is an intruder and call the police. The shower is not opened with a screwdriver but with a silver spoon that in the dream belongs to her and in reality is a spoon her parents brought from abroad.

Miss T.'s association to the shower that is opened with a screwdriver led immediately to the gas chambers. This dream demonstrates the dilemma of the child who is afraid that she can be loved only if she is the dead relative. Later, Miss T. complained about being trapped in her own personality and, after the analyst's vacation, reported that at its very beginning, she had caught some disease that was afflicting a group of people who came from the Old World. Still later, after destroying the link to children of survivors, she thought that analysis for herself alone was a waste. From this concern it becomes apparent that Miss T.'s sense of worth was intimately linked with her identification with someone else.

The dream and the illness Miss T. shared with survivors illustrate two types of identification corresponding to two different attempts at gaining love. In one she had to be the lost object of the parent, and in the other she shared in the fate of the parents themselves. The latter is identification with the object rather than restitution of the lost ones, but neither leads to the kind of giving up of the object which is seen in melancholia.

These patients try to change themselves in order to defend against the trauma of their experiences with their parents. They cannot confront those experiences, since the defenses of their parents aim at abolishing the reality of their own suffering. Thus, these patients maintain repression while entertaining the hope that, through some psychic manipulation, events will be converted into non-happenings. This is different from the obsessive compulsive attempt to undo an event by action on an external object; here the wish is to change the inside so as to abolish the external event.

Unlike other cases who have been more or less damaged, hysterogenic parents are likely to have been able to adapt to the postwar world; but for them the past presented so many problems that their adaptation could not be more than on the surface, in the service of procreation and survival. Hence, the ability to adapt is often so well-developed in their children, as Kestenberg has pointed out. These patients are different from others whose fantasies about the Holocaust, sadism, and persecution constitute a greater disruption with present-day reality. The hysterical patient shares with his parents the ability to create for himself a surface normality and conformity to the culture in which they live. When the events of the past intrude into the relationship, they are rationalized to signify something else in order to maintain the repression.

One has survived death and destruction to take one's place in a society that attempts to affirm life. In order to do this, one has had to undergo profound transformations involving change of culture (very few survivors settled in the country of origin), change of language, and sometimes change of names. Some survivors forgot their original birthdates and took on another date or stopped celebrating. During the war, their survival was often predicated on their taking on false names, secret residences, conversion to Christianity, and a different moral code. E. De Wind (1968) says that the ability to switch quickly from one level of functioning to another has great survival value. This flexibility also proves to be one of the conditions for facilitating readaptation to normal life. But this asset could also become a liability, as described by Saul Friedländer:

I was destined, therefore, to wander among several worlds, knowing them, understanding them . . . but nonetheless incapable of feeling an identification without any reticence, incapable of seeing, understanding, and belonging in a single, immediate total movement. (1979, p. 155)

This experience shows how, in a world such as that in which the survivors lived, identity becomes something like a garment that one can change at will: the more garments one has, the more likely one is to survive.

In the same vein, survivor-parents hoped that they could raise children who were adapted to the postwar world while gratifying their, the parents', wish that

they [the children] should return as saviors into the psychotic world of the concentration camp and to see to it that the parents do not emerge as damaged, humiliated victims, this time . . . to be as if petrified in their own lives, to bear witness as a memorial to the crimes. (Grubrich-Simitis 1979, p. 1008)

From the point of view in which one identity does not preclude another, these wishes do not seem incompatible. The children were led to create strange fantasies, such as the one in which a young man was entering the pre-history of another person and tried to steal that person's identity. This fantasy corresponds again to something that A. Metcalf wrote about aspects of hysteria as being:

in response to parental expectations that the child be a protagonist in scenes from the parents' unconscious fantasies—fantasies that are almost always a sadistic distortion of narcissistic struggles for survival with objects from the parents' past. (1977, p. 259)

Paul-Claude Racamier, also commenting on the dynamics of hysteria, wrote:

The hysteric and the child substitute miracles for mastery. That is to say something which cannot be communicated. . . . He is pushed to live more than he is capable . . . to affirm himself through a life of substitutions, that of others. (1952, pp. 142, 146)

Themes of resurrection, of reincarnation, or of being the savior abound in the material obtained through the treatment of children of survivors. These children have a sense that all good people have died; and that to be loved, one has to be dead or bring back to life the prewar world. The generations are often reversed, and the children take on the identities of the lost objects as well as their own. This is the life of substitutions, as described by Racamier; the absence from oneself, as it was called by Khan; the life of hysterical materialization, as we have come to know it from classical psychoanalytic literature.

## Hysterical Identification

In the children's search to help replace the lost objects of their parents and identify with the parents' suffering, there seems to be both an attempt at restitution for losses and a defense against the oedipal competition with a parent whom the child considers too vulnerable. These are two separate processes aimed at gaining love and freeing the child from the parents without the implied aggression of an oedipal victory. These are two forms of identification for which clinical vignettes have already been given, but which have always had some puzzling aspect: for while in one case they are identifications with lost objects, they should not be confused with those identifications that lead to the giving up of the object in the outside world. Those are neither the dynamics of hysteria nor do they apply to those patients who are being studied here. In these cases, the tie to the object is maintained, and those objects whom they attempt to resurrect are not their own lost objects but those of their parents. The second type of identification—that with the suffering of the oedipal object—is the partial identification observed in Naomi T. who caught a disease that was at the time infecting a group of survivors, but it is similar to the first in that it, too, does not lead to object loss. Traditionally, the second type has been called "partial identification," and the first type—that with the lost object of the parents—must be assumed to be a special case of the second type.

As was mentioned earlier, the first type aims at some form of restitution stemming from the parents' belief that the losses can be undone. The dilemma was poignantly stated by this remark: "I can't discard it since it is already irretrievably lost." The belief that losses can be undone leads to a reversal of generations, as exemplified by Peter Y. who successfully imposed on his parents the religious practices that they had consciously abandoned; when he later started to waver in his beliefs, he felt guilty as if he were the first to abandon a tradition. If the classical cases of hysteria are re-examined to test whether they, too, yield some evidence of this reversal of generations, we are reminded that Anna O. nursed (mothered?) her father during his last illness, and that Dora was her father's companion. It is not easy to assert with conviction that in those cases there was an identification with the lost objects of the parents, since the analyses never went in that direction; but it is conceivable that this was indeed true. In children of survivors, the evidence is overwhelming that there is such identification; hence, there is additional reason for the children not to show an evidence of being victimized. Otherwise, instead of being the restitution for the loss, they might become its confirmation. This can go to ludicrous extremes, as in the case of the parents who referred to their aggressive child as "little Hitler" but punished the less aggressive one for not fighting back. Nothing is permissible that might evoke the fantasy that the survivors abandoned their objects to their death; and the children are often indoctrinated to be aggressive toward a world that is depicted as hostile and menacing. Through their intactness, the children can alleviate some of the guilt of the parents, as was demonstrated clearly in the transference of a patient who was angry at and wanted to punish the analyst: "I would kill myself if it would not give pleasure to all those who say that analysis is no good."

In the hope that the survivors had for their children, there is an implicit interdiction; as victims, they did not want to serve as models; if, however, they lived out their survival as a heroic achievement, they also made identification impossible, since the image they built was of superhuman proportions and required circumstances that would have to be re-created in order to be mastered. We know how many children attempted precisely that: to create circumstances in which the parents' heroic deed could be duplicated. Other children gave evidence of reluctance to identify with the survivor-parent by other means: for example, a patient who studied all languages but the ones that his father spoke fluently. This rebellious attitude is as much because of the aggression (anal castration, according to Bela Grunberger) against the parent as because of the father's own conflicts about assuming his rightful place, for which the son would have to compete in order to attain maturity. "During adolescence, detachment from the parents is tantamount to persecuting or destroying them" (Bruggeman, unpublished manuscript, 1977). Axelrod and her co-workers confirmed this observation: "Hospitalized survivor children have usually been unable to form any significant identification. . . . For this subgroup, parents have effectively banned links with their heritage, seriously interfering with their children's sense of identity" (1980, p. 10). It is apparent that clarity is needed when the word *identification* is used, since hysteria is considered the realm of identification par excellence. But as was seen before, hysterical identifications resemble what one patient called "wearing constantly changing costumes," and serve to obscure the lack of identification that would come from having competed and finally compromised in such a way that the individual feels one with his sexual and procreative functions. Green (1972) says about hysteria that the fundamental conflict resides in the impossibility of making compatible, through sexual experience, the union to a new object having phallic significance with the conservation of the parental objects. According to him, sexuality is the privileged domain for the expression of this conflict, since the attainment of sexual gratification, which would mean a realization of the subject's own personal aspirations, signifies the overcoming of the fixations on the parental objects without the feeling of cutting, separation, and mourning. New ties threaten the disappearance of the old ones in hysteria. Also, the good object is always the one who takes part in the enjoyment of another; therefore we have the identification with another object which permits satisfaction only through a third. This notion of attaining satisfaction through the intermediary of an identification with the parents on the level of sharing their suffering is unconsciously encouraged by many of the parents, who in their lifetime have experienced the mutability of identity, and who perhaps themselves are parents without ever identifying themselves with that function and what it implies. They experience separation as permanent loss and cannot tolerate that particular aggression that leads to a permanent separateness. For many of them it represents only an example of castration, humiliation, or punishment.

Contrary to people's expectations, the problems presented by these survivors' children are ordinary. At the workshop of the International Psycho-Analytical Association Congress in Jerusalem in 1977, the comment was made that the problems presented by these patients were banal. This may be the most pervasive hysterical identification that they make—that with their own culture. The shallow conventionality has also been mentioned as being characteristic of the hysteric. If individuality is thwarted, why not copy the most pervasive pattern around? These survivors' children made "new lives" often in such a way that when they finally made contact with each other and could discuss some of the issues which made them feel so isolated because they were not like everyone else, they felt great relief. This has been documented in much of the literature by the children themselves. Only when making contact fails—when either some somatic problem, a failure in a career, or problems in a love relationship bring them into treatment—does it become apparent that the adaptation was a token of love offered to their parents in order to spare them yet another trauma—the suffering of their children. "Having these complaints is felt as a reproach against the parents, about which there are intense guilt feelings since they say that the war was not their parents' fault" (John Bruggeman, unpublished manuscript, 1977). The conventional adjustment of the child serves to bolster the feelings of innocence on the part of both parent and child.

The part that does indeed receive the mother's communication of catastrophic anxiety, and is later replaced by sexualized fantasies about the parents' lives before and during the war, does eventually make its claim. It is found in some of the incomprehensible actions that can only be understood as identification with the parents' suffering. It expresses both the wish and the punishment for the wish, and it points up again that these children experience the difference between the generations more keenly and feel more shut out of their parents' lives than do most other children. The wish to take part in that past is therefore overdetermined. Not only does it serve as a typical hysterical symptom, but it also allows a greater sense of having shared something important from which they were excluded.

## The Problem of Aggression

It was pointed out at the beginning that survivors often inflicted considerable damage on their children through extensive pent-up aggression. Judging from the cases that have come to our attention, it is apparent that there were many instances of a parent's calling a child "little Hitler" or "worse than what happened to me during the war." Axelrod et al. (1980) report 30 percent child abuse in the histories of the hospitalized group. Often the children, too, are aggressive and abusive. This attitude does not seem particularly pathogenic to their relationship, since it reaffirms the bond between parents and children and keeps alive the victim and executioner scenario. Where both parties seem much more vulnerable is in the area of loosening ties through growth. Emotional growth of the children through treatment may be experienced as a loss by parents, just as does a college education or a marriage. Events that most parents usually greet with pleasure, survivor-parents often react to negatively, as they lack the trust to regard separations as matters of degree. As the danger is loss but not necessarily aggression, parents and children can be tied to each other by the repetition of a pattern of persecution and innocence which reaffirms ties through guilt. One patient, who was subjected to cruelty and abuse in childhood, said that she does not like to think of the Germans as human, since then she would have to think of all that cruelty as human, too. She clearly used the image of the Nazi as a screen for some of the cruelty inflicted on her by her own parents.

Some literature suggests that aggression is not a factor in hysteria, and it places the emphasis on dependency and submissiveness. But anyone recalling the case of Dora, who placed her aggression in the service of defeating Freud and who did not get along with her mother and for whose death was called by Felix Deutsch (1957) a relief to those who had to cope with her, knows that the picture is far from simple, and that those early cases did not yield much material on aggression because the emphasis was on the repressed sexuality. Again, the picture is no simpler with the children of survivors; and basically only that aggression is avoided that would inflict upon the parents damage or loss. In this light, competition seems to be one of the forms of aggression most threatening to the object. A patient who had gone to a job interview asked the interviewer whether she feared that she, the patient, might compete with her. She was not accepted for the position and linked the whole episode to the fact that her mother had been in a concentration camp.

The oral receptivity, dependency, and passivity usually attributed to the hysteric, and also evident in some of these cases, is basically more the expression of the wish to enjoy vicariously through the intermediary of an object with whom one can identify than a genuine malleability. In general, children of survivors have not been a reliable patient population, which fact is further proof that the "dependency" consists of maintaining the tie to the parents rather than its more infantile prototype which would appear in the transference. In this again, these children are similar to those hysterics who have shown great resistance to analytic treatment and who find it difficult to accept certain impulses as being their own. The hysterical children prefer to seduce the analyst into their way of thinking in order to assert their innocence.

As a group, children of survivors described here may only incidentally mention sexual difficulties or actually deny their import if they surface in treatment. Rather, along with the rest of the population, these patients can achieve a superficial eroticism common in the culture today, but this seems to serve as a mask for the anxieties attached to a better-integrated sexuality. Since concern about this malfunction would signal abnormality both in the sense of admitting to sexual strivings and in the failure of the defense against them, this aspect does not seem to be prominent in many cases. It seems rather that the proof of normal sexuality is yet another way in which to establish innocence in the same way as frigidity did at the time of Freud.

Because of the dissociation between their sexual fantasies and the ego functions, hysterics remain passive, in expectation, waiting for someone who will help them act this strange amalgam of pregenital and genital sexuality which is theirs. . . . The hysteric needs, so to say, a sexual facilitation from the other in order to act out the latent and repressed sexual fantasies. That is why he always feels innocent in everything that is actualized in his life as sexual. (Khan 1974b, p. 153)

Unfortunately defenses against the understanding of this mechanism are very resistant to interpretation and may well be recognized without leading to personality changes. This is where analysis and its emphasis on the transference interpretation may be the only effective method of treatment.

## Specific Treatment Issues

Many of the issues are implicit in what we have said before. It has been a repeated observation among those treating children of survivors that they tend to play down the impact of their parents' past even if it is mentioned during the initial interview or is actually known to have been an important factor in their lives. As one patient said, "I don't mind talking about it, but when you bring it up in another context, I don't want to hear about it." Therefore we know of cases that were treated without highlighting the survivor issue. As Bruggeman points out, a child tends to experience the integration of his parents' lives into his own difficulties as an accusation against them. In order to avoid this, survivor children use the analyst and the analytic treatment at times to prove their innocence and that of the parents; and in the process, the analyst becomes the fascist or the Nazi, or he may be called upon to watch scenes passively and thereby confer upon what he is witnessing the stamp of innocence. It becomes apparent that the transference difficulties encountered with hysterics certainly pertains to those problems encountered with children of survivors: that is, their wish to bring into the relationship to the analyst the dimension of victim and victimizer.

De Wind says:

An interpretation can only be "mutative" if it includes three frames of reference: the transference, the patient's actual situation in life, and the infantile relationships. We may add that in the case of traumatized patients the interpretation may have curative meaning only if the way in which the patient unconsciously experienced the trauma of persecution has been included. (1968, p. 175)

The fact that the trauma of persecution belongs to the life of their parents alters only slightly the problem of interpretation but does not change the necessity of bringing into the formulation some reference to events during the war. It is in this context that a thorough familiarity with the problems relating to the treatment of hysteria can be helpful in confronting the issues concerning these patients.

Psychoanalysis admonishes the patient to remember the past, just as the parents of the patients wanted them to remember; but in many cases these two processes run counter to each other. While there is a wish to immortalize the dead Jews, there is the injunction against remembering a childhood full of painful fantasies and anger against the parents. Thus, the memories called forth by the process of analysis have a forbidden quality which spells out disloyalty to the parents. What is to be remembered has been handed down by the parents and becomes part of the child's fantasies, which he then integrates in specific ways that have been repressed. Despite their holding on to a past, these patients may feel that trying to remember is crazy.

While much has been said about not entering into a "pact of silence" with the patient, a word is needed about the other extreme, which is often induced by hysterical patients. Racamier warns: "Who has not felt, when confronted with a hysteric, this secret inclination which tempts him to play doctor? All of a sudden we are imbued with a function" (1952, p. 7). The analyst cannot afford to perform as the Holocaust expert, much as one might be tempted. An interpretation cannot take the place of proper suspension of judgment, and one may have to be alert to the countertransference tendency induced both by the need to be of help and the patient's to have the analyst perform.

**15**

# Thoughts on Superego
# Pathology of Survivors
# and Their Children

## Introduction

This chapter will focus on superego pathology transmitted by the traumatized Holocaust parents to the children of the postwar reconstituted family. A
number of interconnected ideas have become clear as a result of the re-
searches of the Group for the Psychoanalytic Study of the Effect of the Holocaust on the Second Generation. Some hypotheses regarding superego pathology have emerged which will be developed in a profile study of survivors
and their children.

Not all survivors, however, reacted to their camp experiences and other
traumata in the manner described here; nor did all their children. The need
to externalize events from a painful past and relive them repeatedly is not specific to these cases. Many case reports have demonstrated, however, that as
soon as survivors of the Holocaust had created a new family—a "holding environment," in D. W. Winnicott's sense (1965)—they internally confronted
former traumatic losses once again.

The new external environment provided a nonpunitive affective milieu for
the reliving of traumata. It furnished a less threatening atmosphere where the
parents could test and internalize new experiences, newly found capacities for
mirroring, and selective identifications with objects. Under new conditions,
perceptions and affective experiences could be validated afresh. When traumatic events related to the Holocaust past resurfaced (sometimes after years
of suppression)—and were subject to reality testing in a saner and more stable
environment—a thread to the pre-Holocaust past could be restored.

The parents lived out their present fantasies about the past, or illusions colored by real experiences, in interaction with their children whom they cast

into roles that would require them to restore the psychic reality of the parents. The children were unconsciously expected to undo affectively charged traumata, which had damaged a parent's psychic structure and had destroyed superego guidelines and functions. Themes of disillusionment related to a formerly cohesive ego ideal were prominent.

In an attempt at "self-healing," traumatized people use their families as a means of psychic recovery to a far greater extent than less traumatized individuals do. In most cases studied, two major fantasies were transmitted from parent to child. In the first, the child is a replacement of a beloved lost family member—as a rule, a child from a former family, a parent, or an idealized relative. The second fantasy states that the child has a special mission: his or her life goals are to be directed at restoring family pride by personal achievement, in order to heal past injuries.

A fantasy role of a narcissistic nature is cast upon survivors' children: by being special, they have to make up for the traumatic losses, disappointments, shame, and defeat that had led the parents to narcissistic self-devaluation; the children's success thus plays a decisive role in establishing a new, coherent value system, with new ideals for the parents; the children are expected to develop identical values.

The mechanisms described here are also found in traumatic parent-child relationships without a Holocaust background. However, the Holocaust experience is a paradigm for the study of universal phenomena related to trauma. Although persecution of people for religious or ethnic reasons, ending in genocide, is characteristic of Holocaust traumata, responses to persecution, resulting in shock and strain traumata, are followed by known manifestations of the psychopathology of the traumatized person.

The person traumatized by Holocaust experiences or the child of a survivor will create personal myths or fantasies different from other types of traumatized persons. Myth-making will contain memories from the past and may have the function of preserving a traumatic screen (E. Kris 1956a), hiding massive amounts of hostility unleashed by brutalization, anxieties, or personal symptomatology. Hillel Klein* has stated that there is a personal myth about his or her traumatization by every survivor. One may add that the myth influences the modes of displacement of affect in survivor-parents, which are then transmitted to their children. When a person is engaged in myth-making and magical thinking, only a certain part of ego capacities and cognitive processes are turned toward present-day reality. The relationship of the self to reality

* Yale Symposium on the Holocaust, 26 September 1981.

has been altered and frequently expresses itself in nonverbal behavior as concrete acts symbolizing internal conflicts. Myth-making is thus related to coping mechanisms both during and after traumatization. Myths may not be the same for survivor and child, but each has great difficulty comprehending the Holocaust trauma as experienced by the parents.

It is hoped that what follows will open up areas of greater understanding of psychic responses to trauma in general and its interactional effects on parent-child relationships. In the vast literature on trauma, there has been insufficient emphasis on the effect of trauma on the superego structure of the traumatized victim; on superego functioning after the external traumatic agent has ceased to exist; and on the transmission of parental superego pathology to the second generation. This chapter will address itself to some of these issues.

A likely hypothesis presents itself that the unconscious need of the survivor-parent to put a child into the role of replacing a lost loved person, and to respond with merciless threats toward the child who seems to fail in his or her mission, represents an aspect of *superego values that became externalized in order not to be lost.* By being re-enacted in the new family milieu, and thereby maintained, these values, once preserved (a variation on repetition to master trauma), are displaced upon the children *and thereby retained.* Trauma makes repression impossible. Externalization and concretization of thinking and action in favor of fantasy helps to preserve an established value system and protect it from being lost as a result of trauma.

As survivors' children are drawn into the parents' psychic reality, superego and ego-ideal elements constitute a central organizing principle of their involvement in parental readaptation. This involvement interferes with the development of the child's self-representation and the autonomy of the child's developing superego and ego ideal.

Parent-child interaction cannot be explained as having had the *purpose* of self-healing (which would be a teleological argument). Traumatized parents, under the sway of the repetition compulsion, may have been unconsciously motivated to use their new objects—primarily their children—to confront traumatic themes from the past; to recathect a new world through interaction with their children, so that new coping mechanisms related to internal structure and external phenomena could develop.

Pre-Holocaust and post-Holocaust themes merged in Holocaust survivors, which led them to misread the motivations of others and to become confused in interpreting reality. Thus, a reality-testing burden was placed on the children, who also were slated to rectify the horrors the parents brought to light. Not only parental needs but also confusions were transmitted to the children, particularly where "the pact of silence" prevented verbalization and explanation of past experiences; and thus the children's uncertainty increased, and the ground was prepared for the emergence of flourishing fantasies.

In many children of survivors, feelings of pressure to return to the survivor-parent what he or she has lost grow at the expense of the independent development of the self. Because of this conflict, the parent-child bond may turn into a hostile obligation, creating a lasting hostile bond in which the child's superego tries to fulfill the child's perception of parental needs. In this case, only an intrapsychic act of separation from an imposed fate can free the child; a new freedom from the shared bond of guilt can strengthen a separate identity and feelings of healthy narcissism, and consolidate the child's sense of autonomy.

## The Superego under the Impact of Traumatization

We have learned from Freud that under favorable conditions the superego has an organizing function, promoting ego development and reality testing (Freud 1923, 1926; Jacobson 1964; Stein 1966). What are the unconscious impulses that the normal superego prevents from reaching consciousness?

In spite of the infinite variety of social, cultural, and pathological problems that characterize the human condition anywhere in the world, id wishes are predictably few: they are incestuous, cannibalistic, and murderous. They encompass the sexual wishes of the Oedipus complex and those of earlier regressive needs, bisexual wishes, and perversions. The superego does not permit possession of the oedipal love object or removal of the rival. The superego also suppresses revenge fantasies and narcissistic triumphs; the latter are often based on omnipotent or megalomaniacal fantasies, with themes of frustrating experiences between the self and early objects.

Whether expressed in developmental, phase-specific terms, in terms of object relations that may have led to developmental arrest, or as intrapsychic conflict or symptoms, these themes are limited in content. Although specificity of meaning needs to be clarified in the therapeutic work with each patient, love-hate wishes, splits, or unconscious fantasies defensively isolated from each other remain guarded by the superego and do not become conscious with the full implications, except in psychosis. In analysis of neurotic patients, unconscious fantasies appear as derivatives of id impulses, and conflicts reach consciousness only as a result of arduous therapeutic work.

Unconscious sadistic wishes normally forbidden by the superego emerge in treatment with a great deal of pain and under the aegis of the therapeutic alliance. Usually such forbidden fantasies have not been reported as having conjured up details of human cruelty—for example, the making of soap or lampshades from human skin, and the use of gas ovens for mass murder.

Questions have arisen whether most people repress successfully their most archaic or paranoid fantasies or whether their id wishes simply do not contain such elements in the first place.

## Effects of Massive Traumatization on the Psychic Structure of Holocaust Survivors: The Parents

Observers of the traumatizing effect on the survivor's psychic structure reported: muted affects, sometimes to the extent of paralysis resembling a catatonic state; depressive reactions; sexual dysfunction; psychosomatic symptoms; and phobic states. There was a generally diminished capacity to use ego functions, to anticipate and register anxiety-producing situations, and to judge perceptions related to reality. There was affect withdrawal to the point of depersonalization; destruction of feelings of individual identity; cognitive regression; and a marked loss of a sense of time and causality (Krystal 1968; Krystal and Niederland 1971; see also Grubrich-Simitis 1979). Without the reliable use of the anxiety signal for the registration of potential danger, the camp survivor gradually moved from a hyper alert state—forever ready to register danger of death—to a state of inhibition and blocked emotions (Sandler 1967; Krystal 1971).

A constant state of terror (Stern 1959) overwhelmed the intactness of ego functions and theatened their extinction (Keiser 1967). Impairment of verbalization of emotions lowered or abolished the capacity for symbolization, and fantasy formation became impaired or came to a halt. H. Krystal (1978) has pointed out how the settling in of the chronic traumatic state, with its numbing and closing off of affects, afforded a certain relief from constant pain and anxiety to the persecuted individual.

The way of life centered on the here and now rather than on the future. While the survivor's own aggression was minimized experientially because it had become too dangerous to deal with, there was simultaneously an ever-present focus on escape from death. Sometimes the belief in an existence after death modified anxiety. Often there was a narcissistic gain in having survived one more day (De Wind 1968).

Under the aegis of death anxiety, functions became automatized, and an inability to relate to others became manifest. A marked loss of empathy (Grubrich-Simitis 1979) and, with it, a blockage of the mourning process, followed the loss of the capacity to cathect other individuals.

With loss of basic trust and healthy narcissism, hostility was readily turned against the self. The first signs of fragmentation and regression in the capacity to symbolize brought with them the loss of necessary self-protection and alertness for survival. Sometimes this regressive process left a "psychomotoric" organism, whose automatized functions were the first signs of impending death. On the other hand, there were concentration camp inmates who, after a period of deepest regression, experienced a reorganization that permitted a part of the personality to be recathected libidinally and become directed toward survival once more (De Wind 1968).

Massive assaults of hostility from an external source created an affective disturbance of overstimulation that constituted a central strain trauma. It appears that whatever sadistic fantasies or retaliatory wishes may have broken through from within the individual psyche, needed to be suppressed. And, the signal function to respond adequately to imminent danger or violence from the side of the environment had lost its reliable anticipatory function when needed. Thus, the psyche found itself helpless and unprepared, and the superego's normal function of guardianship became ineffective. Familiar moral guidelines proved useless. A constant fear of death became the basis for registration of affects and external perceptions; thus a curtailed capacity for verbal communication and symbolic function robbed the self and object representations of their uniqueness. As a result, narcissistic self-cathexis and a sense of identity gave way to identification with the rules of the aggressor, which created a new system of anticipation geared toward survival.

This extraordinary capacity for adaptation among those who survived may be called "emergency morality." Self-renunciation, which had the advantage of creating distance between the victimized and the victimizer, so that disaster could sometimes be anticipated and avoided (at least in the short run), was a means of a new type of self-protection. When succcessful, this emergency "moral code" apparently was learned, without feelings of disillusionment or hostility toward the internal parental representations. In the case histories studied, these very disillusionments and resentments surfaced decades later, and were observable after the survivor had reconstituted a new family. It was upon the new family members, particularly the children, that the traumatic reactions, silenced by the emergency morality, were later revived and projected.

Three brief vignettes, retold by colleagues from personal experience, high-light the gradual unfolding of "emergency morality." They also demonstrate how one needed to suppress empathy with others in order to become less vul-nerable, and how only through secret assistance—mostly from the outside, as well as by mutual aid of concentration camp inmates toward each other—some normal narcissistic self-cathexis could be maintained, and aid survival.

A colleague reported:

When I was first taken to the concentration camp I wore a suit with a warm jacket, and another woman had on a summer dress. She was very cold and asked to borrow my jacket, which I gave her. When she felt warm, she returned it. I thought, two months later, now she would not have asked for the jacket any more, and I would not have lent it to her.*

And:

A woman was ladling out food which passed for soup. On the bottom there were a few pieces of meat. I thought: "On this meat one could avoid starvation." The woman skillfully kept the pieces of meat until the end and ate them herself. I was in-furiated. Then I thought: "Why should not *she* survive instead of someone else?"*

Another person reported that there was a great premium on having books smuggled into camp. They aided in preserving a person's intellectual identity as a counterforce against Nazi barbarism. The reporter said: "I often thought: as long as I can read Goethe I know I am not crazy."

It is likely that the emergency morality gradually converted into a "moral absolutism" (Piaget 1932), based on a regression to superego precursors and fear of external authority. Primitive, magical, and unrealistic identifications, experienced within an ever-narrowing frame, were used to protect one's psy-chic core from injury and death. It may have been that the pressure of such an atmosphere of danger and torture, brought about by the constant use of violent force, led the victims toward re-externalization of formerly interna-lized superego representations. After liberation, the superego of the survivor was left in a precarious state—in danger of further regression and de-differen-tiation. Against this danger the victims undertook a series of defensive ma-neuvers in the environment.

---

* Discussion at International Psycho-Analytical Congress, Jerusalem, August 1977.

## Superego Pathology in the Postwar Family of the Survivor: Parents and Children

In evaluating case material, it must be asked how superego functions and superego pathology may be assessed. The ego is known by its functions and is closer to consciousness than is the superego. The id is known by drive derivatives, affects, impulses, and fantasies. In order to assess the level and quality of superego functioning vis-à-vis other objects, the following questions helped to assess superego pathology:

Are there superego lacunae?
Is there a capacity to experience guilt when causing injury?
Does one differentiate between acts and wishes and is self-punishment as severe for the former as for the latter?
Does the person wish to evoke guilt?
Does the superego give a warning signal before one commits prohibited acts, or does one realize consequences and dangers only belatedly?
Does one experience feelings of love from one's superego, or is the superego only a criticizing agency?

In many instances, superego functions appeared more disturbed than ego functions: one could function adequately in the external world, but one's understanding of people's motivations, value judgments, or unfamiliar environmental phenomena was often confused.

The superego structure of the survivor-parent was frequently found to have undergone severe destruction by the invasion of Nazi ideology. In many case histories, splitting of self and objects in the superego representations became manifest: the survivor-parent at times identified with Nazi morality but also condemned it. Because of such splitting, parental messages to children were often confused.

Ego-ideal pathology also has to be considered. To what extent does the survivor project his or her disillusionment on the children?

How is the Holocaust theme transmitted by parental demands to restore the narcissistically injured self-image of the parent?

Does the survivor's child feel that he or she cannot aspire to fulfill the ideals set by the parents?

Independence and autonomy from both the social group and parental authority depend, as a rule, on the extent to which the superego has been internalized. But the strain trauma of upbringing by survivor-parents disturbed internalization processes of superego components and, therefore, frequently led the survivor's child toward external acts that were destructive or self-destructive.

Externalization of superego and ego-ideal features may have put the realization of the survivor's child's values and goals into a utopian realm, and the child who has thus suffered will remain dependent on the parents and on approval from an external authority.

In reconstituting the new family with a new generation of children, a shift of values and norms of behavior has taken place once again. In the traumatic past, affective signals and wordless behavior substituted for language and resulted in the loss of symbolic functions. In the new family, typically, the parents are outspoken in making demands on the children: they tend to identify the children with exterminated family members; and in a resurrection fantasy, the child is cast into a mold of living up to the expectations the parents had for the lost child. The new child tends to acquiesce, feeling that he or she owes a debt for being alive.

## The Survivor's Child

The survivor's child has come into a family of parents who lived in a world before the child was born—a world described as having provided a sense of belonging, a chance for personal achievement, and "ideal children." This world (which in memory seems like a dream) was suddenly lost and replaced by cruelty, loss of loved ones, and a constant fear of death.

The miracle of the parent's survival led to the miracle of the survivor's child's birth and survival. As a rule, the fact that parents and children are alive is taken for granted by both. But survivor-parents frequently remain incredulous that they are alive, an idea they transmit to their children. A child in such a family does not take existence for granted and feels "special"—an exception (Jacobson 1959).

Such a child feels that one has to "pay" for having been born and surviving when so many others had been killed. A fantasy that puts a child into the role of a former lost child later becomes concretized in certain life goals or practices. As a result, dead or lost children from a former family may become part of the survivor's child's self-representation in his or her superego and ego ideal.

In spite of the fact that survivors' children were Jews, we noted in our studies a strikingly frequent identification with Christ. One may venture a guess that the recurring fantasy in which a survivor's child has identified with the suffering Christ, suggests an identification not only with an innocent victim who suffered and died for the crimes of others, but with a child miraculously born, whose later life was destined to fulfill special acts of saving others. Christ's miracles reduced suffering and redeemed the worthy. He took over the fate of the victims, setting them free. Identification with Christ also offered a successful momentary silencing of hostile parent-child interactions, comparable with Freud's description (1921) of the beloved and idealized leader to whom the group submits uncritically; thus its members are allowed a temporary relief from sin, as he takes responsibility for all actions.

A survivor's child who has taken a deceased child or other lost family member into his or her self-representation is unconsciously attempting to establish a bridge to the traumatized parent's inner life. The child takes on the parents' conviction that deceased family members are superior to the living. To establish an enduring emotional tie to the parents, the child has to submerge his or her own narcissistic strivings and share parental fantasies that are kept alive within the family and that refer to an idealized dead child. This process transforms the survivor's child's ego ideal. That the survivor's child has come to share the parental fantasy is exemplified by his or her attempts to resemble the dead child or other lost person, at times even in physical ways. In both parent and child, a fantasy becomes entrenched in which the lost child is seen as having been more lovable. The contemporary child maintains himself or herself as lovable or narcissistically valued by trying to fulfill the destiny of the lost child. Yet it is impossible to compete with an idealized rival whose sins have all been paid for by death. Thus, the dead child becomes a hated "sibling" who destroys the autonomy of the survivor's child's ego ideal. A genuine ego ideal can develop only after resolving survivor's guilt, formerly shared with the parents, and after a severing of the legacy of commitment to the dead. Shared fantasies sacrifice the autonomy of the child in order to preserve the value system of the parents and may lead to some narcissistic self-healing of the parents.

When shared fantasies become entrenched during the growth process, an unconscious narcissistic union with the parents makes survivors' children rescuers of dead brothers or sisters. In addition, parental goals set for the living child's future are expected to be carried out and are not looked upon as mere wishes. The child hopes to restore narcissistic defects (engendered by parental expectations and by survivor's guilt) through bringing new honor to the parents by trying to fulfill their expectations for him or her or to replace what they have lost (a variant on Freud's categories in "On Narcissism" [1914]). It is possible that the superior adaptability and achievement in many survivors' children has been motivated by unconscious adaptation to such parental goals and by the wish to obtain the love earlier bestowed on the dead child.

Identification with the parent's past through a shared fantasy concerning a dead person may provoke the child to become a victim and to develop masochistic fantasies. The child may become self-destructive instead of destructive. Destructiveness toward the parent and straightforward hostility are often impossible for the survivor's child to express because of constant awareness of the parents' suffering. In addition, the parents have difficulty helping a child to learn impulse control because they have lost the scale of values related to the expression of hostility and to deprivation. Thus, in severity of punishment, they fluctuate between undue pressure and excessive leniency.

The severity of superego pressures sometimes leads to psychopathic traits in the children, who, in turn, frequently have been found to believe that the parents survived because they "got away with something." Such a fantasy may then strengthen the child's psychopathic tendencies.

As the parents place tasks of fulfilling a restitutional role upon a child early in life, it can be assumed that magical expectations toward self and parents, representing archaic superego fantasies, live on as part of the psychic reality of the growing child.

Although survivors' children grow up under special imposed superego pressures, colored by rescue fantasies, they also rebel against these pressures. However, shared fantasies, while active, curb hostile aggression, reduce the child's guilt toward the parents, and promote object constancy, loyalty toward the dead, and an adaptation toward a life that becomes a substitute for mourning.

In view of their great fear of object loss, the parents discourage the child's efforts to separate. Archaic superego identifications, shared with the parents, relating to feelings of victimization and narcissistic injury heighten the intrapsychic conflict of the survivor's child by strengthening incestuous ties instead of promoting their repression. Thus, having to be special in order to fulfill a parent's unrealized wishes, instead of one's own destiny, interferes with individuation on rapprochement and later pre-oedipal and oedipal levels and with the formation of an oedipal and a post-oedipal superego. The oedipal fantasy becomes infused with themes of aggression and early narcissistic magical goals stemming from the myth of the parental past. Triangulation is interfered with by hostility and guilt "imported" from an earlier reality.

In the survivor's child, empathy and identification with the parent as a persecuted victim, or as a Nazi aggressor, lead to mechanisms of splitting in the ego and superego representations. Frequently the child cannot idealize the parent who was victimized, particularly if the child has witnessed the latter in a subservient role vis-à-vis an official or authority.

After devaluation of parental authority, one's superego cannot internalize one's parent as a protective agent on one's own behalf. The fantasy common to many survivors' children, that they ought to be given special privileges or dispensations, probably stems from a feeling of being unprotected by a reliable parental imago. In this way, a reciprocal conflict has become established: a defeated parent requires the child to restore honor and strength to the family; if the survivor's child, in turn, suffers from premature disillusionment in the parent (in Jacobson's sense [1946] as an idealized and protective force), the child will feel disappointed and unable to act on meeting parental needs.

## On Trying to Be a Dead, Beloved Child

Following Holocaust traumatization as transmitted by the parents, the child may reproject upon the environment superego components that initially had been internalized. This seems to occur particularly after the child has identified with parental suffering and losses.

The child who is psychotic may develop messianic delusions. In a nonpsychotic survivor's child, the fantasy may be somatized—as in the case of Rachel M. (chapter 7), who felt that she had to carry the Jews of the world inside her stomach in order to protect them. Survivors' children, whether primarily neurotic or afflicted by a more damaged psychic structure, give evidence of phobic states and anxieties stemming from an effort to implement or combat the tormenting tasks demanded by the parents. Frequently hostility created by these pressures turns into passivity, a stance of victimization in identification with the dead children, so that the parents' fantasies of restitution cannot be fulfilled. Or a conflict ensues when one "goes along" with the parents' wishes by striving for an exalted career, thus making idealization of the dead children a personal task. At the same time, because of the role-playing aspect, these efforts interfere with the development of individuation and result in a sense of fragmented reality.

Aaron C. said he had felt overwhelmed by having to take the place of a dead relative. It appeared to Mr. C.'s analyst that in identifying with his family, Mr. C. was genuinely mourning those he had never known. The patient described how an atmosphere of loss had prevailed at home. One relative had demonstrated a constant preoccupation with death and performed compulsive rituals to avoid thoughts related to death. In lovemaking Mr. C. himself treated his beloved as though he were holding a dead body. He sexualized death. He suffered from obsessive dreams that revealed his wish that those family members who had attempted to put him into the role of former lost relatives would die themselves. Mr. C. found it difficult to succeed in his own career; an exalted profession had been chosen for him, but he was afraid to become successful as he had the conviction (a conscious fantasy) that success put a person on the side of the Nazis.

A variant on this theme has been observed in cases where a living parent behaves as if he or she were already dead—an attitude that undermines the child's capacity for communication with the parent and may create verbal and cognitive disturbances from early childhood on. The child will feel guilty when there is an opportunity to enjoy life. When one parent behaves as though "already dead," the child may develop difficulties in thinking and reality testing, because it is not clear what is real and what is not. An identification hunger (Greenson 1958) frequently sets in.

Rachel M. said, "If none of my family is alive, how come I'm alive?" (chapter 7). This patient alternated between body feelings that confirmed life and others that confirmed for her that she was already dead. She also fantasied that she, *in fact*, represented a dead beloved relative, and that she had a life to lead in which she would rescue not only this relative but all the Jews who needed to be saved.

Edna D., a young woman who was attempting to help her father mourn his wife and their dead children from his former marriage whom he had lost in the Holocaust, tried to come closer to him emotionally by working in a morgue and washing the dead. At one point, she joined a group of people who performed a chanting and dancing ritual in a cemetery. She was fascinated by the suffering of the tormented Christ and loved pictures in which he was portrayed as having been cruelly beaten and as bleeding and about to die. She admired painters of the suffering Christ, such as Matthias Grünewald— particularly his painting of the suffering Madonna. The patient expressed her oedipal relationship to her father by attempting in symbolic ways to be close to him and experience what he had lost. She expressed the feeling that in these ways and by certain sublimations—her studies—she could help carry and share her father's grief.

Leah F.'s survivor-father had a habit of communicating with the dead on Sabbath in a kind of gibberish, a language that he had created himself, and that was not meant to be followed by his current, living family; it seemed to be a private communication with those he had once known. Miss F. felt very excluded. In a state of great longing for her father, she took medication and alcohol and had herself hospitalized in a confused state. In her therapist's judgment, she was not psychotic, although it was difficult to convince the hospital staff. The therapist sensed, and Leah F. later confessed that, out of a deep longing for closeness with her father, she had tried to enter the world where the father communicated with the dead "in gibberish." By talking an incoherent language, as if in a trance, she hoped to reach him in the innermost aspects of his former world.

Concrete action gives an aura of reality to one's fantasy that a dead person or an idealized parent is part of one's self. Sometimes it gives credence to a fantasy that the opposite can be true: one can be a rebel and avoid becoming part of a dead person. James Herzog (chapter 5) has called some aspects of concretization of fantasy a "world beyond metaphor"—a particularly apt term which demonstrates the temporary regression or loss of symbolic capacity and its translation into external action. It is likely that this action contains—whether expressed directly or in code—a central aspect of the major trauma.

### "Little Hitler"

When the child identifies with and then externalizes the role of parental introjects, he or she becomes the parent of his or her own parent, as it were. This also may happen when the survivor's child identifies or is being identified with the aggressor.

Survivors of concentration camps have frequently called their children "little Hitler" when the child was hostile or misbehaved. The motivation for such parents' behavior may be not only their identification of the child with an introjected aggressor, but an attempt to externalize a disavowed aspect of his or her self-representation, internalized under extreme stress, when identification with the aggressor was the only major adaptational means for survival.

Although the feeling state expressed by parent and child that gives rise to the image of "little Hitler" naturally varies in each family, it does not seem far-fetched to deduce that a "little Hitler" can survive only in a "little camp." While the reliving of the camp atmosphere may be an attempt to teach the children survival mechanisms, it translates a former experience into a concrete mode. Those aspects of the camp atmosphere that made normal inter-action and object relationships impossible, because hostility had to be sup-pressed in order to survive, seem to motivate this hostile reliving.

Children who were rebellious and called "little Hitlers," were also warned that if they did not make good, the parents would suffer a fate worse than under the Nazis! Children raised under such pressures gave evidence of great inner conflict and confusion.

In reliving Holocaust traumata, the parents needed to feel that even if they expressed rage repeatedly, it would not be lethal for their children. Outbreaks appeared to be an active reliving of passively experienced hostile assaults in ghetto or camp.

Parents frequently felt that the treatment they had had to suffer, had been their own fault, and that therefore they needed to expiate their guilt (after which the superego would relent). Feelings aroused by victimization can be shed only by masochistic surrender (self-destruction or special "tortures or labors" to be borne with the aim of being pronounced "not guilty"). Under the impact of traumatic reliving, the sadistic component of the superego be-comes externalized and converted into acts of discharge against contem-poraries and by practices and rituals of expiation. The same code was trans-mitted to the survivor's child. The readiness to suffer passively when assaulted has a long tradition in Jewish history:

> The Talmud began to develop in the first traumatic period of Jewish powerlessness, after the destruction of the Second Temple. The rabbis addressed themselves, not just to timeless pieties but by political indirection also to the political realities con-fronting them so as to evolve an appropriate posture and *modus vivendi* that would ensure Jewish survival. "Belong ever to the persecuted rather than to the persecutors," the Talmud taught. "God loves the person persecuted and hates the persecutors." To compensate for lost natural autonomy, the religious tradition elevated powerlessness into positive Jewish value. (Dawidowicz 1976, p. 465)

When parents and child relived the parents' survival mechanisms, the child unconsciously hoped to save the parents by his or her participation. The restitutional fantasy, even if totally unrealizable, often acted as an organizer of the child's psychic motivational life—even if it alternated between rebel-lion and submission in an expression of inner conflict—because it represented an unconscious wish to save the parents. Thus, the child was made a part of the expiation ritual which, it was hoped, would in turn ensure his or her own survival.

## Shared Superego Pathology

### CONCRETIZATION

Normal identification from the pre-oedipal and oedipal periods formed from abandoned object cathexes leads to internalization, desexualization, and de-aggressivization of objects and to consolidation of the psychic structure.

The sudden assault on the personality from the external world led to traumatization wherein former stable internalizations were weakened or suffered destruction. Excessive hostile assaults on individuals created traumatic overstimulation. An unconscious link between external arousals and the individual's own unconscious sadistic fantasies promoted splitting mechanisms and heightened sexualization, pre-oedipal regressions, or perversions. Thus damaged, the superego became unable to protect the personality from within.

As emphasized earlier in this chapter, it seemed that for survivor-parents the process of externalizing the past created a mechanism for preserving a link to the pre-traumatic past. The need to externalize the past led to the expression of psychic conflicts and fantasies in a concrete mode.

It has been observed repeatedly that massive traumatization in survivors and their children has destroyed the capacity for fantasy formation. It appears that this is the reason why so many fantasies shared between parents and children have to be concretized and lived out in the environment before an affective connection to their inner representations with symbolic meaning can return in the psychic reality of the survivor, or be established in the survivor's child. When this succeeds, new internalization processes may gradually replace tendencies toward concretization and acting out.

The behavioral phenomenon defined here as *concretization* refers to fantasies lived out, grafted upon the environment, and woven into current reality, rather than verbalized. The action contains unconsciously expressed themes of the original trauma. Concretized fantasy may symbolize reanimation or deanimation—bringing one back to life, or "making" someone dead. Judith Kestenberg has commented that the superego has a "wooden quality" when the person is given to concretization.* She described one case in which everything had to be analyzed from at least two points of view, with the Holocaust fantasies more entrenched than the others because (of their concreteness) "sadistic attitudes invaded ... [the patient's] superego in a concrete fashion" (1980). Concretization occurs when reality appears worse than

* Personal communication, 1981.

fantasy: action, it is hoped, will ameliorate or undo a terrible reality, or help deny it.

Concretizing an unreal situation is an assertion of omnipotence; it helps to deny hostility engendered by experiences of loss, by traumatizing exposure to sadistic experiences, or by the struggle against sadistic fantasies. Concrete action creates a situation that appears to be under the person's control and, in its wishful aspects, suppresses rage and anxiety.

It is characteristic of concretizing activity that an important person is unconsciously assigned a role, and that a particular response is solicited in interaction with that person. A current object relationship is used to relive traumatic aspects of a previous one. A defensive externalization contains an unconscious dialogue with objects and carries an important affective message; sometimes a projection of inner feelings upon the environment or manipulation of the environment itself serves to validate fantasy. There may be a loss of differentiation between death wishes or frightening external events—that is, between inside and outside.

When a hostile person becomes equated with a Nazi or with Hitler, internal conflict has lost its symbolic function. Confusion between past and present, fantasy and reality, internal and external abound; external reality becomes drive-laden and overstimulating. Under such conditions, the protective and anticipatory functions of the superego are likely to become paralyzed. Reprojecting problems onto the realm of the external interaction with objects may permit some discharge of frightening affects and can substitute for the loss of more reliable internal defenses. Survivors' children often respond to the primal scene by having sadistic or perverse fantasies about parental activity in the past: the parents appeased the Nazis by sexual intercourse with them, which accounts for their survival. The children may not recognize these as fantasies; but by their overcathexis, such fantasies thus concretized reach the status of a conviction. Concretization facilitated by the "pact of silence" prevents the parents' Holocaust past from being discussed with the children and thereby gives aspects of reality an unreal cast.

MOURNING

Freud (1917) thought that one detaches oneself from what one has lost; but when one has gradually done the work of mourning, libido flows back into the self. It is possible that in some cases survivors have been so traumatized that they have lost the ability to decathect external objects and thus have made the mourning process impossible.

Under normal conditions, the mourned *external* object becomes internalized; however, when the lost object is not mourned and its death is denied, other objects may be sought as substitutes. Restitutional behavior may take the place of mourning (cf. Loewald 1962, p. 484).

Although survivors are often too traumatized to mourn their lost loved ones, they engage in a variety of displacement mechanisms that might be called survivor's "substitute-for-mourning" mechanisms. Symbolic displaced actions, lived out with current *real* objects (children), are unconsciously addressed to lost love objects.

The concretization of the mourning process fuses past and present: the living out of assigned roles can "actualize a wish-fulfilling object relationship" (Sandler and Sandler 1978, p. 285).* A fantasy may represent a dialogue with an object which has become externalized. Externalization and concrete action ward off hostility against internal objects, particularly if such action repeats traumatic events in symbolic form.

The concept of concretization used here includes actualization but is broader in scope. Although all persons may be inclined to act in favor of verbalization in times of stress, traumatization gives the concretizing need a particular urgency. Trauma lowers the capacity for cognitive and affective control; there is a regression in the capacity for symbolization and in the use of words in favor of action. A loss of cognitive capacity and an inability to express affect without reactivating a situation that contains the trauma in symbolic form may also occur. Concretization of traumatic themes, expressed in favor of fantasy, may be without affect or with excessive affect: reality may be distorted as a means of expressing an inner need or drive pressure.

The survivor's child, when cast into the role of a deceased person, identifies with the parent's past which the child shares in fantasy. In such a fantasy, via symbolic acts, the child "resurrects" former objects in the service of mastering the parent's traumata. Mourning is thereby circumvented.

Paradoxically, this constant preoccupation with the deceased, with death and survival, makes the reality of *actual* death unreal, as it becomes "a living reality" among the family members from day to day. Excessive preoccupation with life and death may lead to magical acts that symbolize an undoing of what is most feared. When magical acts are represented by concrete action, they are designed to cover underlying anxieties. A patient who was at-

---

* J. and A. M. Sandler say that striving for actualization "is a part of all object relationships" (1978, p. 289). Daydreams and fantasies can be converted into action and can be played out as a wish-fulfilling function. Concretization differs from the Sandlers' concept of actualization, which they use to explain when a person provokes another—for instance, the analyst—to act in a certain way rather than expressing a wish in words. It appears that this type of actualization may happen in analysis in relation to material that the patient cannot yet verbalize, and often corresponds to traumatic themes from the past.

tempting to help her parents work out what they had lost in the past, said to her therapist, "My parents' history is more real to me than my own life."

When survivors' children mourn the sudden loss of their own parents, no substitute objects can easily be found; and the existing internalization of the lost parents becomes blurred or repressed. Rapprochementlike behavior may be disturbed or skipped each time a young child loses a parent. Since traumatic losses have made internalization processes unstable, there may be no mourning. Ambivalent conflicts may be avoided, and object constancy impaired; there may be an impoverishment of the capacity for fantasy. The search for the lost parental object may begin in the outside world; and as this task is taken on, it replaces internal processes: stabilization of object cathexes and the capacity to mourn. A fantasy of finding the idealized lost parent takes the place of mourning. If guilt has been externalized, it perpetuates the illusion that the dead person is alive, and mourning seems unnecessary.

As long as fantasies are active, both parents and children can deny that members of the parents' previous families had been killed. When idealization of the dead takes the place of mourning, archaic fantasies related to the dead which have been taken into the superego, continue to exert an influence on affects and actions. Keeping the dead alive in fantasy necessitates concretizing action to "prove" that they *are* still alive. Concretization promotes living in two realities and results in splitting ego and superego representations of self and object.

Although concretization has been found to be more common among traumatized survivors than among survivors' children, it seems to appear in survivors' children in particular ways: as a result of the creation of shared fantasies. If fantasies of children are not shared with parents there may be a prohibition on fantasy formation for the child altogether.

SURVIVOR'S GUILT

Survivor's guilt was the leitmotif of continuity and was transmitted to the children as such. In the literature on survivors, guilt feelings that have been universally found to exist as a core affective state have been ascribed to identification with the aggressor (Krystal 1978) and to ambivalence or death wishes toward siblings and parents. Survivor's guilt probably reactivated oedipal themes in a regressive form and absorbed some of the hate and love feelings survivors might have felt toward their own parents when they were children.

There is an analogue between survivor's guilt and certain oedipal problems.

The oedipus complex is reawakened phase-specifically during many periods of the life cycle (Loewald 1962), influences important life events, and causes psychic change throughout life. The Oedipus myth deals with both themes of love and death. A successful development of the oedipal conflict during any period of a person's life includes an oedipal victory over the parents, accomplished by a lessening of the ambivalent conflicts toward them, permission from the superego to triumph over their achievements without undue guilt, and de-sexualization of the parent-child relationship. With the reaching of maturity as a result of internal separation from the parents, there is a greater acceptance of the inevitability of death. (Analysts are familiar with this sequence of inner events from the termination phase of analyses.)

However, survivors, once traumatized severely, try to stave off death through concrete acts and omnipotent fantasies in their myth-making. Shared fantasies which interlock parent-child relationships sexualize their relationship unconsciously, cement their bond, and reaffirm a mutual dependency and denial of ambivalent feelings. The inability to express hostility openly without becoming " a little Hitler" may increase death anxiety and survivor's guilt in the child.

Mr. Aaron C., who told his analyst that "for a man to become successful puts him on the side of the Nazis," was unable to free himself from the survivor's guilt shared with his parents by making good and trying thereby to change their past. He also was unable to reach a post-oedipal independence to start an entirely new life, as his guilt feelings toward his parents were excessive.

On the other hand, children are capable of reaching an independent oedipal equilibrium in spite of their involvement with survivor-parents where individuation is not unconsciously associated with killing the parents. Such children have given evidence of empathy toward their parents, which cannot surface when there is too much guilt. Such children also have demonstrated an increased capacity for play, fantasy, and sublimation, and a new ability to enjoy life.

After the Holocaust, uniqueness centered on survival itself; and in a majority of cases studied, marriage partners were selected on the basis of having experienced a comparable fate during the war years. Survivor's guilt, related though it was to actual events during the Hitler period, nevertheless provided a screen for earlier feelings of ambivalence and death wishes toward the survivor's parents.

From the time cruel assaults by the Nazis against the Jewish population began, there was a constant psychic affect-laden experience that provided inner continuity and was unshakable: it was survivor's guilt. This guilt comprised a segment of innermost, guarded, affectively overdetermined psychic experiences, which tied the individual to those who had been lost. Guilt constituted an obstacle to integrating current life with the nontraumatic past. As guilt was overcome, the threads to the pre-Holocaust past could emerge.

Survivor's guilt became and remained intimately related to the person's core identity: *it preserved the inner core of the superego*. As a psychic phenomenon, it became a primary organizer that retained basic importance for the maintenance of inner continuity of self and object representations established before the Holocaust. It introduced a time element into the traumatized psychic structure, including the pre-Holocaust and Holocaust periods; however, it also constituted an obstacle to adaptation into a new world. It protected the victim from identification with the aggressor and thereby from potential psychopathic tendencies. As such, it constituted an example of emergency adaptive function. The tenacity of survivor's guilt seemed to say: one thing no one can take away from me—my guilt feelings toward those who have perished. This guilt, therefore, could, under all conditions, remain an *internalized* part of the psyche, *protecting the core of psychic representations.*

The enormous burden of survivor's guilt constituted the most important and recurrent theme of shared fantasies between survivors and their children. The children continued to be in the position of having to be "forgiven for something." By having taken a dead child into the self-representation, expiation of guilt was sought in the name of the parents as well as for a narcissistic restoration of the self.

The impact of shared survivor's guilt resulted in the creation of a "double reality," in which the parent's past and the child's present needed to be amalgamated for purposes of adaptation to current life. By identification with the parent as a victim, the survivor's child became a "survivor" as well. The extent to which survivors' children took upon themselves the burden of parental needs varied as did their needs to concretize fantasies related to past traumata or current conflicts.

Many survivors' children who could not lead their own lives fully, were inclined to think of themselves as failures. In some cases, survivor's guilt was exacerbated by hostility toward the parents, resulting in an inability to fulfill an assigned role. In view of the narcissistic problems that ensued in survivors' children, it remained difficult for them to find a way toward the *real self.* Thus, the survivor's child often remained alienated from his or her own ego ideal and in conflict between wishing to play a role and realizing his or her own needs and wishes.

For reasons of excessive guilt, survivors' children were often afraid to acquire professions of their own choosing or to hold on to what they had achieved: good and bad, success and failure became polarized. Frequently, being successful, so ardently pressed for by the parents, meant to the child an alignment with the Nazis; failure was an attempt to express strivings toward individuation. The child became enmeshed in a destiny imposed upon its development which concentrated life and death on a personal mission to vindicate the parent; but it was not an autonomous choice based on personal freedom. The survivor's child had to make good or be told, "You are the death of me." The joint attempt to cope with survivor's guilt created within the family a concretized replication (in T. Lipin's sense [1963]) of an unconsciously repeated situation of being dominated, of inequality, traumatic dangers, and archaic fantasies. This often brought about an arrest on the level of superego precursors, and the need for externalization of hostile fantasies and wishes became common.

Survivor's guilt gave the survivor's child the restitutional role that became infused with earlier omnipotent fantasies. A split image of the self (from the viewpoint of the observer), where the child is at once linked to the past of the parent as well as to his or her own reality, was thus created. By being linked to the parents and by reliving their problem, the child unconsciously took on a share of the parent's survivor's guilt. By sharing survivor's guilt, phase-specific separation and individuation needs on the part of the child would threaten the parents and create a superego conflict in the child. Thus, the child was likely to remain tied to the parent via archaic narcissistic fantasies which would interfere with various phases of autonomous development and particularly (as stated earlier) with the achievement of an oedipal victory.

The child's feeling of being "an exception" will remain emphasized in favor of renunciations demanded by a successful passing of the oedipal conflict.

Shared fantasies about the past are significant for superego formation. If they were formed as a result of a strain trauma, they break the barrier of superego censorship, by permitting themes of excessive cruelty, perversions, or incestuous wishes toward important objects to become conscious.

The most feared unconscious fantasies are not as bad as the destructive forces the survivor-parent encountered in reality. Thus, reliving traumata in a concretized situation takes the place of discharge and attempt at mastery (Lipin 1963; Krystal 1978). There is a lifelong unconscious expectation that the trauma will recur unless new internalizations have reached a level comparable to a pre-Holocaust core of the individual's psychic structure. In the case of children, differentiation from the Holocaust past of the parents was possible after they had distinguished themselves in their current lives or found other means of individuation and a new identity.

Concretization, as discussed, is a phenomenon that serves the repetition compulsion. It is also an attempt at self-healing: it represents an externalization of an *inner* meaning. This meaning, rescued from a traumatic constellation, becomes crystallized first as an *action*. The person *has* "*to do it*": first, in order to experience it affectively; and then, to understand it and translate the action into a cognitive mode. As soon as the symbolized action becomes intelligible, it may receive a new mental representation and may then be internalized. Awareness of the unconscious meaning of actions strengthens symbol formation and internalization is facilitated.

The dialogue with an object previously lost may require the re-establishment of an inner representation before a genuine mourning process can begin. Mourning facilitates the resolution of traumata related to losses, in contrast to concretization, which has the function of avoiding or postponing mourning and separation.

If new internalizations take place, admission of death takes on a normal function: a unified picture of a coherent reality may permit completion of oedipal strivings; and, as a result of mastery of survivor's guilt, an oedipal victory over the parents may be achieved.

Superego pathology has been traced in shared fantasies between survivors and their children. The hypothesis emphasized here is that superego components, when externalized as a result of traumatic stress, could be preserved by being concretized and played out. Externalizing action probably contains the major traumatic themes in symbolic form. Reintegration of the psychic structure becomes a possibility when such action can be understood and can receive a psychic representation.

For the survivor, the tenacity and intensity of survivor's guilt toward those who have perished may have permitted continuity with pre-Holocaust inner representations and constituted a core psychic organizer which prevents destruction of the psychic structure under traumatic stress.

Survivors' children can embrace a new life only insofar as they can free themselves from participation in the unconscious self-healing process of the parents and from the burden of sharing survivor's guilt. Treatment successfully accomplishing processes of separation from a guilt-laden past, shared in fantasy with the parents, encompasses the primary treatment problems and goals in such cases.

As survivors' children are brought up to identify with wishes for self-healing and recovery, they may be better able to use treatment that facilitates psychic reintegration.

# *Epilogue*

THE AIMS AND GOALS that prompted the editors and contributors in planning this book were not clearly formulated from the start. Some crystallized only gradually, as the task of assembling and analyzing data proceeded. The earlier work of psychiatric and psychoanalytic observers had indicated that in many instances the traumatic impact of the Holocaust is transmitted to the children of survivors. We wished to know in greater detail how this transmission takes place. The case material presented offers some valuable data and conclusions about this complex problem.

Some survivors transmit Holocaust trauma by the very fact that they continue to live in its shadow. Others continually compare their children with the children who died in the Holocaust, forcing the "revenants" to live, as it were, two lives—one in present-day experience and one in the "time tunnel" of an imposed identity with the dead children. Another group unconsciously equates the child with the persecutor, and still another turns to their children for parenting, some out of disappointment with the inability of their own parents to protect them from victimization. Survivors may have transformed the Holocaust into a personal myth, and may transmit this myth to their children. In other cases, children have created a myth about the Holocaust experiences based on their own fantasies, particularly in families where parents had been silent about their personal experiences.

Two of the problems that confront children of survivors are of special significance. What is the status of the Holocaust experience of the parents in the psychic life of their children? Is it a trauma comparable to such catastrophes as major illness or loss of a parent in early childhood? Our data suggest that the Holocaust experience of the parents was the kind of trauma that organized around itself other life experiences of the children. There are many kinds of trauma, but the human being's capacity to respond to trauma may be limited.

The second problem that we encountered concerns the controversial question whether it is possible for any child of a survivor to remain psychically healthy—that is, capable of loving and enjoying work and leisure. Throughout this book we assumed that there are survivors who have mastered their

Holocaust experience to such an extent that they have not passed on its sequelae to the second generation. As therapists we did not have direct access to such cases. However, one case of a child of a survivor who sought analysis for didactic rather than therapeutic purposes, was presented to us. A highly successful professional man, he was free from symptoms. However, as the analysis proceeded, it became clear that he suffered from a state of hyperalertness and attention to every detail in his environment—a state that is usual in instances of personal danger. He lived in what we called a "double reality." Events such as student riots were experienced as taking place simultaneously in the contemporary world as well as in the world of the Holocaust of his parents. We realize that such a pessimistic view will evoke criticism; but so far as our own experience goes, it is not possible for a child to grow up, without becoming scarred, in a world where the Holocaust is the dominant psychic reality. With few exceptions, the mental health of children of survivors is in jeopardy; and our community owes them the second chance of recovery through psychological treatment.

The basic psychological mechanisms involved in the transmission of trauma may be the same as those encountered in patients who have been traumatized by personal tragedies. However, the patterns of response observed in Holocaust survivor families have qualities that differ from those emerging as a result of other natural or man-made disasters. Currently there is no available psychoanalytic literature that would make it possible for psychoanalytic investigators to compare the Holocaust with, for example, Hiroshima or Stalin's reign of terror, in terms of the transmission of trauma from the first generation to the second. Comparisons are painful to contemplate, but the human potential for aggression persists, as do social catastrophes in various parts of our world, all of which may yield further significant findings. This is a direction for psychoanalysts and interdisciplinary researchers to take in the future.

The investigators involved in this project were impressed by the fact that psychoanalysts and psychotherapists have failed frequently to note how clinical material may relate to the Holocaust, and to employ the necessary sensitivity required for an understanding of the special challenges posed by the problems of survivors and their children. This lapse in recognition may have accounted for an unnecessarily large number of therapeutic failures. It is important to learn what might have gone wrong in therapy and how therapeutic technique may be refined so that further difficulties can be avoided (see chapter 13).

When a survivor or a child of a survivor meets a therapist, there is always

# Epilogue

more than just a personal encounter; it matters who the therapist *is*. One of the most moving encounters reported in our group discussions, one that required unusual tact, occurred between a Jewish child of a survivor and a German analyst. It is an eloquent tribute to the skill and sensitivity of the analyst that the treatment moved favorably.

Regrettably, this case could not be included here. As one of our German colleagues has stated, the analysis of survivors and children of survivors, as well as of children of Nazis, has forcibly reminded us that, whether we like it or not, the psychoanalytic relationship is always a social relationship. The dynamics of almost all the cases here presented show that Freud's metaphor of the psychoanalyst as an opaque mirror, only reflecting back what a patient says, could not be adhered to when unusually strong emotions were evoked in the therapist.

The most controversial part of this book has been our decision to include a section on children of Nazis. Behind the controversy on the relevance of this section, we encountered an indignation, at times coming close to a feeling of sacrilege, that we dared compare the two groups.

Our belief that the comparison would be fruitful has been justified. Vast differences remain; but striking similarities have also emerged, many that we did not suspect. We obtained the case history of a daughter of a Nazi who, out of protest, married a Jew; but the husband's rigidity and sadism came close to being that of a Nazi. Therefore, she both rebelled against and refound her Nazi father.

Controversy emerged around the definition of the term *survivor*, with Judith Kestenberg arguing in favor of a broad definition that would include also refugees and their children. Others of the contributors preferred a more stringent definition of survivors: those who were either in a concentration camp or in hiding and exposed daily to the danger of death as well as to multiple losses of close family members. We did not minimize the fate of refugees, but we felt that their problems and the problems of their children have been part of human suffering throughout history, whereas the dangers and destruction of Hitler's Final Solution were unprecedented. As a matter of choice, all cases included in the textbook fall within the stringent definition.

All the chapters except chapter 3, on indemnification, were written by psychoanalysts. Milton Kestenberg's chapter is written with the lawyer's sense of outrage—a feeling we share, but we are less inclined to blame the petty, rigid, and sadistic bureaucrats. To us, the very fact that the German government thought that survivors could be judged and compensated as a result of a medical examination, as would be the case in an industrial accident, demonstrates that the unprecedented meaning of the Holocaust, as it emerges from this and other books, was never grasped by the German government.

Therapists who work with children of survivors require special skills, guidance, and preparation, some of which this study offers. One issue is to discern what psychoanalytic models have been found most useful in conceptualizing clinical findings. The data that were accumulated seem to indicate that the metapsychological model of trauma presented by Sigmund Freud in *Beyond The Pleasure Principle* (1920)—where he spoke of a stimulus barrier that has been pierced or overrun by a trauma—was not sufficiently explanatory. On the other hand, Freud's clinical observations on processes of identification, first described in *Mourning And Melancholia* (1917), were, in retrospect, important and helpful. Of special significance as well were some insights arrived at concerning the functioning of characteristics of the post-traumatic super-ego of survivors (chapter 15) and the transmission of values to their children.

In comparison with other books on the Holocaust, the focus here is narrow, and the concentration is on clinical issues. However, the Holocaust has larger dimensions that the therapist cannot afford to neglect. A major group of families, described as survivors, and their children was Jewish. The Holocaust therefore has to be considered as an event that takes place within the Jewish community and Jewish history. In the Prelude to this volume it is noted that the very term *Holocaust* has a profound psychological meaning. The names of these events—"Holocaust" (*shoa* in Hebrew) or "destruction" (*churban* in Hebrew, after the term designated in Jewish history as describing the destruction of the Temple and the end of the Jewish secular state)—have a strong passive connotation. In contrast, such titles as *The War Against the Jews* (Dawidowicz 1976) may seem more acceptable to many who find the passive implications of other terms offensive. This semantic and linguistic polarization in titles has its counterparts in other matters as well. Within the Jewish community as in the world at large, there are pressures to forget, even to deny, the Holocaust, and to escape from the burdens of being born a Jew. There are pressures, too, in the opposite direction: one is enjoined to remember, to commemorate, never to forgive or forget the trauma; to keep it alive and to use dramatic and forceful educational methods to achieve this aim. An important task of the therapeutic-educational community must be to discover ways of remembering the Holocaust without transmitting its traumatic potential.

One of the problems that confront children of survivors is the conflict between achieving autonomy on the one hand, and discharging their responsibilities to their bereaved and traumatized parents. In this connection the views of the Israeli psychoanalyst Hillel Klein are of special significance.

# Epilogue

Klein called attention to the mistaken tendency to use the term *survivor's guilt* in a pathological sense and thus to give it a pejorative meaning. In many instances it may be appropriate to use the term in that sense. But in Klein's view there is also a healthy survivor's guilt as it links survivor and offspring to the past, to those who died, to a sense of belonging to the Jewish group in a life-affirming way. The conviction that one owes something to the dead need not be a pathological burden. One hopes that the work of colleagues who collaborated to produce this volume draws upon such an affirmative point of view.

The Holocaust is also a part of German history. It was because of a wish to understand the impact of the Nazi heritage not only on the children of survivors but on the children of the perpetrators, that the section on the children of Nazis was included in this book. We did not anticipate the frequency with which the children of Nazis would, in the eyes of their parents as well as in their own eyes, identify with Jewish victims.

Finally, the Holocaust is also an event in world history. The twentieth century must find a way of mastering the incredible events that happened under the rule of Hitler. The Holocaust has profoundly affected our view of man's capacity for evil, and the dangers of succumbing to the seduction of a pathological leader who demands total obedience. The question (raised in chapter 15) whether the Nazis merely expressed and acted out what is universal in the instinctual life of every human being, or whether they went beyond the wildest range of what is ordinarily repressed in an average expected conglomerate of libidinal and aggressive instincts, is one that is with us still and that remains unresolved.

Clinical material relating to young people who were neither children of survivors nor children of refugees but who nevertheless made the Holocaust a central psychic event, in that they behaved as if they lived under Nazi rule, were also studied. Although they could not be included within the framework of this book, these patients deserve special investigation. The way in which various individuals express their oedipal and sado-masochistic conflicts by borrowing from the events of the Holocaust is also a challenging field for further inquiry.

Hitler's legacy has made it possible to imagine another, even wider Holocaust of worldwide atomic destruction. The six million Jews and the other victims who died have thus attained the symbolic significance of a potential world-encompassing devastation. The actuality of the past and the possibility for the future are psychologically linked.

This book appears at a time when literature about the Holocaust is on the increase. As a whole, this is a necessary development, enabling us all to master the trauma. Inevitably, though, there are undesirable by-products. The

Holocaust can be exploited for a variety of purposes. It can become a source of erotic, masochistic, and sadistic fantasies. It can be trivialized, cheapened, and degraded. The authors trust it is the expression of their own personal ways of working through their patients' and their own traumata that enables them to present a book that will not be sensational, that will respect the dead and honor their memory, and that will help the living fulfill their potential.

## EVERYONE HAS A NAME

Everyone has a name
given to him by God
and given to him by his parents
Everyone has a name
given to him by his stature
and the way he smiles
and given to him by his clothing
Everyone has a name
given to him by the mountains
and given to him by his walls
Everyone has a name
given to him by the stars
and given to him by his neighbours
Everyone has a name
given to him by his sins
and given to him by his longing
Everyone has a name
given to him by his enemies
and given to him by his love
Everyone has a name
given to him by his holidays
and given to him by his work
Everyone has a name
given to him by the seasons
and given to him by his blindness
Everyone has a name
given to him by the sea
and given to him
by his death.

*By Zelda, an Israeli poet*
*Translated from the Hebrew by* MARCIA FALK

# Bibliography

ABELIN, E. L. 1971. "The Role of the Father in the Separation-Individuation Process." In John B. McDevitt and Calvin F. Settlage, eds., *Essays in Honor of Margaret Mahler*, pp. 229–52. New York: International Universities Press.

ADORNO, T. W.; et al. 1950. *The Authoritarian Personality*. New York: Harper & Brothers.

ALEKSANDROWICZ, DOV. 1973. "Children of Concentration Camp Survivors." In *The Child in His Family* (Anthony and Koupernik: 1973: 385–92).

ALEXANDER, FRANZ; and STAUB, HUGO. 1929. "Der Verbrecher und seine Richter." In *Psychoanalyse und Justiz*. Edited by Tilman Moser. Frankfurt: Fischer, 1971.

ANTHONY, E. JAMES; and KOUPERNIK, CYRILLE. 1973. Eds. *The Child in His Family: The Impact of Disease and Death*. New York: John Wiley.

APPELFELD, A. *Hadoar*. 23 Tishre, Tashlach.

ARENDT, HANNAH. 1958. *The Origins of Totalitarianism*. New York: Harcourt Brace Jovanovich.

ARLOW, J. A. 1979. "Metaphor and the Psychoanalytic Situation." *Psychoanalytic Quarterly*, 48:363–85.

AXELROD, SYLVIA; SCHNIPPER, O. L.; and RAU, J. H. 1980. "Hospitalized Offspring of Holocaust Survivors: Problems and Dynamics." *Bulletin of the Menninger Clinic*, 44(1):1–14.

BAEYER, W. 1960. "Uber die psychiatrische Begutachtung von Gesundheitschaden aus der national." In *Sozialishischen Verfolgung* (Festschrift H. Muthesius). Frankfurt: Neue Wege der Forsorge.

BAEYER, W.; HAFNER, H.; and KISKER, K. P. 1964. *Psychiatrie der Verfolgten*. Berlin; Gottingen; Heidelburg.

BAROCAS, H.; and BAROCAS, C. 1979. "Wounds of the Fathers: The Next Generation of Holocaust Victims." *International Review of Psychoanalysis*, 6:331–41.

BENEDEK, T. 1949. "The Psychosomatic Implications of the Primary Unit: Mother-Child." *American Journal of Orthopsychiatry*, 19:642–54.

BENN, GOTTFRIED. 1979–80. *Letters to P. W. Oelze, 1945–56*. Edited by Harald Steinhagen and Jürgen Schroeder. Munich: Limes Verlag.

BERES, D. 1958. "Vicissitudes of Superego Functions and Superego Precursors in Childhood." In *Psychoanalytic Study of the Child* (R. Eissler 1945–79, 13:324–51).

BERGLER, EDMUND. 1952. *The Superego: Unconscious Conscience*. New York: Grune & Stratton.

BETTELHEIM, BRUNO. 1943. "Individual and Mass Behavior in Extreme Situations." *Journal of Abnormal Social Psychology*, 38:417–452.

BICK, E. 1968. "The Experience of the Skin in Early Object-Relations." *International Journal of Psychoanalysis*, 49:484–86.

BLACKER, K. H.; and TUPIN, J. P. 1977. "Hysteria and Hysterical Structures: Developmental and Social Theories." In *Hysterical Personality* (Horowitz 1977:95–142).

BLOS, P. 1962. *On Adolescence: A Psychoanalytic Interpretation*. Glencoe, Ill.: Free Press.

BLOS, P. 1967. "The Second Individuation Process." In *Psychoanalytic Study of the Child*. (R. Eissler 1945–79, 22:162–83).

BLOS, P. 1968. *Minutes of Discussion Group 7*: "Children of Social Catastrophe." Sequelae in *Survivors and the Children of Survivors*. Meeting of the American Psychoanalytic Association, New York. December 1968.

BLUM, H. P. 1978. "Psychoanalytic Study of an Unusual Perversion: Discussion." *Journal of the American Psychoanalytic Association*, 26:785–92.

BORNSTEIN, B. 1967. *Die lange Nacht*. Frankfurt: Europaische Verlagsanstalt.

*317*

# Bibliography

BRENMAN, ERIC. 1973. Panel on hysteria today. Twenty-eighth Congress of the Psycho-Analytical Association, Paris. Unpublished manuscript.

BREUER, JOSEF; and FREUD, SIGMUND. 1893. *Studies on Hysteria*. In *Standard Edition* (Freud 1953–74, 2:1–335).

BRODY, S. 1973. "The Son of a Refugee." In *Psychoanalytic Study of the Child* (R. Eissler 1945–79, 28:169–91).

BROSZAT, MARTIN. 1963. *Kommandant in Auschwitz*. Munich.

BRUCKNER, WINFRIED; FERRA MIKURA, VERA; et al. 1978. *Damals war ich vierzehn*. Munich–Wien: Jugend und Volk.

BURLINGHAM, DOROTHY. 1951. "Present Trends in Handling the Mother-Child Relationship during the Therapeutic Process." *Psychoanalytic Study of the Child*, 6:31–37.

CHODOFF, PAUL. 1963. "Late Effects of the Concentration Camp Syndrome." *Archives of General Psychiatry*, 8:323–33.

DAHMER, HELMUT. 1979. " 'Holocaust' und die Amnesie." *Psyche*, 33:1039–45.

DANIELI, YAEL. 1980. "Families of Survivors of the Nazi Holocaust: Some Long and Short Term Effects." In *Psychological Stress and Adjustment in Time of War and Peace*. Edited by N. Milgram. Washington, D.C.: Hemisphere Publications.

DANIELI, YAEL. 1981. "Countertransference in the Treatment and Study of Nazi Holocaust Survivors and their Children." *Victimology: An International Journal*. Vol. 5, no. 3–4.

DAVIDSON, SHAMAI. 1972. "The Treatment of Holocaust Survivors." In S. Davidson, ed., *Spheres of Psychotherapeutic Activity* (Jerusalem: Medical Department, Kuput Cholim Center).

DAWIDOWICZ, LUCY S. 1976. *The War Against the Jews, 1933–1945*. New York: Bantam Books. *First edition:* New York: Holt, Rinehart & Winston, 1975.

DES PRES, TERENCE. 1976. *The Survivor*. New York: Oxford University Press.

DEUTSCH, FELIX. 1957. "A Footnote to Freud's Fragment of an Analysis of a Case of Hysteria." *Psychoanalytic Quarterly*, 26:159–67.

DEUTSCH, HELENE. 1942. "Some Forms of Emotional Disturbance and their Relationship in Schizophrenia." In *Neuroses and Character Types: Clinical Psychoanalytic Studies*. New York: International Universities Press (1965).

DE WIND, EMMANUEL. 1949. "Confrotatie met de dood." *Folia Psychiatrica, necrl. Trans.*: De Wind (1968).

DE WIND, EMMANUEL. 1968. "The Confrontation with Death: Symposium on Psychic Traumatization through Social Catastrophe." *International Journal of Psychoanalysis*, 49:302–5.

DE WIND, EMMANUEL. 1971. Quoted in *Spätschäden nach Extrembelastungen*. (Herberg 1971:332).

DONAT, ALEXANDER. 1978. *The Holocaust Kingdom*. New York: Holocaust Library: Holt, Rinehart & Winston.

EISNER, J. 1980. *The Survivor*. Edited by Irving A. Leitner. New York: William Morrow.

EISSLER, KURT R. 1960. "Variationen in der psychoanalytischen Technique." *Psyche*, 13:609–24.

EISSLER, RUTH S.; et al. 1945–79. Eds. *Psychoanalytic Study of the Child*. Vols. 1–25, New York: International Universities Press. Vols. 26–33, New Haven: Yale University Press.

EITINGER, LEO. 1961. "Pathology of the Concentration Camp Syndrome." *Archives of General Psychiatry*, 5:371–79.

EITINGER, LEO. 1962. "Concentration Camp Survivors in the Postwar World." *American Journal of Orthopsychiatry*, 32:367–75.

EL-GHUSEIN, FA'IZ. 1975. *Martyred Armenia*. New York: Tankian Publishing Corp.

EPSTEIN, HELEN. 1977. "Heirs of the Holocaust." *New York Times Magazine*, 19 June 1977:12–15; 74–77.

EPSTEIN, HELEN. 1979. *Children of the Holocaust: Conversations with Sons and Daughters of Survivors*. New York: G. P. Putnam's.

ERIKSON, E. H. 1959. "Identity and the Life Cycle." *Psychological Issues*. Vol. 1, no. 1, monog. 1. New York: International Universities Press.

# Bibliography

FOGELMAN, E.; and SAVRAN, B. 1979. "Therapeutic Groups for Children of Holocaust Survivors." *International Journal of Group Psychotherapy,* 29:211–36.

FOGELMAN, E.; and SAVRAN, B. 1980. "Brief Group Therapy with Offspring of Holocaust Survivors: Leaders' Reactions." *American Journal of Orthopsychiatry,* 50(1):96–108.

FREEDMAN, A. 1978. "Psychoanalytic Study of an Unusual Perversion." *Journal of the American Psychoanalytic Association,* 26:749–78.

FREUD, ANNA. 1946. *Das Ich und die Abwehrmechanismen,* p. 52. London: Imago Publishing Co., Ltd. *U.S. edition: The Ego and the Mechanisms of Defense.* New York: International Universities Press, 1966. *Trans.:* Cecil Baines.

FREUD, ANNA. 1960. Discussion of Dr. John Bowlby's Paper in *Psychoanalytic Study of the Child* (R. Eissler 1945–79, 15:53–62).

FREUD, ANNA. 1965. "Normality and Pathology in Childhood: Assessments of Development." In *Writings of Anna Freud,* vol. 6. New York: International Universities Press.

FREUD, ANNA. 1967. "Comments on Trauma." In S. Furst, ed., *Psychic Trauma.* New York: Basic Books.

FREUD, ANNA; and DANN, S. 1951. "An Experiment in Group Upbringing." In *Psychoanalytic Study of the Child.* (R. Eissler 1945–79, 6:127–69).

FREUD, SIGMUND. 1900. "The Interpretation of Dreams." In *Standard Edition* (Freud 1953–74, 4–5.)

FREUD, SIGMUND. 1901. *The Psychopathology of Everyday Life.* In *Standard Edition* (Freud 1953–74, 6:1–279).

FREUD, SIGMUND. 1905. "Fragment of an Analysis of a Case of Hysteria." In *Standard Edition* (Freud 1953–74, 7:3–122).

FREUD, SIGMUND. 1912–13. *Totem and Taboo.* In *Standard Edition* (Freud 1955, 13:1–162).

FREUD, SIGMUND. 1914. "On Narcissism: An Introduction." In *Standard Edition* (Freud 1953–74, 14:69–102).

FREUD, SIGMUND. 1915. *On Transience.* In *Standard Edition* (Freud 1953–74, 14:305–7).

FREUD, SIGMUND. 1916a. "Trauer und Melancholie." In *Gesammelte Werke* (Freud 1946 10, 428–46).*Trans.:* Freud (1917).

FREUD, SIGMUND. 1916b. "Some Character-types Met with in Psychoanalytic Work." In *Standard Edition* (Freud 1953–74, 14:310–34).

FREUD, SIGMUND. 1916c. "Introductory Lectures on Psychoanalysis." In *Standard Edition* (Freud 1953–74, 15–16:15–463).

FREUD, SIGMUND. 1917. "Mourning and Melancholia." In *Standard Edition* (Freud 1953–74, 14:239–58). *German Text:* Freud (1916a).

FREUD, SIGMUND. 1920. "Beyond the Pleasure Principle." In *Standard Edition* (Freud 1953–74, 18:3–64).

FREUD, SIGMUND. 1921. "Group Psychology and the Analysis of the Ego." In *Standard Edition* (Freud 1953–74, 18:67–143).

FREUD, SIGMUND. 1923. "The Ego and the Id." In *Standard Edition* (Freud, 1953–74, 19:3–66).

FREUD, SIGMUND. 1925. "Negations." In *Standard Edition* (Freud 1953–74, 14:234).

FREUD, SIGMUND. 1926. "Inhibitions, Symptoms and Anxiety." In *Standard Edition* (Freud 1953–74, 20:77–174).

FREUD, SIGMUND. 1927. "The Future of an Illusion." In *Standard Edition* (Freud 1953–74, 21:3–56).

FREUD, SIGMUND. 1930a. "Civilization and Its Discontents." In *Standard Edition* (Freud 1953–74, 21:59–145).

FREUD, SIGMUND. 1930b. "Das Unbehagen in der Kultur." In *Gesammelte Werke* (Freud 1968, 14:421–506.) Frankfurt: Fischer.

FREUD, SIGMUND. 1932a. "Why War?" In *Standard Edition* (Freud, 1953–74, 22:197–215).

FREUD, SIGMUND. 1932b. *New Introductory Lectures on Psychoanalysis.* In *Standard Edition* (Freud 1953–74, 22:3–182).

FREUD, SIGMUND. 1937. "Constructions in Analysis." In *Standard Edition* (Freud 1953–74, 23:256).

FREUD, SIGMUND. 1937–39. "Moses and Monotheism." In *Standard Edition* (Freud 1953–74, 23:3–137).

# Bibliography

FREUD, SIGMUND. 1940a. "An Outline of Psycho-Analysis." In *Standard Edition* (Freud 1953–74, 23:141–207).

FREUD, SIGMUND. 1940b. "Splitting of the Ego in the Process of Defense." In *Standard Edition* (Freud 1953–74, 23:273).

FREUD, SIGMUND. 1953–74. *The Standard Edition of the Complete Psychological Works of Sigmund Freud*. 24 vols. Translated from the German under the general editorship of James Strachey. In collaboration with Anna Freud. Assisted by Alix Strachey and Alan Tyson. London: Hogarth Press and The Institute of Psycho-Analysis.

FREUD, SIGMUND. 1966–78. *Gesammelte Werke*. 17 vols. Edited by Anna Freud, E. Bibring, and W. Hofer. Frankfurt: Fischer.

FRIEDLÄNDER, SAUL. 1979. *When Memory Comes*. New York: Farrar, Straus & Giroux.

FRIEDMAN, P. 1948. "The Road Back for the D.P.'s." *Commentary*, 6:502–10.

FRIEDMAN, P. 1949. "Some Aspects of Concentration Camp Psychology." *American Journal of Psychiatry*, 105:601–5.

FUEHMAN, F. 1981. "Meine Schulzeit im dritten Reich (8). Den katzenartigen wollten wir verbrennen." *Frankfurter Allgemeine Zeitung*, 25 July, no. 169.

FURMAN E. 1973. "The Impact of the Nazi Concentration Camps on the Children of Survivors." In *The Child in His Family* (Anthony and Koupernik 1973, 2:379–84).

FURMAN, E. 1974. *A Child's Parent Dies*. New Haven: Yale University Press.

FURST, S. S. 1967. Ed. *Psychic Trauma*. New York: Basic Books.

GEBARSKI, B. 1963. "A Letter to my Turkish Friend." From the Polish *Kierunki*, 26 November 1961. Baikar Press.

GEBHARDT, BRUNO. 1962. a.a.O. zit. nach Hans Adolf Jacobsen u. Hans Dollinger (Hrsg.): Der zweite der Weltkrieg. München 1962, darin: Dokumentation v. 31.8.1939.

GEBHARDT, BRUNO. 1970. *Handbuch der Deutschen Geschichte*. Vol. 4. Stuttgart: Klett-Cotta.

GREEN, A. 1972. "De l'esquisse à l'Interpretation des Rêves." *Nouvelle Revue de Psychanalyse*, 5:155–80.

GREEN, A. 1973. Panel on hysteria today. Twenty-eighth Congress of the Psycho-Analytical Association, Paris. Unpublished manuscript.

GREENACRE, PHYLLIS. 1950. "General Problems of Acting Out." *Psychoanalytic Quarterly*, 19:455–67.

GREENACRE, PHYLLIS. 1969. "Conscience in the Psychopath." In *Trauma, Growth, and Personality*, pp. 165–87. New York: International Universities Press.

GREENACRE, PHYLLIS. 1971. "The Influence of Infantile Trauma on Genetic Patterns." In *Emotional Growth: Psychoanalytic Studies of the Gifted and a Great Variety of Other Individuals*. 2 vols. New York: International Universities Press.

GREENSON, R. R. 1958. "On Screen Defenses, Screen Hunger, and Screen Identity." *Journal of the American Psychoanalytic Association*, 6:242–62.

GRINBERG, L. 1968. "On Acting Out and Its Role in the Psychoanalytic Process." *International Journal of Psychoanalysis*, 49:23.

GRINBERG, L., and GRINBERG, REBECCA. 1971. *Identidad y Cambio*.

GRUBRICH-SIMITIS, ILSE G. 1979. "Extremtraumatisierung als kumulatives Trauma." *Psyche*, 33:991–1023.

GRUBRICH-SIMITIS, ILSE G. 1981. "Extreme Traumatization as Cumulative Trauma." In *Psychoanalytic Study of the Child*, 36:415–50.

GRUNBERGER, BELA. 1979. *Narcissism*. New York: International Universities Press.

GYOMROI, E. L. 1963. "The Analysis of a Young Concentration Camp Victim." In *Psychoanalytic Study of the Child* (R. Eissler 1945–79, 18:484–510).

HAYS, D.; and DANIELI, YAEL. 1976. "International Groups with a Specific Problem Orientation Focus." In *The Intensive Group Experience*. Edited by Max Rosenbaum and Alvin Snadowsky. New York: Free Press.

HERBERG, E. 1971. Ed. *Spätschäden nach Extrembelastungen*. Herford: Nicolaische Verlagsbuchhandlung.

HERZOG, JAMES. 1978. Presentation in the workshop on children of survivors. *Meeting of the*

# Bibliography

*American Psychoanalytic Association*. Chaired by Martin Bergmann and Milton Jucovy. December 1978.

HERZOG, JAMES. 1980. "Sleep Disorder and Father Hunger: The Erlkonig Syndrome." In *Psychoanalytic Study of the Child* (R. Eissler, 1945–79, 35:219–33).

HERZOG, JAMES. 1981. "Father Hurt and Father Hunger: A Son's Experience with His Aging Survivor Father's Declining Years and Death." *Journal of Geriatric Psychiatry*. (Submitted for publication.) Presented to the 32nd International Psychoanalytic Meeting. Helsinki, July 1981.

HITLER, ADOLF. 1940. *Mein Kampf*. Munich: Zentralverlag der NSDAP.

HOFMANNSTHAL, HUGO VON. 1959. *Aufzeichnungen*. Frankfurt: Fischer.

HOPPE, KLAUS. 1966. "The Psychodynamics of Concentration Camp Victims." *The Forum*, 1:76–86.

HOPPE, KLAUS. 1968. "Re-somatization of Affects in Survivors of Persecution: Symposium on Psychic Traumatization through Social Catastrophe." *International Journal of Psychoanalysis*, 49:324–26.

HOROWITZ, M. J. 1977. Ed. *Hysterical Personality*. New York: Jason Aronson.

JACKSON, FRED. 1980. *New Statesman*, 4, April 1981.

JACOBSON, E. 1946. "The Effect of Disappointment on Ego and Super-Ego Traumata in Normal and Depressive Development." *Psychoanalytic Review*, 33:129–47.

JACOBSON, E. 1959. "Exceptions: An Elaboration of Freud's Character Study." In *Psychoanalytic Study of the Child* (R. Eissler 1945–79, 14:135–54).

JACOBSON, E. 1964. *The Self and the Object World*. New York: International Universities Press.

JUCOVY, MILTON. 1978. "Countertransference and technical issues in the treatment of Holocaust survivors and their children." Contribution to the *Symposium on the Psychology of the Jewish Experience (The Holocaust: Psychological Effects on Survivors and their Children)*. Organized by the Combined Jewish Philanthropies of Greater Boston, 21 May 1978.

KEILSON, HANS V. 1979. *Sequential Traumatization of Children*. Stuttgart: Ferdinand Enke. *German Text*: Keilson and Sarphati (1979).

KEILSON, HANS V.; SARPHATI, R.; and HERMANN. 1979. *Sequentielle Traumatisierung bei Kindern*. Stuttgart: Ferdinand Enke. *Trans.*: Keilson (1979).

KEISER, S. 1967. "Freud's Concept of Trauma and a Specific Ego Function." *Journal of the American Psychoanalytic Association*, 15:781–94.

KERNBERG, OTTO. 1980. *Internal World and External Reality*. New York: Jason Aronson.

KESTENBERG, JUDITH S. 1972. "Psychoanalytic Contributions to the Problem of Children of Survivors from Nazi Persecution." *Israel Annals of Psychiatry and Related Disciplines*, 10:311–25. *German Text*: "Kinder von uberlebenden der Naziverfolgungen (Kestenberg 1974:249–65).

KESTENBERG, JUDITH S. 1973. "Introductory Remarks: Children of the Holocaust." In *The Child in His Family* (Anthony and Koupernik 1973:359–67).

KESTENBERG, JUDITH S. 1974. "Kinder von uberlebenden der Naziverfolgungen." *Psyche*, 10:249–65. *Trans.*: "Psychoanalytic Contributions to the Problem of Children of Survivors from Nazi Persecution" (Kestenberg 1972:311–25).

KESTENBERG, JUDITH S. 1975. *Children and Parents: Psychoanalytic Studies in Development*. New York: Jason Aronson.

KESTENBERG, JUDITH S. 1977. "The Psychological Consequences of Punitive Institutions." In *Humanizing America* (Knopp 1977:113–29). Reprinted in a modified form in *Israel Annals of Psychiatry and Related Disciplines* (1981a, 18:15–30).

KESTENBERG, JUDITH S. 1978. The parents' past in the life of survivors' children. Presented to the *Symposium on the Psychology of the Jewish Experience (The Holocaust: Psychological Effects on Survivors and their Children)*. Organized by the Combined Jewish Philanthropies of Greater Boston. Boston, 21 May 1978.

KESTENBERG, JUDITH S. 1979a. Aus Analysen der Kinder der Verfolgten: ein Vergleich zwischen Analysen der Erwachsenen und der Kinder. Vortrag Gehalten am *Kongress Kinderpsychoanalyse und Sozialarbeit*. Gesamthochschule Kassel am 21.11.

# Bibliography

KESTENBERG, JUDITH S. 1979b. Aus Psychoanalysen der Kinder vom Uberlebenden vom Nazi-Massenmord. Vortrag gehalten vor der Schweizer Psychoanalytischen Gesellschaft in Zurich am 22:4.

KESTENBERG, JUDITH S. 1979c. Workshop at the Berlin Institute.

KESTENBERG, JUDITH S. 1980. "Psychoanalyses of Children of Survivors from the Holocaust: Case Presentations and Assessment." Journal of the American Psychoanalytic Association, 28:775–804.

KESTENBERG, JUDITH S. 1981a. Revised reprint of "The Psychological Consequences of Punitive Institutions." Israel Annals of Psychiatry and Related Disciplines, 18:15–30.

KESTENBERG, JUDITH S. 1981b. "The Development of Paternal Attitudes, with Hershey Marcus, Mark Sossin and Richard Stevenson, Jr." In Anthology of Fatherhood. Edited by S. Cath, A. Gurwitz, and J. Ross. New York, Boston: Little, Brown.

KESTENBERG, JUDITH S.; MARCUS, H.; ROBBINS, E.; BERLOWE, J.; and BUELTE, A. 1971. "Development of the Young Child as Seen through Bodily Movement." Journal of the American Psychoanalytic Association, 19:746–63. Reprinted in Children and Parents (Kestenberg 1975:195–214).

KHAN, M. MASUD R. 1963. "The Concept of Cumulative Trauma." In Psychoanalytic Study of the Child (R. Eissler 1945–79, 18:286–306).

KHAN, M. MASUD R. 1969. "On Symbiotic Omnipotence." Psychoanalytic Forum, 3:137–58.

KHAN, M. MASUD R. 1974a. The Privacy of the Self. London: Hogarth Press.

KHAN, M. MASUD R. 1974b. "La rancune de l'hystérique." Nouvelle Revue de Psychanalyse, 10:151–58.

KHAN, M. MASUD R. 1979. Alienation in Perversions. London: Hogarth Press.

KHERDIAN, D. 1979. The Road from Home. New York: Greenwillow Books.

KISKER, K. P. 1961. "Die Psychiatrische Begutaghtung der Opfer Nazionalsozichistischer Verfolgung, Koyr, d." Psychiatria et Neurologia. Dresden: Gesselloch.

KLEIN, H. 1968. "Problems in the Psychotherapeutic Treatment of Israeli Survivors of the Holocaust." In Massive Psychic Trauma (Krystal 1969:233–48).

KLEIN, H. 1973. "Children of the Holocaust: Mourning and Bereavement." In The Child in His Family (Anthony and Koupernik 1973:393–409).

KLEIN, H.; ZELLERMEYER, J.; and SHANAN, J. 1963. "Former Concentration Camp Inmates on a Psychiatric Ward." Archives of General Psychiatry, 8:334–42.

KNOPP, JOSEPHINE. 1977. Ed. Humanizing America: A Post-Holocaust Imperative (Proceedings of the Philadelphia Conference on the Holocaust). Philadelphia: Institute of the Holocaust, Temple University.

KOGON, E. 1950. The Theory and Practice of Hell. New York: Farrar, Straus.

KOGON, E. 1979. "Der S. S. Staat." In Das System der deutschen Konzentrationslager XXI. Munich: Kindler.

KOHUT, HEINZ. 1971. The Analysis of the Self. New York: International Universities Press. German Text: Kohut (1973).

KOHUT, HEINZ. 1973. Narzissmus. Frankfurt: Suhrkamp. Trans.: Kohut (1971).

KOHUT, HEINZ. 1977. The Restoration of the Self. New York: International Universities Press. German Text: Kohut (1979).

KOHUT, HEINZ. 1979. Die Heilung des Selbst. Frankfurt: Suhrkamp. Trans.: Kohut (1977).

KRIS, ERNST. 1952. Psychoanalytic Exploration in Art. New York: International Universities Press. German Text: Kris (1977).

KRIS, ERNST. 1956a. "The Personal Myth: A Problem in Psychoanalytic Technique." Journal of the American Psychoanalytic Association, 4:653–81. Reprinted in Selected Papers of Ernst Kris (Kris, 1975:272–300).

KRIS, ERNST. 1956b. "The Recovery of Childhood Memories in Psychoanalysis." Reprinted in Selected Papers of Ernst Kris (Kris 1975:301–40).

KRIS, ERNST. 1975. Selected Papers of Ernst Kris. New Haven: Yale University Press.

KRIS, ERNST. 1977. Die asthetische Illusion: Phanomene der Kunst in der Sicht der Psychoanalyse. Frankfurt: Suhrkamp. Trans.: Kris (1952).

KROHN, A. 1978. Hysteria: The Elusive Neurosis. New York: International Universities Press.

KRYSTAL, HENRY. 1968. Ed. Massive Psychic Trauma. New York: International Universities Press.

# Bibliography

KRYSTAL, HENRY. 1978. "Trauma and Affects." In *Psychoanalytic Study of the Child* (R. Eissler 1945–79, 33:81–116).
KRYSTAL, HENRY; and NIEDERLAND, WILLIAM G. 1971. *Psychic Traumatization: After Effects in Individuals and Communities*. Boston: Little, Brown.

LAING, R. D.; and ESTERSON, A. 1964. *Sanity, Madness and the Family*. London: Tavistock Publications.
LAPLANCHE, J. 1970. *Life and Death in Psychoanalysis*. Baltimore: Johns Hopkins University Press.
LAUFER, M. 1973. "The Analysis of a Child of Survivors." In *The Child in His Family* (Anthony and Koupernik 1973:363–73).
LEYTING, GISELA. 1980. Kriegserleben—Erfahrunger und Ueberlegungen zum Betroffensein. Lecture given at the *Meeting of the Middle-European Psychoanalytic Societies*. Bamberg, 1980.
LICHTENSTEIN, HEINZ. 1964. "The Role of Narcissism in the Emergence and Maintenance of Primary Identity." *International Journal of Psychoanalysis*, 45:49–56.
LIEBLICH, A. 1978. *Tin Soldiers on Jerusalem Beach*. New York: Pantheon.
LIFTON, ROBERT JAY. 1967. *Death in Life: Survivors of Hiroshima*. New York: Random House.
LIFTON, ROBERT JAY. 1969. "Observation on Hiroshima Survivors." In *Massive Psychic Trauma* (Krystal 1969:168–89).
LIPIN, T. 1963. "The Repetition Compulsion and Maturational Drive Representatives." *International Journal of Psychoanalysis*, 44:389–406.
LIPKOWITZ, M. H. 1973. "The Child of Two Survivors. A Report of an Unsuccessful Therapy." *The Israel Annals of Psychiatry and Related Disciplines*, 2(2):363–74.
LOEWALD, H. 1962. "Internalization, Separation, Mourning, and the Superego." *Psychoanalytic Quarterly*, 31:483–504.
LOEWALD, H. 1965. *Twenty-fourth International Psychoanalytical Congress*. Amsterdam, 1965.
LORENZER, A. 1968. "Some Observations on the Latency of Symptoms in Patients Suffering from Persecution Sequelae." *International Journal of Psychoanalysis*, 49:316–18.

McDOUGALL, JOYCE. 1970. *Plaidoyer pour une certaine Anormalité*. Paris: Editions Gallimard.
MAERTHESHEIMER, PETER. 1979. *Im Kreuzfeuer–Der Fernsehfilm Holocaust*. Frankfurt: Fischer.
MAHLER, MARGARET S.; and FURER, MANUEL. 1968. *On Human Symbiosis and the Vicissitudes of Individuation*. Vol. 1: Infantile Psychoses. New York: International Universities Press. German Text: Mahler and Furer (1972).
MAHLER, MARGARET; and FURER, MANUEL. 1972. *Symbiose und Individuation*. Stuttgart: Klett. Trans.: Mahler and Furer (1968).
MAHLER, MARGARET S.; PINE, F.; and BERGMAN, A. 1975. *The Psychological Birth of the Human Infant*. New York: Basic Books.
METCALF, A. 1977. "Childhood: From Process to Structure." In *Hysterical Personality*. (Horowitz 1977:223–81).
MITSCHERLICH, ALEXANDER. 1979. "Die Notwendigkest zu trauern." *Im Kreuzfeuer–Der Fernsehfilm Holocaust* (Maerthesheimer 1979:207).
MITSCHERLICH, ALEXANDER; and MITSCHERLICH, MARGARET. 1970. *Die Unfähigkeit zu trauern*. Munich: R. Piper.
MOOR, PAUL. 1972. *Das Selbstporträt des Jürgen Bartsch*. Frankfurt: Fischer.
MOSES, R. 1978. "Adult Psychic Trauma: The Question of Early Predisposition and Some Detailed Mechanisms." *International Journal of Psychoanalysis*, 59:353–64.

NAGERA, HUMBERTO; and FREUD, W. E. 1965. "Metapsychological Assessment of the Adult Personality: The Adult Profile." In *Psychoanalytic Study of the Child* (R. Eissler 1945–79, 20:9–41).
NES-ZIEGLER, J. van. 1971. "Einführung." In *Spätschäden nach Extrembelastungen*. (Herberg 1971:10).

# Bibliography

NIEDERLAND, WILLIAM G. 1961. "The Problem of the Survivor." *Journal of the Hillside Hospital*, 10:233–47.

NIEDERLAND, WILLIAM G. 1964. "Psychiatric Disorder among Persecution Victims: A Contribution to the Understanding of Concentration Camp Pathology and Its After-effects." *Journal of Nervous and Mental Diseases*, 139:458–74.

NIEDERLAND, WILLIAM G. 1968. "Clinical Observations on the 'Survivor Syndrome': Symposium on Psychic Traumatization through Social Catastrophe." *International Journal of Psychoanalysis*, 49:313–15. German Text: Niederland (1980).

NIEDERLAND, WILLIAM G. 1969. "The Psychiatric Evaluation of Emotional Disorders in Survivors of Nazi Persecution." In *Massive Psychic Trauma* (Krystal 1969:8–22).

NIEDERLAND, WILLIAM G. 1980. "Folgen der Verfolgung: Das Überlebenden Syndrome." In *Seelenmord*. Frankfurt: Suhrkamp. *Trans.*: Niederland (1968).

ORGEL, D. 1978. *The Devil in Vienna*. New York: Dial Press.

PANDSKY, WALTER. 1965. *Richard Strauss: Partitur eines Lebens*. Munich: R. Piper.

PANKOW, GISELA. 1974. "The Body Image in Hysterical Psychosis." *International Journal of Psychoanalysis*, 55:407–14.

PIAGET, JEAN. 1932. *The Moral Judgment of the Child*. Glencoe, Ill.: Free Press.

PILICHOWSKI, C. 1980. *No Time-limit for These Crimes*. Warsaw: Interpress Publishers.

PODIETZ, L. 1975. "The Holocaust Revisited in the Next Generation." *Analysis: Jewish Institute for Policy Studies Bulletin*, pp. 1–5.

PORTER, J. N. 1978. The survivor syndrome. Unpublished manuscript.

PORTER, J. N. 1979. "Social Psychological Aspects of the Holocaust." In *Encountering the Holocaust*. Edited by B. L. Sherwin and G. S. Ament, pp. 189–222. Chicago: Impact Press.

RACAMIER, Paul-Claude 1952. "Hystérie et Théâtre." In *De Psychanalyse en Psychiatrie*, pp. 135–64. Paris: Payot, 1979.

RAKOFF, V. 1966. "Long Term Effects of the Concentration Camp Experience." *Viewpoints*, 1:17–21.

RAKOFF, V. 1969. "Children and Families of Concentration Camp Survivors." *Canada's Mental Health*, 14:24–26.

RAKOFF, V.: SIGAL, J. J.; EPSTEIN, N. B. 1966. "Children and Families of Concentration Camp Survivors." *Canada's Mental Health*, 14 (July–August).

RAPAPORT, DAVID. 1957. "A Theoretical Analysis of the Superego Concept." In *Collected Papers of David Rapaport*. Edited by Merton M. Gill, pp. 685–709. New York: Basic Books, (1967).

RAPPAPORT, E. 1968. "Beyond Traumatic Neurosis." *International Journal of Psychoanalysis*, 49:719–31.

RAUSCHNING, HERMANN. 1939. *Gespräche mit Hitler*. Vienna: Europaverlag, 1973.

RICHTER, HANS PETER. 1974. *Damals war es Friedlich*. Munich: Deutscher Taschenbuch.

RIEBESSER, PETER. 1979. Discussion of the paper by Judith S. Kestenberg entitled "Aus Psychoanalysen der Kinder der Uberlebenden vom Nazi Massenmord." Held at the *Meeting of the Swiss Psychoanalytic Society*. Zurich.

ROBINSON, S. 1979. "Late Effects of Persecution in Persons Who—as Children or Young Adolescents—Survived Nazi Occupation in Europe." *Israel Annals of Psychiatry and Related Disciplines*, 17:3.

ROIPHE, H. 1978. "Discussion: Psychoanalytic Study of an Unusual Perversion." *Journal of the American Psychoanalytic Association*, 26:779–83.

ROSEN, V. H. 1955. "The Reconstruction of a Traumatic Childhood Event in a Case of Derealization." *Journal of the American Psychoanalytic Association*, 3:211–21.

ROSENBERGER, L. 1973. "Children of Survivors." In *The Child in His Family* (Anthony and Koupernik 1973:375–77).

ROSENKÖTTER, LUTZ. 1979. "Schatten der Zeitgeschichte auf psychoanalytischen Behandlungen." *Psyche*, 33:1024–38.

SANDLER, J. 1967. "Trauma, Strain, and Development." In *Psychic Trauma* (Furst 1967:154–74).

# Bibliography

SANDLER, J.; and SANDLER, A. M. 1978. "On the Development of Object Relations and Affects." *International Journal of Psychoanalysis*, 59:285–93.

SCHIEFFER, I. 1978. *The Trauma of Time.* New York: International Universities Press.

SCHLINGENSEIDER, JOHANNES. 1976. *Widerstand und verborgene Schuld.* Berlin: Jugenddienstverlage. *Trans.*: Schlingenseider (1977).

SCHLINGENSEIDER, JOHANNES. 1977. *Resistance and Hidden Guilt.* Berlin: Jugenddienstverlage. *German Text:* Schlingenseider (1976).

SCHUR, MAX. 1953. "The Ego in Anxiety." In *Drives, Affects and Behavior.* Edited by R. M. Loewenstein, pp. 67–103. New York: International Universities Press.

SIGAL, J. 1971. "Second Generation Effects of Massive Trauma." *International Psychiatry Clinics,* 8:55–65. Reprinted in *Psychic Traumatization* (Krystal and Niederland 1971:55–65).

SIGAL, J. 1973. "Hypotheses and Methodology in the Study of Families of Holocaust Survivors." In *The Child in His Family* (Anthony and Koupernik 1973:411–18).

SIGAL, J. 1978. Discussion of Judith Kestenberg's paper entitled "From the Analyses of Children of Survivors." Montreal, October 1978.

SIGAL, J.; and RAKOFF, V. 1971. "Concentration Camp Survival: A Pilot Study of Effects on the Second Generation." *Canadian Psychiatric Association Journal,* 16:393–97.

SHENGOLD, LEONARD L. 1979. "Child Abuse and Deprivation: Soul Murder." *Journal of the American Psychoanalytic Association,* 27:533–59.

SIMENAUER, ERICH. 1968. "Late Psychic Sequelae of Man-made Disasters: Symposium on Psychic Traumatization through Social Catastrophe." *International Journal of Psychoanalysis,* 49:306–9.

SIMENAUER, ERICH. 1978. "A Double Helix: Some Determinants of Self-Perpetuation of Nazism." In *Psychoanalytic Study of the Child* (R. Eissler 1945–79, 33:411–25).

SIMENAUER, ERICH. 1979. Commentary on Fred Grubel's article entitled "Zeitgenosse Sigmund Freud." *Jahrbuch der Psychoanalyse,* 11:166–70.

SIMENAUER, ERICH. 1981. "Die zweit Generation—Danach. Die Wiederkehr der Verfolgermentalität in Psychoanalysen." *Jahrbuch der Psychoanalyse,* 12:8–17.

SOLNIT, ALBERT J.; and KRIS, MARIANNE. 1967. "Trauma and Infantile Experiences." *Psychic Trauma* (Furst 1967:175–220).

SONNENBERG, S. M. 1974. "Workshop Report: Children of Survivors." *Journal of the American Psychoanalytic Association,* 22:200–4.

STEIN, M. 1966. "Self-Observation, Reality and the Superego." In *Psychoanalysis: A General Psychology.* Edited by R. M. Loewenstein; L. M. Newman; M. Schur; and A. Solnit, pp. 275–97. New York: International Universities Press.

STERBA, E. 1968. "The Effect of Persecution on Adolescents." In *Massive Psychic Trauma* (Krystal 1969:51–59).

STERN, M. 1959. "Anxiety, Trauma and Shock." *Psychoanalytic Quarterly,* 34:202–18.

STEVENS, WALLACE. 1972. *The Palm at the End of the Mind: Poems and a Play.* Edited by Holly Stevens. New York: Random House.

STRAUSS, HERBERT. 1957. "Resonderheiten der nichtpsychotischen seelischen Storungen bei Opfern der nationalsozialistischen Verfolgung und ihre Bedeutung in der Begutachtung." *Nervenarzt,* 28:344–50.

STRAUSS, HERBERT. 1961. "Psychiatric Disturbances in Victims of Racial Persecution." *Third World Congress of Psychiatry.* Montreal.

STRAUSS, RICHARD; and HOFMANNSTHAL, HUGO VON. 1978. *Briefwechsel.* Edited by Willi Schuh. Freiburg: Atlantis.

SYMPOSIUM of the ISRAEL PSYCHOANALYTIC SOCIETY. 1967. Chaired by H. Zvi Winnik. Published in *Israel Annals of Psychiatry and Related Disciplines,* 1:99–100.

TASHJIAN, J. H. 1965. *Turkey: Author of Genocide.* Boston: Commemorative Commission on the Fiftieth Anniversary of the Turkish Massacres of the Armenians.

TOLAND, JOHN. 1976. *Adolf Hitler.* New York: Doubleday.

TORBERG, FRIEDRICH. 1978. *Die Erben der Tante Jolesch.* Vienna: Langen Müller.

# Bibliography

TOYNBEE, A. J. 1975. *Armenian Atrocities: The Murder of a Nation.* New York: Tankian Publishing Corp.

TROSSMAN, B. 1968. "Adolescent Children of Concentration Camp Survivors." *Canadian Psychiatric Association Journal,* 12:121–23.

VENZLAFF, ULRICH. 1960. Basic observations as to the evaluation of psychic damages caused by racial and political persecution. Wiederfutm Berl d. Allg. Wochenzeitung Der Juden. Germany, May 1960.

VENZLAFF, ULRICH. 1968. "Forensic Psychiatry of Schizophrenia in Survivors." In *Massive Psychic Trauma* (Krystal 1969:110).

WANGH, MARTIN. 1962. "Psychoanalytische Betrachtungen zur Dynamik und Genese des Vorurteils, des Antisemitismus und des Nazismus." *Psyche,* 16:273–84.

WANGH, MARTIN. 1968a. *Minutes of Discussion Group 6:* "Children of Social Catastrophe." Sequelae in *Survivors and the Children of Survivors.* Meeting of the American Psychoanalytic Association. Boston, May 1968.

WANGH, MARTIN. 1968b. "A Psychogenetic Factor in the Recurrence of War: Symposium on Psychic Traumatization through Social Catastrophe." *International Journal of Psychoanalysis,* 49:319–23.

WANGH, MARTIN. 1969. Workshop on children of survivors. *International Congress for Psychoanalysis.* Rome. August 1969.

WANGH, MARTIN. 1971. "Die Beurteilung von Wiedergutmachungsanspruchen der wahrend der nationalsozialistischen Verfolgung geborenen Kinder." In *Spätschäden nach Extrembelastungen* (Herberg 1971:270–74).

WIESEL, ELIE. 1972a. *One Generation After.* New York: Bard Books.

WIESEL, ELIE. 1972b. *Souls on Fire: Portraits and Legends of Hasidic Masters.* New York: Random House.

WIESEL, ELIE. 1977. "The Holocaust: Three Views." *ADL Bulletin,* November.

WIJSENBEEK, H. 1977. Lecture held at the *Netherlands-Israel Symposium on the Impact of Persecution.* Jerusalem. October.

WILLIAMS, M. 1970. Discussion of M. Laufer's paper entitled "The Analysis of a Child of Survivors" (Laufer 1973).

WILLIAMS, M.; and KESTENBERG, JUDITH. 1974. Introduction and discussion in workshop on children of survivors. Summarized in *Journal of the American Psychoanalytic Association,* 22:200–204.

WINNICOTT, DONALD W. 1955. "Clinical Varieties of Transference." In *Through Paediatrics to Psycho-analysis* (Winnicott 1975).

WINNICOTT, DONALD W. 1965. *The Maturational Processes and the Facilitating Environment.* New York: International Universities Press.

WINNICOTT, DONALD W. 1971. *Die therapeutische Arbeit mit Kindern.* Munich: Kindler. *Trans.:* Winnicott (1973).

WINNICOTT, DONALD W. 1973. *Therapeutic Consultations in Child Psychiatry.* London: Hogarth Press. *German Text:* Winnicott (1971). *U.S. edition:* New York: Basic Books, 1971.

WINNICOTT, DONALD W. 1975. *Through Pediatrics to Psycho-analysis.* New York: Basic Books.

WINNIK, H. ZVI. 1967a. "Psychiatric Disturbances of Holocaust Survivors: Symposium of the Israel Psychoanalytic Society." *Israel Annals of Psychiatry and Related Disciplines,* 5:91–100.

WINNIK, H. ZVI. 1967b. "Further Comments Concerning the Problems of Late Psychopathological Effects of Nazi Persecution and their Therapy." *Israel Annals of Psychiatry and Related Disciplines,* 5:1–16.

WINNIK, H. ZVI. 1968. "Contributions to Symposium of Psychic Traumatization through Social Catastrophe." *International Journal of Psychoanalysis,* 49:298–301.

WOLFFHEIM, NELLY. 1966. *Psychoanalyse und Kindergarten und andere Arbeiten zur Kinderpsychologie.* Munich: Ernst Reinhardt.

WUTTKE-GRONEBERG, WALTER. 1979. "Medizin und Technik." *Der Spiegel.* Hamburg 33.5. v.29.1.1979.

# Index

Aaron C. (case history), 298

abandonment, 6, 44, 48, 49, 90, 98; as significant traumatic experience, 98

abuse, 233; in Nazi mentality, 243

acculturation, of survivors in Israel and other countries compared, 22

achievement, in survivors' children, 19, 296–97

acting-out behavior, 91–93

actualization, 304n

adaptability, and survivor syndrome, 11

adaptation, 278–79, 296–98, 300, 307; and emergency morality, 292, 293; and post–Holocaust adjustment, 105

adaptive behavior, in second generation and general population compared, 19

adaptive regression, 98

Adenauer, Konrad (Chancellor of Germany), and indemnification laws, 63–64, 77–78

adjustment: post–Holocaust, 105; mechanisms of, in survivor-families, 269

adolescence, 23, 100, 265

adolescents, 19, 38, 49

adolescent survivors, 44, 51, 85, 91–94; identification of, with Nazis, 44, 91, 92; psychological disorders of, 69

adult survivors, see survivor-parents

adult trauma, 47

affective deficiency, 21, 48

age of trauma, 83, 105; and effect on offspring, 158

aggression, 20, 22, 146, 175, 176; in children of survivors, 19, 20, 281, 283–85, 302–3; in child-survivors, 84; in concentration camp syndrome, 134; in survivor-families, 10, 281, 284

aggressors, 22; identification with, 44, 91, 92, 94, 294, 300; see also Nazis

Akedah, 3

Aleksandrowicz, Dov R., 21, 48

alienation, feelings of, 21

Allied forces, and liberation, 4, 57

America, and Holocaust survivors, 58–59

American Joint Distribution Committee, 7

anal aggression, Nazi mentality, 168

anal period, problems during, in survivor-families, 23

anal-sadistic phase, 99, 224

analysis, 14, 34, 36, 44, 119, 249, 286; aggression in, 284; classical, 26, 265, 280; and ego-syntonic behavior, 210; and emergence of sadistic wishes, 291; importance of history in, 41; of Nazis and offspring, 167, 170, 174, 175, 231–35; see also children of Nazis; neurotic conflict in, 173; patient rejection of Holocaust impact in, 285; survivor-family reaction to, 35n; symbiotic omnipotence in, 209

analyst, 10, 36, 38, 40, 127, 166, 175, 201, 261–62; and attitude toward psychological disorders of survivors' children, 27–28; and avoidance of Holocaust-related topics, 92; and denial, 34, 92; and disbelief, 250; effect of cultural trends on, 162; and identification of Holocaust-related symptoms, 197, 314; non-neutrality of, 165; relation to survivors' children, 285; role of, and drive-affect-fantasy configuration, 157; survivors' attitude toward, 17; and theorizing, 251; threatening situations, 175; and treating children of Nazis, 163; see also analysis; countertransference; therapist

analysts, Israeli, Holocaust-related symptoms, 269

analytic interpretation, and change, 288

anger, normal, 146

Anna L. (case history), 72

Anna O. (Freud's case history), 271, 281

anniversary reaction, 93, 97, 270, 277

Anthony, E. J., 20

anti-fascist Nazi offspring, 231

anti-Jewish terrorism, and fear among Holocaust survivors, 61

anti-Semitism, 49, 61, 168, 170, 195, 196, 222, 247

anxiety, 23, 146, 276; and superego malfunction of, 259; and survivor syndrome, 11; transmission of, 273, 276

# Index

# Index

and mourning, 297, 312; and narcissism, 103, 288, 307; and Nazis' children compared, 164–65; nightmares of, 103; and the Oedipus complex, 256–57, 280–81; and parents' experience, 44, 84, 120, 265; persecution, and effect on, 158; phobic responses in, 19; and preoccupation of, 44, 164, 267; and pseudo-schizophrenic episodes, 92, 270; and psychic reality, 288; psychosexual disorders of, 18–29, 156, 298; psychosexual stages, and disturbances in (*see specific stages*); psychotic symptoms, 121, 270; and reality, 289, 299; and reality of trauma, 271–73; and rebellion, 19, 297; and reliving the past, 265, 267; as replacement of lost object, 95, 96, 273, 276, 288, 298–300, 304, 311 (*see also* lost object); as repudiation of Nazi ideology, 57–58, 95; as self-object, 106; and separation/individuation conflict, 308; silence and effect on (*see* Michal M.; Liora N.; silence); stress tolerance in, 122; and superego, 289, 297; tasks of, 61, 226, 279–80, 289, 298–301, 308; traumatization of, 47 (*see also* trauma); treatment of, 257–60, 285, 309; and verbal disturbances, 299; and vindication of parents, 277; *see also* hospitalized children of survivors; second generation

child survivors, 7, 34, 68, 69, 84–87; and effect of degradation of parents, 94; and latency-phase victims, 49, 69, 70; and loss of trust in parents, 50; nightmares of, 70; placement of, following liberation, 57; precocity of, 84

child survivors of concentration camps: and confusion with displaced persons camp, 56; and impact of separation from parents, 69; during latency phase, 49; psychic damage in, 85; psychological problems of, 7; of Theresienstadt, 84; and treatment of offspring, 85–86

Chodoff, Paul, 9

chosenness, 173; and survivor/persecutor similarities, 224

Christ, identification with, 295, 299

Christian conversion, 57, 279

Christian religious teachings, and anti-Semitism, 195

Christians, and protection of child survivors, 34

chronic depression, in survivors, 10, 11

chronic traumatic state, in camp survivors, 291

classical analysis, 26, 265, 280

Clinic for the Development of Young Children and Parents (Boston, Mass.), 103

cognitive disturbances, 11, 291, 299

communication, 104, 225, 230, 295; *see also* silence

Communist countries, indemnification for survivors in, 76

competition, and aggression, 284

concentration (mental), impairment of, 231

concentration camps, 9, 291–93; adolescent survivors of, 49, 93–94; and children in latency period, 49; child survivors from, and sadistic fantasies, 85; deprivation in, 52; and psychic damage, 85, 291; release from, 4, 5–6; *see also* emergency morality; morality; and *specific camps*

concentration camp survivors, 4, 22, 85, 93–94; reaction of analysts, to, 250; and symptoms of massive traumatization, 291, 292

concentration camp syndrome, 9, 134

concretization, 289, 299, 302–4, 304*n*, 305, 309

Conference of Jewish Material Claims, 77

conflicts, 152, 164–65, 224, 228, 242, 286; *see also* confusion

conflictual overflow, transmission of, to offspring, 105

confusion, in survivors' children, 289–90, 294

Congress on Child Analysis and Social Work, 76

Congress of Child Psychiatry, 21

Congress of the International Psychoanalytic Association, on "Sequelae of Man-Made Disasters," 167

conspiracy of silence: and analysis, 175, 249; and confusion in survivors' offspring, 290; in Nazi families, 230; *see also* silence

consulting physicians, in indemnification procedures, 73–76

containment, and shared safe space, 106

contradictory identifications, 225

conventionality, in children of survivors, and hysterics compared, 282–83

coping mechanisms, 22

countertransference, 180, 197, 226, 249; and analysis of children of Nazis, 163, 223–24; in analysis of Nazis, 174–75; in analysis of survivor-family members, 35*n*, 286; and analysis of survivors, 18

culture: change in, survivors and, 279; differences in, and second generation, 21, 41; discrepancies in, and problems for children of Nazis, 163–64; mores of, and superego development, 165

cumulative trauma, 47, 155, 222, 226–27; *see also* trauma

Cyprus, internment camps on, 4

Dachau (concentration camp), 78

Dahmer, Helmut, 169

# Index

Danieli, Y., 27, 35n, 37, 48
David P. (case history), 110–18
Davidson, Shamai, 37
dead children, see lost object
death, 299, 304, 306; idealization of, 277, 280; role of, in life of Hitler, 243
death anxiety, 291-92
decathexis, 12
deception, 66, 78
decoding, and ego splitting, 122
decompensation, and identification, 121–22
defense mechanisms, 5, 6, 20, 132, 170, 275; and children of Nazis, 29, 78, 180, 231; concretization of, 289; and ego ideal, 242, 244; and ego splitting, 121–22; and latency period, 269; and Nazi mentality, 168–70, 171, 172–73; and repression, 5, 6, 168, 279; of second generation Germans, 78; in survivor-families, 289; of survivors, 5, 269
defensive depersonalization, 269
defensive identification, with aggressor, 94
degradation, 65, 220
degradation of parents, 55, 98, 265; and effect on offspring, 91, 94, 97
dehumanization, of Jews, by Nazis, 53
delayed disorders, 71–73
delusions, 212; of chosenness, and Nazis, 173 (see also chosenness); of omnipotence, 244
denial, 5, 6, 7, 87, 177; by analysts, 34, 92; by Germans, 62, 74, 162, 169–70; during latency period, 34; and persecutors' mentality, 172; and refusal of restitution, 60; second generation as confirmation of, 48; see also mass denial
dependency, 284, 295
depersonalization, in survivors, 291
depression, 6, 12, 134, 256; second generation, 19, 231; in survivors, 11, 12, 69, 231; see also chronic depression
deprivation, 25, 52, 84–85, 132
de-realization, 271
Des Pres, Terence, 265
destructurization of society, and Nazi grandiosity, 217
Deutsch, Felix, 284
Deutsche Christen: and Third Reich, 198
developmental arrest, 8
developmental phase-linked events, and children of survivors, 98–101
developmental process, normal, 302
De Wind, Emmanuel, 10, 267, 279, 286
Dietrich L. (case history), 198, 222–24
disability, and indemnification laws, 65
discipline, in survivor-families, 297
disillusionment, in survivor-families, 288
disorganization, and trauma, 8
displaced persons camps, 4, 56, 70, 98

displacement: of parental omnipotence, 94; as substitute for mourning, 306; see also transference
distrust, universality of, 97
doctors, in indemnification proceedings, see Beratender Arzt; Vertrauensarzt
Donat, A., 49
Dora M. (case history), 74
double reality, 165, 307
dreams, see Elsa B.; fascism dreams; nightmares
drive-affect-fantasies configuration, in survivor's-child complex, 136–37
drive development, 146–48, 165
drive expression, transmission of, to offspring, 104, 105
drive theory, and Nazi mentality, 167–68
dual existence, see double reality
Dutch children, and wartime separation from parents, 69

Eckstaedt, Anita, 162
economic recovery, as mourning substitute, 172
Edna D. (case history), 299
education: about the Holocaust, 37; in displaced persons camp, 70
ego, 52, 265, 291, 294; development of, 84, 290; impaired, and the second generation, 148–50, 225; integration of, 165; restriction of, 22, 170; splitting of, 121–22, 297–98, 305; strength of, 137, 270, 271; and the superego, 174; in survivors' children, 148–50, 270, 271; see also ego ideal
ego function, 27, 231, 291, 294
ego ideal, 165, 174, 176–82; in children of survivors, 289, 296, 307; and externalization of superego, 295; in Nazis and offspring, 168, 178–79, 242, 244; and survivor-parents, 52
ego-syntonic behavior, in analysis, 210
Eichmann, Adolph, 251
Eicke, Martha, 161
Eissler, Kurt, 68, 71
Eitinger, L., 9
Elsa B. (case history), 231–42
emergency mortality, 292, 293, 307
emotional growth of children, 284
emotional impairment, and indemnification, 67–68
empathy, 293, 306
Epstein, Helen, 37, 149
escape, effect of, 98, 99
Esterson, A., 121
ethical teaching, and ego ideal, 176
"Everyone Has a Name," 315
excitability, 231
expectations, in children of Nazis, 231

330

# Index

extermination, 62, 247, 257; Nazi attitude toward, 168, 242; *see also* Final Solution
externalization: as defense mechanism, 289; of hostile fantasies, 308; and mourning, 304; and superego, 295, 301
external reality, and fantasy of survivors' children, 272
external support, for survivors, 56

failure, in survivors' children, 308
family: lost, restoration of, 23, 95; need for following liberation, 5, 56; non-Holocaust, 288; numb, 48; pathology of, 105; pre-Holocaust, 57, 94, 96; *see also* survivor-families; survivor-parents
fantasies, 20, 22, 252, 288, 302–3, 308, 309; concretization of, 299; and double reality, 307; shared, 296, 297, 306–9 passim; somatization of, 300; in survivors' children, 101, 122, 156–57, 290, 297, 311
fascism dreams, 235–42
father hunger, 110–18
fatigue, in survivor syndrome, 11
fear, 23; in child survivors, 84; of Holocaust return, 11, 23, 48, 58, 61, 308; transmission of, 89–91
Federal Indemnification Law of 1953 (West Germany), 63–79
Federn, Paul, 29n
Federal Republic of Germany, *see* Germany, economic recovery of; indemnification laws
Field Security Service, 168
fighter families, 48
Final Solution, 4, 5, 244, 247
fixation point, 270, 274
flexibility, survival value of, 279
Fogelman, E., 27, 37
food, obsession with, 48
Franco-Prussian War, 175
Franz M. (case history), 252
Freedman, Abraham, 13–14, 250, 276
Freud, Anna, 47, 69, 145, 170; on trauma, 9, 85
Freud, Sigmund, 168, 176, 182, 244, 261–62, 269; on aggressive impulses, 4; *Beyond the Pleasure Principle*, 8, 312; and case history of Anna O., 271, 281; and frigidity, 285; on hypnoid state, 269; on idealized leader, 296; on mourning, 172, 303; *Mourning and Melancholia*, 169, 312; and Oedipus complex, 156; "On Narcissism," 296; on repression, 172; on superego, 174, 290; *Totem and Taboo*, 169; *Transitoriness*, 169; on trauma, 8–10, 46, 226
Frieda T. (case history), 186–94
Friedländer, Saul, 279
Friedman, Paul, 7
Furman, E., 26

Gambetta, Léon, 175
gastrointestinal disorders, and survivor syndrome, 11
generation reversal, *see* reversal of generations
Gerhard H. (case history), 181
German-Jewish soldier, case of, 68
German language, under Hitler, 171
German people: attitudes of, 62–63, 170; and Jewish persecution, 49; and mass denial, 35, 62, 74, 169; and silence, 162
German psychoanalysts, 161
German race, under Nazis, 51
Germany, 33, 41, 63, 78, 312–13; anti-Semitism in, 170, 171; and collective silence, 175; economic recovery of, 172; latency period in, 167; *see also* indemnification; indemnification laws
German youth, 51, 78; explaining Holocaust to, 162; guidelines for rearing, 179, 204, 218
Goethe, 251
grandiosity, 154, 165, 215–16, 217, 220, 242; infantile, 219
Green, André, 272, 282
Greenacre, Phyllis, 9
Gretchen B. (case history), 94
Group Project for Holocaust Survivors and Their Children, 37
Group for the Psychoanalytic Study of the Effect of the Holocaust on the Second Generation, *xi*, 36–37, 38, 42, 197, 287
Grubrich-Simitis, Ilse, 47, 48, 161, 248, 277
Grumbel, Erich, 267
guilt, 33, 53, 301, 306–7, 313; and children of survivors, 19, 277, 296; collective, 33; externally forced, 172; survivors' feelings of, 14, 16, 53, 93, 305–8

Hampstead Clinic (England), 36
Hannah V. (case history), 256–57
Hardtmann, Gertrud, 78, 162
Harry R. (case history), 86–87, 97, 101
hate: addiction to, 267; ideology of, 4
healing, *see* self-healing
health, 10, 47, 57; *see also* psychosomatic disorders; survivor syndrome
Helmut E. (case history), 179
helplessness, and effect of ego, 52
heroism, 98, 218; as theme of survivor-families, 98
Herzog, James, 148, 299
Hessen (West German state), 75
hiding, 28, 87; and methods of survival, 279
Hiroshima victims, and Holocaust victims compared, 52
Hitler, Adolf, 54, 243, 244, 247, 252
Hitler youth, 51, 52
Hofmannsthal, Hugo von, 228–29

# Index

Holland, restitution in, 76
Holocaust, 3, 20, 44, 87, 167, 268, 312–13, 314; adolescent interest in parents' experience, 38; denial of, by analysts, 34, 92; and etiology of psychopathology, 14–18, 268: fear of return of, 23, 58, 61, 308; immediate aftereffects of, 4–8; memories of, and transmission without trauma, 313; non-German bystanders, 166; pathology from, and personal pathology, 250–53; patients not involved in, 314; re-enacted by second generation, 88, 281; repetition of, in survivor-families, 90, 301; silence about, *see* silence; *see also* Holocaust trauma
"Holocaust" (television series), 134
Holocaust Study Group, 37
Holocaust trauma, 16, 34, 52–55, 265, 288; and double registry, 254–56; and Freudian explanation of, 8–10; and influence on second generation, 28, 311; transmission of, xi, 311
Hoppe, Klaus D., 10, 132
hospitalized children of survivors, 27, 97, 268, 282, 284
Höss, Rudolf, 168, 242
humiliation, and indemnification procedure, 65
hypnoid state, 269
hysteria, 12, 267–86; adaptation in, 279; and children of survivors, 271, 284; and pseudoschizophrenic episodes, 92
hysterical conflict, 282
hysterical identification, 280–83
hysterical materialization, 280
hysterical mechanisms, in survivors, 269
hysterical neurosis, 226–27
hysterical psychosis, 269, 270, 275
hysterogenic mother, 273
hysterogenic parents, 278–79

id, 265, 290, 294
idealization, 152, 154, 295; of the dead, 298, 305
idealized leader, survivors' children as, 296
ideals, formation of, 176–77
identification, 278, 280–81, 297, 302, 305, 308; with aggressors, 44, 91, 92, 94, 294, 297, 300; with attitudes of persecutor, 23, 51, 292; in child survivors, 86, 94; with Christ, 295; and decompensation, 121–22; with lost objects, 277, 278, 280, 281, 295, 298, 299; of Nazi children with victims, 313; with pre–Holocaust family, 96; with primary objects and ego ideal, 176; rebellion against, 282; of survivor-parents with children, 48; of survivor-parents with the dead, and effect of offspring, 299; of survivor's children with dead family members (*see* identification with lost objects); and transmission of anti-Semitism, 196

identification, hysterical, 280–83
identification hunger, 299
identificatory participation, and children of Nazis, 174
identity problems, 94, 134, 275, 279, 291
ideology: construction of, 222; of hate, 4
idolization, 218–19
*Impact of Disease and Death* (Anthony and Koupernik), 20
"Inability to Mourn" (Mitscherlich and Mitscherlich), 169
indemnification, 7, 59, 66–68, 78, 314
indemnification laws, 33–34, 35, 63–79; and delaying tactics, 68–69, 75–76; intention of, 63–64, 77–78; survivor reactions to, 59, 60
indemnification officers, attitudes of, 73
individual pathology, factors influencing, 29, 182
individuation, 265, 308; *see also* separation
infant survivors, 68, 69, 85
Inge, Orgel's story of, 50–51
initiative, 231
inner-genital phase disturbance, 99–100
innocence, 285, 286
insight, 131, 173
insomnia, 231
Institute for Holocaust Studies in Tel Aviv, 37
integration, in survivors' children, 156
intellectualizing, in Nazi offspring, 180
internalization, 23, 302, 307, 308
internalization of values, effect of reversal in, 176–77
International Congress on the Psychological Adjustment in Time of War and Peace, 37
International Psycho-Analytical Association, 10, 282–83
internists, role of after war, 33
interpretation, 262–64, 286
interviews, as research method, 21, 35
intrapsychic conflict, 8
*Introductory Lectures* (Freud), 8
introjection, of aggressor, 300
irritability, 231
isolation, feelings of, 11, 56
Israel, 4, 21–24, 34–35; effect on Jewish self-image, 61; and national day of mourning, 24; second generation in, 21, 41, 267; wars, 23, 34–35, 193
Israel Psychoanalytic Society, 10

Jackson, Fred, 168
Jacob C. (case history), 15–18
Jacobson, E., 260
"Jew," as defamatory word in Germany, 171
Jewish community, and polarization on attitudes relating to Holocaust, 313

# Index

# Index

# Index

psychic reality, 273–74, 288
psychic strength, 11
psychic traumatization, 7, 291–93
"Psychic Traumatization through Social Catastrophe" (symposium), 10
psychoanalyst, *see* analyst
Psychoanalytic Congress in Jerusalem, 267
psychoanalytical methodology, and Nazi mentality, 174
psychoanalytic data, lack of, 37
psychological care, lack of, 7
psychological disorders, 7–8, 25, 69, 70, 85; analysts' attitude toward, 27–28; in children of Nazis, 23, 244; indemnification for, 67–70; *see also* psychopathology
psychological tests, 21
"psychomotoric" state, in camps, 292
psychopathology, 8–9, 10, 12, 212, 275; in concentration camp survivors, 292; etiology of, 7, 14–18, 28, 251; and mourning, 24; in second generation, 27–28; and sexualization of mother-child relationship, 274; in survivors, 68; *see also* psychological disorders; psychosis
psychosexual development: parents' Holocaust memories of, 250, 256; phase linked events, 98–101; *see also specific psychosexual stages*
psychosis, 252–53, 268, 270, 298
psychosislike episodes, in survivor-families, 92
psychosomatic disorders, 11, 134, 231, 291
psychotherapy, and research, 21, 35
punishment, 297

Racamier, Paul-Claude, 280
Rachel M. (case history), 137–55, 156, 256, 298, 299
racism, in post-war Nazis, 230
Rakoff, V., 18–19
Rappaport, E., 6
rapprochement, 88, 305
rationalization, and repression, 279
Rau, J. H., 27
Rauschning, Hermann, 244
readaptation, 289
reality, 272, 289, 298, 299, 308; "double," 312; *see also* psychic reality
reality distortion, 304
reality testing, 254, 289, 290, 299
rebellion, 19, 297
recathexis, 23
refugee agencies, 33
refugees, 56
regression, 27, 98, 171, 177; and Nazi mentality, 168, 177, 244; under Nazi persecution, 49, 292; rehabilitation of survivors, 7; and traumatization, 302, 304
reincarnation, 57, 94, 280

rejection: of indemnification application, 66; of pre-Holocaust family, 57
religion, and ego ideal, 176
religious conversion, of survivors, 94, 279
repetition compulsion, 98, 133, 167, 289, 309
replacement, of lost object, 94, 105, 298; *see also* lost object
repression, 7, 225, 267, 279, 289; as defense mechanism, 5, 6, 168, 278; Freud on, 172; during latency period, 34
research data, 35, 36, 39
resettlement, problems of, 58
resilience, and survivor syndrome, 11
resistance: in analysis, 175, 249, 284–85; and denial, 6–7
restitution, *see* indemnification
resurrection guilt, 98
return-of-the-persecutor mentality, 174
revenge, and superego, 290
reversal of generation, 280, 281, 302, 311
Rheinland-Pfalz (West German state), 75
Riebesser, Peter, 75–76, 161
Robinson, Shalom, 85
Roiphe, H., 13
Rosen, V. H., 249
Rosenberger, L., 25, 48
Rosenkötter, Lutz, 161, 162, 165, 175
Russia, occupation of post-war Germany, 62

sacrifice, in Jewish history, 3–4
sadistic drive, and superego, 301
sadistic fantasies, 85, 291, 292
sadists, 22
sado-masochism, in concentration camps, 52
safe space, *see* shared safe space
Sandler, A. M., 304n
Sandler, J., 304n
Sarah D. (case history), 69
Sara R. (case history), 254–56
Savran, Bella, 27, 37
Schieffer, I., 251
schizophrenia, 68, 270, 275
Schlingenseider, Johannes (Reverend), 62–63
Schnipper, O. L., 27
schools, and influence on superego, 165
Schur, M., on Gretchen B., 94
scribble therapy, 233
second generation, 21, 41, 43, 44, 164–65, 169, 224–27 passim, 267; and anal sadistic phase, 99, 224; analysts' relationship with, 36; and awareness group, 37; and defense mechanisms of in Germans, 78; etiology of pathology in, 25; and mourning, 48, 297, 312; and psychopathology, 27–28; and reenactment of Holocaust experience, 88, 281; and silence, 20; studies of, 18–19, 161; trauma in, 47, 226–27; *see* children of Nazis; children of survivors

*335*

# Index

security, 22, 47, 90
seduction theory of hysteria, 272
self, 242, 290, 292, 307
self-concept, disorders of, 231
self-deprecation, 14, 16, 23, 69
self-destructiveness, 295, 297
self-esteem, 57, 84–85, 100, 103
self-healing, 106, 288, 309
self-image, 51, 61
self-object, 106
self-realization, through offspring, 229
self-reliance, in child survivors, 84
self-representation, 22, 296
separation: and adolescence, 265; and child survivors, 69; and conflict in survivor's child, 308; and hysteria, 282; problems of, in survivor-families, 23, 38, 47, 101, 297; and survivor-parents, 276, 284; in therapy, 127, 265
separation-individuation, 84–85, 244
sexual dysfunction, 291
sexual fantasies, 303
sexualization, 274, 275, 302
sexual perversion, and identity problems, 275
shared fantasies, 296, 297, 306–9 passim
shared safe space, 104, 106, 107, 109–10
shared superego pathology, 302–9
shock trauma, 8, 47
sibling loyalty, 85
Sigal, J., 19, 47, 48
silence, 33, 38, 59, 162; and case histories, 120–21, 122–36; and children's fantasies, 311; collective, 175; as defense mechanism, 5, 6; and second generation, 20; in German families, 162; of world community, 6; see also conspiracy of silence
Silverman, Martin, 36n
Simenauer, Erich, 10, 161, 162, 259
simultaneous double existence, 141
slavery, in the United States, 53
sleep disorders, 11, 231; see also nightmares
Snake Pit (film), 92
social catastrophe, and individual pathology, 29
somatic illnesses, etiology of, in Holocaust survivors, 10
somatization: of fantasies, 300; of Holocaust trauma, 16
Sonnenberg, S. M., 34
son of survivor (case history), 110–18
soul murder, 231
Spätschäden, see delayed disorders
splitting mechanism: and Nazi ideology, 222; and traumatization, 302
splitting of self, 294
splitting of superego, 152, 165, 290, 297–98
sterility, among survivors, 23
strain trauma, 47

Strauss, Richard, 228, 229
stress, 271
structural theory, and Nazi mentality, 174
sublimation, 156
submission, 242, 243
success, 288, 308
suffering, in survivors' children, 267
superego, 165, 225, 289–94 passim, 302; and anxiety, 259; and concretization, 305; distortion of, 218; and ego, 174, 176, 290, 294; and externalization, 289, 295, 301; formation of, and shared fantasies, 308, 309; Freud on, 174, 290; and sadistic drive, 301; splitting of (see splitting of superego); and survivors' guilt, 307, 308; and trauma, 265, 290–91; and treatment, 257–60; and unaltered attitudes of, 174
superego pathology, 162, 297–309; case history of, 151–53, 258–59; shared, 302–9; treatment of, 257–59
superiority, 165, 230
survival, 102, 249, 279, 300, 301; experiences of, and problems in offspring, 43; and question of morality, 98; suspiciousness of, 297
survival of species, 105
survivor, definition of, 313
survivor-families, 19, 21, 22, 23, 48–49, 98, 149, 269, 288, 289, 295, 296; and aggressiveness, 10, 281, 284; discipline in, 297; disillusionment, 288; holding environment for, 287; hysteria in, 269; and internalization of Hitler, 252; in Israel, 21–24, 34–35; and mourning, 225; and nightmares, 46–47; and oedipal triangle, 277; and passivity, 281, 284, 298; pseudo-psychotic episodes in, 92; and psychiatric help, 25; reaction to analyses, 35n; recathexis in, 23; and re-creation of Holocaust experience, 90, 96, 301; and restoration of lost family, 23, 95; resurrection guilt in, 98; and self-healing, 288; separation in, 47; superego pathology, 294–95; and theme of genocide, 83; and trauma, 311; treatment approach for, 100; see also parent-child relationships
survivor-fathers, 87–90; case history of son of, 110–18; fear of sadism, 22; and impaired safe spaces, 106; and regression into sado-masochism, 52; and survivor-mothers compared, 158; suspicious attitude of, 20, 90
survivor-marriage, 105, 106, 109, 306
survivor-mothers, 23, 47; and hysterogenic mothers compared, 273; and shared safe space, 106; and survivor-fathers compared, 158; and transmission of anxiety, 276
survivor-parents, 25, 42, 48, 56–61, 291–93, 297; and aggression toward children, 10; and analysis of offspring, 35; anxiety in, 276; attitude toward offspring, 23, 47; atti-

# Index

tude toward parenting, 57; behavior toward offspring, 97; and child abuse, 283; from concentration camps, 93–94; and displacement of affect, 288; and ego ideal, 52; and emotional growth of offspring, 284; and feelings of degradation, 55; and goals for offspring, 296; and guilt-producing threats, 301; and Holocaust experience, 43, 49–52, 84; and identification of offspring with aggressors, 311; and linking, 43–44; and marriage of children, 284; and overprotectiveness, 19, 276; identification pattern of (see identification); post-Holocaust experiences, 56–61; and protection, 12; protective shield and, 122; and psychopathology in offspring, 28; and regression, 98; rehabilitation of, 45; and repetition-compulsion, 133; and silence toward children, 38; superego structure of, 294; and tasks of offspring, 279–80; and transmission of Holocaust experience, 44; and treatment of children, 94–96

survivors, 5, 11, 23, 38, 56, 57, 231, 269, 291; attitude toward death, 306; and attitudes toward imdemnification, 59; attitude toward psychoanalysts, 17; and children of Nazis compared, 226; in concentration camps and others compared, 85; depression of, 10, 11; and etiology of psychopathology, 7; and fear of anti-Semitism, 170; goals of, 57; and guilt feelings, 53, 93, 305–8, 313; identification, with Nazis, 23, 300; and illness, 47; isolation of, 56; latency period for, 5, 34, 269; and material wealth, 25, 57; and Nazi offspring compared, 231; paranoid projections of, 262; problems in new cultures, 59; procreation, and attitudes of (see procreation); and projection, 262; pseudo-schizophrenic episodes in, 92; and psychiatric help, 25; psychological recovery, 22; psychopathology of, 7, 22, 24, 68; reaction of people to, 33; reality testing in, 254; rehabilitation of, 7; religious conversion, 94; and replacement of pre-Holocaust family, 96; and repression, 5, 6; and self-deprecation, 14, 16, 23; and splitting of self, 294; therapy for, 10, 14, 260–64

survivor's-child complex, 136–57; and cross-cultural comparison, 41; and ego strength, 137, 270, 271; identification of, 38–39; and impaired safe space, 109–10

survivor's-child syndrome, lack of, 44

survivors' guilt, 305–8, 309

survivor syndrome, 10–12, 13, 21, 34, 48

symbiotic omnipotence, 209, 222, 225

symbiotic transference, 226

symbol formation, 311

symbolic capacity, and trauma, 302

symptoms, failure to recognize Holocaust relation to, 314

taboos, and silence about Holocaust in Germany, 162

tension tolerance, 122

terror, effect on ego, 291

Terry, Jack, 43*n*

theory of affects, 174

therapeutic sharing, in survivor marriage, 105

therapeutic technique, problems of, 262–64

therapists, importance of personal background with Holocaust patients, 312; reaction to survivor-families, 248–50

therapy, and timing, 260–61

Theresienstadt (Czechoslovakia), 69, 251; child-survivors from, 84

third generation, effect of Holocaust on, 94

Third Reich, see Nazi ideology

time tunnel, 225

togetherness in survivor-families, 48–49

toilet training, 43

Torberg, Friedrich, 168

torture, 52, 98

*Totem and Taboo* (Freud), 169

traditions, role of superego in, 174

transference, 23, 56, 112, 231, 265; in analysis, of Nazi offspring, 231–35; of guilt, and children of Nazis, 164; symbiotic, in children of Nazis, 226; see also displacement

transient psychosis, 270

transmission of trauma, xi, 98, 103–19, 155, 274, 298, 311; case histories of, 107–119; model for, 103, 104, 311

transmitting experience to second generation, 101–2

transposition, 148, 149, 157, 225

trauma, 8, 11, 47, 98, 273–80, 289–309; adult and infantile compared, 47, 49; age of, and effect on offspring, 158; chronic state of, 291; classic theory of, 67; and concretizing, 304; developmental stage of, and effect on second generation, 99–101; effect on survivor-families, 311; fear of recurrence, 308; Freudian theory of, 8–10, 46, 226, 269; Holocaust and non-Holocaust compared, 288; lack of sharing, and overflow, 109–10; and loss of trust in parents, 50–51; metapsychological model of, 312; period of latency, 269; reality of, 271–73; recovery from, 85; reliving of, in survivor-families, 44; and repetition compulsion, 98; and repression, 289; and seduction theory of hysteria, 272; severity of, and parenting ability, 83; sexualization of, 274–75; and shared dreams, 46–47; silence as defense mecha-

*337*

# Index

trauma (continued)
 nism against, 5; and superego, 265, 290; and symbolic capacity, 300; transmission of (see transmission of trauma); and withdrawal, 16; see also cumulative trauma; Holocaust trauma; traumatization
trauma reaction, 293
traumatic conditions, 9
traumatic memories, and avoidance of psychological help, 7–8
traumatic neuroses, 9, 46
traumatic toilet experience, 99
traumatization, 47, 302; and developmental stages, 101; and fantasy, 302–3; and mother-child relationship, 47, 132; and psychic structure, 291–93; superego and, 290–91, 302–3; universal, in Germany, 171; see also anniversary reaction; cumulative trauma; transmission of trauma
treatment: case history of, 15–18; with Holocaust survivors, 14, 260–64; and mourning, 10, 12, 265, 312; superego problems in, 257–59; with survivors' children, 257–60, 285, 309
treatment, classical for traumatic neuroses, 46
triangulation, 297
Trossman, B., 19
trust: loss of, 50–51, 292; and trauma, 132
Turkish slaughter of Armenians, and Holocaust experience compared, 53–55 passim

unconscious material, transmission of, 103, 104
United Nations, and State of Israel, 4
United States, and cross-cultural comparison of survivor's-child complex, 41
uprooting, and assault on ego, 52
urethral phase, disturbance in survivors' children, 99

value system, and defense mechanism, 289
Venzlaff, Ulrich, 68
verbal disturbances, 299
verbalization, of traumatic events, 12
Vertrauensarzt, in indemnification proceedings, 64–65
victim envy, in children of Nazis, 164

vindication, 224
visibility, of survivors after war, 5
Volker M. (case history), 182
vulnerability, of child survivors, 25, 103

Wagner-Jauregg, Julius von, 168
Wahrgenommen, 172n
Waiting for Godot (Beckett), 221
Wangh, Martin, 10, 68, 69, 227, 269
war-related catastrophes, and Holocaust compared, 52–53
Warsaw ghetto, 13
Weizsaecker, Victor von, 171
Weltanschauung, and perpetrators as victims, 173
Werner C. (case history), 178–79
West Germany, indemnification of victims, 59
Why War? (Freud), 4
Wiedergutmachung, and restitution to survivors, 7
Wiesel, Elie, 3, 6–7, 37
Wijsenbeek, H., 85
Williams, M., 25, 34
Windermere, England, resettlement camp, 85
Winestine, Muriel, 43n
Winnicott, D. W., 233, 287
Winnik, H. Zvi, 10, 149
withdrawal, 11, 16, 69
Witzelspitzel (Brentano), and Nazi ideology, 215–16
Wolfheim, N., 85
Woman without a Shadow (Hofmannsthal and Strauss), 228, 229
Women's International Zionist Organization (WIZO), 130, 132
World War I, 9, 55, 62

xenophobia, 16

Yale Symposium on the Holocaust, 288n
Yoav C. (case history), 148–49
Youth Alija, 57

Zimmermann, Ingeborg, 161
Zionist youth organization, 22